Governing Intellectual Property Rights Within Publicly Funded Biobanks

Governing Intellectual Property Rights Within Publicly Funded Biobanks

R. Neethu

Wolters Kluwer

Published by:
Kluwer Law International B.V.
PO Box 316
2400 AH Alphen aan den Rijn
The Netherlands
E-mail: international-sales@wolterskluwer.com
Website: lrus.wolterskluwer.com

Sold and distributed in North, Central and South America by:
Wolters Kluwer Legal & Regulatory U.S.
7201 McKinney Circle
Frederick, MD 21704
United States of America
Email: customer.service@wolterskluwer.com

Sold and distributed in all other countries by:
Air Business Subscriptions
Rockwood House
Haywards Heath
West Sussex
RH16 3DH
United Kingdom
Email: international-customerservice@wolterskluwer.com

ISBN 978-94-035-0621-0

e-Book: ISBN 978-94-035-0622-7
web-PDF: ISBN 978-94-035-0623-4

To
My loving parents and PK

About the Author

Dr R. Neethu (RajamNeethu) is a fellow under the NNF grant on Collaborative Research Programme in Biomedical Innovation at the faculty of Law, University of Copenhagen, Denmark. She is also a part of the project on policy, practice and patient experience in the age of intensified data sourcing (POLICYAID) funded by the European Research Council. Previously, she was engaged with the University of Copenhagen's Excellence Program for Interdisciplinary Research called Global Genes and Local Concerns examining legal issues in the area of genetic research. She has been junior academic Fellow at the University of Oxford, as well as Visiting Research Fellow at the Max Planck Institute of Intellectual property and competition law, Munich, Germany and the Global Trust Fellow under the European Research Council. She holds a PhD in Law from the University of Copenhagen, an LLM in Intellectual property rights and technology law from the London School of Economics, UK, and a Law Degree from India. She is teaching and widely researching in the area of intellectual property law, Big Data and emerging technologies.

Table of Contents

Foreword

When in 2013, the University of Copenhagen decided to fund the interdisciplinary research project Global genes, local concerns: *Legal, ethical and scientific challenges in cross-national biobankingand translational exploitation* I (being the (then) PI) knew that whoever would be lucky and good enough to get the research fellowship on '*commercialisation aspects and IPR*' faced a tall order. Even though it is generally agreed that big, international biobanks containing vast collections of human biological samples and data are crucial to academic research and it is accepted that the development of new drugs and treatments based on biobanks is immensely costly, little had been written on the involvement of intellectual property rights within biobank. Clearly, these are murky waters to navigate and anyone setting sail to do so must navigate with an eye both to legal and ethical norms but also involve the interests and values of the multitude of stakeholders involved in biobanking (donors, doctors, scientists, etc.). Moreover, the concern over biobank's research involvement is heightened when industrial partners are involved in such research and publicly funded biobanks also have important obligations for sharing of resources and dissemination of information. In the face of such obligations, commercial partnerships within biobanks make a hard line for biobanks to cross. Often, it is, however, necessary to do so in order to release the full potential of the knowledge contained in the biobanks.

I was, therefore, thrilled to find Neethu amongst the applicants. Her papers were impeccable and her academic skills and personal perseverance had already made it possible for her to add an LLM from LSE on top of the legal education she received in India. The marriage between this skilled lawyer with the challenging topic and the interdisciplinary nature of the overall project turned out to be a happy and fruitful one. Neethu quickly developed a passion for the topic and this in combination with her excellent legal, analytical skills, natural curiosity and a lot (!) of hard work not only made it a joy to be Neethu's supervisor and colleague. It also resulted in many fruitful and interesting discussions, public presentations and eventually became an excellent research work. which not only demonstrates the author's excellent academic skills, covers new ground, provides new legal knowledge and is useful and necessary but also lets the reader *see* the author and gives voice to their own values, hopes and concerns.

In this way, the research is not just a work of high value in itself. It also contributes in an important and a substantial way to the overall aims of the Global Genes project.

Dr Neethu deals with the overall topic of commercialization aspects and IPR in a both comprehensive and original way. One of the major limitations for biobanks to successfully engage with intellectual property rights in biobanks is dearth in understanding how various IPRs function. The ability of the biobanks to share, access and reuse data, as well as to integrate data from diverse sources for research or other purposes requires effective technical and legal interoperability rules and practices. Such understanding is also essential for big data research paradigm within which biobanks function as systemic tools for research engagement. The same applies in handling of human biological samples. In this regard, the book offers an extensive understanding of the role of different IPRs particularly, patents, database rights, copyright and trade secrets within the realms of genomic research. It also identifies the gaps in IP laws to deal with biomedical research. The book, furthermore, examines the potential consequences for involvement of intellectual property rights within research partnerships in biobanks. In this process, the author draws on the foundational principles of research and commercialization. These principles include the concept of stewardship over resources, public trust for research and finally valorization or seeking value for the research. The research finds that the only way to manage the knowledge emanating from the use of biobank's resources is to manage the intellectual property inputs and outputs effectively. With this realization, the research draws attention to the creation of research environment of sharing without affecting the protection of research results through Intellectual property rights in Europe.

Professor, LL.D., PhD Jens Schovsbo
Center for Information and Innovation Law (CIIR), University of Copenhagen

Preface

The journey towards the writing of this book has been nothing but a challenging one. This was partly on account of the rapidly changing world of genomic research coupled with the slower and phase by phase change within biobanks as resource research infrastructures. When I began the research in early 2014, biobanking was in its formative phase and BBMRI was just awarded an ERIC status as an independent legal entity only in December 2013. There were number of other concerns for biobanks to consider during that period rather than commercial involvement or intellectual property rights. From the mid of 2015 onwards there emerged a growing discussion towards sustainability of biobanking institutions. The failure of certain biobanks and the rapidly diminishing funding of many biobanks in Europe forced a move towards the discussion of sustaining biobanks and commercialization as a means to achieve this. Since then there was a swift movement in practice and literature in seeking measures that suit the changing needs of biobanks. Nevertheless, such discussions in literature did not offer a meaningful understanding of intellectual property rights (IPR) to address the impact and implications of IP from a subjective focus. The Global Genes Local concerns project under the University of Copenhagen's Excellence Programme for Interdisciplinary research offered a highly interdisciplinary outlook to study this topic. This research put forward the challenge of understanding the organizational and legislative choices for biobanks. Particularly it focused on the question as to whether publicly funded biobanks should engage in tech-transfer and the protection of research results through IPR. Addressing this challenging research involved not just a view of intellectual property rights. Instead, it required an assimilation of various issues that subsist within biobanks such as consent, anonymization, privacy, sustainability, technical issues relating to sample and data storage, ownership, commercialization and benefit sharing. Therefore the issues within the biobank can be visualized as a Danish layer cake with IP and commercialization being the cream within those layers of interrelated elements. I have tried to accommodate these diverse points within the focus of the research. In addition, I have also strived to incorporate the expanding critical literature over many aspects such as biobank commercialization, data management practices and collaborative partnerships.

In writing this work I am deeply indebted to a number of humans who have guided, inspired and supported my research with time and valuable resources. In particular, I would like to thank Prof. Jens Schovsbo, Prof. Dr Klaus Høyer, Dr Tine Sømmer, Prof. Dr Thomas Riis, Dr Imogen Goold, Prof. Paul Torremans, Dr Brian Clark, Dr KarineSargsyan, Dominic Allen, MerikeLeego, K. Rajam for the comments relating to the research and the chapters. I would also like to thank Dr Andres Metspalu, Dr Graeme Dinwoodie, Dr RichardLiwicki, Dr Fay Betsou, Prof. HelleK-runke, Prof Jacob Graff Nielsen, Dr Janis Klovins, Dr TimoMinssen, K. MohanaKuma-ran Nair, P.K Jena, Soren Thuen for their valuable support. I would also like to extend my sincere thanks to the publishing team of Wolters Kluwer in particular Christine Robben for her patience and ongoing support towards the realization of this book.

List of Abbreviations

BBMRI	Biomolecular Resource Research Infrastructures
BCR-ABL	Breakpoint Cluster Region-Abelson
BHB	British Horseracing Board
BIMS	Biobank Information Management System
BRCA1/BRCA2	Breast Cancer Type 1/Type 2
CD3	Center for Drug Design & Discovery
CHM	Common Heritage of Mankind
CIOMS	Council for International Organizations of Medical Sciences
CJEU	Court of Justice of the European Union
CML	Chronic myelogenousleukemia
CNR	National Research Council
CORBEL	Coordinated Research Infrastructures Building Enduring Life-Science Services
CR	Corporate Responsibility
CRISPR	Clustered Regularly Interspaced Short Palindromic Repeats
CSR	Corporate Social Responsibility
DDF	Danske Dagblades Forening
DNA	Deoxyribonucleic Acid
DRMs	Digital Rights Management Technologies
DTA	Data Transfer Agreement
EAGDA	Expert Advisory Group on Data Access
EC	European Commission
ECHR	European Convention of Human Rights
ECtHR	European Court of Human Rights
EGCUT	Estonian Genome Center of the University of Tartu
EHR	Electronic Health Record

ELSI	Ethical Legal Social Implication
ELIXIR	European Life-Sciences Infrastructure for Biological Information
EMMA	European Mouse Mutant Archive
EPC	European Patent Convention
EPO	European Patent Office
ERIC	European Research Infrastructure Consortium
ESFRI	European Strategy Forum on Research Infrastructures
ESHG	European Society of Human Genetics
EU	European Union
EUIPO	European Union Intellectual Property Office
FIC	Free Informed Consent
GAVI	Global Alliance for Vaccines and Immunization
GDPR	General Data Protection Regulation
GEN-AU -	Genomeforschung in osterreich -The Austrian Genome Research Program
GWAS	Genome-Wide Association Study
GTC	Genetic Therapy Center
HBGRD	Human Biobanks and Genetic Research Databases
HBM	Human Biological Material
HGP	Human Genome Project
HGRA	Human Genes Research Act
HUGO	Human Genome Organisation
IBBL	Integrated Biobank of Luxembourg
ICT	Information and Communication Technology
IMI	Integrated Medicines Initiative
IP	Intellectual Property
IPRs	Intellectual Property Rights
ISBER	International Society for Biological and Environmental Repositories
ISO	International Organization for Standardization
IRDiRC	International Rare Disease Consortium
IT	Information Technology
LCSB	Luxembourg Centre for Systems Biomedicine
LIH	Luxembourg Institute of Health
LIMS	Laboratory Information Management System
MMV	Medicines for Malaria Venture
MTA	Material Transfer Agreement
NDA	Non disclosure Agreement
NHS	National Health Service
NIA	National Institute on Ageing
NITD	Novartis Institute for Tropical Diseases

OECD	Organisation for Economic Co-operation and Development
P3G	Public Population Project in Genomics and Society
PPP	Public Private Partnerships
PM	Personalized medicine
QMS	Quality Management Systems
RAIDs	Rational Molecular Assessments and Innovative Drugs Selection
R&D	Research and Development
RIs	Research Infrastructures
RRI	Responsible Research and Innovation
SFIRS	SocietàFinanziariaRegioneSardegna (Finance Corporation of the Region Sardinia)
SGC	Structural Genomics Consortium
SNPs	Single Nucleotide Polymorphisms
SPCs	Supplementary Protection Certificates
TA	Technology Assessment
TEC	Treaty Establishing the European Community
TFEU	Treaty on the Functioning of the European Union
TMS	Transcranial magnetic stimulation
TRIPS	Trade-Related Aspects of Intellectual Property Rights
UNESCO	The United Nations Educational, Scientific and Cultural Organization
VAT	Value-Added Tax
WCT	WIPO Copyright Treaty
WMA	World Medical Association
XNAT	Extensible Neuroimaging Archive Toolkit

Part I Definition, Principles and Evolving Models of Governance for Biobanks

CHAPTER 1

The Definition of Biobanks: Finding the Focal Points

§1.01 INTRODUCTION: BIOBANKS AS RI AND THE PRECOMPETITIVE PHASE OF GENETIC RESEARCH

Collection of scientific specimens has always been a pursuit towards the bewildering paradoxes of nature and sciences.[1] However, the advent of genomic studies opened up new directions towards creating, collecting and storing resources. Biobanks have thus emerged as 'Big Science' as sizeable undertakings with facilities involving large storage for cryopreservation, large sequencing coupled with bioinformatics platforms for genomic and proteomic analysis.[2] What are biobanks? While a detailed definition is discussed elsewhere in this chapter, the basic idea of biobanks are that they are organized collection facilities for storage of different types of samples human, animal and plants.

It is only over a decade, that serious thoughts on standardized practices found voice within biobanking landscape in Europe. The strength behind this effort has been the creation of European Strategy Forum on research Infrastructure (ESFRI) that identified the needs for Research infrastructures (RIs)[3] in priority fields of scientific

1. For instance the cabinets of curiosity of Ulisse Aldrovandi (1572) who was an Italian Naturalist. Encycl Br. Available at: http://www.britannica.com/EBchecked/topic/13659/Ulisse-Aldrovandi (accessed on 23 April 2015). While the collection of pathological tissues often started sporadically and out of curiosity, with the advent of public health as a political concern for nation states in the late eighteenth and early nineteenth century, collecting pathological tissues took on a broader political significance in Europe (*Biobanks and the Public Governing Biomedical Research Resou rces in Europe.* A Report from the BBMRI Project).
2. *Ibid.*
3. The term 'research infrastructures' refers to facilities, resources and related services used by the scientific community to conduct top-level research in their respective fields, ranging from social sciences to astronomy, genomics to nanotechnologies. Examples include singular large-scale research installations, collections, special habitats, libraries, databases, biological archives, clean

research.[4] In its first road map, the ESFRI recognized the research biobanking as an area of strategic interest and this resulted in the formation of Biomolecular Resource Research Infrastructures (BBMRI) in 2008.[5] In 2013, legal status was accorded to the European Research Infrastructure Consortium (ERIC)[6] under the Council Regulation (EC) No. 723/2009,[7] with the aim of creating a pan-European facility for biobanks in Europe. Two reports from the Commission highlighted some of the pressing challenges faced by biobanks.[8] These included technical, legal, regulatory and ethical concerns such as consent, ownership over biological samples, disposition of samples, handling of data, public engagement, cross-border exchange, confidentiality, intellectual property rights (IPR), commercialization investment and business strategies. While these challenges were identified, it was not fully address in literature. Caulfield, observes that 'Industry involvement could also increase the need to clarify issues that are associated with the ownership and control of samples, the regulations regarding access to samples and participant information ... thus policy should be informed of further analyses'.[9] Other prominent writing also notes that the increasing significance of biobanks in an era of rapid advances in translational medicine requires an understanding of not only important organizational and ethical questions, but also an understanding of dealing with IPRs that might arise out of the creation or later use of such biobanks.[10] The European Commission also recommended[11] that in *developing and using world-class research infrastructures, one of the major aspects to take into account is the protection of Intellectual Property Rights.*[12] Towards this reality the committee of

---

rooms, integrated arrays of small research installations, high-capacity/high speed communication networks, highly distributed capacity and capability computing facilities, data infrastructure, research vessels, satellite and aircraft observation facilities, coastal observatories, telescopes, synchrotrons and accelerators, networks of computing facilities, as well as infrastructural centres of competence which provide a service for the wider research community based on an assembly of techniques and know-how. RIs may be 'single-sited' (a single resource at a single location), 'distributed' (a network of distributed resources), or 'virtual' (the service is provided electronically). *See*: http://ec.europa.eu/research/infrastructures/index_en.cfm?pg=what (last accessed on 13 September 2018).

4. A Calzolari et. al., 'The European research infrastructures of the ESFRI Roadmap in biological and medical sciences: status and perspectives'. *Ann Ist Super Sanita.* 2014; 50(2).
5. *Supra* note 4.
6. The community legal framework for a European Research Infrastructure Consortium (ERIC) entered into force on 28 August 2009. This specific legal form is designed to facilitate the joint establishment and operation of research Infrastructures of European interest. BBMRI was given ERIC status under Commission Implementing Decision of 22 November 2013 on setting up the Biobanks and Biomolecular Resources Research Infrastructure Consortium (BBMRI-ERIC) as a European Research Infrastructure Consortium.
7. Council Regulation (EC) No. 723/2009 of 25 June 2009 on the Community legal framework for a European Research Infrastructure Consortium (ERIC).
8. Biobanks for Europe: a challenge for Governance, 2012 and Biobanks in Europe: Prospects for Harmonisation and Networking, 2010.
9. T. Caulfield et al., Industry Involvement in publicly funded biobanks, *Nature Reviews Genetics.* 2014; 15(4): 220.
10. J. Schovsbo et al., Legal aspects of biobanking as key issues for personalized medicine and translational exploitation, *Personalized Medicine.* 2014; 11(5): 497–508.
11. European Commission, A vision for strengthening excellent research infrastructures on the ERA: report of the Expert Group on Research Infrastructures, Brussels, 2010.
12. *Ibid.*, Point 6.4 Recommendations, at p. 41.

ministers, Council of Europe in May 2016 adopted *Recommendation CM/Rec(2016)6* which urged 'the importance of earning trust and stressing the role of good and transparent governance of biological materials of human origin stored for research purposes'.[13] It requires Member States 'to adapt their laws and practices to ensure the implementation of the guidelines'.[14]

The World Medical Association (WMA) in October 2016, adopted the Declaration of Taipei on Ethical Considerations regarding Health Databases and Biobanks, which called for '*Special considerations should be given to the possible exploitation of intellectual property*'.[15] In this regard questions of 'balancing' the usage of sample, 'possibilities' of exploitation of IPR along with assessing the 'special consideration' becomes immensely essential. Equally, it is also important to understand the phase of research within which the biobank-based research functions. This is essential for addressing the specific concerns relating to the protection of research results. Biomedical research proceeds in different phases of knowledge creation[16] and knowledge transfer.[17] The nature of new knowledge particularly in genomic research and the nature of its scattered creation within different public research projects act as barriers to knowledge transfer. This means that additional efforts are necessary to overcome such limitations.[18] To this end, there is an increasing focus on improving the quality and the standardization of the early phase of research. Understanding such basic research is also essential in terms of improving innovation within translation medicine paradigms. Precompetitive research and partnerships within these spaces enable knowledge transfer more effectively for biomedical research. Biobanks acts as effective tools in this process. Mining biobanks with technology and research provides the opportunity to identify risk and exposures prospectively as well as retrospectively in a representative sampling of a large population.[19] However, as noted above there exists several barriers not only for biobanks but for also evolving precompetitive research and partnerships within biobanks such as standardization, privacy, confidentiality and

13. Adopted by the Committee of Ministers on 11 May 2016 at the 1256th meeting of the Ministers' Deputies, available at: http://www.coe.int/en/web/portal/-/research-on-biological-materials-of-human-origin-new-recommendations-to-member-states (last accessed on 20 July 2016).
14. *Supra* note 13.
15. Adopted by the 53rd WMA General Assembly, Washington, DC, USA, October 2002 and revised by the 67th WMA General Assembly, Taipei, Taiwan, October 2016, available at: http://www.wma.net/en/30publications/10policies/d1/ (last accessed on 3 January 2017) *see* point 18.
16. Knowledge creation may proceed in the direction of codification of information or can be a part of implicit personal knowledge also called tactic knowledge. In the present context, knowledge creation is used in the sense of research and development and codification of results particularly within a publicly funded basic research environment. *see* I. Nonaka et al., A theory of knowledge creation. *International Journal of Technology Management*. (1996); 11: 833–845. Special Issue on Unlearning and Learning for Technological Innovation.
17. Knowledge transfer as the dissemination of research results via multiple channels from one individual or organization to another, D.V. Gibson and E.M. Rogers. R&D collaborations on trial, Harvard Business School Press 1994.
18. E. Verena Christiane and D. Engel, How to benefit from publicly funded pre-competitive research: an empirical investigation for Germany's ICR program. *Journal of Technology Transfer* (2011); 36: 292.
19. Establishing Precompetitive Collaborations to Stimulate Genomics-Driven Product Development: Workshop, Institute of Medicine (US) Roundtable on Translating Genomic-Based Research for Health. Washington: National Academies Press (US) 2011.

management of IPR. The urge to protect IPR may also pose challenges for innovation and collaboration in precompetitive paradigms. In this regard, it is important to understand the organizational and legislative choices biobanks may involve particularly while engaging in protection of research results and tech-transfer within a publicly funded setting. While the international initiatives call for special attention to IPR, there are no further guidance as to how Intellectual property (IP) policies ought to be framed to meet the needs of the biobanks including principles if any that are required in research partnerships within biobanks. This gap is addressed by the present work by interlinking research, innovation and collaboration within a precompetitive biobank-based research.

[A] Aims of the Book and Explanation of Structure

Biobanks combine collections of human tissue linked with genetic information and other health information gathered with the aim of securing enhancement in treatment methods, diagnosis and cure for various diseases. Thus being a finest resource of genetic information biobanks must strategize their resources towards effective utilization for biomedical research. The European Commission's 'Recommendation on the Management of Intellectual Property in Knowledge Transfer Activities and a Code of Practice for Universities and Other Public Research Organisations', 10 April 2008 (IP Recommendation, often also referred to as 'IP Charta') lays down that:

> An effort should be made to better convert knowledge into socio-economic benefits. Therefore, public research organisations/ entities need to disseminate and to more effectively exploit publicly funded research results with a view to translating them into new products and services. The means to realise this effectively is through academia-industry collaborations and collaborative or contract research conducted or funded jointly with the private sector.

Similar approach resurfaced in 'A vision for Europe: open innovation, open science, open to the world' published in 2016, which sought the use of intellectual property before making knowledge publicly available in order to ensure translation of research results into innovation. These insights from the Commission reflects the changing paradigms of research and forms the objective for the current work. The shift in public sector research is aimed not only at improving research in general but also at the economic sustenance of public research to enable them to play an active role in making social contribution. Hence, it is pertinent that research in general and biomedical research in particular must respect the participants and should be conducted in a manner that upholds human dignity, fundamental freedoms, human rights and must be carried out in a responsible manner.[20] Within these broader visions, the present work examines the role of IPR in biobank-based research. This examination involves an identification of all the stakeholders involved and their distinctive role within research. This work acknowledges the foundational rights of the donors (research participants) particularly the right of self-determination and privacy. However, these

20. OECD, Guidelines 2009 on Human Biobanks and Genetic Research Databases.

rights come only under a limited purview in present work while examining the legal relationship of donors with respect to the research process. Thus, without going into the depths of the concept of consent and by excluding the discourse on the ethics of commercialization of human genetic materials, the book tries to examine the role of IPR within biobanks including research partnerships where IPR may be involved to protect the results.

IPR are 'double-edged' in both acting as enablers and restrictors of progress. This gives impetus to an understanding of various factors such as the legal, governance, innovation and publicly funded research within biobanks. In establishing these elements, the possibilities for structuring new models of research with integrated principles of ethics and laws could emerge. Research and commercialization of results may involve involving different incentive structures of research. Such incentives may vary based on the research paradigm within which such innovation proceeds. First, consider the question 'what kinds of incentives exist for protecting research results within biobanks?' This directs one to think in terms of the traditional and most prominent incentives, which are IPR. IPR are of different types, and then the next question arises as to 'whether different IPR can play a role in biobanks?' The innovation outcomes of biobank-based research may be protected by IPR however time consuming it may be.[21] However, there could be multiple challenges for involving IPRs within biobank based research and personalized medicine. Despite this there exists different types of IPR like sui generis rights or copyrights that have useful implications for protecting the data and data sets within biobanks. Thus identifying different IP rights and their challenges enables strategizing an effective IP policy for biobanks. Another question that invariably arises in the mind of the reader would be if there could be any potential consequences for involving IPRs within publicly funded biobanks? While protecting the interest of innovators, IPRs can foster an environment in which creativity and innovation can flourish, provided the private interests are adequately balanced with social benefits. At the same time IPRs may tend to restrict access to research results particularly within a precompetitive space where knowledge is much more fluid. However, the sustenance of biobanks rests on finding use of the attenuated resources held by the biobank.[22] In finding use for attenuated products, there exists '*a fortiori*', a case for commercialization of the results of biobank-based research. On this account biobank, based research also needs to address the potential consequences in involving IPR within biobanks. This assessment needs to be done with reference to the mixed experiences within Europe with an intention to identify the possible strategies and pitfalls in balance IP policies within publicly funded biobanks.

21. J.E. Olson et al., Biobanks and personalized medicine. *Clinical Genetics*. 2014; 86(1): 50–55. Biobanks can provide critical research and infrastructure support for clinical genetics in the era of personalized medicine. Studies using biobanks can effectively support discovery and validation of genetic associations and gene-environment interactions, which will inform general biological insights on disease pathogenesis and can ultimately be translated for risk assessment/stratification, new diagnostics, pharmacogenomics and drug development, all are important to supporting the practice of clinical genetics.
22. A product is considered to be attenuated if a donor does not subjectively *see* the human tissue product as significant; *See* Tonti-Filippini, J Transplant Technol Res 2013, 3:2, http://dx.doi.org/10.4172/2161-0991.1000e12.

While there are possibilities to secure property rights over materials and data, what matters is how well the interests of different stakeholders are balanced.

With the above directions, the present work considers that biobanks must seek an IP policy, which considers two important points namely:

(1) The obligations towards participants while endeavouring the commercial use and exploitation of resources held within the biobanks.[23] This is on account of the sensitive nature of such repositories.[24]
(2) The obligations towards other researchers working in the area of biomedical research. While an IP policy may protect research results, it should also ensure that the rights of other researchers are not to be hampered in the process. Hence there arises important issues in relation to access, data sharing[25] and experimental use of patented discoveries.[26]

Policy development in the field of biobanking must be informed of realities involved in research/industrial partnerships. To this end it is essential that the governance of research partnerships adheres to internationally accepted legal and ethical standards. However, since law does not conclusively deal in all aspects of biobanks based research, it is essential to have an understanding of the different legal and quasi-legal frameworks in place along with a mosaic view of different issues that

23. As pointed out in under Principle 9 C of the OECD Guidelines on biobanks, 'The operators of the HBGRD should have a clearly articulated policy and explicitly indicate to participants whether they and/or the HBGRD retain any rights over the human biological materials and/or data and the nature of such rights.'
24. C. Heany et al., The perils of taking property too far. *Stanford Journal of Law Science and Policy.* May 2009. While the European Convention on Human Rights and Biomedicine(Oviedo, 4 April 1997) and the Universal Declaration on Human Genome and Human Rights(11 November 1997) explicitly prohibit commercial gains from human body parts as such however it does not exempt commercialization of products such as cell lines or other process used in extraction and storage of samples. There has been a diversity as to commercialization as an approach in the field of biobanking. Some writers (D. Chalmers, et.al., Has the biobank bubble burst? Withstanding the challenges for sustainable biobanking in the digital rra. *BMC Medical Ethics.* 2016), content that public trust in biobanks is inevitably reduced where there is a commercial partner, particularly an international commercial partner. Indeed, loss of public trust has been connected with the demise of certain biobanks in the past, however the present needs a realistic view on balancing commercial interests with the needs of the biobanks. The use of the resources (actual or and potential) have been the strength behind the donation of samples. This argument invariably finds strength in industrial partnerships as well while learning the pitfalls from previous experiences.
25. E. Richard Gold and D. Nicol, 'Beyond open source: patents, biobanks and sharing', in G. Pascuzzi (ed.), 'Comparative issues in the governance of research biobanks', Springer 2013; considers that, there is a growing recognition that greater reliance on research collaborations and data sharing are necessary to increase productivity. Collaborations bring together individuals and institutions possessing different skills and knowledge sets, opening up opportunities for creative approaches to drug discovery. Data sharing allows for the more efficient deployment of resources by avoiding duplication of research and the use of standard software tools. Together, collaborations and data sharing offer important tools to rationalise the cost in time and money of drug discovery ... However *in the light of IP rights the pro and cones as well as reality of data sharing along with privacy concerns needs to be addressed* [Emphasis added].
26. B.M. Simon, How to get a fair share: IP policies for publicly supported biobanks. *Stanford Journal of Law, Science and Policy.* 2009.

involved in the process. Such an approach offers stability to the vision of the European Commission in seeking a complete integration of a pan-European infrastructure to support medical research and healthcare.[27]

To accomplish this aim, the structure of the work is spread out in four parts and a conclusion consisting of nine chapters. The core issues divided between samples and data following the definition of biobanks. Part I. (Chapters 1 and 2) Chapter 1 thus sets out the background for the research questions, theoretical approaches, definitions of biobanks, foundational principles and limitations. Chapter 2, explores the legal landscape, governance models within which biobanks operate giving a foundation for the research landscape of biobanking in Europe. Part II (Chapter 3) examines patent law and the legal and ethical issues surrounding the use of human biological materials (HBMs) within biomedical innovations. In particular the chapter examines the concept of 'ownership' over resource and the use of samples in pre-patent research. Broadly, this chapter thus deals with the IP issues over samples. Part III, deals in different perspectives over protection of genomic data and databases. This consists of Chapters 4, 5 and 6. Chapter 4 is devoted to the analysis of IP issues over genomic data within biobanks. Chapter 5 is devoted to copyrights over genomic data including copyright policies for digital integration within biobanks. Chapter 6 deals with the growing importance of Trade Secrets in Europe and its implications for public research. These chapters unpack the question of data in its varying manifestations including the status of biological material as 'data'. Part IV consisting of Chapters 7 and 8 deals in commercial collaboration, practices, consequences and policies for governance of biobank-based research and collaborations. Chapter 7 under this part considers the IP management as identified through the collaboration contracts and material transfer agreement (MTA) with a view to appreciate if the considerations for involving IP and balancing them out with the ethical needs for commercialization of biobank research are fully met. Chapter 8 examines the mixed experiences in Europe over commercial involvement within biobanks and considers models for commercial involvement particularly the public private partnership model, which is widely being recognized as a balancing model. It also considers an IP policy that may be developed within a PPP (Public Private Partnership) model in biobanks. Finally, Part V concludes with Chapter 9, with recommendations devoted to evolving solutions to balance the needs of public research and private interests. The chapter focuses on two key areas namely seeking a distinct role for IP (unlike the traditional discussions) within biobanks and drawing the focus on building a research climate suited to balance IP within biobank-based research.

27. *Ibid.*

[B] The Definition of a Biobank

The use of the term 'biobank' is comparatively new and is still in the process of gaining its repute.[28] The Eurobarometer study[29] of 2010 reports that 66% have not heard about biobanks prior to the survey. The inconspicuousness of the term among general public coupled with the increasingly extensive usage of biobanking facilities in biomedical research in the scientific world, calls for a greater attention to the understanding of the nature and scope of biobanking. This part addresses the problem of defining the system or institution of 'biobanks'. By examining the prominent definitions, the paper seeks to address the conclusiveness or non-conclusiveness of the definition of a biobank. It also seeks to consider whether it is imperative to reconstruct a comprehensive definition for biobanks. Even so, the novelty of the concept may offer certain confines to the concept in itself. The literary structure of the term rests on two distinct words 'bio' and 'bank'. 'Bio' is a combination form meaning 'life' from its Grecian origins.[30]'Bank' on the contrary refers to an establishment for custody. It gains its usage from English and Scandinavian origins of the thirteenth century.[31] A synthesis of the two terms thus refers to a storage unit for matters containing life or an establishment for storage of stratum of life. It is also pertinent to examine the meaning of the term beyond its literary bounds and for purpose of the present discussion. To this end three distinct sources may be examined namely acts and guidelines from different jurisdictions, explanations by biobanking organizations and finally views from literature in the area of biobanking.

[1] Regulatory Definition

Not many jurisdictions have settled on to an extensive regulation on biobanks. Few countries have settled laws while others are in the process of developing standards for biobanking regulations. In some jurisdictions the ethical guidelines for biomedical research is largely used as a standard rather than separate legislation on biobanking mechanism. One of the first legislations developed in the field is from Iceland. The Iceland Biobanks Act[32] was developed in 2000 and has been amended twice since then in 2008 and 2009. The act apart from offering a general definition of biobank also classifies biobanks into two distinct categories namely research biobank and clinical biobank. As per the act, '*a biobank is a collection of biological samples which are permanently preserved*'.[33] Though this definition offers no clarity as to the nature of the biological samples, the objective clause of the act explains that it is aimed to authorize the collection, keeping, handling and utilization of human biological samples. Under

28. H. Simonsen et al., Neonatal screening in Denmark, Status and future perspectives. Ugeskr. Laeger.1998; 160: 5777–5782.
29. Special Eurobarometer survey 73.1 Report on Biotechnology, 2010.
30. http://dictionary.reference.com/browse/bio-.
31. http://www.merriam-webster.com/dictionary/bank.
32. No. 110/2000, as amended by Act No. 27/2008 and Act No. 48/2009.
33. Article 3[5.], Iceland, The Biobank and health database Act 2000, Inserted by Act No. 48/2009, Art. 1.

the same article, a research biobank is defined as *'a collection of research samples to be preserved for more than five years'*[34] and a Clinical biobank as a *'collection of clinical samples to be preserved for more than five years'*.[35] The distinction between 'clinical' and 'research' is based on the nature and use of the collection. While clinical samples are acquired for the purpose of health services, the research samples are used for scientific purposes like study of population or specific symptoms and so on. The Swedish Act on Biobanks[36] defines the concept 'biobank' as 'biological material from one or several human beings collected and stored indefinitely or for a specified time and whose origin can be traced to the human or humans from whom it originates'.[37] According to the Swedish Act on Biobanks, the size of the sample collection has no significance; a single human sample may form a biobank. There is no difference between samples collected for research or during routine medical care.[38] Another distinctive feature of the definition is that the human biological sample must be traced to a human being, thus a sample taken from an unidentified corpse may not come within the premise of the Swedish biobanks. In Denmark, The Act on Research Ethics Review of Health Research Projects, 2012[39] lays down the legal framework for the research ethics evaluation of health research projects. The act defines a research biobank as a structured collection of HBM that is kept with a view to a concrete health research project, and which may be accessed according to defined criteria and where information bound in the biological material may be traced to individuals.[40] The provision aims at essentially strong health research project that has been duly approved by the committee under the act and must be taken from identifiable donors as in the Swedish Act.

Under the Finnish Act[41] a biobank is visualized a biobanking carrier maintained by the unit, which will gather and store samples and associated information for the future research biobank (biopankkitutkimusta). It also defines research biobanks as those which use stored biobank samples and associated data and the purpose of which is to promote health, understanding disease mechanisms or health and medical products used in the development and management practices.[42]

Under the Spanish Royal Decree 1716/2011,[43] a 'Biobank for biomedical research' is defined as public or private, non-profit establishments home to one or more collections of biological samples of human origin for biomedical research, organized as a production unit with quality criteria by and destination, regardless of samples

34. Article 3[6], Iceland, The Biobank and health database Act, 2000.
35. Article 3[7], Iceland, The Biobank and health database Act, 2000.
36. (SF 2002: 297).
37. 2 §, The Swedish Act on Biobanks, 2002.
38. http://www.biobanks.se/biobank.htm (last accessed on 12 March 2014).
39. Came into force on 1 January 2012, the act contains provisions that implement parts of Directive 2001/20/EC.
40. Part 2, section 2(1) 13, The Act on Research Ethics Review of Health Research Projects, 2012.
41. The Finnish Biopankkilaki Act, 2012 688/2012, Finland.
42. Article 3(8), Biopankkilaki, 2012.
43. Issued in 2011 to clarify Law 14/2007, of 3 July, on Biomedical Research.

harbouring other purposes.[44] These definitions offer clarification the nature and size of biobank apart from enjoining the basic requirements for authorization and operation of biobanks for biomedical research. Some of the definitions also offer to include ethical and research oriented focus of biobank in the larger public interest. Commentators point out that most biobanks have been guided predominantly by the 'quest for research' rather than by conventional supply-and-demand mechanics.[45] Thus offering a definition of public and private biobanks without any room for commercialization may prove detrimental to the subsistence of the biobanks.[46] Other prominent European jurisdictions to look upon various aspects of biobanks include Belgium[47] and Estonia,[48] Norway and Switzerland. The Norwegian Biobank Act, 2003[49] defines biobanks on similar lines to the Iceland biobank by making a classification into diagnostic and research biobanks. The terms diagnostic biobank and treatment biobank as used in the act means a *collection of human biological material contributed for the purpose of medical examination, diagnosis and treatment.* The term research biobank as used in the act *means a collection of human biological material and data obtained directly by the analysis of this material, and that is used or is to be used for research purposes.* Further, under the Norwegian biobank law it is possible to use the biological samples that had been originally collected for the purposes of diagnosis for research as well, to study for instance the nature of genetic or rare diseases.

In many jurisdictions, the term 'biorepository' is also used.[50] The term denotes a 'collection of human biological material collected and stored during the execution of a specific research project, in accordance with regulations or predefined technical, ethical and operational standards under the management of a researcher and for non-commercial purposes'.[51] Though the distinction between the two appears to be nominal, its importance is meaningful. While biobank is an institutional facility having

44. Article 2(b), Royal Decree 1716/2011, Art. 3(d) Law 14/2007 of the prior Act of 2007 on Biomedical research offered for a slightly different version of the definition. Under the prior act a biobank was defined as a public or private non-profit establishment which has a collection of biological samples conceived for biomedical diagnostic or research purposes and organized as a technical unit with criteria of quality, order and destination.
45. J. Vaught et al., Biobankonomics: developing a sustainable business model approach for the formation of a human tissue biobank, DOI: 10.1093/jncimonographs/lgr009.
46. The bankruptcies of private population biobanks in Canada and Iceland is illustrative of the problems raised in the context of a complete exemption of commercialisation. For more discussion on the aspect, *see* T. Caulfield et al., A review of the key issues associated with the commercialization of biobanks. *Journal of Law and Bioscience*. 2014.
47. The law on procurement and use of human biological material for therapeutic or research use, 2008 outlines bank of human biological material as organized structure for various transactions like procurement, testing, processing, preservation, storage or distribution, including import and export of human biological material.
48. In Estonia the Human Genes Research Act, 2000 does not use the term biobank as such instead uses the term 'Gene Bank' to mean a database established and maintained by the chief processor consisting of tissue samples, descriptions of DNA, descriptions of state of health, genealogies, genetic data and data enabling the identification of gene donors.
49. Entered into force on 1 July 2003 pursuant to Royal Decree of 23 May 2003.
50. Article 3 III, Brazilian Ordinance No. 2,201 of 2011. See also G. Marodin et al., Biobanking for health research in Brazil: present challenges and future directions, Rev Panam salud publica, 2012 June 31 (6) 523–528.
51. *Ibid.*

an organized collection, which may be used for future studies, a biorepository is essentially limited to a single project. Such distinction in the definition has implications for ethical procedures such as consent, which could be given for specific projects as opposed to a general consent.[52]

In Switzerland, guidelines for biobanking involving human participants have existed since 2006,[53] which defines biobanks as 'systematic collections' of samples of human body substances (e.g., organs, tissue, blood, cells, etc.) and Deoxyribonucleic acid (DNA) as carrier of genetic information. Data that contain information on the donor (demographic data, type of disease, etc., but also genetic data) are stored, either together with the samples or separately. A new act called the Human Research Act, complementary to the above-mentioned guidelines have come into force from 1 January 2014[54] that deals in the ethical matters related to use of human biological samples.

[2] Organizational Definition

The proliferation of genomic testing and involvement of human participants have led to many interest groups and international bodies to achieve standardization in the exploitation of human biological samples. The BBMRI was one of the first projects entering the European Research Infrastructure which aimed to develop an infrastructure for biobanking and biological research in Europe and worldwide.[55] The BBMRI considers the aim of biobank as a coordinated, large-scale European infrastructure of biomedically relevant, quality-assessed collection of collected samples (with the possibility to link to related clinical and epidemiological information), to enhance therapy and prevention of common and rare diseases, including cancer.

Yet another initiative is the Public Population project in genomics and society or the Public Population Project in Genomics and Society (P3G).[56] It is a 'not-for-profit' consortium that provides the international research community with access to the expertise, resources and innovative tools for health and social sciences research. According to the P3G Biobank Lexicon,[57] a biobank is an organized collection of HBM and associated information stored for one or more research purposes. The Organisation for Economic Co-operation and Development (OECD) Recommendation on Human Biobanks and Genetic Research Databases, 2009[58] views human biobanks and genetic research databases ('HBGRD') as 'structured resources' that can be used for the

52. *Supra* note 50.
53. Biobanks: Obtainment, preservation and utilisation of human biological material Medical-ethical guidelines and recommendations 23 May 2006 Switzerland.
54. Organization Regulation for Human Research Act (Organization Regulation HFG, OV-HFG) of 20 September 2013.
55. J. Reichel et al., ERIC: a new governance tool for biobanking. European Journal of Human Genetics. 2014; 22: 1055–1057.
56. http://p3g2.org/ (last accessed on 14 September 2018).
57. B.M. Knoppers and T.J Hudson. The art and science of biobanking. *Human Genetics.* 2011 130: 329. https://doi.org/10.1007/s00439-011-1067-9.
58. www.oecd.org/sti/biotech/44054609.pdf (last accessed on 8 March 2014).

purpose of genetic research and which include: (a) HBMs and/or information generated from the analysis of the same; and (b) extensive associated information.

The definition of biobanks have been considerably expatiated by German National Ethics Council[59] on similar lines as the OECD guidelines and it is considered as a collection of samples of human bodily substances that are or can be associated with personal data and information on their donors. Examples of bodily substances include cells, tissue and blood, as well as DNA as the physical medium of genetic information. The twofold character of biobanks serving as collections of samples and data forms its distinctiveness. Thus a facility cannot be regarded as a biobank if it merely records and stores personal data derived from bodily samples e.g., laboratory values from blood tests or the results of genetic analyses.[60] Further the new guidelines enjoin that every collection should be the subject of the statutory provisions for biobanks if it satisfies the following three criteria:[61]

(1) It contains genetic material originating from humans with related data.
(2) Its samples are linked electronically to personal information and further information, in particular relating to health.
(3) Its samples and data are collected, preserved or used for purposes of scientific research.[62]

This explanation fortifies the stricter adherence to the ethical guidelines particularly when it has personal patient data attached to it. Another definitional distinction worth mentioning herein is the difference between 'health data base' and 'biobanks' which is interchangeably used. While both give rise to the similar legal and ethical issues, they are essentially different. A health database is a system for collecting, organizing and storing health information. It enables the subsequent retrieval of information in a structured manner with appropriate algorithmic support.

[3] Literature

The literature in the field of biobanking is also exhaustive with conceptions as the nature and structure of a biobank. Biobanks are defined as facilities that hold biological material and associated data in an organized manner.[63] These enable research activities in such a way that it would be possible for combining clinical studies and research collections with similar international collaborations thus facilitating the exchange of

59. German National Ethics Council guidelines 2004 https://www.ethikrat.org/fileadmin/Publikationen/Stellungnahmen/englisch/DER_StnBiob_Engl_Online_mitKennwort.pdf (last accessed on 14 September 2018).
60. http://ec.europa.eu/research/biosociety/pdf/ethikrat_opinion_biobanks.pdf (last accessed on 5 March 2014).
61. *Supra* note 59.
62. *Ibid.*
63. A. Cambon Thomson, The social and ethical issues of post-genomic human biobanks. *Nature Reviews Genetics.* 2004; 5: 866–873.

genetic resources and data for biomedical research in the long run.[64] This convergence of molecular and digital advances requires a global view and policy re-engineering for biobanks. In this sense biological specimen collections, often considered a treasure house of information, for genetic components.[65] In considering the need for enhanced studies and finding more cases in the interest of medical cure, some writers have also suggested a move from biobank towards biobank networks or as a consortium study with increased collaboration within public research.[66]

The exhaustive definitions discussed above from various statutory and other sources offers some directions towards identifying the role of biobanks.

First, almost all regulatory guidelines seem to view biobank as a 'collection', 'unit' or 'structure', which is systematically arranged or organized. They may be also considered as a 'network' or 'consortium'.[67] This generally implies existence of different biobank models.[68]

Second, such collection contains samples of human origin. Though some of the definitions examined above are not inclusive of this view for instance biobanks for biodiversity and wild life preservation also exist e.g., The wildlife Biological Resource Centre, South Africa. Thus, the standardization also differs based on the nature of the collection.

Third, such samples are essentially accompanied by associated information or data pertaining to the said samples. This forms a crux of most definitions on account of the fact that much of the concerns on privacy and data protection rely on the donor information attached to the samples collected.

Fourth, the most important reflective aspect of every definition seems to be the purpose for which the sample collection is made. It may be solely for clinical or for research, purposes. Sometimes the samples derived from clinical studies may also be used in diagnostic research. The purpose also tends to identify the usage of the samples and data in research cohorts and collaborations. Based on the nature of usage, the type of consent obtained from donors may also vary.[69]

Another interesting view point raised by many stakeholders and commentators[70] is that the usage of the term 'biobank' may be sometimes misleading.[71] Bank may refer not only to establishment for storing but may also mean in common parlance an institution where transactions may be conducted. The money, an account holder has in

64. J. Kaye et. al. Governing biobanks, Hart Publishing, 2012.
65. Robin J.R Blatt, Banking biological collections: data warehousing, data mining, and data dilemmas in genomics and global health policy, *Community Genetics*. 2000; 3(4): 204-211.
66. M.M. Morente and S. Alonso, Current challenges of human tumour banking. *Hematological Oncology*. 2005; 23: 54-56.
67. *Ibid.*
68. D.M. Shaw et al., What is a biobank? Differing definition among biobank stakeholders, Clinical Genetics, 3 2013 September. Doi:10.1111/cge-12268, 2013.
69. R. Hewitt and P. Watson, Defining Biobank, Biopreservation and biobanking. October 2013; 11(5): 309-315; *see also* J. Schovsbo et al., Legal aspects of biobanking as key issue for personalized medicine and translational exploitation'. *Journal of Personalised Medicine*; 11(5): 497-508.
70. *Supra* notes 68 and 69.
71. J. Sandor et al., The case of Biobank with law: between a legal and scientific fiction. *Journal of Medical Ethics*. 2011.

his bank account may be utilized and transacted in different ways; likewise the usage 'biobank' may suggest an inference that the donors have ownership over their respective samples. Such an interpretation subverts the existing notions on biobanks while giving strength to the claims of informed consent and larger public participation. Although law prohibits commercialization of tissue samples,[72] the exercise of consent in collecting the tissue samples from donors' amounts to transfer of ownership.[73] Thus, the adequacy of the term in itself is questionable. The conceptual divergence in the definition of biobanks also suggests attention to standardization of norms governing biobanking.

[C] Types, Models of Biobanks

Just as there are varying differences in the definition of biobanks, the type of biobanks also differs widely.[74] They may vary based on its content, purpose or size. Based on their organizational structure there may be public, private or non-profit biobanks (e.g., UK Biobank). Based on their purpose biobanks may be classified into population studies, disease specific (e.g., rare disease consortium biobank or national rare disease biobank, Spain), clinical cohorts or even considered as a general biobank.[75] Likewise, the nature of access arrangements can also determine a differing type of biobank[76] e.g., closed access, controlled access or public open access.[77] In order to avoid getting lost in the wilderness of the various types of classification the present work appreciates each biobank based on the type of role pursued by it, irrespective of its purpose (i.e., as population collection or disease specific). This would enable one to easily identify the perspective under discussion in different parts of this work. Biobanks can be categorized into three:[78]

(1) Biobanks as service providers.
(2) Biobanks as a product developer.
(3) Biobank as biomedical research infrastructure/consortium.

Biobank in its role as a service provider offers technical services relating to collection, processing and storage of biological samples. While involving in research

72. Article 21 – Prohibition of financial gain, Oviedo Convention 1997; *See also Greenberg v Miami Children's Hospital*, 264 F. Supp. 2d.1064, 1077.
73. *Ibid.*
74. *See* S.M.C. Gibbons, Regulating biobanks; A twelve point typological tool. *Medical Law Review*, Autumn, 2009; 17: 313–346; H. Gottweiss and K. Zatloukal, Biobank governance: trends and perspectives. *Pathobiology*. 2007; 74: 206–211.
75. J.E. Olson, et al., Biobanks and personalized medicine. *Clinical Genetics*. 2014; 86(1): 50–55. PMC. Web. 16 January 2017.
76. *Supra* note 75.
77. *See* for more discussions on categories *see*: Stratum WP 7 Report on Financing UK biobanks: rationale for a National. Biobanking Research Infrastructure; *see also* Biobanks in Europe: Prospects for Harmonisation and Networking Report at p. 11.
78. Idea acknowledgement Dominic Allen Chief Operating Officer, IBBL (Integrated BioBank of Luxembourg).

activities biobanks engage in product development involving methods and processes thereby being involved in commercially viable activities. As a part of a larger structure, biobanks may be obliged to follow rules pertaining to such consortium. In such roles there would also be collaborative/join research arrangements with different biobanks or research units. This would enable identifying the distinctive functions performed and would offer to clarify the relationships between different stakeholders. This will eliminate a one-sided perspective which is quite often reflated in literature relating to biobanks being just 'banks' collecting samples for future uses with possible commercial interest.[79] Thus in avoiding a narrow view of biobanks, such classification opens up the possibilities and enables an understanding of how IP law may function within these roles.

[D] HBMs: The 'Sample' in Biobanks

Cells and tissues derived from human donors are increasingly used in different types of research. For such purposes, the samples are being processed and stored through special cryogenic procedures. As seen from the definition above biobanks mainly comprise of samples and data and together they form an essential resource for biomedical research. Although, HBMs are widely used in research, they not always defined.[80] Under Article 2, of the, draft instrument on the use of archived HBMs in biomedical research[81] *'human biological materials shall mean materials of human origin whether identified, identifiable or not'*. While this is not much illuminating, Article 3 sub Clause 3.2 of the same draft instrument provides that:

> This instrument shall not apply to research:
>
> i) that comes under the scope of the Protocol on Biomedical Research.
> ii) On unlinked anonymized human cell lines or stem cell lines.
> iii) On human foetuses, embryos, sperm, eggs and their precursors.

However, this view taken in 2002 in the draft proposals vanished from the Rec(2006)4[82] which only provided under Article 2, that the recommendation did not apply to *'embryonic and foetal tissues'*. Thus, the mentioning of only embryonic and foetal tissues and avoiding the rest of samples like human cell lines or stem cells meant a larger scope for the term HBM[83]. In the more recent recommendation

79. J. Sandor, The case of biobank with law: between legal and scientific fiction, *Journal of Medical Ethics*. 2011.
80. C. Trouet, New European guidelines for the use of stored human biological materials in biomedical research. *Journal of Medical Ethics*. 2004; 30: 99–103.
81. Proposal for an instrument on the use of archived human biological materials in biomedical research, CDBI/INF (2002)5.
82. Recommendation Rec(2006)4 of the Committee of Ministers to Member States on research on biological materials of human origin (Adopted by the Committee of Ministers on 15 March 2006, at the 958th meeting of the Ministers' Deputies).
83. *Supra* note 80.

CM/Rec(2016)6[84] this approach was restructured to exclude '*embryonic and foetal biological materials*' from its purview. This by far avoided any materials relating embryonic and foetus by removing the word tissue. While it may be safe to consider that HBM would include all other HBMs except the embryonic and foetal, it is still ambiguous. The WMA declaration of Taipei[85] considers biological material to include a sample obtained from an individual human being, living or deceased, which can provide biological information, including genetic information, about that individual (*see also* Chapter 4).[86] Thus, HBMs may include tissue, cell lines, blood, organ parts and DNA, etc.[87] For the present discussion, it is best to find a definition of HBM closer to the sphere of IPR and innovations. In respect of the present discussion, I propose using the definition under the biotech directive (Directive 98/44/EC).[88] Article 2 of the biotech directive provides that, *'biological material' means any material containing genetic information and capable of reproducing itself or being reproduced in a biological system*; this definition is broad enough to include all types of biological materials (including embryonic), animal materials and plant materials. However, the Directive also makes certain exclusion, which are noted under Article 6 of the Directive such as 'human embryos'. Under the biotech directive, '*biological material which is isolated from its natural environment or produced by means of a technical process may be the subject of an invention even if it previously occurred in nature*'.[89] In applying the definition of biological materials as in the biotech directive, plant and animal biological materials will be excluded for the present enquiry and any reference to biological material shall be limited to those originating from human beings unless otherwise specifically mentioned.

[E] Data, Data Types and Database

The exploration and appreciation of genetic data sets of individuals helps in understanding the causes for proximity or remoteness to or the modifiability or non-modifiability of risk factors. Such studies require a digital integration of data along with analytics, which enables cutting out pieces of information of interest from a mass of data elements.[90] Over the last decade, rapid advancement in genomic technology has enabled the creation of scientific platforms for collecting, processing genomic data and collaboration with international counterparts with a realization that the power of

84. Recommendation CM/Rec(2016)6 of the Committee of Ministers to Member States on research on biological materials of human origin(Adopted by the Committee of Ministers on 11 May 2016 at the 1256th meeting of the Ministers' Deputies).
85. Preamble 4, WMA Declaration of Taipei on Ethical Considerations regarding Health Databases and Biobanks, 2016.
86. WMA declaration on ethical consideration regarding health databases and biobanks, 2015.
87. M.B. Kapp, Biobanking human biological materials: issues surrounding the collection of samples for use in future research, Pharmaceutical Medicine. 2008; 22: 75.
88. Directive 98/44/EC, 6 July 1998 on the legal protection of biotechnological inventions.
89. Article 3(2), Directive 98/44/EC.
90. A-M. Tasse, ´Legal and ethical implications of data sharing in international biobanking research: Toward a global response. *Biopreservation and Biobanking.* 2016 14(3), Mary Ann Liebert, Inc.

individual studies is limited.[91] The structure of such digital integration often evolves from discovery of a fact to its biological analysis and finally its translation into clinically useful data (Figure 1.1 below). In this process, the function of a database is to accelerate discovery of disease susceptible genes through an integrated analysis using large-scale data sets and a range of experimental designs, within computer assisted analytic programs. The ultimate goal of the process is to find new and novel disease pathways and biomarkers.[92]

Figure 1.1 Data Integration Within Biomedical Research[93]

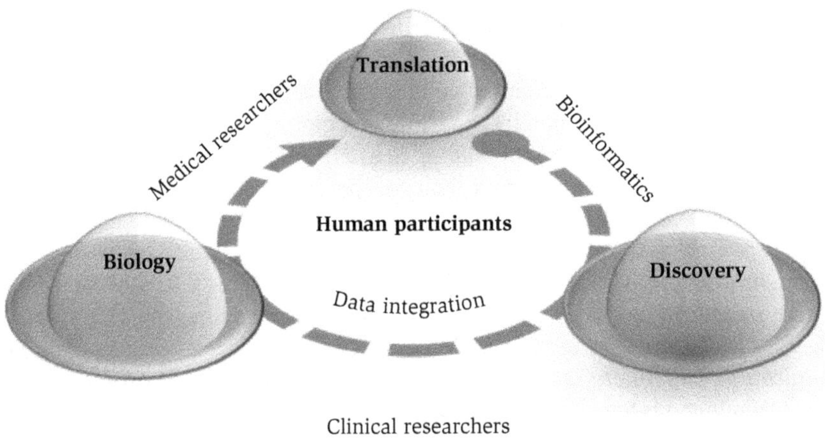

A pragmatic view considers social genomic studies as 'quantified self', wherein the approach is to record and store multiple data that reflect factors of human existence. Thus as aptly put in by Gregory and Bowker human beings now live algorithmically as 'data citizens' whose identities are necessarily caught up in the cloud.[94] However, the authors consider affiliating the 'data' pertaining to an individual to the plain self as misplaced concretism. Thus, physical objects are at the most causes of perception. Nevertheless, human beings are sense-objects, thus being at the heart of perception itself. This seems to be the most important reason for dissent over genetic resources even though factually the interaction with the actual data may not exist at all. This concern seems to be escalated with the change in scale of sample collection (e.g., large population collections), which raises a number of other concerns both legal and

91. European Network for Genetic and Genomic Epidemiology summary report 2012, available at http://www.euengage.org/press.html (last accessed on 15 July 2016).
92. L. Peltonen and A. Victor, McKusick, Dissecting human disease in the postgenomic era. *Science.* 16 February 2001; 291(5507): 1224–1229.
93. Acknowledgement: ALLPPT.com _ Free PowerPoint Templates, Diagrams and Charts.
94. J. Gregory and G.C. Bowker, The data citizen, the quantified self, and personal genomics, in Dawn Nafus, Quantified, Biosensing Technologies in Everyday Life, MIT Press, 2016.

ethical.[95] Nevertheless, before going into the depths of the discussion, it is essential to clarify few concepts, which would be further expanded in the chapters that follow.

[1] Data

'Data' in the scientific front data implies results collected using specific methods for a specific purpose of studying or analysing and obtained by a process of scientific observation and experimentation. Thus, data involves elements like names, words and numbers that categorize, calculate or quantify facts collected. When these are linked to concepts, they become information.

Data integration as a process involves discovery, biological analysis and translation thus involving multiple scores of data in each phase. Hence, 'Data' in the context of biobanks is often viewed as 'universal language' across the discipline of biobanking.[96] Quality assurance and thereby the value of a biobank often depends not only on the samples but also that of the data relating to it. The greater the quality of data linked to a biospecimen, the better a sample will be characterized and qualified for future use.[97] The international standard, ((International Organization for Standardization) ISO 9001), which sets out the internationally accepted requirements for quality management systems (QMS) requires data and documentation as one of the main elements to ensure quality. According to the definition provided by ISO, '*Data is a representation of facts, concepts or instructions in a formalized manner suitable for communication, interpretation or processing by human beings or by automatic means*'.[98] Whether it is 'electronic' or 'physical', data has to be recorded in a systematic manner for the purposes of communication or interpretation. Irrespective, in some cases the mere fixation in a systematic form may not be enough as a data having the quality. For e.g., while the ISO standard has been applied by biobanks, it has however been argued that utility or 'fitness for the purpose' must also be ensured as a mark of quality both in terms of wet and dry data.[99] Therefore the value of a 'biobank' is based on the quality of the associated and attributed information i.e., information used to describe, and authenticate the biospecimen as well as the data that provides a record of the processing and pre-analytic variables to which it has been exposed.[100] This implies that connotation of what is essentially a data of standard may differ widely.[101]

95. KL Hoeyer, Size matters: the ethical, legal, and social issues surrounding large-scale genetic biobank initiatives. *Norsk Epidemiologi.* 2012; 21(2): 211–220.
96. Sara Y. Nussbeck et al., 'Life in data'–Outcome of a multi-disciplinary, interactive biobanking conference session on sample data. *Biopreservation and Biobanking*, 2016; 14(1).
97. A. Carter and F. Betsou, Quality assurance in cancer biobanking. *Biopreservation and Biobanking.* 2011; 9(2): 157.
98. ISO 2382-1:1984 (1 January 2001).
99. *Supra* note 95 *see also* P.H.J Riegman et al., Biobanking for better healthcare. *Molecular Oncology.* 2008; 2(3): 213–222. *PMC.*, on the Marble Arch Working Group report on International Biobanking (MAWG) June 2006.
100. *Supra* note 96.
101. For more discussion on legal status of data *see* Chapter 4.

[2] Big Data

'Big Data' refers to large amounts of data produced very quickly by a high number of diverse sources; Such data can either be created by people or generated by machines, such as sensors gathering climate information, satellite imagery, digital pictures and videos, purchase transaction records, GPS signals, etc. It covers many sectors, from healthcare to transport and energy.[102] The meaning of 'Big Data' differs based on the technical frontier where it finds application. However, it is generally acknowledged that big datasets have large volumes, high velocity of information inception and variety or diversity of uses or potential uses in any given industry.[103] While its usefulness is often lauded, the underlying challenges are equally forthcoming.[104] Sheila Jasanoff, argues that framing the policy implications of Big Data is difficult precisely because it manifests in multiple contexts that each call up different operative concerns. These include Big Data as property (who owns it); Big Data as common pool resources (who manages it and on what principles); and Big Data as identity (it is us ourselves, and thus its management raises constitutional questions about rights).[105] In the context of large-scale sample collection, the use and exploitation of it in medical research would imply both the wet samples as well as its algorithmic information stored with a database. Hence, any reference to 'big genomic data research' in the present work would imply a referral to samples stored in biobanks. In other words, it would imply the use of human biological samples including the data and its ethical handling during research. On the contrary, a simple use of 'Big Data' would imply algorithmic data. Ownership, management and rights of access are issues in both Big Data and Big Data research and will be each separately examined elsewhere in this book within the context of IPR.

[3] Bio Medical Data

The 'biomedical research data' is a subset of personal, sensitive data relating to genetic information relating to individuals.[106] Such data may offer information that may provide important insight into disease susceptibility, disease status, or response to specific medicines. Biomedical data can serve as invaluable resources for researchers. There is often a justified enthusiasm about the potential use of such data to meet the

102. European Commission, https://ec.europa.eu/digital-single-market/en/big-data (last accessed on 18 July 2016).
103. Big Data: Seizing Opportunities, Preserving Values – Report of the Presidential Big Data and Privacy Working Group, May 2014.
104. European commission, https://ec.europa.eu/digital-single-market/en/making-big-data-work-europe.
105. Executive Office of the President, 'Big Data: Seizing Opportunities, Preserving Values' (The White House Washington 2014).
106. The European Molecular Biology Laboratory (EMBL) training module on Biomedical data: Ethical, legal and social implications, avaliable at: https://www.ebi.ac.uk/training/online/course/biomedical-data-ethical-legal-and-social- implicati/biomedical-data- collection-use-and-sharing.

ends of medical research.[107] However, the sensitive nature creates a need for its controlled use through legal and policy changes in any given community where its importance is realized. Thus, what distinguishes biomedical data is its content, which is often 'personal' and 'identifiable'. Any reference to 'data' within the present context would imply biomedical data relating to human samples that are used in medical research. The significance of the potential of this type of genetic data has been noted by the European court of human rights (ECtHR) in *S. and Marper v United Kingdom,*[108] wherein it was observed that genetic data of an individual is integral owing to its sensitivity and its interaction with individual,. The court further observed thus:

> Indeed, bearing in mind the rapid pace of developments in the field of genetics and information technology (IT), the Court cannot discount the possibility that in the future the private-life interests bound up with genetic information may be adversely affected in novel ways or in a manner which cannot be anticipated with precision today'. As envisioned by the European court, it is indeed a matter of great concern in using sensitive data in biobank-based research. Handling such data and using them for different purposes ought to have essential standards as the book argues.

[4] Database

The definition of database discussed herein represents a view from science and not the legal definition of database given under Chapter 4. The aim here is to distinguish the scientific concepts in science in gaining perspectives for the legal discourse that is developed in Chapter 4. A database is a collection of related data, which are organized so that useful information may be extracted. The effectiveness of databases derives from the fact that from one single, comprehensive database much of the information relevant to a variety of organizational purposes can be obtained. In healthcare, the same database may be used by medical personnel for patient care; recording information, assessing patient status, treatment advice; researchers in assessing the effectiveness of drugs and clinical procedures, etc. It may even be used by administrative personnel in cost accounting and by management for the planning of service facilities.[109] From a structural perspective database consists of the actual data, the software used to program its contents and hardware to store the database. In its functional perspective database involves different types of data namely '*primary data*' (i.e., those data obtained from direct observation e.g., DNA and protein sequences, genetic mapping data and data resulting from functional analysis) and or '*derived data*' (i.e., the data generated from analyses or functional combinations of two or more other data e.g., Human BMI, Body Mass Index). Another important set of data is '*Analysis Data*' these are data generated from analyses of other data or data generated out of research

107. S. Hoffman and A. Podgurski, The use and misuse of biomedical data: is bigger really better?'. 2013. Faculty Publications. Paper 606.
108. [2008] ECHR 1581 at para. 71.
109. G. Wiederhold, Database in Healthcare, Stanford Computer Science Department Report No. STAN-CS-80-790.

projects using primary data. This apart there could also be *'clinical data'*,[110] obtained at the point of care at a medical facility, hospital, clinics or practice containing demographic information, and *'assay data'* or biochemical assessment data which qualitatively assess or quantitatively measure the presence, amount and/or functional activity of a particular analyte,[111] (e.g., the presence of lipids, enzymes, density, molarity, etc.).[112]

Biobanks as research resource infrastructures are initiatives to accumulate resources for medical researchers. Biobanks are currently being used for a variety of research initiatives wherein there is a collection and storage of tissue samples within hospital-based comprehensive centres or as large biobank consortiums with multicentre research networks.[113] In order to utilize the data several tools have also been developed which makes it easier to analyse, verify and correlated different types of data. It is important to note that there is a subtle distinction between 'database' and 'database management systems'. While the term database refers to the actual collection of '*data*', the '*database management system*' on the contrary refers to the software that organizes, manages such database and controls the access of data within the database. In other words, the software tools to manage a database. Thus, database management systems are factually 'computer program' for the purposes of IPR. Whereas IPR in such databases, are governed by the database rights, which will be discussed in detail elsewhere. Examples of database management systems include Laboratory Information Management System (LIMS),[114] XNAT,[115] BIMS,[116] TMS,[117] etc. The advantage of such systems lies in the ease of configuring multiple data sets, which can also be used by researchers to develop new data. For instance, derived data from a cancer biobank could be used to enrich the researcher's own data relating to her project or cross-sectional data from a population biobank to study complex disorder in certain ethnic groups[118] (*see* Figure 1.2). Hence examining ownership rights particularly IPR may be often complex particularly in the context of bigger data sets. While the terms 'Data' and 'Database' explained above reflects a general scientific conception, the implications of it in context of IPR shall be dealt with under Chapter 4.

110. Data resources in health sciences http://guides.lib.uw.edu/hsl/data/findclin (last accessed on 21 July 2016).
111. Analyte is a substance whose chemical constituents are being identified and measured.
112. UK Biobank/ Data Management & Sharing Plan, December 2012.
113. H.U. Prokosch et al., IT infrastructure components for biobanking. *Applied Clinical Informatics*. 2010; 1(4): 419–429. doi:10.4338/ACI-2010-05-RA-0034.
114. Laboratory Information Management System, *see* Case Study: Effectively Storing and Analyzing Biological Data at UK Biobank, available at https://tools.thermofisher.com/content/sfs/brochures/CS-615-LIMS-Biological-Data-UK-Biobank-UKBIOBK-CS615-EN.pdf (last accessed on 23 July 2016).
115. eXtensible Neuroimaging Archive Toolkit (XNAT) is an open source platform for Neuroscience data repositories.
116. (the 'biobank information management system for the 21st century') applied at Karolinska Institute (Stockholm).
117. German Telematics Platform for Networked Medical Research. For more information *see Supra* note 113.
118. B. Nicholl et. al., Ethnic differences in the association between depression and chronic pain: cross-sectional results from UK Biobank, *BMC Family Practice* 2015; 16:128, DOI: 10.1186/s12875-015-0343-5.

Figure 1.2 Categories of Data Flow Within Biobanks

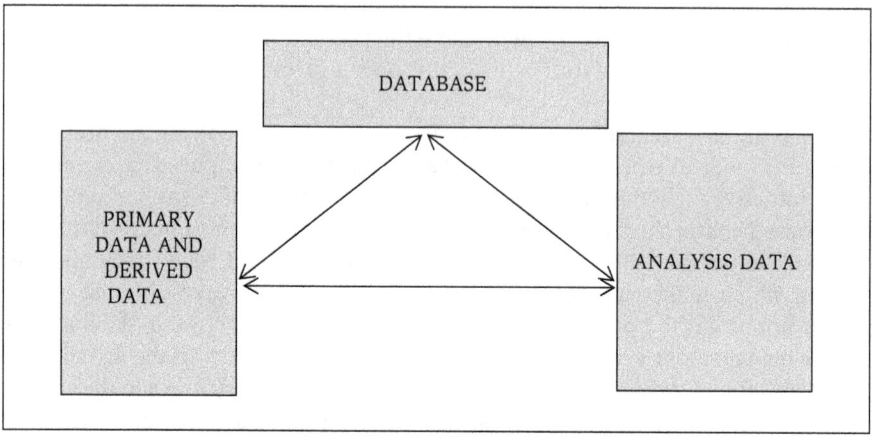

§1.02 STAKEHOLDERS IN THE RESEARCH 'USE'

Stakeholders are individuals, groups, organizations or interest groups who are interested in or in some ways affected by act or process or an event.[119] The definition of biobanks (*see* §1.01[B] above) reveals that research within biobanks involve different stakeholders which are inevitable on account of different types of human involvement in the research. At the factual level, this includes the biobankers including the scientific and technical staff engaged in the process of collecting, processing and storage of samples. It also involves the hospitals or clinics from where such samples are collected. Biobanks also involve scientific researchers including industrial partners who access or use the samples in scientific research either independent or in cohorts. At the heart of biobanking and its associated research is the contribution of the patients or the donors who have voluntarily contributed the samples for research purposes.[120] There are other stakeholders such as ethicists, lawyers, media, funding partners and the like who may also possess differing interests in the process and results of biobanking in general. Although distinguished by characteristic roles and interest, stakeholders bring forth knowledge and interests, which is core to the essential balance of research within

119. For instance, research participants who may be potentially affected physically or emotionally by the conduct of research. Hence there is a greater emphasis on the process of research involving such participants.

120. A. Husedzinovic et al., Stakeholders' perspectives on biobank-based genomic research: systematic review of the literature. *European Journal of Human Genetics*. 2015; 23: 1607–1614.

biobanks.[121] Biobanks assume a central role in initiatives related to health research including PM using the samples and data. In this regard, it is essential for biobank governance to be informed by diverse perspectives that such activities may tend to influence.[122] It is therefore essential to appreciate different interests of stakeholders in any efforts to harmonize legal and governance frameworks for biobanks. This is possible only when the stakeholders are educated of the trade-offs between privacy, progress, human rights, and security.[123] So also, stakeholder identification and engagement is highly essential to the very existence and continuance of biobanks.[124] Nonetheless, the perspectives of stakeholders differ and sometimes they may be diametrically opposing that of another. For instance, the donors of samples may have concerns regarding security and privacy of their genetic information; the researchers on the contrary may be concerned on access and exploitation of such resources without too many restrictions. The industry may be structured on enhancing profits. Seated at the midst of these differing views and aspirations is the biobanks which need to constantly and dynamically monitor their activities in their efforts to balance such differing interests. Bjugn and Casati[125] in an analysis of stakeholders in biobanks consider that a stakeholder analysis ought to include (i) identification, (ii) attributing values, (iii) prioritizing, (iv) plans for engagement and (v) monitoring. Identification is a process to be pursued by a brainstorming session of the various interests involved in or affected in a biobank. However according to the author's this is not just enough, instead it is also essential to understand the proximity of such interest to the biobank (i.e., finding the value of interest) along with a prioritization list before devising plans for engaging with such stakeholders. In this exercise, it is possible that some stakeholders will have more interest and ability to affect a biobank project than others will, giving impetus for the project to establish some form of interaction with such stakeholders.[126]

121. S. Dodds and R. Ankeny, Regulations of hESC research in Australia: promises and pitfalls for deliberative democratic approaches. *Bioethical Inquiry*. 2006; 3: 95–107.
122. M. Murphy et al., Engaging diverse stakeholders to inform biobank governance. *Biopreservation and Biobanking*. 2017; 15(4).
123. S. MacLean and M.M. Burgess, In the public interest: assessing expert and stakeholder influence in public deliberation about biobanks, Public Understanding of Science. 2010; 19(4): 486–496.
124. G. Pa'lsson, 'The rise and fall of a biobank: The case of Iceland', in H. Gottweis and A. Petersen (eds) 'Biobanks: governance in comparative perspective', Routledge, 2008: 41–55.
125. R. Bjugn and B. Casati, Stakeholder analysis: A useful tool for biobank planning. *Biopreservation and Biobanking*. 2012; 10(3).
126. *Ibid.*

Figure 1.3 Stakeholders in a Biobank Based Research Structure

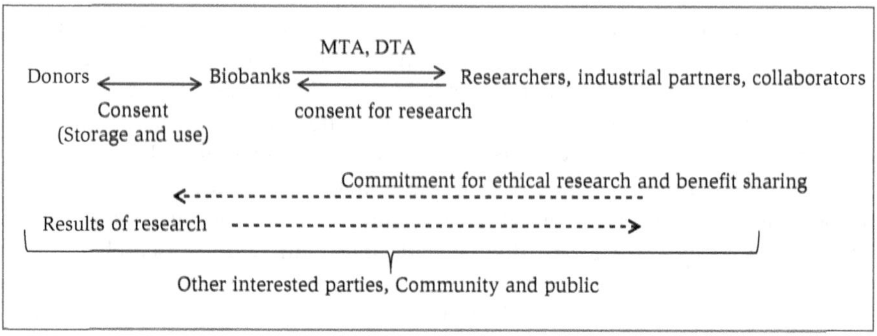

Within these multiple concerns, issues such as privacy and consent often seek prominence within biobanks and forums such as BBMRI.[127] Linking biological materials to personal data for enabling genomic research raises the concerns over 'use' of the resources in research without exploitation.[128] Thus, self-determination of participants essentially rests on the attitude of the donors towards making such contributions. This is essential for the systemic functioning of biobanks as a storage unit and in offering; such resources for the purposes of research see Figure 1.3. On the contrary, mere storage of resources respecting the consent of donors does not offer a use for such resources such as cure for serious or rare diseases. So also, it tends to affect the sustainability of biobanks, which are expensive to maintain. This requires that researchers and industrial partners be equally offered access to resources of study cohorts provided they meet the requisite ethical standards of research. Industrial partnership also demands accuracy of information related to biological resources, access to clinical data, follow-up of patients, financial and regulatory conditions and the IPR.[129] The Icelandic experience reveals appropriate management of stakeholders is one of the best ways to avoid project failure (*see* Chapter 7). It is therefore essential that any discussion on an IP policy must indulge the finer balance between the needs of the industry/researchers with those of the contributors of the resources.

From the point of 'use', the primary stakeholders are biobanks and the researchers including researchers from industry. This does not mean that the rights of the contributors (donors or patients) of the samples are diminished in importance. Instead, the contribution of donors forms the cornerstone of the biobanking sector because without samples no research or innovation could proceed in the area of genomic studies. It is however, also essential that the distinction as to the streams of bioethics and innovation be distinct though not completely independent. Such an approach

127. BBMRI: A step closer to Stakeholder's Forum report, 2010.
128. *Supra* note 124.
129. P. Hofman et al., Public-private relationships in biobanking: a still underestimated key component of open innovation, Springer-Verlag Berlin Heidelberg 2013.

would require the researchers, industrial partners and policymakers to pay more attention to heuristic principles of ethically acceptable research.

§1.03 FINDING THE FOCAL POINTS: PRINCIPLES FOR 'USE' OF BIOBANKS AS A RESOURCE

In tracing the nature of biobanks for the present enquiry and in identifying the stakeholders of research within biobanks, it is also important to find the focal points to the discussion, which will also be revisited in the conclusion. This is required in exploring a role of IPR within biobank-based research because, biobanks seek a unique integration of the personal and professional values along with the knowledge it generates.[130] Balancing the various stakeholder and their concerns also require an understanding of the foundational principles and values governing genetic research. Assimilating these principles and values can be achieved at different phases of collection, storage, use and exploitation of samples and data. This will in turn ensure the potential return on public investment in genomic research is realized in an ethical way.[131] To achieve this goal three focal points are identified by the present work which lays the foundations for commercialization and IP involvement within biobanks. These principles are stewardship, public trust and valorization each of which will be touched upon herein along with its significance in the context of the present enquiry.

[A] Principle of 'Stewardship'

A 'steward' is defined as an officer placed instead of another.[132] Steward has also been defined as a ward or keeper, or a person appointed in the stead of another.[133] It has been noted that the term 'steward' has thirteen distinct meanings from its dictionary usage.[134] The term stewardship can be applied to a multiplicity of legal relationships.[135] Historically the concept has its origin in medieval common law usage with land being transferred to a trustee for the sake of a beneficiary.[136] Remoter origins have also been sought in the Roman *fideicommissa* (Trust), the canonical concept of steward as a holder of another's faith, the Germanic Treuhandanstalt ('Trust agency') or the Islamic waqf.[137] Such arrangements under common law ensured that the land or the property in temporary possession of the steward was preserved for the sake of the benefactor.[138]

130. A. Brand et al., 'Biobanking for public health', in P. Dabrock et al., 'Trust in biobanking dealing with ethical, legal and social issues in an emerging field of biotechnology, Springer 2012.
131. *Supra* note 129.
132. Blacks law dictionary online.
133. D. Milman, Governance of distressed firms, Edward Elgar 2013 at p. 20.
134. S. Holm, From steward to stuart: Some problems in deciding for others, 62 *Northern Ireland Legal Quarterly*. 2011: 617, 632.
135. D. Milman, 'Governance of Distressed Firms', *Edward Elgar* (Corporations, Globalisation and the Law series), UK 2013.
136. S.N. Kantz, The oxford international encyclopedia of legal history. 2009; 6.
137. *Ibid.*
138. G.S. Alexander, The transformation of trusts as a legal category, 1800–1914. *Cornell Law Faculty Publications*. 1987; 469.

A more specialized variant is the concept of bailment. *Bailee* is responsible for the goods entrusted to his custody by the *bailor.*[139] Thus, the concept of Stewardship presupposes:

(a) Existence of a relationship on behalf of someone who is unable to express themselves.[140]
(b) Existence of a beneficiary who seeks to earn the benefits at the end of such relationship.
(c) In relation to the above, two that such relationship may be fulfilled its end at some definite point in future.

Holm however notes that stewardship may also be uncoupled from a particular beneficiary and being expressed merely as a mode/attitude for decision-making.[141] In all such relationships or attitudes, the elements of trust, faith and responsibility govern the equation.[142]

The diffusion of this concept into governance of HBMs and the health sector in general has been held as the struggle of the law to find an acceptable solution to the treatment of HBMs.[143] This struggle is visible even within the legal paradigms discussed in the present context both in terms of the HBMs and the data derived from them.[144] Hence, it is important to consider this upfront in laying out an IP policy for biobanks. Starting with defining the concept stewardship and its importance, the principle will again be revisited in appraising the role of IPR under Chapter 7. This will enable a discussion as to whether the concept of stewardship essentially suits the needs of commercial relationships, particularly the use of HBMs in research leading to commercially viable results. In understanding the essence of applying the principle of 'stewardship', it is also essential to understand why and how it came as a matter of choice for the HBMs.

[1] Property as a Legal Paradigm for Biological Materials

Before the advancements of science as we witness today, the deceased human body was rarely offered for research purposes to hospitals. The breakthrough in scientific research in the twentieth century also brought out a fundamental shift in value of HBMs for the purposes of biomedical research and understanding of the secrets of

139. Sir W.R. Anson et al., Anson's law of contract, OUP 2010 ed. at p. 657.
140. *Ibid.*
141. S. Holm, From steward to Stuart: Some problems in deciding for others. *Northern Ireland Legal Quarterly*. 2011; 62: 617, 632.
142. J. Popp, The role of biotechnology in a sustainable food supply, Cambridge University Press 2012 at p. 37.
143. E.E. Appel Blue, Redefining stewardship over body parts. *Journal Law & Health*. 2007; 21: 75, 122.
144. *See* Chapters 3 and 4 on the status of Biological materials and data.

human race.[145] This gave rise to not only quests for seeking such materials but also quests for seeking control over such resources. Most importantly, such change also rippled within the legal system as need for regulating the use and exploitation of resources. The predominantly visible legal model that governed, 'things' acquired by humans or belonging to them is the instrument of 'property'. Although 'property' was easier to fit within the normative frames, the regulatory environments have often been faced with the dilemma of finding a sense to applying a 'property' paradigm for HBMs.[146] The need to find a common denomination for the sake of dealing in dead bodies, to sort the customary rituals and in dealing with the wishes of the dead, led law to provide for a certain means to support the responsibility of a living.[147] While these rights were in the form of a limited possessory rights, its application to other types of samples such as tissues from living donors were never harmonious. This has been vividly illustrated by the prominent decisions from around the world like for instance *Moore v Regents of the University of California*,[148] *Roche v Douglas*[149] or *Washington University v William Catalona* et al.[150] or the *Hel La* cell controversy.[151] These decisions not only reflect the tension of involving property rights paradigm to HBMs but also the limitation a property rights discourse has in the context of exploitation of such resources for the purposes of scientific research.[152] The reason for the limitation of property law to govern biological materials according to the bioethical view is that 'body is so inseparable from the person'.[153] The argument against commodification often arises because such views involve an innate notion of human dignity which has been strongly attached to the notion of property.[154] J.W. Harris points out that this notion of sale and property need not always go together. It is quite possible that one can have property interests that fall short of a 'commercial' interest; see for example, the 'mere property use-privileges and control-powers'.[155]

On the contrary treating HBM as property not only weighs down convention but also the long-standing respect to altruism. Further, such a strict property right regime also poses threat to scientific research and development. The right over *'one's own'* questions the use of such materials in research, which may involve IPR, held by another. It is this sentimental perception of someone else profiting from what is regard as *'one's own'* which has initiated public defiance in the prominent cases cited above.

145. I. Goold and M. Quigley, 'Human Biomaterials: the case for a property approach', in I. Goold et al. (eds) 'Persons parts and property, how should we regulate human tissues in the 21st century?' Hart Publishing, 2014.
146. J.K. Mason and G.T. Laurie, Consent or property? Dealing with the body and its parts in the shadow of Bristol and Alder Hey. *The Modern Law Review*. September 2001; 64(5): 710–729.
147. *Supra* note 145.
148. 793 P 2d 479 Cal SC (1990).
149. [2000] WASC 146 (WASC).
150. No. 4:03CV1065 (E. Dist. Mo. 14 April 2006), on appeal Nos 06-2286 & 06-2301 (8th Cir.).
151. R. Skloot, The immortal life of Henrietta Lacks, Crown Publishing Group 2010.
152. L. Skene, Proprietary rights in human bodies, body parts and tissue: regulatory contexts and proposals for new laws. *Legal Studies*. March 2002; 22(1): 102–128.
153. Paul Ramsey, as cited in Elizabeth E. Appel Blue, Redefining Stewardship over Body Parts, 21 *Journal of Law & Health* 75, 122 (2007).
154. J.W. Harris, Property and justice, OUP, 1996, at p. 352.
155. *Ibid.*

Thus creating a property right poses significant risk to the notions of what it means to be human by evaluating everything virtually in the sense of a commodity.[156] The supporters of the property regime on the other hand consider that property rights are essentially malleable to involve the concept of self-determination. Inversely the very notion of altruism in donation of tissues rests on the idea of a sense of belongingness of the material to the donor.[157] So also, the idea of tissue being offered as gift cannot be conceived without the notion of property.[158] Spite of the divergence existing in academic opinions on the possible application of a property regime,[159] an essential element for consideration is the fiduciary duty between the donor of the samples and the biobanks which have been sworn to protect the wishes of the donor. So also, a property regime is evasive with regard to the donor's relationship to a user who uses such resources for the purposes of scientific research. For instance in the Moore case the researcher and the doctor being one and same, the court while ignoring the claim for a share of patent rights in the patented research, considered the doctrine of fiduciary duty.[160] The concept of fiduciary duty applies to only special relationships such as doctor and his patient. The existence of layers of relationships (other than those within a traditional fiduciary relationship) within the biomedical research with different actors in the biomedical industry necessitates consideration for other principles apart from the norms of property.[161] Against this backdrop, the principle of 'stewardship' calls for an attention in addressing the role of biobanks as well as researchers involved within the field of medical research.

[2] The Principle of Stewardship and Biomedical Research

In the recent years, the idea of stewardship has become an essential principle in addressing regulatory environments in differing fields.[162] Increasingly it is being

156. *Supra* note 151.
157. *Ibid.*
158. *Ibid.*
159. G. Laurie, Consent or property? Dealing with the body and its parts in the shadow of Bristol and Alder Hey. *Modern Law Review* 2001; 710–729; D. Morgan, Issues in Medical law and Ethics (Cavendish Publishing, 2001), pp. 83–104; J.W. Harris, Property and Justice (1996); I. Goold, Property or not Property? The spectrum of approaches to regulating the use of human bodily materials. *Journal of Law and Medicine.* 2013; 21: 299.
160. *Supra* note 158; The term Fiduciary is derived from the Roman law, and means (as a noun) a person holding the character of a trustee, or a character analogous to that of a trustee, in respect to the trust and confidence involved in it and the scrupulous good faith and candour which it requires. Thus, a person is a fiduciary who is invested with rights and powers to be exercised for the benefit of another person (Black's Law Dictionary).
161. *Supra* note 151.
162. Health, environmental law, company law, management of estates and the like. *See* for instance C. Rodgers, 'Natures place? Property rights property rules and environmental stewardship. *Cambridge Law Journal.* November 2009; 68(3): 550–574; Paul J.A. Withers et al., Stewardship to tackle global phosphorus inefficiency: The case of Europe, *Ambio.* 2015; 44(Suppl. 2): S193–S206; S.J. O'Brien, Stewardship of human biospecimens, DNA, genotype, and clinical data in the GWAS era, *Annual Review of Genomics and Human Genetics.* 2009; 10: 193–209. *See also* R. Brownsword et al., Public health interventions: Liberal limits and stewardship

applied in the context of health and related research.[163] However so the notion in which it is being applied needs special attention.[164] The principle of stewardship may have ethical or regulatory manifestation. Brownsword classifies the applicability of the principle of stewardship in a regulatory framework into three types or registers as he terms it, namely:

- Normative register.
- Moral register.
- Prudential register.

The normative register dictates how regulators ought to act if they are to do the right thing; the moral register signals the regulatees (i.e., those bound by a regulation) that certain acts are not practicable or unwarranted. The prudential register on the contrary conceives the idea that regulators (acting as proxies for their regulatees) have a prudential responsibility to ensure that, wherever there is reason to suppose that risks to health, safety and environment might be presented by new technologies, then such risks are expertly assessed and adequately managed.[165] Regulators in governing technologies often use these registers interchangeably. While Brownsword focuses on the role of the state in framing his stewardship concept, he also acknowledges that some environments are regulated in a top-down law-like fashion (with regulators clearly distinguishable from regulatees). Others are more bottom-up, more self-regulatory and more reliant on 'governance' than hard law. Whilst so some regulatory environments are reasonably stable and well formed, others are unstable or overlapping.[166] There could thus be other actors like 'institutions' or 'stakeholders' whose actions or responses govern the growth of a given environment. In the context of the present enquiry, the normative and prudential registers may be considered in framing and understanding the role of 'stewardship' in context of biobanks and commercialization. In particular the prospective role of the 'other actors' apart from the state such as biobanks (both as an infrastructure and as a resource) or the stakeholders of the research community, need attention herein(*see* Figure 1.4). In this regard, the analysis will proceed in two parts to examine the role of other actors and the role of the state in the context of biobanking.

---

responsibilities. *Public Health Ethics*. 2013; 6(3): 235–240. D. Milman, Governance of distressed firms, Edward Elgar 2013, at p. 20; D. Plotkin, reviewed by A.S. Coronado, Data stewardship: An actionable guide to effective data management and data governance, Journal of Information Privacy and Security, 2014; 10(4): 236–238.

163. The increasing academic discussion on stewardship in health is witnessed by the fact that the special issue of the *Northern Ireland Legal Quarterly* in 2011 vol. 62 part 5 was devoted to stewardship in the medical context. In addition, its importance was noted by the 'WHO health report', 2004 and Nuffield council of ethics in the context of public health (London: Nuffield Council on Bioethics 2007).
164. Mark L. Flear, 'Supra-Stewardship: A tool for citizen participation in European Union pandemic preparedness planning'. *Northern Ireland Legal Quarterly* 2011; 62: 569, 572.
165. R. Brownsword, Responsible regulation: Prudence, precaution and stewardship. *Northern Ireland Legal Quarterly*. 2011; 62: 573, 598.
166. *Ibid.*

Figure 1.4 Essential Role of Biobanks as Stewards

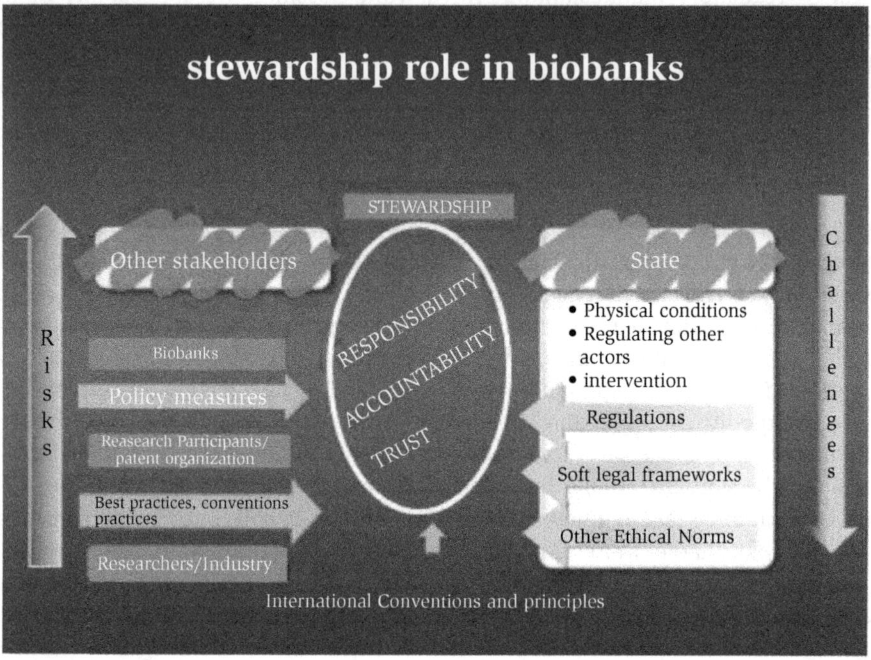

[3] Conditioning Stewardship Role of Stakeholders (Other than State) in Biobanking

Biobanking presents a conflux of relationships and issues at the same time. Governance of such relationships calls for enhanced responsibility of varying actors in the maintenance and utilization of biobanks. The individualistic stewardship theory models an individual as a steward whose behaviour is ordered such that pro-organizational, collectivistic behaviours have higher utility than individualistic, self-serving behaviours.[167] Thus given a choice between self-serving behaviour and pro-organizational behaviour, a steward's behaviour tends to disregard self-serving behaviour in its entirety.[168] The prudential course of action of individual actors in a stewardship role would seek cooperation over self-interests.[169] However, in actual practice the prudential decisions of one actor in a relationship may not coincide with that of another. In such cases, regulative norms ought to be applied by the legislators in conceiving an acceptable course.[170] In the context of biobanks for instance, the role and purpose of creating such resources is to act as a tool for biomedical research. On

167. J.H. Davis, F.D. Schoorman and L. Donaldson, Toward a stewardship theory of management. *Academy of Management Review*. 1997; 2: 22.
168. *Ibid.*
169. *Supra* note 164.
170. *Supra* note 163.

the contrary offering an open, uncontrolled access of such resources to third parties, tends to affect the rights of privacy of individuals. Regulation in the form of the data protection law governs the rules of consent and anonymization to regulate the relationship between biobanks and the donors. Alternatively, the individual actor may themselves consider measures to modulate other relationships or to equip their own prudential actions and decisions. For instance, biobanks are seeking to develop their own mechanism or policies for governance with regard to donor aspirations or resource and data management. By contributing towards self-governance, Biobanks thus also contribute to the law making in the process. To illustrate this we can take the example of the Life Gene stewardship policy[171] a study cohort based on the Swedish population. Its access and IP policy provides:

> LifeGene will serve as the steward of its resource, maintaining and building it for the public good in accordance with its purpose. This implies both the judicious protecting and sharing of the resource. It also extends to the careful management of any transfer of parts or all of the database or sample collection. Participants will not have property rights in the samples ... . LifeGene will act in accordance with the Personal Data Act and all other relevant legislation, including the Biobank Act.[172]

The above statement reflects the goals of the organization, which will in turn govern the research and, actions of its scientific employees to the ends laid out by the organization. In this way, they act as stewards of common good as defined by their organization. On the contrary whether a steward will act in an ethical manner, therefore depends upon whether the goals of the organization are ethical.[173] This will however be determined by the normative registers by the legislators in defining the contours of an organizational action. This is reflected in the LifeGene example where the policy draws its organizational commitment in normative foundations. Biobanks thus have legal, moral and practical obligations in its stewardship role and these may overlap in many ways.[174]

While the biobanks and related research may find self-regulatory and normative goals for a stewardship approach, the question remains how other participants such as individual researchers or industrial partners would be obliged to act as stewards of such resources in common good.

Normative registers of the state ensure individual obligations to statutory requirements or to soft legal conventions like Oviedo Convention on Bioethics.[175] So also even principles of policy such as Responsible Research and innovation (RRI) regulates

171. LifeGene is prospective cohort based on the Swedish population for epidemiological studies https://www.lifegene.se/For-scientists/Call-for-proposal/.
172. LifeGene access and IP policy *see supra* note 169.
173. *Supra* note 164.
174. C. Heaney et al., The perils of taking property too far. *Stanford Journal of Law, Science and Policy*, 2009; 46.
175. The Convention for the Protection of Human Rights and Dignity of the Human Being with regard to the Application of Biology and Medicine, Convention on Human Rights and Biomedicine (ETS No. 164), was opened for signature on 4 April 1997 in Oviedo. *See also* M.L. Flear and A Vakulenko, A human rights perspective on citizen participation in the EUs governance of new technologies. *Human Rights Law Review*. 2010; 10: 661.

societal actors (researchers, citizens, policymakers, business, third sector organizations, etc.) to work together during research and innovation process in order to better align both the process and its outcomes with the values, needs and expectations of society.[176] While these obligations are conditioned normatively, Brownsword notes that there are other regulatory signals such as social norms, market signals, architecture and codes which could also function normatively in governing actions or conduct of given individuals within a systemic functioning. For instance, 'autonomy', 'privacy' and 'freedom from harm' are social norms of cultural societies, which have found a place in the normative legal structures.[177] So also the research market involved in genomic research are bound by the scientific norms of genomic research, practices as well as protocols that require an ethical approval subject to certain predefined standards for such research.[178] Such practices ensure that no research proposal can seek access to the biobank resources unless such standards are clearly demonstrable from the access requests. In a latent sense, best practices evolving from the pitfalls and issues faced within given industry also ensures adherence to obligations and norms of the research community without deviance.[179] The example of Icelandic model of biobanking has enabled many biobanks to frame polices effectively to ensure transparent and consensual participation.[180] This has in turn enabled researchers to commit to obligations, which under normal circumstances they may not such as the 'return of research results'.[181]

[4] State Stewardship in Biobanking

World Health Organization (WHO) addressed 'state stewardship', in relation to health-related policies in its seminal report on health systems.[182] In this report, 'state stewardship' is defined as a '*function of a government responsible for the welfare of the population and concerned about the trust and legitimacy with which its activities are viewed by the citizenry*'. '*The Ultimate responsibility for the performance of a country's health system lies with government. The careful and responsible management of the*

176. https://ec.europa.eu/programmes/horizon2020/en/h2020-section/responsible-research-innovation.
177. *Supra* note 164.
178. These may include internal polices or accepted practices by such biobanks or research institutions dealing with the genomic research. *See* The international charter of principles for sharing biospecimens and data, http://rd- connect.eu/platform/ethics/sharing-bio-specimens-and-data/; *See also* V. Sandow et al., 'Conflicts of Interest in Medical Research: What Can Ethics Contribute?', in J. Schildmann, V. Sandow, O. Rauprich & J. Vollmann (eds) 'Human Medical Research', Springer, Basel, 2012.
179. J. Vaught and N.C. Lockhart, The evolution of biobanking best practices. Clinica Chimica Acta. Elsevier, B.V; 9 October 2012 [cited 4 March 2014]; 413(19–20):1569–1575.
180. *See* www.ukbiobank.ac.uk.
181. http://www.ukbiobank.ac.uk/wp-content/uploads/2011/06/Return-of-Results_Guidance-Note_v2.pdf; *see also* J.S. Forsberg, Changing perspectives in biobank research: From individual rights to concerns about public health regarding the return of results. *European Journal of Human Genetics*. 2009; 17: 1544–1549.
182. The world health report 2000 – Health systems: improving performance, available at: http://www.who.int/whr/2000/en/ (last accessed on 18 September 2017).

well-being of the population –stewardship–is the very essence of good government. The health of people is always a national priority: government responsibility for it is continuous and permanent'.[183]

In a similar vein, the Nuffield Council drew the concept of state-stewardship to mean '*that liberal states have a duty to look after important needs of people individually and collectively. It emphasises the obligation of states to provide conditions that allow people to be healthy and, in particular, to take measures to reduce health inequalities. The stewardship-guided state recognises that a primary asset of a nation is its health: higher levels of health are associated with greater overall well-being and productivity*'.[184]

The concept of stewardship thus envisions an oversight of the way the entire system functions without a tunnel vision and without having a blind eye to a system's failures.[185] In outlining the role of state stewardship in health, the Nuffield Council also noted that with regard to third parties involved in health research, that although they may have different motivations for pursuing social responsibility strategies, there is increasing recognition that they have obligations beyond simply complying with relevant laws and regulations. Whilst so if industry fails to meet these obligations and the health of the population is significantly at risk or if the market fails to act responsibly, the state in its stewardship role has the right to intervene. Thus, the role of the state is double-edged in the sense that it not only has to pursue its own goals of stewardship in the interest of its population but also to ensure the effective role of other actors in the process. The state thus has an extensive role, which involves:

- Creating conditions essential for development.
- Promoting and balancing the role of different actors.
- And active participation and intervention where necessary.[186]

In the context of biobank-based research and particularly in the larger perspective of 'Big Data research' the state has an increased role in creating the appropriate climate for the functioning of such research in the interest of health of its population. For instance in Europe ten years back biobanks were known to limited circles, so also its potential as we know today was not realized to the fullest extent. The evolution of resource research infrastructures to ERICS and centres of excellence has been a long set of initiatives in preparing research and development in the context of Big Data.[187] However this has also led to increased interaction of differing paradigms, which affect

183. *Ibid.*; Return of research results arises from a stewardship obligation that when research is done using the resources of another the researcher has a duty to communicate findings in a responsible manner to the other from whom the resources were sought (Nuffield Council on Bioethics, public health: Ethical issues (London: Nuffield Council on Bioethics 2007). Although it may have been conditioned by the research industry, yet it is also a responsible research obligation of the scientific researcher.
184. Nuffield Council on Bioethics, public health: Ethical issues (London: Nuffield Council on Bioethics 2007).
185. *Ibid.*
186. The third point noted by Brownsword in Rights Responsibility and Stewardship, in Heather Widdows and Caroline Mullen, 'The Governance of Genetic Information who Decides?', Cambridge University Press 2009.
187. https://ec.europa.eu/programmes/horizon2020/en/area/research-infrastructures.

the role, and functions of actors involved in the process; for example, balancing the rights of patients with that of research.[188] Biobanks as resource of genetic information offer invaluable support for health research including commercial entities of the biotech industry that are responsible for bringing innovation into the health market.[189] The subsistence of such resource for research also rests on public support.[190] This requires state intervention in the form of normative registers in ensuring a balance of interests and needs of different stakeholders. Brownsword goes further in his conception of intervention, in requiring that such intervention must essentially be for the achievement of a community's perception as a moral community.[191] In this sense, the correlative conditions that may tend to affect the community such as vulnerability, perceptions of control and like tend to affect the community interest. Genomic research has had fair share of unfortunate instances affecting community interests.[192] Against this background state responsibility with regard to genomic research involves a careful weighing of the boundaries and linkages between bioethical questions and legal measures, including IP laws.[193]

[5] Stewardship and IPR

While the role of the state and other actors in the context of biobanks may seem more visibly aligned to stewardship, its significance to IPR may be less obvious. The traditional role of a steward is to conserve the said property and secure the returns from such property for the beneficiaries. An IP owner being steward of the resources in relation to an innovation may even seem paradoxical. On the contrary, IPR do not create rights that are beyond the purview of the concept of property, instead it sits juxtaposed to one another.[194] An IP owner utilizes the resources from the common stock of information and produces an invention or a creative work.[195] In addition, such innovation or work need not necessarily conserve the resources in the same form. Hence prima facie stewardship as an approach appears to have minimal scope in the context of IPR. However, in a larger perspective it can be considered that IPR offer incentive to creative contributions from a common stock of knowledge. The aim of creating such IP rights offers two tenable results namely a) value additions to the common stock of knowledge and b) innovations that contribute to the health and

188. *See* Regulation (EU) 2016/679 (General Data Protection Regulation) recital 4.
189. OECD, Guidelines on Human Biobanks and Genetic Research Database, 2009.
190. Biobanks for Europe a challenge for Governance, 2012.
191. The idea of a moral community refers to a community's own self-perceptions as striving to be a moral community.
192. http://www.wipo.int/wipo_magazine/en/2006/05/article_0008.html.
193. H. Howe, 'Property, sustainability and patent law -could the stewardship model facilitate the promotion of green technology?', in H. Howe (ed.) Concepts of property in intellectual property law. Cambridge University Press, 2013.
194. S. Frankel, 'Attempts to protect indigenous culture through free trade agreements'. in C.B. Graber, K. Kuprecht, J.C Lai (eds), 'International trade in indigenous cultural heritage: Legal and policy issues'. Edward Elgar, 2012, 118–143; *See also* J. Lai, Indigenous cultural heritage and intellectual property rights, learning from the New Zealand experience?, Springer, 2014.
195. This idea is developed further in Chapter 7 in finding the role of IP.

welfare of a community.[196] IP thus ensures development of marketable products and services, which may prove as useful to the community.[197] Nonetheless, a component of every creative work or innovation is not the product of individual effort. This sphere can be called 'periphery', which is distinct from the individual efforts and results from a host of social factors.[198] Where the subject of the IP right is of particular significance for the community, or where the value of the property has been partially contributed by the community, the rights of the IP owner to exploit the property for personal gain will be perceived in a different sense by the peripheral stratum.[199] With respect to genetic materials the concerns over ownership and property rights, sits differently with the argument over 'common heritage' or 'public property' in such genetic materials.[200] The principle of stewardship as a model seeks to accommodate community interest in the property.[201] IP law has endeavoured to be incorporative of such interests, for instance the issues surrounding research on human embryos has to be dealt by both by judicial[202] and legal measures.[203] Inventions commercial exploitation would be contrary to ordre public or morality has been strictly regarded unpatentable.[204]

Biobanks contain biological materials that enable extraction of valuable information, which can be applied for health-related research. In this, way both the biobanks (offering the resources) and the researchers (accessing such resources) are engaged in a participatory role in 'innovation'. The researcher not only uses the biobank resource but also other common stock of knowledge related to the field of enquiry. The peripheral contribution involves the contribution of donors who donated the samples for the research. Contributing to such research also gives an opportunity for individual belonging to the community, a sense of self-realization to the common good, which such genomic research has to offer.[205] Hence, such research participation is based on

196. Gowers Review of Intellectual Property, 6 December 2006; Creating value from intellectual assets - OECD, 2008.
197. Carolina Lasén Díaz, Intellectual Property and Biological Resources An Overview of Key Issues and Current Debates, 2005.; *see also* WIPO-UNEP Study on the Role of Intellectual Property Rights in the Sharing of Benefits Arising from the Use of Biological Resources and Associated Traditional Knowledge, 2004.
198. R.P. Merges, Justifying intellectual property, Harvard University Press June 2011; Mergers considers that every IP right contains two components an inviolable individual contribution, called the 'deserving core' of the work covered by the right and the periphery. The periphery represents that part of a work or innovation over which society, as opposed to the individual creator, has a legitimate claim. This periphery as a sphere is used by mergers to discuss the foundation of intellectual property rights applying the Rawls theory of distributive justice.
199. *Supra* note 197.
200. T. Caulfield et al., A review of the key issues associated with the commercialization of biobanks. *Journal of Law and the Biosciences*. 2014; 1(1): 94–110. *PMC*. Web. 20 September 2017.
201. H. Howe, 'Property, sustainability and patent law -could the stewardship model facilitate the promotion of green technology?', in Helena (ed.), 'Concepts of property in intellectual property law Howe', Cambridge University Press, 2013.
202. Judgment in *Oliver Brüstle v Greenpeace* (Case C-34/10) and Judgment in Case C-364/13, *International Stem Cell Corporation v Comptroller General of Patents, Designs and Trade Marks*.
203. Article 6 of Directive 98/44/EC, on the legal protection of biotechnological inventions, makes certain inventions unpatentable.
204. *Ibid.*
205. E. Christensen, 'Biobanks and our common good', in J. Solbakk, S. Holm and B. Hofmann (eds) 'The ethics of research biobanking', Springer, Boston, MA, 2009.

voluntary altruism, which is respected through the rules of autonomy and self-determination. Within this interrelationship, the expectations of such future benefit helps to shape the scientific domain and participant motivation towards such research.[206] Such benefit-sharing expectations may also be higher in certain cases.[207] The Human Genome Organisation (HUGO) Ethics Committee considers that '*benefit is a good that contributes to the wellbeing of an individual and/or a given community* (e.g. *by region, tribe, disease-group.). Benefits transcend avoidance of harm (non-maleficence) in so far as they promote the welfare of an individual and/or a community. Thus, a benefit is not identical with profit in the monetary or economic sense*'.[208] On a reverse outlook, this implies that the research community is not expected to bring in monetary profits for the research participants. Researchers ought to be bound by a responsible research and ethical protocols in ensuring that such research attains its goals in the form of a cure or a possible prognosis of a genetic disorder affecting the community. This also places a vital responsibility on the researchers to appreciate the needs, values, priorities and cultural expectations of the community in pursuing such research. Examples have also shown that disregard to such expectation may not enable a successful research commercialization even with an IP at hand. In Hagahai patents, for instance the patent over cell line of an indigenous population had to be returned as the research was conducted without proper respect for consent.[209] So also, the failure of Myriad patents demonstrates that aggressive legal tactics may also not serve the interest of IP holders without being accommodative of the community concerns.[210] Seeking a stewardship model alone does not enable resolving community concerns. Researchers involved in genomic research must play a proactive role in ensuring that the research adheres to the norms and standards of genetic research. So also, academic and industrial partners within collaborating in research must actively seek measures to ensure access and sharing of results with the community. While these are policy measures for research partners to resolve, the role of IP as a steward of community resources involves support innovation and research for human health, progress, generating employment, trade, etc.[211]

[B] Public Trust and Scientific Research

Trust pervades personal, social and political life and has many meanings and effects. In its basic sense trust is a perception of security,[212] which also creates a sense of goodwill

206. G. Haddow et al., Tackling community concerns about commercialisation and genetic research: A modest interdisciplinary proposal. *Social Science & Medicine.* 2007; 64(2):272–82.
207. Example where resource of a particular community or tribe or a specific disease cohort is involved in the research the level of expectation for the peripheral community may be on a higher threshold.
208. http://www.eubios.info/BENSHARE.htm (last accessed on 14 September 2018).
209. S. Lehrman, US drops patent claim to Hagahai cell line. *Nature.* (12 December 1996); 384: 500.
210. *Supra* note 199.
211. Intellectual property rights intensive industries and economic performance in the EU, Publication date: October, 2016.
212. S. Camporesi et al., Investigating public trust in expert knowledge: Narrative, ethics, and engagement, *Journal of Bioethical Inquiry* 2017; 14.

from the other person who is being trusted.[213] Trust is an expectation or a 'cognitive state' that one will not be exploited by another.[214] Trust helps to determine the effectiveness of committed relations. A lack of trust in relations has negative consequences because almost all economic transactions have embedded within them.[215] In this sense, trust also evolves cooperation amongst the participants within such relationship. 'Public Trust' is the willingness or perception of the community in its engagement with the activities of individuals, institutions or government bodies. Trust thus involves the information about the event along with a willingness to engage in such event that may even involve risks with the confidence in the entity being trusted.[216] In the context of biomedical research, the concept of trust has been on delicate bedrock.[217] This has been both on account of faith and on account of perception. Trust can be deeply imbibed in relation to fiduciary roles such as doctors and other healthcare professionals.[218] This can also be called a 'conditioned attitude'. Such trust tends to be affected on account of a fiduciary duty governing the relationship between the public and the person holding such position of trust. For instance, the Tuskegee Syphilis Study in the United States (US) where health professionals knowingly withheld diagnostic details and treatment of African-American rural workers was a great setback to the trust in medical professionals. It led to serious discussions on preventing exploitation within such relationships and lead to the Belmont Report, which articulated three pillars of research involving human subject namely respect for persons, beneficence and justice.[219] On the other hand, public trust could also be a perceived sense of how an institution works within the systemic order. For example, the Icelandic biobank's over indulgence in research and the bankruptcy and mismanagement of the Sardinian biobank[220] have led to suspicions over the research directions

213. T. Simson, What is trust?. *Pacific Philosophical Quarterly*, volume 93, 2012.
214. *Infra* note 214.
215. S. Teraji, Property rights, trust, and economic performance. *The Journal of Socio-Economics*. 2008; 37: 1584–1596.
216. C. Richter, Biobanking, In: P. Dabrock, J. Taupitz and J. Ried (eds) Trust in Biobanking. Dealing with Ethical, Legal and Social Issues in an Emerging Field of Biotechnology, Springer, Heidelberg, 2012.
217. *See*: K. Dierickx and P. Borry, New challenges for biobanks: ethics, law and governance, *Intersentia*, 2009; H. Gottweis and G. Laus, Biobank governance in post-genomic age, *Personalized Medicine*. 2010; 7(2): 187–195; M. Otlowski et al., Biobanks Information Paper, *Journal of Law, Information and Science* 2010; 5; G. Laurie, Reflexive governance in biobanking: on the value of policy led approaches and the need to recognise the limits of law, *Human Genetics*; 2011 September; 130(3): 347–356.; O'Doherty et al., From consent to institutions: designing adaptive governance for genomic biobanks, *Social Science & Medicine* 2011; J. Kaye et al., Governing biobanks: understanding the interplay between law and practice, Hart Publishing 2012; T. Caulfield et al., A review of the key issues associated with the commercialization of biobanks, *Journal of Law and the Biosciences*, 94–110, 2014; B.M. Knoppers et al., A human rights approach to an international code of conduct for genomic and clinical data sharing. *Human Genetics* 2014; 133(7): 895–903, 2014.
218. E.D. Pellegrino, Toward a virtue-based normative ethics for the health professions. *Kennedy Institute of Ethics Journal*. 1995; 5(3): 253–277.
219. Ethical Principles and Guidelines for the Protection of Human Subjects of Research, The National Commission for the Protection of Human Subjects of Biomedical and Behavioral Research, 18 April 1979.
220. N. Nosengo, DNA heist that was not sparks data questions, *Nature Biotech*, 16 September 2016.

of biobanks. The lack of trust or diminishing 'public trust' in biobanks and biobank-based research have been associated to several factors such as fear of exploitation, nature of investments (for e.g., private in public research), the type of organization-(public versus private),[221] the realization of lack of direct benefits, lack of feedback or results.[222] The question then is 'how public trust needs to be addressed?' In the present context, public trust can be viewed in two distinct ways:

(1) The public trust that the biobanks must fulfil.
(2) Public trust which the research sector needs to maintain.

Often these two perspectives are entangled within the general perception of biobank's environment because ultimately the collection of samples and data are to be used for research purposes. However, there exists a distinctive role for different stakeholders, which enable the maintenance of public trust.

A biobank's stability and sustainability with regard to its research activities is fundamentally based on the public support. Nevertheless, the mode of public engagement within a 'science-society' relationship have been often been questioned on its purpose in terms of being educational or participatory role that it seeks to fulfil.[223] Such public engagement within biobanks may however need different sets of consideration based on the nature, purpose of the biobank along with the local concerns, which needs to be addressed. Trust in a biobank's activities manifest itself through the decisions or policies it undertakes to address questions of risk, security of and responsibility towards the research participants and the community who are involved in the process.[224] Engaging the community strengthens local ownership of the research and builds confidence in the ability of biobanks to negotiate various aspects of the research, such as recruitment strategies, care for the health needs of study participants, site selection, data collection and sharing.[225] This calls for attention to information, transparency and participation of the public in biobanks. With regard to biobank-based research the OECD guidelines[226] recommend that the operators of the HBGRD should have a clearly articulated policy and explicitly indicate to participants whether they retain any rights over the HBMs and data including the nature of such rights. Similar clarity must also exists for policies relating to commercialization of biobank's own resources, research results or commercial products, if any, that may arise from research use of such resources.

221. C.R. Critchley, Public opinion and trust in scientists: The role of the research context, and the perceived motivation of stem cell researchers. *Public Understanding of Science.* July 2008; 17(3): 309–327.
222. *Supra* note 199.
223. H. Gottweis and A. Petersen, Biobanks governance in comparative perspective, Routledge 2008.
224. *Supra* note 219.
225. Council for International Organisations of Medical Sciences International Ethical Guidelines for Health-related Research Involving Humans (2016).
226. OECD, *supra* note 188.

Researchers and innovators who work in close association with biobanks or use the biobanks for their research also have a responsibility to maintain public trust.[227] This is critical for biomedical research for its continuance as it involves sensitive information of human subject. The credibility of scientific researchers needs to be proved when the public pays IP as the price for seeking better cure and treatments. This responsibility of maintaining trust and credibility of biomedical research will be revisited in the ensuing part in relation to the discussion of RRI measures. Building a 'research cultural ethos' of trust suiting the pursuit of advanced in health research in Europe is the only way IPR can evolve itself more positively.

[C] Valorization

The term 'Valorization' means the creation of Value for a source.[228] The concept of valorization in the present context stands for value creation for innovations. It stems from the Marxian view of '*surplus value*', which in his 'Critique of political economy', is explained to be the unpaid surplus labour performed by the worker for the capitalist, serving as a basis for capital accumulation. In other words, total 'surplus value' is equal to the sum of net distributed and undistributed profit, net interest, net rents, net tax on production and various net receipts associated with royalties, licensing, leasing, certain honorariums, etc.[229] While Marx focused on the capitalistic profit making, his idea of surplus value guides the use of such surplus in social value creation. 'Value' is certainly not a quality of a substance, but it is also not a result of the subject's valorization. Rather, value is generated by the generalized exchangeability made possible by networks of communication in which subjects and things are embedded.[230] Similarly HBMs in its innate self, do not offer information in any manner. The altruistic contributions towards biobanks and its use for the purposes of research offer potential for resources to become 'valuable'.[231] Even though the research potential creates value for such attenuated parts, its commercial exploitation is prohibited as such.[232] However, mere collection and storage of biological materials also does not bring about the knowledge of the human genome needed to translate them into clinically relevant research outcomes.[233] Against this backdrop, HBMs are indirectly enabled to give rise to marketable knowledge and products.[234] In a Lockean sense the value of genetic information develops with the research work based on the genetic information. The

227. Larry I. Palmer, Should Liability Play a Role in Social Control of Biobanks?. *Journal of Law, Medicine and Ethics*, 2005.
228. Oxford, Dictionary of Business and Management.
229. https://www.marxists.org/archive/marx/works/1867-c1/index.htm.
230. M Vatter, The Republic of the Living: Biopolitics and the Critique of Civil Society, Fordham University Press, 2014.
231. P.H.J Riegman, et al., The Marble Arch, International Working Group on Biobanking for Biomedical Research, 2008.
232. Article 21, Oveido Convention on Human Rights and Biomedicine, 1997.
233. M.J Murtagh, et al., Realizing the promise of population biobanks: a new model for translation. *Human Genetics*. 2011; 130(3): 333e345.
234. K Evers, Commercialization of Biobanks. *Biopreservation and Biobanking*. 2012; 10(1).

labour involved in innovation seeks to be rewarded by IPR.[235] On the contrary John Locke, in his '*Second Treaties on Government*' laid down the labour theory of property which says that, whilst individuals have a right to homestead private property from nature by working on it, they can do so only '... at least where there is enough, and as good, left in common for others'. In other words the 'surplus' value out to benefit common good.[236] This philosophy is of growing importance in the context of genomic research. This philosophy is now much more refined and is called 'Valorization'. The process of value creation out of knowledge, by making knowledge suitable and available for economic or societal utilization with the aim of translating it into high-potential products, services, processes and industrial activity.[237] With the changing paradigms of academic and publicly funded research towards increased collaborative research, partnerships with the industry commercialization of research results have become increasingly prominent in Europe.[238] Genomic research has also been moving with the wave of commercialization in the interest of sustenance of biobanking as a resource for research.[239] Commercialization is seen as the process of extracting economic value from new products process and knowledge using IPR, licensing or spin-off research.[240] However, biobanks presents a unique situation wherein 'trust' as discussed in the previous section is essential to its subsistence, which is often affected by efforts towards commercialization owing to the fear of exploitation of resources. As Turner notes 'Biobanks are caught directly between the values and rights of participants and the potential commercial and scientific value of the samples and data and at the same time having to construct a business model that will ensure the long term sustainability of the biobanks.'[241] Balancing such needs of biobank-based research requires a holistic approach to commercialization. Valorization seeks to enable this both as a goal and as an approach to commercially oriented research within biobanks. *Valorization* is the process of securing value added products out of genomic research in the form of novel technologies, devises or genetic testing for diagnostic and therapeutic products for social benefits. It is also a process of a complex interaction between public institutions and business entities with better integration of all stakeholders in the process. It thus envisions the flow of knowledge from science to its practical application with active involvement in public–private collaboration and active support of

235. J Hughes, The Philosophy of Intellectual Property. *Georgetown Law Journal*. 1988; 77: 287.
236. Second Treaties on Government, 1689.
237. S.D. Jong, Engaging scientists: Organising valorisation in the Netherlands. Rathenau Institute, 2015-09-10.
238. *See* for instance: D. Charles and J. Howells, Technology transfer in Europe: Public and private networks, Belhaven Press 1992; M. Jacob et al., Entrepreneurial transformations in the Swedish university system: The case of Chalmers University of Technology'. *Research Policy*. 2003; 32(9): 1555–1568., F. Kitagawa and C. Wigren, From basic research to innovation: entrepreneurial intermediaries for research commercialization at Swedish 'Strong Research Environments' Center for Innovation, Research and Competence in the Learning Economy (CIRCLE), Paper No. 2010/02, Lund University, 2010.
239. A. Turner et al., 'Biobank Economics and Commecialization Problem'. *spontaneous generation*. 2013; 7(1): 69–80.
240. Y. Jolly et al., Moving Beyond Commercialization: Strategies to maximize the Economic and Social impact of genomic research, policy brief, 5, 212.
241. *Ibid*.

knowledge protection and technology transfer and sharing of genetic information.[242] Thus valorization focuses on societal value, created by contributions aimed at improving clinical practices and economic value, created by collaborations with business partners.[243]

The growth of 'large-scale biobanking' marked a trend in genomics with new societal dimensions[244] and valorization of such large biobanks has been seen to be essential. The interest in this European concept have led to many initiatives like the EAPM (European Alliance on personalized Medicine), Genetic Alliance UK, the Malariagen Project, Duchenne research, etc. to adopt it as a matter of policy. While these initiatives were directly not involved in biobanking, yet the principle could be a guide contextually. A report was also submitted to the European Commission in 2012 on developing this concept in the context of patent law, which aimed at creating value from patents by capturing and extracting their latent economic potential through developing and commercializing the underlying technology.[245] The principle of 'valorisation' offers an understanding of the challenges involved in commercialization and in seeking solutions to such challenges by focusing on socially productive outcome for research than other parameters such as innovation or exclusive rights in research. This process however involves seeking an equilibrium of 'knowledge creation' 'knowledge exchange' and 'knowledge translation'. Such a balancing act may arise only in combined interactions of IP, ethical values and contractual refinements.[246]

242. D Stemerding and R Nahuis, Implicit and explicit notions of valorization in genomics research. *New Genetics and Society*. (2014); 33(1): 79–95.
243. CMSB. 2004. Annual Report 2004. Leiden: Centre for Medical Systems Biology.
244. D. Chalmers et al., Has the Biobank bubble burst? Withstanding the challenges for suistainable biobanking in the digital era, *BMC Medical Ethics* (2016) 17: 39.
245. Options for an EU instrument for patent valorisation, European Union 2012.
246. *Supra* note 239.

CHAPTER 2

Evolving Governance and Structural Frameworks for Biobanks: Regulation, Guidelines and Policy

§2.01 LEVELS OF BIOBANK GOVERNANCE

The growing importance of biomedical research and commercialization along with different concerns it raises have contributed to a focused attention towards legal and ethical norms particularly within European Union (EU). Research using HBMs not only involves a concern for the samples but also the data generated from such samples. The stability of research using HBMs is in fact a challenge as biomedical innovation is in itself a multi-scalar process, which seeks the coordination of differing relationships.[1] Addressing these challenges at different fronts has given rise to increasing governance within biomedical research. While there is a dearth in literature for a more refined definition of the term 'governance' in the context of biobanks, there are multiple interpretations that have evolved from a political, economic and administrative front.[2] Governance in general terms refers to some kind of body, which would provide oversight, regulation and guidance for biobanks.[3] However, this body is not often visible being spread out at different levels. In order to avoid the cul-de-sacs of viewing law merely by the visible regulations, statues and law reports, it is also essential to view the deeper structures that cause the changes in the governance front. Under a critical legal positivist approach normative law's external connections to social sciences needs special attention. In the words of Kaarlo Tuori, *Legal concepts form the grid through*

1. K. Birch, Innovation, regional development and the life sciences: Beyond clusters, Taylor & Francis 2016, at p. 129.
2. OECD, DAC Guidelines and Reference Series Applying Strategic Environmental Assessment: Good Practice Guidance for Development Co-operation, OECD 2006.
3. A. Hawkins and K. O'Doherty, Biobank governance: A lesson in trust. *New Genetics and Society*. 2010; 29(3): 311, 327.

which social reality is observed and interpreted.[4] An understanding of legal science may also involve recourse to social practices.[5] Biobanks as social actors in the field that seek attention to the social realities because of its confrontation with different subjects like donors, researchers, biobankers, pharmaceutical companies, etc. An understanding of legal science may also involve recourse to social practices[6] like the customary principles of 'trust' or 'stewardship', which are core to the concept of biobanking. In addition, need-oriented roles (like consumers, donors, researchers, etc.) can contribute to differing perspectives and principles for governance. Tuori's legal structuring enables an understanding of phenomenon of legal and social evolution in the context of biobanks (see Figure 2.1 below). In applying the level of legal process in the issues of biobanking and commercial partnerships through an IP lens, one has to consider different elements of governance, the structures involved in such governance and most importantly the normative structures.[7] Therefore, it is essential to consider how legal norms are created, implemented and applied. In this sense, the governance of biobanks involves the structurization, processes and relationships involved in the pursuit of the goals defined by biobanking institutions.[8] Governance reflects the exercise of authority by state actors to steadily and effectively manage the development of biobanks.[9] They may also involve self-regulatory practices evolved by biobanks themselves. The governance paradigm for biobanks are multilayered consisting of formal legal instruments and regulatory bodies at national and European levels, as well as more informal types of governance such as 'professional guidelines' and 'best practice'.[10] The governance of biobanks and research in life sciences in general are to a greater extent influenced by ethical norms. Some of these are codified into practice while others are followed as good clinical or laboratory practices and are institutionalized within the conduct of public research. This chapter will explore some of the evolving mechanisms that relate to the functioning of biobanks. Nevertheless, the true challenge for biobanks is to ensure that both sourcing of samples and its use proceeds within a RRI standard. It is equally important that specific policy visions relating to biomedical research are enacted as policy strategies and priorities in knowledge-based commodity chains or any other value chain in the translation of public research.[11] Such an approach also contributes to strengthening procedures, commercial strategies and trust in research, which abides to these legal and soft legal parameters. Increasingly there is a call for

4. T.K. Touri, Critical legal positivism, Ashgate 2002 at p. 302.
5. *Ibid.*, at p. 144.
6. *Ibid.*
7. This view distinguishes governance from regulatory frames as such *see* for instance: J. Kaya et al., Governing biobanks, Hart Publishing 2012.
8. J. Kaye et al., Governing biobanks: Understanding the interplay between law and practice, Bloomsbury Publishing 2012.
9. K. Nana et al., Challenges for the sustainability of university-run biobanks, *Biopreservation and Biobanking*. August 2018; 16(4):312–321.
10. H. Gottweis, Biobanks for Europe a challenge for governance, Routledge, 2012.
11. *Ibid.*

involving participatory governance measures that reflects the interests of the stakeholders involved in this process.[12] Governance in this emerging role must ensure the long-term commitment, sustainability, legitimacy and commitment to biobanks.[13]

Innate to the structuring of governance are differing levels that one can find (see fig 2.2.)[14] A surface examination of the biobanking sector reveals different types of law like data protection laws, patent rights, copyright and database rights, rules of procedure, national laws, statutory arrangements of different legal notions,[15] decisions of European court of Justice, European Patent Office (EPO) board of appeal decision, etc. The subsurface layer consists of various policy paradigms rooted to the legal culture like Standard operating procedures (SOP's) or guidelines formulated by biobanks.[16] Finally, at the core of this or the deep structure lies actors or the stakeholders whose relationships govern the process of lawmaking in the context of biobanks. As this process is, still formative one can find a lot of evolving actions from social organizations that are involved in this process like patient's organizations, WMA, BBMRI, ESFRI, etc. These organizations acts as platforms for evolving concerns of different stakeholders and have largely been the basis for structuring the legal practice. The present inquiry considers protection of research results through an IP and commercialization paradigm, which is largely based on its impact on the legal culture, and the deeper structures of governance. (*See* Chapter 8)

12. M. Murphy et al., Engaging diverse stakeholders to inform biobank governance. *Biopreservation and Biobanking*. 2017; 15(4): 393–395.
13. H. Gottweis and G. Lauss, Biobank governance in the post-genomic age. *Personalized Medicine*. 2010; 7(2): 187–195.
14. Following the theme of levels of law developed by Touri, *Supra* note 4 at p. 151.
15. For example As Petrini points our variations in the way donations are construed under law (*see* C. Petrini, Ethical and legal considerations regarding the ownership and commercial use of human biological materials, Dove Medical Press 2012).
16. *Supra* note 10.

Figure 2.1 The Foundational Basis for Addressing Governance in the Context of Biobanking

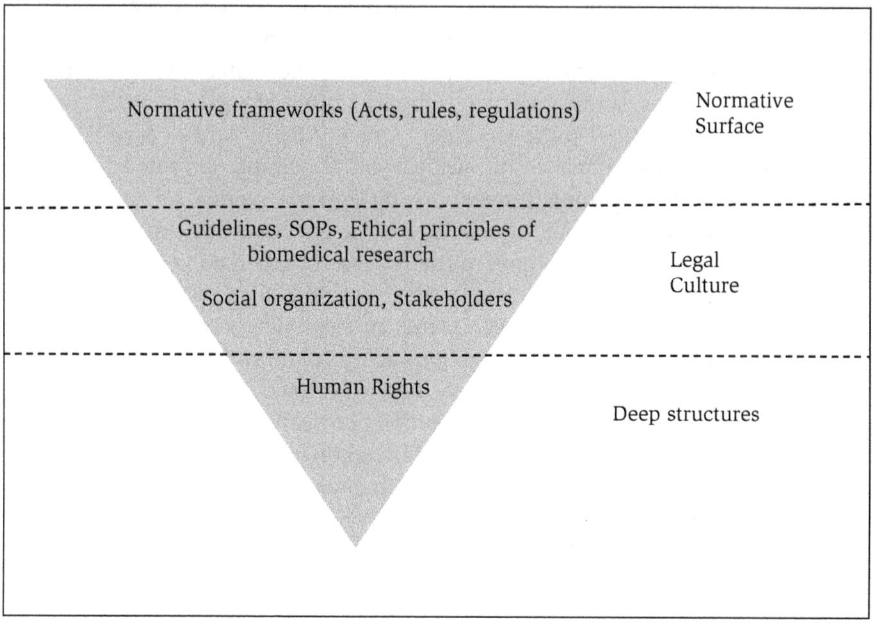

The different layers of formal regulation can be discussed under different heads (Figure 2.2) namely: (1) EU level; (2) international level; and (3) national levels.

Figure 2.2 Differing Levels of Governance

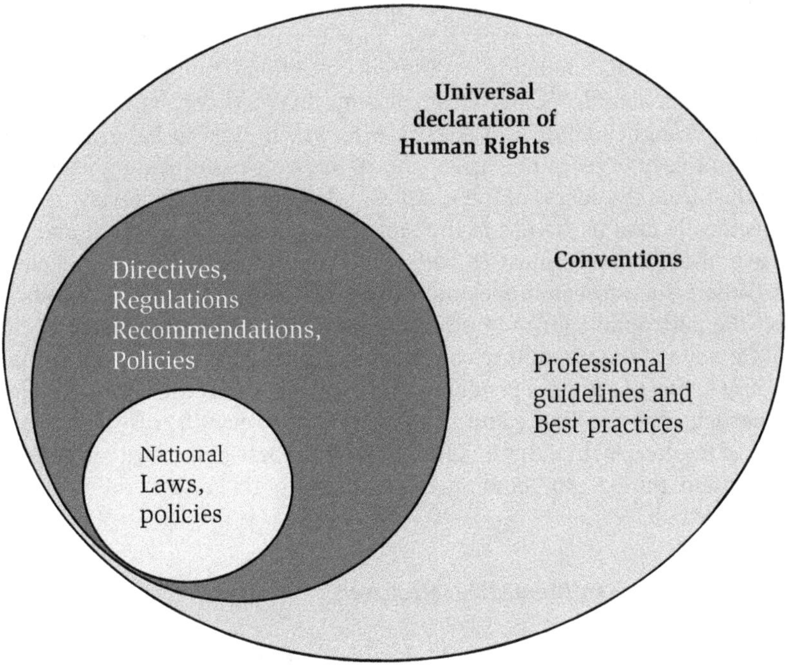

[A] Ethical and Legal Governance at EU Level

At the European level governance mechanism consist of directives, regulations, recommendations and other policies which govern the ethical as well as legal aspects of biobank-based research in general and biomedical research in particular both in terms of use of samples as well as the data.

[1] Use of Samples in Biomedical Research

There is no EU law so far dealing in the aspects of biobanking and this according to some commentators makes it more complex to address what governance mechanisms governs the biobanks as such.[17] Although human tissue were regulated through the Directive 2004/23/EC, yet it did not deal in research using such tissues.[18] The Rec(2006)4 was the first official European statement applying to research with HBMs. Though not legally binding, it provides orientation, especially in countries without

17. A. Hawkins and K. O'Doherty, *supra* note 3, *see also*: K. Beier et al., Biobanking strategies and regulative approaches in the EU: Recent perspectives, Dove Medical Press 2015.
18. Directive 2004/23/EC of the European Parliament and of the Council of 31 March 2004 on setting standards of quality and safety for the donation, procurement, testing, processing, preservation, storage and distribution of human tissues and cells.

domestic regulations, on a range of issues.[19] However, the recommendation had to be aligned to the new developments in the field of biobanking. As the increasingly diverse origin of biological materials stored in collections and the difficulty to guarantee non-identifiability of such samples along with the increasing amount of research involving such materials coming from different collections, along with the importance of research on biomaterials removed from persons unable to consent.[20] Hence this was revised into Recommendation CM/Rec(2016)6, which aims to balance the dignity, integrity and privacy of research participants along with ensuring a rightful benefit to the researched from the access of the samples.[21] Articles 21–23 of the new recommendation specifically deal in the use of the biological samples for research and requires that the use of the samples must fit within the consent given by the participants of research. Where such research does not fit with the consent, the researches have to re-contact the participants for the purpose of assessment of such consent to the new research. However if the attempts to contact such participants fail then the samples can be used only subject to an independent ethical evaluation as the efforts to reconnect with the participants, the nature and importance of the scientific research in question and nature of the consent in terms of its support for the research activity in general. The recommendation though not binding is an effort to reflect a certain standard in biomedical research.

[2] Use of Data in Biomedical Research

The European Parliament adopted on 27 April 2016, the much-awaited 'Regulation of the European Parliament and of the Council on the Protection of Natural Persons with regard to the Processing of Personal Data and on the Free Movement of Such Data'(GDPR).[22] This new regulation repeals Directive 95/46/EC, the general data protection directive that was first implemented in 1995. The Regulation has applicability within the EU and supersedes national statutes in individual EU Member States. This new EU regulation aims to protect not only individuals against abuse of personal data collected by outside entities but also the transborder flow of such data outside the EU. Its adoption has several implications for biomedical researchers working on data derived from EU citizens and for the rights of the citizens themselves. The regulation applies both to electronic as well as non-electronic databases that store personal data. The regulation requires that processing of personal data is performed in accordance with principles of 'lawfulness', 'fairness' and 'transparency'. Processing health data, as defined by the GDPR, evolves further obligations and restrictions, because health data

19. Recommendation Rec(2006)4 of the Committee of Ministers to Member States on research on biological materials of human origin and its Explanatory Memorandum (Adopted by the Committee of Ministers on 15 March 2006 at the 958th meeting of the Ministers' Deputies).
20. https://www.coe.int/en/web/bioethics/-/research-on-biological-materials-of-human-origin-new-recommendations-to- member-stat-1?desktop = true.
21. Recommendation CM/Rec(2016)6, of the Committee of Ministers to Member States on research on biological materials of human origin (Adopted by the Committee of Ministers on 11 May 2016 at the 1256th meeting of the Ministers' Deputies).
22. http://ec.europa.eu/justice/data-protection/reform/index_en.htm.

is considered sensitive data. The processing of sensitive data is by default prohibited (Article Art. 9, Art.4(13-15))

Under the new EU legislation, data subjects now have enhanced rights, such as 'data rectification' (Article16) – the ability to rectify any inaccuracy in relation to their personal data. Another important right offered to data subjects is the '*right to be forgotten*' or a '*right of erasure*' in cases where the personal data are no longer necessary in relation to the purposes of the research or where they were not processed lawfully or where the data subject withdraws her consent (Article 17). The researchers handling human data are thus bound by request from data subject for removing personal data collected by them. However, this right shall not apply in certain cases such as processing of information carried out in public interest, exercise of legal authority, assessment of occupational health of employees or assessment of public health concerns particularly in ensuring high standards of quality and safety of healthcare. In addition, where archiving of data was made for scientific purposes and in public interest, the right of erasure may not be offered wherein it is 'likely to impair the achievement of the objectives' of that processing. This may mean that researchers working in publicly funded research activities within biobanks may still be able to retain data related to donors, even if they get a request for withdrawal or erasure provided the conditions in the exemption are met. In addition with the realms of emerging technologies such as AI and blockchain secured genome data management platforms the scope protection of personal data may be limited on account of technological limitations.

The exemption provided in the case of processing for archiving purposes in the public interest, scientific or historical research purposes or statistical purposes implies an exemption even when applying new technologies within such research (Article 89). In all other instances the GDPR requires consent for the collection of data in the research limited to one or more specific purposes in a manner that is clearly distinguishable from the other matters, in an intelligible and easily accessible form, using clear and plain language. Thus, there is a requirement for explicit and informed consent for the processing of personal data, unless public interest or scientific, historical or statistical purposes are served by a broader consent. The regulation acknowledges that it is often not possible to fully identify the purpose of data processing for scientific research purposes at the time of data collection. Therefore, data subjects should be allowed to give their consent to certain areas of scientific research while in keeping with recognized ethical standards for scientific research. In such cases, data subjects should have the opportunity to give their consent only to certain areas of research or to parts of research projects based on purpose.[23] Thus, it may be essential for researchers to secure a re-consent as to other parts of the research if the aims of the study differ from the time when data was originally collected and consented. The GDPR is in fact a major step to meet the challenges for protection of personal data in the context of Big Data research and increased cross-border flow of data within shifting paradigms of research alliances. While regulating the processing of

23. Recital point 33, General Data Protection Regulation, 2016.

data in research, the New Regulation also ensures that the processing of personal data for scientific research purposes should be interpreted in a broad manner in the interest of technological development, development of fundamental research and applied research as well as privately funded research. For instance the general principle of the GDPR that sensitive personal data be essentially processed only for the specified purposes for which the data subject offered consent; however in the interest of research, the Regulation offers the researcher the possibility to process such data for a subsequent legitimate purpose by ensuring appropriate standards and safeguards while processing such data.[24] These include weighing considerations like the initial purpose of the collection, the nature of data and the possible consequences of processing such data for a new purpose.[25]

Apart from GDPR there are policy-based instruments such as the *Council of Europe steering committee on Bioethics, proposal for an instrument on the use of archived human materials* dealing in both samples and data in biomedical research and the FAIR data management rules relating to findable, accessible interoperable and reuse ability of research data[26]. Even though these principle may not involve personal data yet it supports the use and sharing of rich metadata to facilitate discovery.

So also, the European Convention on Human Rights[27] plays a key role in ensuring the right to life and freedom of human beings, particularly in terms of their privacy and family. The ECtHR plays a vital role in this process in addressing the use of human biological data in violation of the rights of such persons.[28]

[B] Governance for Biobank-Based Research at the International Level

At the international level, a general but powerful foundation exists in the form of universal declaration of human rights, which governs the basic rights of all individuals.[29] Parallel to this exists, the Universal Declaration on Bioethics and Human Rights adopted by the United Nations Educational, Scientific, and Cultural Organization (UNESCO) on 19 October 2005. It is an important step in the search for global minimum standards in biomedical research and clinical practice.[30] The Belmont Report created by the National Commission for the Protection of Human Subjects of Biomedical and Behavioral Research (USA) became acknowledged in terms of the fundamental principles of respect for human beings, justice and beneficence that had to stand as threshold for any health-related research involving human participants including use

24. Article 6(4) General Data Protection Regulation, 2016.
25. R. Neethu, What the role out of EU data protection means for you. *Nature Biotech.* 2017.
26. Council of Europe. Steering Committee on Bioethics (CDBI) Strasbourg, 17 October 2002; See also M.D. Wilkinson et al., The FAIR Guiding Principles for scientific data management and stewardship. *Scientific. Data* 3:160018 doi: 10.1038/sdata.2016.18 (2016).
27. Convention for the Protection of Human Rights and Fundamental Freedoms, 1953.
28. *Elberte v Latvia*, Application No. 61243/08, 2015. *See also*: R. Neethu, Elberte V. Latvia: The to be or not to be question of consent. *Medical Law Review.* 1 August 2017; 25(3): 484–493.
29. 1948, http://www.un.org/en/universal-declaration-human-rights/.
30. R. Andorno, Global bioethics at UNESCO: In defence of the universal declaration on bioethics and human rights. *Journal of Medical Ethics.* 2007; 33(3): 150–154. PMC. Web. 30 September 2017.

of their samples in such research.[31] Another more prominent and widely cited regulatory document is the Oviedo Convention[32] along with four additional protocols dealing in biomedical research,[33] cloning,[34] transplantation of tissues and organs[35] and genetic testing for health purposes.[36] The Oviedo Convention is the first legally binding international text designed to preserve human dignity, rights and freedom, through a series of principles and prohibitions against the misuse of biological and medical advances. The convention considers that the interests of human beings must come before the interests of science or society and lays down a series of principles and prohibitions concerning bioethics, medical research, consent, right to private life, etc.[37] In addition, the research involving human subjects must also adhere to the WMA's Declaration of Helsinki, which considered that medical progress is based on research that ultimately must include studies involving human subjects, however such research must also ensure ethical standards to ensure that the participants of such research are not harmed in any way.[38] The Council for International Organizations of Medical Sciences (CIOMS) has also been publishing international ethical guidelines for health-related research involving humans since 1993 and a latest version of this was published in 2016.[39] Another important document which addresses biobank-based research is the 'WMA's *Taipei Declaration on Ethical considerations regarding health databases and Biobanks*'.[40] This document is regarded as a complementary tool to the Helsinki Declaration and takes into account the need for the medical profession to have guidance about how to ethically approach the rapidly growing agendas of health databases and biobanks.[41] The Declaration of Taipei calls for special attention to the possible exploitation of IP. Accordingly, it requires that protection over ownership of materials, rights and privileges be addressed and contractually defined before collecting or sharing the material. Intellectual property issues should be addressed in a policy that covers the rights of all stakeholders and should be communicated in a transparent

31. https://www.hhs.gov/ohrp/regulations-and-policy/belmont-report/index.html.
32. The Convention for the Protection of Human Rights and Dignity of the Human Being with regard to the Application of Biology and Medicine: Convention on Human Rights and Biomedicine (ETS No. 164) was opened for signature on 4 April 1997 in Oviedo (Spain).
33. Additional Protocol to the Convention on Human Rights and Biomedicine, concerning Biomedical Research, Strasbourg, 25 January 2005.
34. Additional Protocol to the Convention for the Protection of Human Rights and Dignity of the Human Being with regard to the Application of Biology and Medicine, on the Prohibition of Cloning Human Beings, 1 March 2001.
35. Additional Protocol to the Convention on Human Rights and Biomedicine concerning Transplantation of Organs and Tissues of Human Origin, 1 May 2006.
36. Additional Protocol to the Convention on Human Rights and Biomedicine concerning Genetic Testing for Health Purposes, Strasbourg, 27 November 2008.
37. *Supra* note 32.
38. Adopted by the 18th WMA General Assembly, Helsinki, Finland, June 1964.
39. https://cioms.ch/shop/product/international-ethical-guidelines-for-health-related-research-involving-humans/.
40. Adopted by the fifty-third WMA General Assembly, Washington, DC, USA, October 2002 and revised by the sixty-seventh WMA General Assembly, Taipei, Taiwan, October 2016, available at: http://www.wma.net/en/30publications/10policies/d1/ (last accessed on 1 October 2017).
41. http://www.bbmri-eric.eu/news-events/new-wma-declaration-of-taipei-on-hdb-published/ (last accessed on 1 October 2017).

manner.[42] Thus as can be seen both at the EU level and at the international level there is a growing realization for considering the aspects of research within ethical realms. Although the EU and international level of governance consists of many relevant instruments governing biomedical research, they are, supplemented by the guidelines of professional bodies like BBMRI-ERIC along with standards developed by other interested parties relevant to the sector such as OECD,[43] Nuffield council,[44] HUGO,[45] European Society of Human Genetics (ESHG), etc.

[C] National Level

At the national level, many Member States have laws that deal with biobanks, while many others do not have any regulation at the national level. However, in such Member States without specific national legislation, there are other integrative ethical strategies, requisites and conditionalities for the functioning of the biobanks within the national legal structure.[46] With regard to the data, the present general data protection regulation has offered to strengthen the efforts for harmonization as to the processing of data.[47] Although the new regulation is binding upon Member States, yet they are required to clarify provisions in their laws for certain specific exemption for the purposes of research within biobanks in the interest of research for public benefits (e.g., exemptions in relation to data portability or rights of access of data subjects, right of rectification, restriction on processing).[48] Further, since the regulation does not deal with the data of deceased person, Member States may provide for rules regarding the processing of personal data of deceased persons.[49] Apart from these alignments, the law governing data is, fairly settled in EU. However, this has not been the case with regard to the samples. Hence, different national laws on biobanks govern the use of samples in research. Some states have ethical guidelines for the collection and use of samples rather than formal legal framework (*See* table 2.1).

42. Point 18, Declaration of Taipei, 2016.
43. Guidelines for Human Biobanks and Genetic Research Databases (HBGRDs).
44. Nuffield Council, Human Tissue Ethical and Legal Issues, 1995.
45. HUGO Ethics Committee statement on benefit sharing – 9 April 2000.
46. *Supra* note 43.
47. While the regulation is in force since 24 May 2016, it shall apply from 25 May 2018.
48. Recital 53, Regulation (EU) 2016/679 of the European Parliament and of the Council of 27 April 2016.
49. Recital 27, Regulation (EU) 2016/679.

Table 2.1 National Arrangements for Regulating Biobanks in Europe (Figure Modified from Beier K, Lenk C, Biobanking Strategies and Regulative Approaches in the EU: Recent Perspectives, Dove Press, 2015)

Head	*Country Name*
National Law on Biobank	Belgium, Estonia, Finland, Hungary, Latvia, Lithuania, Portugal, Spain, Sweden, United Kingdom (UK)
Other Control than Biobank law	Austria, Cyprus, Denmark, France, Germany, Greece, Italy, Luxembourg, the Netherlands, Poland, Republic of Ireland, Slovenia
Ethical Guideline	Austria, Cyprus, Denmark, France, Germany, Greece, Italy, Republic of Ireland, Slovenia, Sweden, UK

There exists certain similarities and more diversity in approach based on the nature, settings, government policies, etc. For instance Beier has studied the national legal systems based on four focal points namely ownership, consent, privacy and confidentiality and benefit sharing.[50] With regard to the legal status of human tissue samples, the majority of European Member States are most reluctant to grant donors property rights in their biological materials. This is backed up by the international conventions and other European documents that the 'human body and its parts shall not, as such, give rise to financial gain'.[51] In addition, both Continental Civil Law and the Common Law traditions, perceive of the human body as a *res extra commercium.*[52] In spite of such similarities there are also differences; for instance with regard to ownership rights there are those countries whose jurisdictions do not take a stance at all towards this issue (e.g., Sweden). Some countries explicitly exclude any ownership or property rights in tissue samples and data derived thereof (e.g., France). Few countries ascribe a middle path in the right of ownership not to donors, but to the biobank (e.g., Greece) or to the chief processor of samples respectively (e.g., Estonia). Yet in other countries they set out a de facto property right for donors, though bearing on diverging explanations such as the concept of personality rights (e.g., in the German speaking countries).[53] This diversity in national approaches, are also reflected in the outlook towards protection of research results from genetic research. For instance in Sweden the individual (as well as employed) researcher owns the result of his or her research. This applies to what one writes or draws as well as any technical invention.[54] This approach is visible in the MTAs of Swedish institutions.[55] Thus the variety in

50. K. Beier and C. Lenk, 'A unified European approach on tissue research and biobanking? A comparison', in C. Lenk J. Sándor and B. Gordijn (eds) 'Biobanks and tissue research. the international library of ethics, law and technology', Vol. 8. Springer, 2011.
51. Oveido Convention.
52. C. Lenk and K. Beier, Is the commercialization of human tissue and body material forbidden in the countries of the European Union?. *Journal of Medical Ethics.* 2011.
53. *Supra* note 50.
54. Act on the Right to Inventions by Employees (1949: 345), Sweden.
55. MTA of Karolinska Instituttet, Sweden.

national traditions, research cultures contribute to national approach towards regulating research with human biological samples.

Figure 2.3 Emerging Legal and Ethical Governance for Biobanks and Related Research

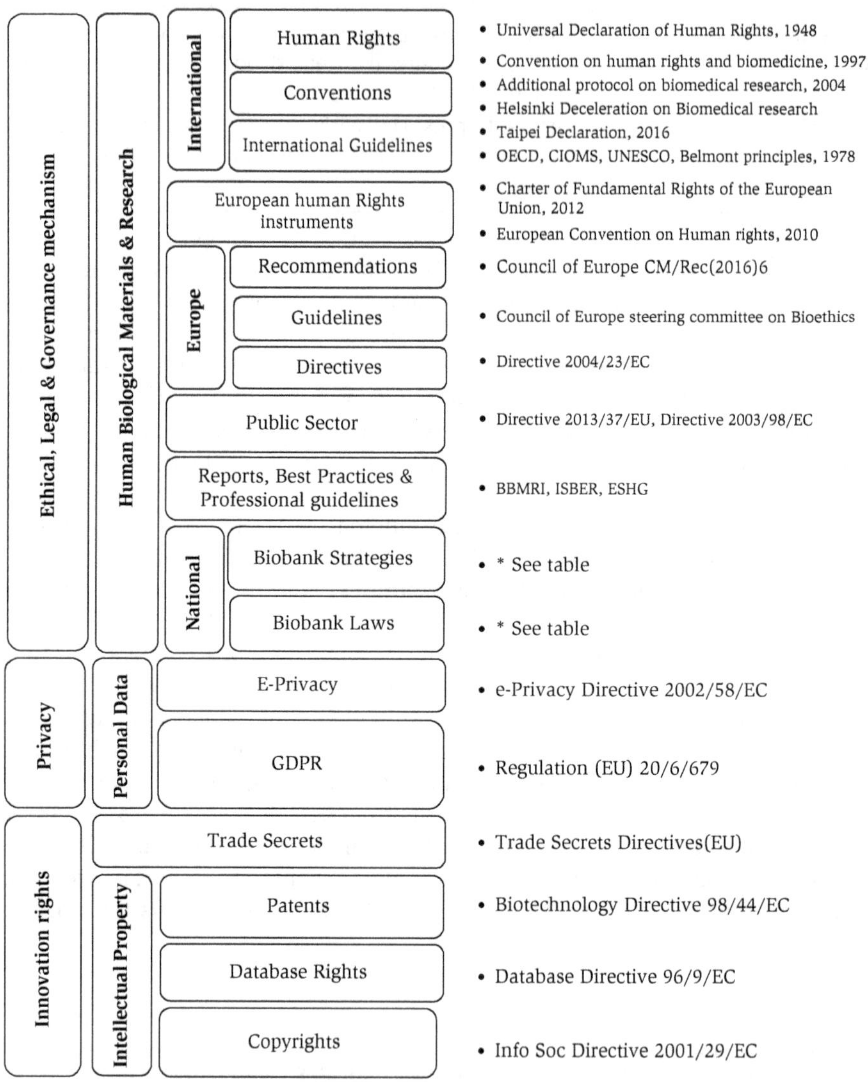

§2.02 OTHER STANDARDS FOR CONDUCT OF SCIENTIFIC RESEARCH

In considering other standards for research, the first thing that comes up is the need for ensuring higher standards. The HeLa cells of which most biomedical researchers are familiar is a befitting example to this end. The HeLa cell line was formulated in 1951 and was taken from a biopsy of a cervical tumor taken from Henrietta Lacks, a working-class African-American woman living near Baltimore. These cells were isolated and preserved without the knowledge or permission of Henriette or her family, and they became the first human cells to grow well in a lab. The bright side of the event is that the cell lines contributed to the development of a polio vaccine, the discovery of human telomerase and countless other advances including more than 75,000 research papers using the cell line.[56] In spite of the prospects contributed by hela cell line, the public outcry in relation to the issue reflects the sense of injustice of the part of the researchers at John Hopkins institute.[57] Such instances reflect ethical dilemmas and conflict of interest in the marriage between scientific research and society. Science forms the foundation for seeking better future and forms the bedrock of a knowledge-based society and a healthy economy. The dialogue between science and society must reflect a state in which research as well as innovation must respond to the needs and ambitions of society reflect its values, and at the same time are responsible.[58] In addition, the diversity in research tradition and culture, seeks to enforce a reasonable standard for the conduct of scientific research, which any research entity public or private needs to abide within biomedical research. In other words, diversity must seek the development of new cultural landscape within biobank-based research. In this regard, it would be of interest to involve **RRI** for epistemic validity in biomedical research. 'RRI' is regarded as a convergence of Technology Assessment (TA) Ethics, including corporate responsibility (CR).[59] The EU commission defines RRI as '*a transparent, interactive process by which societal actors and innovators become mutually responsive to each other with a view on the* (ethical) *acceptability, sustainability and societal desirability of the innovation process and its marketable products* (in order to allow a proper embedding of scientific and technological advances in our society)'.[60] As opposed to systemic reasoning in considering RRI as a down-to-earth concept, for researchers, innovators or policymakers to follow, RRI is seen as systemic reasoning that seeks to create spaces and processes to allow roles for innovation based on certain values.[61] Thus, RRI envisions a research process, which abides by standard conduct of research, which enables the establishment of a proactive scientific community and the

56. E. Callaway, Deal done over HeLa cell line: Family of henrietta lacks agrees to release of genomic data, 7 August 2013; G. Javitt, Why not take all of me?, reflections on the immortal life of henriatta lacks and the status of participaction in research using human specimens, *Minnesota Journal of Law Science and technology*. 2010.
57. *Ibid.*
58. M. Geoghegan-Quinn, European commissioner for research, innovation and science message delivered at the conference 'Science in dialogue – towards a European model for responsible research and innovation' Odense, 23–25 April 2012.
59. K. Iatridis and D. Schroeder, An overview of corporate responsibility tools and their relationship with responsible research and innovation. *Responsible Research and Innovation in Industry*. Springer Briefs in Research and Innovation Governance. Springer, 2016.
60. European commission, Towards a Responsible Research and Innovation in the Information and Communication Technologies and Security Technologies Fields, European commission 2011.
61. R. Owen, Responsible research and innovation: Options for research and innovation policy in the EU.

development of a creative role and responsibility for co-actors.[62] It also visualizes accountability in adhering to standards and ensuring privacy and data protection of research participants. In this process, RRI requires that ethical principles are considered as design principles for technological development.[63]

[A] RRI in EU's Scientific Research

Although researchers have used the dimensions of RRI for more than a decade, its visible figure is more recent.[64] These dimensions revolved around many aspects of research in a number of fields such as ethical legal social implication (ELSI) from genomic research, precautionary principle in environmental laws or corporate social responsibility (CSR) under commercial transactions.[65] Since the fifth and sixth EU framework programmes there have been calls for greater public engagement with the science and technology.[66] The seventh programme framework was decisive with the creation of ESFRI roadmap, which aimed to establish research infrastructures with the aim to serve as a forum for stakeholder participation and maximizing socio-economic benefits through research.[67] Furthermore, RRI is a 'cross-cutting issue' in Horizon 2020. Under the regulation implementing the Horizon 2020 programme the general objectives of the Horizon 2020 shall be aimed at contributing to building a society and an economy based on knowledge and innovation across the union by leveraging additional research, development and innovation funding and by contributing to attaining research and development targets.[68] The general objective of the programme is pursued through (a) excellent science; (b) industrial leadership; (c) meeting the societal challenges.[69] The specific aims in relation to the general objectives are 'spreading excellence and widening participation' of different stakeholders and to build effective cooperation between science and society. In this respect the Horizon 2020 programme aims to develop the governance for the advancement of RRI by all stakeholders (researchers, public authorities, industry and civil society organizations), which is sensitive to society needs and demands, and promote an ethics framework for research and innovation.[70] While many programmes are underway in Europe in this

62. *Infra* note 322.
63. R. Von Schomberg, Towards responsible research and innovation in the information and communication technologies and security technologies fields. Brussels: European Commission.
64. R. Owen et al., Responsible research and innovation: From science in society to science for society, with society, *Science and Public Policy.* 2012; 39: 751–760.
65. *Ibid., see also* J.B. Tucker, The promises and perils of synthetic biology. *The New Atlantis.* Spring 2006; 12: 25–45, J. Stilgoe et al., Developing a framework for responsible innovation. *Research Policy.* November 2013; 42(9): 1568–1580. J. Cameron et al., The precautionary principle: A fundamental principle of law and policy for the protection of the global environment. *Boston College International & Comparative Law Review.* 1991; 14: 1.
66. *Supra* note 64.
67. ESFRI Roadmap 2016.
68. Regulation (EU) No. 1291/2013 of the European Parliament and of the Council of 11 December 2013 establishing Horizon 2020 – the Framework Programme for Research and Innovation (2014–2020).
69. Article 5, Regulation (EU) No. 1291/2013.
70. Annex 1 Part V, Regulation (EU) No. 1291/2013.

respect with the aim of incorporating RRI into research,[71] it is noted by the Rome Declaration that RRI is an ongoing process of aligning research and innovation to the values, needs and expectations of society.[72]

[B] Biobank-Based Research and Commercial Collaborations: RRI Perspectives

Research involves a systematic investigation through observation, experiment and critical thinking.[73] It is an attempt to find results to a scientific hypothesis. It involves collection, gathering of data and information along with facts that contribute to new knowledge. Innovation on the contrary has been defined as an activity or process which may lead to previously unknown designs pertaining either to the physical world (e.g., designs of buildings and infrastructure), the conceptual world (e.g., conceptual frameworks, mathematics, logic, theory, software), the institutional world (social and legal institutions, procedures and organization) or combinations of these.[74] Thus, innovation is more associated with industrial or business relationships. The two activities also signify different relationships in the chain of research activity leading to an innovation. The term responsibility has a philosophical notion of duty and accountability.[75] Thus, it could stem from a state of mind moral, legal or mental.[76] Under an RRI framework, science and innovation are envisaged as being directed at, and undertaken towards, socially desirable and socially acceptable ends, through an inclusive and deliberative process.[77] This implies a sense of responsibility for researchers in terms of carrying out their experiments or observations in seeking results. It also stands for the responsibility of institutions which can regulate such actions including academic bodies, universities, professional bodies or even the state. The commercial collaborators also equally possess a duty of care in applying research results towards valorized outcomes. It is with backdrop one must view biobanking as a scientific technology and biobank-based research as a process of innovation. The obtainment, preservation and utilization of HBM for biomedical research or diagnostics, have been a common practice. However, important technical innovations, especially in the fields of human genetics and electronic data processing, today make it possible to collect, store and compare biological material and personal data obtained from it on a large scale.[78] The epidemiological, diagnostic and therapeutic knowledge derived from such resources enables researchers to contribute to the medical research in many ways.[79]

---

71. *See* footnotes notes 63, 64.
72. http://ec.europa.eu/research/swafs/pdf/rome_declaration_RRI_final_21_November.pdf (last accessed on 2 October 2017).
73. *Supra* note 64.
74. J. van den Hoven, 'Value sensitive design and responsible innovation', in R. Owen, J. Bessant and M. Heintz (eds) 'Responsible innovation'. John Wiley, 2013, pp. 75–83.
75. *Ibid.*
76. *See* definition of responsibility Merriam Webster's.
77. *Supra* note 74.
78. Biobanks: Obtainment, preservation and utilisation of human biological material, Swiss Academies Reports, 2006.
79. *Ibid.*

There are also challenges for such research in biobanks, in particular, the fear that biological material and data may be used for purposes other than those for which the donor has explicitly given consent or that researchers or industrial collaborators could potentially abuse such resources in seeking economic profits through IPR. Such concerns over research and commercialization must be addressed early on to evolve innovation and create an innovation culture that caters to these concerns in an effective manner. The principle of public trust, valorization, stewardship and ELSI approaches forms the foundation for evolving an RRI culture within biobanks. However, RRI moves further steps towards seeking and enforcing responsibility as a mechanism to regulate social commitments towards research and innovation.

[C] RRI in Bridging Science – Society Relationship in Biobanks

Biobanks as a resource for research faces two major societal concerns expressed through literature in the field namely (i) consent – i.e., the selection of appropriate information and consent procedures for different research protocols, (ii) Privacy – the protection of confidentiality of those who submit tissue material or personal information while still facilitating important research.[80] As noted above there are well-laid ethical guidelines and legal rules intended to govern biobanks, particularly with regard to consent and privacy and many biobanks have adopted such standards to varying degrees. However, there remains no consensus as to their legal and ethical appropriateness.[81] Under such circumstances, an RRI paradigm seeks to go beyond what science and innovation 'ought not to do' to 'what can be done'.[82] Thus, the target for research and innovation is to be identified in an ethical, inclusive, democratic and equitable manner.[83] The Declaration of UNESCO addresses ethical issues related to medicine, life sciences and associated technologies as applied to human beings, taking into account their social, legal and environmental dimensions.[84] Although directed towards state actors, it offers ample guidance for the decisions and practices of individuals, groups, communities, institutions and corporations, both public and private.[85] Incorporating such broader visions within biomedical research calls for attention to ensuring and enforcing good research practices and professional rules of conduct in research along with stakeholder engagement to democratically open up and realize new areas of public value for science.[86] Therefore good research practices in handling genetic information must ensure that privacy of individuals is respected by

80. M.G. Hansson, Ethics and biobanks. *British Journal of Cancer.* 2009; 100.1: 8–12.
81. T. Caulfield and B. Murdoch, Genes, cells, and biobanks: Yet, there's still a consent problem. *PLoS Biology* 2017; 15(7): e2002654.
82. *Supra* note 64.
83. *Ibid.*
84. Universal Declaration on Bioethics and Human Rights, 19 October 2005.
85. Z. Menevidis et al., 'Code of conduct for FP7 researchers on medical and biometric data Privacy', in 'Towards responsible research and innovation in the information and communication technologies and security technologies fields'. Brussels: European Commission.
86. J. Wilsdon et al., The public value of science, Demos 2005.

de-identifying data as effectively as possible whenever possible.[87] Ethical collection of identifiable medical data should be carried out only with informed consent, including consent to the length of the data retention period. If the data are de-identified, and an independent ethical approval has been obtained which determines that the data use is in line with the data subject's original consent, only then data may be used without further consent. Data subjects should be able to give broad consent so that their data can be reused; otherwise, consent must be sought for each instance of data collection, use, or retention, or if the purpose has been modified. If consent is not obtained, the data must be removed from any databases.[88] Researchers must also ensure that data subjects understand the implications of taking part and the data collection must be maximally transparent.[89] So also, stakeholder engagement must be sought early on in the cohort planning phase to give the participants an idea of the nature and proposed outcome of research. These efforts must also seek mechanisms for accountability for researchers and their actions. The infrastructures such as BBMRI-ERIC or International Society for Biological and Environmental Repositories (ISBER), could ensure that standards and practices are strictly followed and take actions in case of mishandling such as non-recognition of the biobank as a participant of the infrastructure. Thus, 'responsibility' should also ensure the responsible conduct of other actors in this process.

[D] RRI in Industrial Academic Collaborations in Biobanks

The current research paradigm is one of collaboration and partnerships which seek to achieve mutual interests through joint efforts. Setting up a participatory research agenda has multiple advantages. Apart from helping to identify stakeholders' needs and identifying end users' needs it also helps researchers to include new perspectives in research.[90] Industrial partnership also draws private investment in academic institutions, which have helped to expand and support universities, public research institutions and research cohorts alike.[91] In addition, innovation capabilities (both upstream and downstream) are increasingly dispersed within organizations and may even developed outside the organization. Such collaborations have significant outcomes for the industry as (a) it reduces costs to develop and to market, (b) it broadens the innovation pipeline and (c) improves time to develop and time to market considerably.[92] The literature with regard to industrial collaboration within publicly funded biobanks reveals two major concerns namely: (1) creation of monopolies through IPR;[93] and (2) benefit sharing.[94] The industry also has concerns over public

87. *Supra* note 80.
88. *Ibid.*
89. *Ibid.*
90. RRI Tools.
91. A.E. Shamoo and D.B. Resnik, Responsible conduct of research, Oxford scholarship online 2009.
92. http://www.innovationmanagement.se/2010/05/24/collaborating-downstream-in-emerging-markets/ (last accessed on 3 October 2017).
93. S. Aymé et al., Patenting and licensing in genetic testing recommendations of the European society of human genetics, *European Journal of Human Genetics*. 2008; 16: 405–411.

opinion, investments and modes for seeking a balance while engaging in commercial returns. The prospect of IP protection is just one of the many factors that drive innovation and, translational research in the field of medical genetics.[95] Hence it is not only the task of public bodies but also industrial partners alike to find models and approaches that encourages innovation and promotes sharing of results to the public at large. A RRI approach does not require commercial collaborators to contribute to a better world ideology but to contribute to competitive advantage by strategizing a balance of conflicting interests.[96] To cite an example the Rational molecular Assessments and Innovative Drugs selection (RAIDs) consortium is Europe's first biobanking study with emerging market-oriented results.[97] It conducted 4.5 years of studies on cervical cancer and was successful in building intelligent targeted therapy designs. The RAIDs consortium brought together almost twenty public and private partners from Germany, Netherlands, Serbia, Moldavia, Hungary and Romania, the countries that have the highest prevalence of cervical cancer in Europe in an attempt to study patient's patterns and develop drugs based on molecular profiling.[98] The success of this project was its multidisciplinary cooperation between academic clinical centres, Small and medium scale enterprises (SMEs) and translational research. Along with this, the consortium also focused locally in strategic locations around Europe with increased incidences to cervical cancer and having lesser research contributions.[99] So also effective data collection, patient engagement,[100] target-oriented study and result-oriented approach. The consortium has also sought a patent for therapeutic vaccines for cervical tumor.

From an RRI perspective such examples reflects seeking attention to certain considerations on the part of public funded institutions and the industry alike. These include:

(a) Creating effective models for research collaborations such as public-private partnerships (PPP).
(b) Industrial partners ought to take a leadership role in involving, building and developing RRI.[101] For example in offering access to data and resources for public researchers with whom such collaboration is done, ensuing healthcare

94. T. Caulfield et al., A review of the key issues associated with the commercialization of biobanks. *Journal of Law and the Biosciences*. 2014; 1(1): 94–110. PMC. Web. 20 September 2017; K. Evers, Commercialization of biobanks. *Biopreservation and Biobanking*. 2012; 10(1).
95. *Supra* note 94.
96. https://www.rri-tools.eu/how-to-stk-bi-do-a-business-plan-embedding-the-rri-principles.
97. Pan European Networks – Horizon 2020 – p. 201, http://www.horizon2020publications.com/H6/files/assets/basic- html/page201.html, *See also* http://www.raids-fp7.eu/project-overview.html.
98. https://labiotech.eu/raids-europe-hpv-cervical-cancer/; *See also* C. Ngo et al., From prospective biobanking to precision medicine: BIO-RAIDs – an EU study protocol in cervical cancer. *BMC Cancer*. 2015; 15:842.
99. *Supra* note 97.
100. A patients' working group was organized at Institut Curie around precision medicine issues and also patient-doctor meeting was organized. *See* http://cordis.europa.eu/result/rcn/202706_en.html.
101. *Supra* note 91.

benefits for the research, avoiding unrealistic expectations for the public from research.[102]

(c) IP policies within such partnerships must seek to protect the rights of researchers as well as the interests of the university, industry and the public.[103]

(d) Effectively pursuing CSR (philanthropy) and CR (corporate responsibilityi.e., no harm beyond philanthropy) tools can assist in realizing the goals of the emerging RRI framework.[104]

(e) Focusing locally on the needs of health research within specific regions involving such collaborations.

These aspects of RRI discussed herein within the context of biomedical research pursue a major goal i.e., avoiding irresponsible research as in the case of Hela cell line. RRI in genetic research must not be sought a method of research but instead, as the EU commission noted (in its RRI policy, 2011) as a 'process' which must seek, find and commit to the deployment of mechanisms suiting the needs of the biobank-based research. 'RRI' also posits a reminder that biobanks are not just research resources but are stewards for social commitment in finding better healthcare and treatments to humans within a coordinated effort from stakeholders each with a defined responsibility in such research. RRI draws the focus towards a culture of seeking attention to the principles in handling human biological resources, which will be considered in the next chapter (Chapter 3) particularly in the context of pre-patent research.

§2.03 STRUCTURAL AND INSTITUTIONAL MECHANISMS FOR GOVERNING BIOBANKS

Translating biomedical research into effective medical interventions or developing innovations supporting the treatment cure or prevention of diseases requires not only an effective scientific research but also collaborative efforts on the part of donors, academia, researchers and the industry alike. Biobanks are a result of realizing this common goal in the context of health and innovation within the realms of health.[105] In Europe, this realization of structural support for biomedical research was brought about by the flotation of BBMRI, as a major project of the European Strategy Forum on Research Infrastructures (ESFRI) from 2008 to 2011. Research Infrastructures (RIs) were created with the aim of supporting a coherent and strategy-led structure to

102. R. Wynberg et al., 'Conclusions and recommendations: Towards best practice for community consent and benefit sharing', in R. Wynberg, D. Schroeder and R. Chennells (eds) 'Indigenous peoples, consent and benefit sharing', Springer, 2009.
103. For example Malaria drug discovery at the Novartis Institute for Tropical Diseases, which sought to share benefits for the public in kind from the research: *see* https://wellcome.ac.uk/funding/managing-grant/approach-wellcome trust-managing-intellectual-property – maximis e-public-health-benefit.
104. *Supr* note 64, 65.
105. M. Yuille et al., Biobanking for Europe, brief bioinform. January 2008; 9(1): 14–24. Epub 23 October 2007.

facilitate multilateral initiatives leading to a better use and development of scientific discoveries, technological development and research collaboration from around the world.[106] This however requires a change of culture within both RIs and industry as well. Creating a research orientation towards research infrastructures requires that 'industry should become more RI oriented and RIs more business oriented'.[107] This aim not only enables the realization of the goals of such research infrastructures but also seeks to facilitate the industries with access to a wide range of resources at their fingertips. This is an essential element for research and development in the area of pharmaceutical and biotechnology particularly in Europe as the sector demands the high amounts of R & D investment besides being R & D intensive.[108] The ERIC status was awarded to BBMRI in 2013, which lead to its emergence as an independent infrastructure from ESFRI.[109] BBMR-ERIC operates and develops a pan-European distributed research infrastructure of biobanks and biomolecular resources in order to facilitate the access to resources and to support high quality biomolecular and medical research.[110] A hub and spoke model was established to the federated IT architecture developed to link national biobanks to national nodes that are integrated into BBMRI-ERIC which provides one common access point for users. The national nodes are designated by a Member State and enable the coordination of the national biobanks and biomolecular resources, and link its activities with the pan-European activities of BBMRI-ERIC.[111] The principal task of an ERIC shall be to establish and operate a research infrastructure and operate the infrastructure on a non-economic basis.[112] However, in this process BBMRI-ERIC may carry out limited economic activities, provided that they are (a) closely related to its principal tasks and (b) does not jeopardize their achievements.[113] In interpreting the notion of 'non-economic', the commission relies on the definition of 'economic activities' as developed by the Court of Justice of EU in its decision in competition matters.[114] Thus, an economic activity consists of offering goods and/or services on a given market and being carried on, at least in principle, with a view to profits.[115] In this sense a limited economic activity means economic activity to the extent needed to allow an ERIC to engage in cooperation with industry, carry out technology transfer and contribute to innovation, it may

106. https://ec.europa.eu/research/infrastructures/index_en.cfm?pg=about.
107. ESFRI Annual report 2016.
108. The EU R & D scoreboard, 2016.
109. European Biobanking and Biomolecular Resources Research Infrastructure (BBMRI) business plan, 3 December 2012.
110. *Supra* note 105.
111. *Ibid.*
112. Article 3(2), Commission Implementing Decision, of 22 November 2013, on setting up the Biobanks and Biomolecular Resources Research Infrastructure Consortium (BBMRI-ERIC) as a European Research Infrastructure Consortium (2013/701/EU).
113. Article 3, Commission Implementing Decision, of 22 November 2013, on setting up the Biobanks and Biomolecular Resources Research Infrastructure Consortium (BBMRI-ERIC) as a European Research Infrastructure Consortium (2013/701/EU); *See also* Council Regulation (EC) No. 723/2009 of 25 June 2009 on the Community legal framework for a European Research Infrastructure Consortium (ERIC).
114. Case 118/85, *Commission v Italy*; Case C-35/96, *Commission v Italy;* Case C-309/99 Wouters.
115. Legal framework for a European Research Infrastructure Consortium – ERIC, Practical Guidelines, April 2010.

carry out economic activities under the conditions stipulated under the council regulation for ERIC.[116] The limited character of these activities means that they are secondary and are not to prevail over the execution of the main task of the ERIC and have been considered to be below 25% of the annual activities in a quantified scale.[117] This means a balanced approach to commercial partnerships in relation to ERIC. The ERIC as a legal status enables BBMRI-ERIC to claim appropriate IPR available within applicable national and international jurisdictions over tools, data, products or any other results developed or generated by BBMRI-ERIC while carrying out the Work Programme.[118] On the contrary biobanks functioning as a part of the 'BBMRI National node' are not limited in their commercial approaches although they may be bound by any laws or policies including international conventions relating to IPR or benefit sharing as designated by the relevant ministry or research council of Member State within which such biobank functions.[119]

[A] Role of Expert Centres and Research in Biotechnology and Life Sciences

Although the formation of ERIC as a legal structure for biobanking that enabled it to be an independent legal entity dealing in policy matters and coordination of biobanks, yet it limited the potential for cooperation with commercial and industrial partners. The realization that innovation and industrial cooperation are important factors that strengthen the RIs in terms of long-term sustainability and are essential to the translation of research results into biomedical inventions, the expert centres were formulated which began functioning since 2016 onwards.[120] Expert centres are key intermediaries between public and private sectors performing the analysis of biological samples under internationally standardized conditions. BBMRI-ERIC associated expert centres are designated as 'trusted partners' who enable building the bridge between academic and applied research within a public-private partnership model.[121] Thus the role of expert centres have been to enhance collaborative research on a non-profit basis using limited resources efficiently, sharing data, technology, knowledge and expertise, facilitating innovation and thus: increasing competitiveness in academic science as well as on the marketplace through product innovation and increased R&D efficacy.[122] Industrial partnerships within such expert centres facilitate scientific collaborations. Hence, the BBMRI-ERIC also draws in policy options in this regard by ensuring joint IP

116. Article 3(3), Council Regulation (EC) No. 723/2009 of 25 June 2009 on the Community legal framework for a European Research Infrastructure Consortium (ERIC).
117. *Supra* note 112 and 115.
118. Article 19, Commission Implementing Decision, of 22 November 2013, on setting up the Biobanks and Biomolecular Resources Research Infrastructure Consortium (BBMRI-ERIC) as a European Research Infrastructure Consortium (2013/701/EU).
119. Article 19(1), Commission Implementing Decision, of 22 November 2013, on setting up the Biobanks and Biomolecular Resources Research Infrastructure Consortium (BBMRI-ERIC) as a European Research Infrastructure Consortium (2013/701/EU).
120. http://www.bbmri-eric.eu/services/expert-centre/.
121. BBMRI-ERIC-associated Expert Centres/Trusted Partners, 27 October 2015.
122. *Supra* note 120.

between industrial partners and expert centres on the IP jointly generated.[123] It has also been stipulated that the exploitation of the IP should be as flexible as possible and could be negotiated between the partners on a case-by-case basis. The general policy however should be that industrial partners have optimal freedom to generate value out of IP (e.g., industry as holder/owner of the patents).[124]

Figure 2.4 Role of Expert Centre as Intermediary in Developing Public-Private Partnership

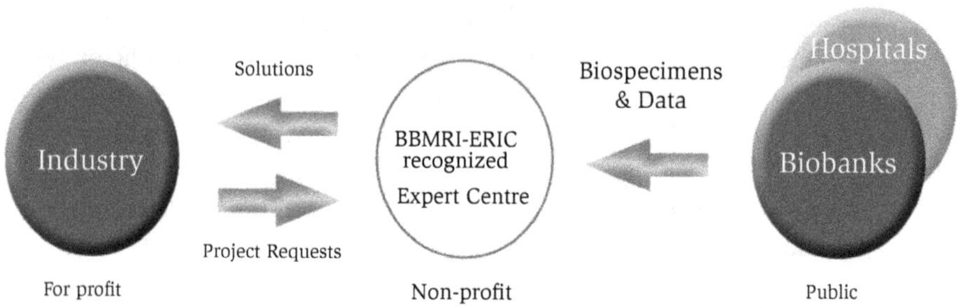

Source CBmed.

In case of joint inventions, the academic partners should benefit in the form of royalties or other benefit-sharing models that properly reflect and reward the contribution of public resources, expertise and work.[125] Thus, the present scenario in Europe exhibits three pathways (*see* Figure 2.5) for collaborative research partnerships via:

(1) BBMRI-ERIC (facilitates collaboration in many ways like ELSI, project planning, IT, coordination with nodal partners).
(2) Expert centres approved by BBMR-ERIC (Expert centres are incorporated companies and works as intermediaries for research collaborations).
(3) National biobanks (samples, data, research cohorts, projects).

BBMRI-ERIC's present model in Europe is thus, aimed at becoming a relevant resource for partners in academic and scientific institutions as well as in the pharmaceutical and life science industries, thereby contributing directly to the strategic goals of research in Europe.[126]

Through the establishment of partner expert centres in Europe it is hope that it will open up new highways for collaborative research with non-EU countries and thus enables significant cooperation in biomedical research.[127] Collaboration between academia, the diagnostics industry and the pharmaceutical industry is particularly

123. *Ibid.*, note 121.
124. *Ibid.*
125. *Supra* note 121 at p. 9.
126. G.J.B van Ommen et al., BBMRI-ERIC as a resource for pharmaceutical and life science industries: The development of biobank-based expert centres. *European Journal of Human Genetics*. 2015; 23: 893–900.
127. *Supra* note 229.

important for successful biomarker identification, validation and application, diagnostic imaging and the like. While BBMRI-ERIC has been attempting to harmonize the approach toward commercialization through new models of expert centres and public-private partnerships, the biobanks still have differing approaches and models in governing their commercial relationships.

The current structure at the EU level, seeks to offer substantial resources, technology and skills for collaborative research with industrial partners. However, the success of endeavours depends on certain crucial factors. Commercial entities will only actively engage in collaboration when the benefit they derive is greater than the effort and time it takes to collaborate, as they are mostly profit oriented in outlook. Thus, suitable policies must seek to govern the alignment of goals between public and private partners particularly with regard to IPR.[128]

Figure 2.5 The Three Broad Pathways to Partnership in Europe

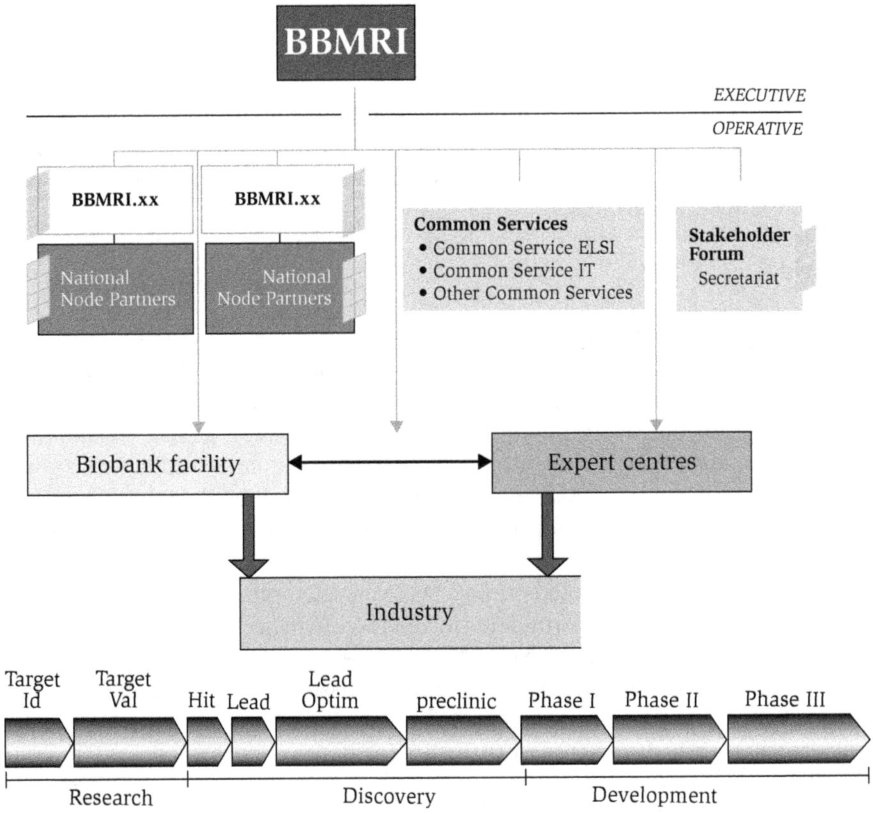

Source: BBMRI-ERIC.

128. K. Asadullah et al., Industry–academia collaborations for biomarkers, *Nature Reviews Drug Discovery* volume 14, pages 805–806 (2015).

[B] Differing Models of Biobanks and Research Partnerships

As seen from the above discussion, institutional arrangements such as the expert centres enable the needs of commercial involvement for translation of research results to research inventions that are socially useful to the society. Since commercialization of human bodily materials is forbidden according to the European Oviedo Convention and by national legislation in most Member States, and public opinion generally does not approve of financial compensation even on a cost-recovery basis, it makes access for industry difficult or even impossible in many cases.[129] Under such circumstances, the only recourse for research is through collaboration. While expert centres facilitate such efforts to a certain extent, biobanks themselves also enter into commercial relationships to meet their needs. However, biobanking operators such as hospitals, research institutes, pharmaceutical companies and patient organizations interpret their own biobanking activities differently, very often according to the background of the founding organization and the particular context in which the biobank is embedded (e.g., geographical location, ability to network nationally or internationally, etc.).[130] This creates diversity not only in the approach to collaboration but also to the governance polices of biobanks.

The biobanking landscape in Europe offers different biobank models for partnership and collaborative research.[131] Biobanks in Europe are also engaged in transnational biobank partnerships along with collaborations with academic or research institutes or industrial partners.[132]

There are different models for biobank partnership and research collaboration. These include:

(1) **Public-private partnership model**

This is widely used as a preferred model for biobank partnerships particularly where it involves the commercial partners. This is seen as a means for balancing public interest with innovation goals. Collaborations within such partnerships are developed and customized to suit the goal of such collaboration. Examples include Danish national biobank, which is funded by Novo Nordisk and contributions from Lundbeck foundation.

(2) **Hub models**

This involves collaboration between different institutional partners or research centres to formulate an alliance for specific or related genomic research. This facilitates easy sharing of resources among the partners. The popularity and effectives of hub model is based on the existence of multiple

129. *Supra* note 229.
130. D. Mitchell et al., Biobanking from the patient perspective, *Research Involvement and Engagement*. 2015.
131. Some biobanks are single (stand-alone) banks or have formed a partnership with other biobanks located either in the same or in a different country, for a variety of purposes such as sharing samples and/or for carrying out research., *See also* Z. Elen, Biobanks in Europe: Prospects for harmonisation and networking, 2010.
132. *Ibid.*

and interrelated resources for research. Formation of common goal also enables policies for partners to abide. For example, Genetic Alliance for rare disease studies. There are also variation of the hub model like the hub-and-spoke model where samples are collected in multiple clinics/hospitals and then sent to the central 'hub' for final processing, storage, and subsequent retrieval for experimental analysis.[133] For example LifeLines initiative.

(3) **Charitable trust model**

In this model 'proprietary interests' associated with tissues are transferred to a custodian or trustee who, together with the proprietary powers, also carries the fiduciary duties of responding to certain predetermined uses of the goods in favour of any third parties or the public.[134] Such model may integrate ethics with innovation and open access policies with patient focus as the centre of research intiatives. For example European Organisation for Research and Treatment of Cancer (EORTC) Charitable Trust to support the creation and funding of a pan-European Biobank for colorectal cancer.[135]

Apart from the above models of collaboration, differing models for biobanks can also be seen in Europe. Biobanks may also evolve from regional or national spectrum within polices of research determined by national laws, policies or other institutional structures. While it may not be possible to discuss all biobanks to a greater length, few examples of biobanks from across Europe can be briefly examined herein to appreciate the structural differences in the functioning of these biobanks. These include Biobank Graz under the Medial University Graz Austria, Integrated Biobank of Luxembourg (IBBL), Estonian Genome Center at the University of Tartu and Auria Biobank established by the University of Turku. Though this is a random selection of biobanks, yet the fact of these being within a publicly funded setting invokes the interest in understanding these models.

The BBMRI-ERIC contributes towards uniform policy standards for biobanks in Europe, yet the key challenge for governance is the lack of structural harmonization within which each of the biobanks function. Establishing biobanks within public structures in Member States required negotiation with regulatory bodies to gain acceptance and approvals for this new way of doing science. As a result, new norms, practices, standards and laws have been developed especially for biobanking amongst different Member States within EU.[136] It is to be noted that the IP laws and technology transfer measures are very much under national laws although there are specific European directives and regulations in place. Accordingly, commercial partnerships arrangements for biobanks are often modelled on the laws of the Member States

133. M. Bruinenberg et al., Comparing the hub-and-spoke model practices of the lifelines study in the Netherlands and the H3Africa initiative. *Biopreservation and Biobanking*. 2014; 12(1): 13–16.
134. D. Winickoff et al., The charitable trust as a model for genomic biobanks. *New England Journal of Medicine*. 2003; 349: 1180–1184. *See also* D. Mascalzoni, Ethics, law and governance of biobanking National European and international approaches, Springer 2015.
135. http://www.eortc.org/strategic-overview/ (last accessed on 26 November 2017).
136. Biobanks for Europe a challenge for Governance, European commission, 2012.

entering into such collaborative relationships. However, it seems that a common approach followed by biobanks is to adhere to the standards set by BBMRI along with national and international laws.

[C] Varying Models of Biobank Structurization

[1] Biobank Graz

The biobank Graz was fundamentally based on the Austrian Genome Programme GEN-AU tissue collection that was developed into a biobank under Medical University Graz by establishing the logistics and technologies for coordinated and standardized collection of various human biological samples, medical and experimental data.[137] The biobank Graz is a publicly funded, non-profit organization. Biobank Graz is one of three independent areas of the 'Organisational Unit for Research Infrastructure' (O-FIS) of Med Uni Graz. Besides Biobank Graz, the 'Center for Medical Research' (ZMF) and the area 'Biomedical Research' are embedded in this organizational unit.[138]

The research scenario of Graz interestingly consists of Federal Government and Local Government sometimes equally working under the same organizational structure. While the Medical University of Graz is under the Federal Government,[139] the LKH- Hospital Graz is governed by a company formulated by the local government of Styria.[140] Thus, research initiatives with the medical university and the hospital associated with the biobank involves researchers from either sectors. Apart from storage and processing of samples, the biobank also functions as a facilitator to enable collaborations between the university, the hospital, university research spin-off and the industrial partners. This enables the biobank to engage in commercially oriented research cohorts without directly involving itself in the process. So also, the model contributes to greater research cooperation in biomedical research. One of the key elements for sustainability adopted by biobank Graz is to ensure that it contributes qualitatively to strategic sample collections. Biobank Graz supports both types of collections using the following collection strategies: (1) A cross-sectional clinical biobank, which contains unselected pathological samples and clinical data from the entire population of south-eastern Austria. This biobank represents all detected diseases at their natural frequency of occurrence, yielding a large amount of epidemiological data; (2) a disease-focused clinical biobank, providing different types of human biological samples of high quality and with detailed clinical follow-up data during the whole disease course, and long-term observation for specifically selected cohorts in

137. *Supra* note 246.
138. Biobank Graz: Leader in Biobanking As a hub for co-operative Medical Research information brochure.
139. https://www.medunigraz.at/fileadmin/mitarbeiten/personalmanagement-entwicklung/pdf doc/MAEingangsphaseEinfuehrungsmappeE_March2016.pdf (last accessed 20 November 20 17).
140. Steiermärkische Krankenanstaltengesellschaft mbH (KAGes).

targeted disease group.[141] This along with a clearer structure and a vision focused on increased research along with the innate openness of the university towards industrial collaboration has effectively contributed to the successful working of the biobank.[142] On the regulatory side there is no Austrian laws on biobanking per se, however the legal foundations of consent, tissue safety and the like are governed by multiple laws such as Genetic Engineering Law (Gentechnikgesetz or GTG), the Austrian Blood Safety Law (Blutsicherherheitsgesetz), Tissue Safety Law (Gewebesicherheitsgesetz), Organ Transplant Law, Hospital Law (Krankenanstaltgestz). The IPR are governed by specific MTAs and other contractual arrangements following the IPAG - Intellectual Property Agreement Guide.[143]

[2] IBBL

The IBBL is an autonomous not-for-profit institute. Its formation was the result of the 'Health Sciences and Technologies Action Plan' by the Luxembourg Government in 2008. The plan aimed at the creation of a Centre of Excellence in Biomedical Research and Development in Luxembourg. This led to the development of IBBL, the LCSB (Luxembourg Centre for Systems Biomedicine). IBBL was merged with 'center de research public' to form the LIH or the Luxembourg Institute of Health a public biomedical research organization.[144] Presently IBBL is an autonomous institute, organized within the LIH. IBBL collaborates with organizations and individuals on biospecimen collection projects, research, industrial projects, through the provision of samples to clients. IBBL enters into partnerships with industrial organizations. These partnerships are aimed to be kept at 'arm's length', in which case IBBL's role is to validate commercial products and processes. In such cases, IBBL retains its independence (if findings are published, for example) and does not accept funding. In other cases, IBBL develops products and processes specifically for, or together with, its partner. Under these circumstances, the partnership involves collaboration and remuneration.[145] One of the key advantages for IBBL is its autonomous status as a foundation and its participation in large consortia projects, such as cancer, personalized healthcare and the like, both as a sample provider and as a research partner and acting as a central biobank for such research.[146] As regards commercializing research, the approach of Luxembourg has been to invest in a risk capital fund to set up a

141. K. Sargsyan et al., Sustainability in biobanking: Model of biobank graz., Biopreservation Biobanking, 2015, 13: 410–20.
142. http://www.medunigraz.at/en/research/cooperations/science-and-industry/.
143. IPAG is a project of 'Universities Austria' supported by the National Contact Point for Intellectual Property (ncp.ip) at the Federal Ministry of Science and Research (BMWF), the Federal Ministry of Economy, Family and Youth (BMWFJ), the Federal Ministry for Transport, Innovation and Technology. Austrian universities and companies jointly designed this set of model agreements to facilitate an efficient transfer of knowledge and technology.
144. https://www.lih.lu/page/aboutus.
145. IBBL Annual report 2012.
146. http://www.innovation.public.lu/en/cooperer/trouver-partenaires/instituts/integrated-biobank-of-luxembourg ibbl/integrated-biobank-of-luxembourg-ibbl/integrated-biobank-of-luxembourg-ibbl-1/index.html.

scouting mechanism within research institutions, to fund early stage start-ups and more generally to allow stakeholders to familiarize themselves with, and create links with, the world of investors.[147] So also the State of Luxembourg has a proactive role in biomedical research in particular. It offers support to research and development particularly in the context of IPR by an advantageous tax exemption regime.[148]

[3] Genome Center Estonia

The Estonian Biobank, founded in the year 2000, is a population-based biobank of the Estonian Genome Center of the University of Tartu or EGCUT. The project is in accordance with the Estonian Gene Research Act and all participants have signed up for a broad informed consent. Its main objectives, as stated in the Human Genes Research Act (HGRA), include the development of genetic research, collection of health and genetic information on the Estonian population, and implementation of genetic research results for the benefit of public health.[149] The initiative for research of the Estonian population came up in an effort to create a bridge to Europe, an opportunity to demonstrate the quality of Estonian Sciences in the European context and to create a strong identity for the Estonian population distinct from the Russian sphere. Thus, it was not just a matter for science but also a broader political implication for Estonians.[150] The HGRA – was passed by the Riigikogu (Parliament of Estonia) in December 2000 (RT I 2000, 104, 685). The HGRA is the superior law that regulates all the activities of the EGCUT. The law is stricter in terms of confidentiality and informed consent. It has incorporated principles from internationally acclaimed guiding documents dealing with genetic research, such as UNESCO's Universal Declaration on the Human Genome and Human Rights and the Council of Europe's Convention on Human Rights and Biomedicine. The chief processor of the Gene Bank is the University of Tartu, who is regarded as the owner of the tissues samples and data contributed to the biobank. Another interesting provision in the act is that the doctor of a gene donor has the right, to obtain the decoded description of the state of health of the gene donor from the Gene Bank in order to treat the gene donor. The HGRA stipulates criminal conviction in cases where the law is broken, i.e., confidential information is disclosed, discrimination occurs, or illegal human genetic research is conducted. Further, the act allows re-contacting the gene donors, collecting their health data from other registries and the application of the results of the research for commercial purposes.[151] Thus, the

147. Luxembourg Strategy for Smart Specialisation, August 2014.
148. Multinational companies: Luxembourg an unrivalled gateway to Europe.
149. Estonian Genome Center booklet.
150. R. Eensaar, 'Estonia ups and downs of a biobank', in H. Gottweis and A. Petersen, 'Biobanks governance in comparative perspectives', Routledge, 2008.
151. For instance the HGRA, § 6. Genetic research and genetic testing (1) Genetic research relating to the Gene Bank is permitted in order to study and describe the links between genes, the physical and social environment and the lifestyles of people, to find medicinal products or methods of treatment on the basis thereof, to assess individual health hazards and to prevent

landscape for research and collaboration is well structured under law and this enable the biobank to enter in research collaborations with other research partners including industrial partners. For instance Estonian Genome Center partners with BioAge a private partner in developing therapies for aging; likewise the biobank also sought strategic partnership from Nestlé Institute of Health Sciences in Lausanne, Switzerland, on studying the biological mechanisms involved in long-term weight maintenance, with a long-term goal to discover targeted nutritional approaches to improve weight management in obese people.[152]

[4] Auria

The Auria Biobank is the first biobank in Finland and started its establishment even before there was a law governing biobanks in Finland. Auria Biobank is situated in Turku, in connection with Turku University Hospital and the University of Turku. The biobank was established by the University of Turku and the hospital districts of south-west Finland, Satakunta and Vaasa and is regarded as a public institution.[153] It was established in 2012. In spring, 2014 it received its operating licence from Valvira, the National Supervisory Authority for Welfare and Health. The biobank's activities are guided by the Finnish Biobank Act, which entered into force in autumn 2013. Auria is one of the eight biobanks in Finland. Auria Biobank is a public and academic institution, and its main purpose is to advance Finnish biomedical research. Auria collaborates closely with universities and research centres. It is also involved in developing commercial activity from biobanking. The key actors in Auria reason that business activities and profitable collaboration with private enterprises and the big pharma corporations are an important way, if not a necessity, in sustaining and developing biobanking activities.[154] Auria Biobank serves both academic research and R&D of medical companies of which 63% are academic and 37% are industries.[155] The uniqueness of Auria Biobank consists of several factors but the three important factors are:

(1) linkage with three different hospitals which enables its ability to build a rich collection of biological information that is connected to clinical data from the hospitals;

illnesses. https://www.riigiteataja.ee/en/eli/531102013003/consolide (last accessed on 29 September 2017).

152. https://www.genomeweb.com/drug-discovery-development/bioage-labs-raises-109m-partners-estonian-genome- center-develop-anti.

153. *Infra* note 270.

154. H. Lehtimaki et al., Commercialization of biobank data: The case Auria biobank, University of Eastern Finland.

155. https://www.auriabiopankki.fi/services/biobank-research/?lang=en (last accessed on 29 September 2017).

(2) existence of the Finnish Biobank Act[156] which seeks the use of biobank samples and data for research while requiring that certain standards are met;[157] and
(3) a proactive outlook towards commercial use of biomedical samples.

The National Genome Strategy of Finland published in 2015 requires that 'advances in genomic technology raise ethical and legal issues relating to people's privacy and the predictive nature of genomic data, among other things. For genomic data to be used effectively in healthcare, research and in commercial activities, the use of data related to the human genome must be safe and governed by law and guidelines'.[158] This encourages biobanks of Finland such as Auria to develop value-oriented research collaboration in biomedical research.

These examples illustrate the differing ways in which institutional arrangements evolve based on a number of factors, which include *inter alia* the structure of the organization, the need and purpose it serves. The commercial arrangements that flow from these biobanks are largely governed by the nature of the organization. Commercialization within biobanks have been controversial both in Europe and globally as well.[159] While the supporters view it as a public good rationale to facilitate health and innovation outcomes,[160] the opponents on the contrary consider that pharmaceutical and biomedical companies are no charitable organizations; their goal is to maximize shareholders' profits which can be seen as a form of 'exploitation' of the tissues altruistically contributed by the donors.[161] In spite of such differing views, there is also a growing realization that the purpose of biobanks is to contribute effectively to genomic research.[162] Therefore, the collaborative activities of biobanks must enable

156. Biobank Act (Biopankkilaki)688/2012, 1 September 2013.
157. Biobank Act (Biopankkilaki)688/2012, Chapter 3: Processing of samples and personal information associated with the samples under section 26: Principles for granting access to samples and information: (1) the intended use corresponds to the research area defined for the biobank and the criteria and conditions established for the processing of the sample; (2) terms and restrictions provided in this act or elsewhere in law and determined by the biobank are observed in the research and in the processing of samples and information; (3) the individual granted access to the samples or information holds the appropriate professional and academic qualifications for processing the samples and information, and the granting of access to the sample or information is in connection with the duties of the recipient.
158. http://www.julkari.fi/bitstream/handle/10024/126940/URN_ISBN_978-952-00-3598-3.pdf?sequence=1 (last accessed on 29 September 2017).
159. T. Caulfield et al., A review of the key issues associated with the commercialization of biobanks. *Journal of Law and the Biosciences*. 2014; 1(1): 94–110.
160. National Statement on Ethical conduct in Human Research (2007) updated 2015, available at: https://www.nhmrc.gov.au/guidelines-publications/e72 (last accessed on 27 September 2017).
161. J. Pirnay et al., Beware of the commercialization of human cells and tissues: Situation in the European Union. *Cell Tissue Bank*. 2012; 13(3):487–498.
162. S.M. Fullerton et al., Meeting the governance challenges of next-generation biorepository research, *Science Translational Medicine*. 20 January 2010; F Betsou, 'Biobanks as producers of reference materials', in P. Hainaut P., J. Vaught, K. Zatloukal and M. Pasterk (eds) 'Biobanking of human biospecimens'. Springer, 2017.

the ability of such biobanks to continue to contribute as a research resource.[163] Hence, long-term sustainability of biobanks calls for collaborative research partnerships in the interest of utilization of resources. It has also been noted that while this is not a universal challenge considering that some biobanks receive funding from the public resources, yet self-sustainability in economic terms is indeed a challenge for biobanks in the long run.[164]

163. D. Chalmers et al., Has the biobank bubble burst? withstanding the challenges for sustainable biobanking in the digital era. *BMC Medical Ethics.* 2016; 17: 39.
164. *Supra* note 162.

Part II Translation Research, Patents and Technology Transfer

CHAPTER 3

Uncertain Legal Status for Use of Biological Materials in Pre-patent Research

§3.01 INTRODUCTION

As indicated in Chapter 1 the definition of 'biobanks' have a conceptual divergence in literature[1] particularly as to the variables involved in them. However, the two constant elements found commonly in these definitions are the 'samples' i.e., the biological materials and the data relating to the samples. In other words, both the wet data and the dry data[2] constitute the foundations of a biobank's structural framework. With the data boom that biomedical research is currently facing, individual identities have been reduced to informational materials. This is least surprising from the point of rapidly changing genetic technologies, which increasingly tends to shift biology to technology and vice versa.[3] This intertwining of physical and life sciences has great implication in the discussions involving biotechnological inventions. In the context of genetic research, technology has offered great impetus to innovations in the field of health. Genomic scientists world over have been able to join in assembling the 'blue print of

1. D.M. Shaw et al., What is a biobank? Differing definitions among biobank stake holders. *Clinical Genetics.* March 2014; 85(3).
2. A.R. Mushegian, Foundations of comparative genomics, Academic Press 2010.
3. W. Brian Arthur, The nature of technology: What it is and how it evolves, Penguin Books 2010. *See also* R. van Est (2014), Intimate technology: The battle for our body and behaviour, Rathenau Instituut, 12 April 2015, explains it as follows: 'The first implies that living systems are increasingly seen as reproducible. Genetically modified bulls, cloned sheep, cultured heart valves and artificially reconstructed bacteria illustrate this trend. It is not only about biological interventions as IT-based interventions are also emerging in techniques to influence brain processes. A well-known example is the use of deep brain stimulation to reduce severe tremor in patients with Parkinson's disease. The reverse trend being that of 'technology becoming biology' is reflected in artefacts that increasingly appear more lifelike or seem imbued with human behaviours.'

life' is often referred to as the Human genome.[4] Revisiting the historical developments in the Human Genome Project (HGP) reveals the greater participatory role of individuals and scientists. Nevertheless, the most important tools that enabled the scientists to produce, store, retrieve, manipulate and isolate the genetic sequence has been the tool of technology.[5] This cultural shift from observational biology to 'Big-Data' science has raised doubts over the extent of exploitation of genetic resources.[6] Involving IPR within this scheme of genetic research creates increased ethical concerns such as free informed consent (FIC) of patients, privacy and patient's rights. In addition, there also exits legal concerns on account of uncertainties with respect of the proprietary rights in inventions based upon biological materials taken from donors or patients. For this reason, this chapter seeks to address some of the legal uncertainties surrounding the use of human biological samples and the related concerns that it raises in the context of patent rights. This part identifies two integrated challenges for biobank-related research namely:

(1) Property Rights.
(2) Ethics.[7]

The complexity of the integration between property and ethics in the context of genetic resources is such that it has been hard for legal authorities to put a finger on the issue. Hence, an attempt will be made herein to deconstruct the issues by focusing on the upstream phase of biobank-based research where IPR are being involved. In doing so the challenges and solutions presents itself greater implications for biobanks and biotechnology-related research in general. The governance of genetic resources within such a conglomerate paradigm has found unsettled equations within traditional property rights. In the same vein, research activities using human biological samples and IPR over such research results have often been viewed in relation to the traditional concept of property and control over genetic resources. Interestingly such an outlook is also the result of an ethical discourse primarily focused on the participants of such research. There is a lack of clarity as to the treatment of these issues both in perception and in literature. This gives impetus to the present discussion, which touches upon property laws and ethics to bring out its overlap with IP law.

4. D.M. Gitter, 'The 1000 Genome project', in Matthew Rimmer and Alison McLennan (eds), 'Intellectual property and emerging technologies, the new biology', Queen Mary Studies in Intellectual Property series, 2012.
5. H. Rose and S. Rose, The promethean promises of the new biology, genes, cells and brains, 2014.
6. P.A. Chow-White, 'Informationalization of race', communication technologies and the human genome in the digital age. *International Journal of Communication.* (2008); 2: 1168–1194.
7. Reference herein to ethics implies code of ethical principles approved internationally or nationally in respect of the usage of human biological materials and human participation in research-related activities e.g., Helsinki Deceleration on biomedical research, International Declaration on Human Genetic Data http://www.unesco.org/new/en/social-and-human-sciences/themes/bioethics/human-genetic-data/, Oviedo Convention on Human Rights and Biomedicine https://www.coe.int/en/web/conventions/full-list/-/conventions/treaty/164 (last accessed on 14 December 2016).

[A] Property Right Versus Patent Rights: Theoretical Justifications

Excised human body parts have a great value in research. Researchers use such biological material for investigating human disease patterns and clinicians use them for diagnosis and treatment studies. For the same reason proprietary rights and exploitation of such biological material has provoked tremendous controversy and condemnation.[8] It is hence least surprising that the European Council in its Convention on Human Rights and Biomedicine[9] states that 'The human body and its parts shall not "as such" give rise to financial gain.' At the same time, the European Commission also lays down that 'An effort should be made to better convert knowledge into socio-economic benefits'.[10] Therefore, public research organizations/entities need to disseminate and to more effectively exploit publicly funded research results with a view to translating them into new products and services. To this end IPR assists researchers by encouraging creation and innovation by incentivizing creativity. At the same time it has been argued that the theoretical or rather the academic justification of IPR have had little in common with its use in the real world and are not fully conclusive in itself.[11] Yet a discussion of these prominent theories offers perspectives to the context of genetic research.

The traditional approach in to IPR in Anglo-Saxon countries were governed by the *'sweat of the brow'* in line with the Lockean labour theory. It is based on the proposition that a person who labours upon resources that are either unowned or 'held in common' has a natural property right to the fruits of his or her efforts – and that the state has a duty to respect and enforce that natural right. This justification was conceptually well accepted because 'property' was innate to the society which encouraged people to work and strive for. Therefore, where such labour resulted in valuable good its value had to be compensated.[12] On the contrary, the personality theory considers IP justifiable because they shield from appropriation or modification of creations in which authors have expressed their wills. Both these consequentialist approaches are based on creation of property based on their intellectual value. The other two important theories justifying IPR are the utilitarian theory and the social planning theory. A utilitarian theory of IPR aims to maximize the social welfare by striking an optimal balance between exclusive rights and public enjoyment of the benefits of such inventions or creations.[13] It calls for a balancing approach by weighing

8. J. Gibson, Intellectual property, medicine and health (Intellectual property, theory and culture), Ashgate 2009, pp. 199–120.
9. Oviedo, 4 April 1997 Art. 21.
10. 'Recommendation on the Management of Intellectual Property in Knowledge Transfer Activities and a Code of Practice for Universities and Other Public Research Organisations'. IP Recommendation, often also referred to as 'IPCharter'. http://eur-lex.europa.eu/legal- content/EN/TXT/?uri=URISERV%3Ari0007 (last accessed on 1 March 2016).
11. G. Parchomovsky and P. Siegelman, Towards an integrated theory of intellectual property. *Virginia Law Review*. November 2002; 88(7): 1455–1528.
12. L. Bernier, Justice in genetics: Intellectual property and human rights from a cosmopolitan liberal perspective, Edward Elgar Publishing 2010.
13. W. Fisher, 'Theories of intellectual property', in S.R. Muzer (ed.), New essays in the legal and political theory of property, Cambridge University Press, 2001, at p. 168.

the potential benefits of the invention to the risks, harm or public unease, if IPR are accorded to such inventions.[14] A less established theory is the 'social planning theory' it differs from utilitarian theory in that it seeks to go beyond the notion of 'social welfare' to a much broader vision of society serviced by IP.[15] In employing this theory policymakers ought to make difficult choices at two levels. The first involves formulating a vision of a just and attractive culture and second understanding the nature of society it seeks to promote, by an adjustment of the various IPR.[16] In this sense, it envisions a phenomenon where IP rights are not just focused on economic parameters but by social justice that the conferral of such rights seeks to achieve. For instance the interests of a plant breeder who cannot acquire or exploit a plant variety right without infringing a patent is offered a just relief through provisions under the law such as a compulsory licence.[17] This in turn limits the possibilities of the patentee to use the patent as a means of restricting access to important breeding material thereby reducing a monopolistic behaviour.

Another way to explain a justification of IPR is to examine it from an economic theory perspective. In this approach, IPR aims to avoid the tragedy of commons or in a contextual sense the free rider problem, which erodes information value in a knowledge society. The concept of the tragedy of commons was developed with Hardin's[18] pasture example which distinctively produced a brand of inefficiency. The 'common' referred to those goods that are owned by a community and which the same community can freely dispose. The notion of commons can thus, be identified as all tangible and intangible resources that constitute a collective heritage of a community.[19] In this sense, genetic resources can be elevated to 'a resource held in common'. While so, it has often been argued that an increase in IP like for instance over human genetic materials may result in patent thickets, royalty stacking and ultimately a tragedy of *anitcommons* in genetics.[20] According to Fennell[21] reason for this is that the aspirational normative structure of science regards new biological discoveries as shared public resources', while 'commercial biotechnology regards such discoveries as potential commodities to be patented, licensed, and marketed through the application of exclusive proprietary rights'. On the contrary a lack of adequate exploitation through intellectual property right incentives will lead to a '*new tragedy of commons*' as will be seen from the discussions in Chapter 8 which highlights examples that was almost closed down owing to underutilization of the genetic resources collected by such bio-repositories. It would at best serve information staking just as galactic libraries without any membership. As a direct result it is argued here that, 'parts of the natural

14. EPO – T 0019/90 (Onco-Mouse).
15. *Supra* note 13.
16. *Supra* note 13 at p. 33.
17. Article 12, Directive 98/44/EC, *see also* G 0001/98 (Transgenic plant/NOVARTIS II) of 20 December 1999.
18. G. Hardin, The tragedy of the commons. *Science.* 1968; 162(3859): 1243–1248.
19. L.A. Fennell, 'Commons, anticommons, semicommons', in K. Ayotte and H.E. Smith, 'Research handbook on the economics of property law', Edward Elgar, 2011.
20. G. Van Overwalle, Gene Patents and collaborative licensing models, First ed. Cambridge University Press 2009.
21. *Supra* note 19.

environment must be removed from the "commons" and used privately if they are to have any significant effect on the comfort and well-being of the individual humans like for instance finding new pathways for personalized medicine'.[22] Thus a theory of IP in HBMs calls for consideration of integrated approaches as leverages opens up possibilities for policymakers to find desirable solutions. In particular, the research work calls for a '*social value*' oriented approach in the context of biobanking. This point would be revisited later towards Chapters 8 and 9.

[1] Tissues and Concept of Ownership

HBMs including human tissues stored in a repository evolves out of a process from collection, storage, preservation to research and use in industrial purposes. The fact that these 'Big Data' sets have great economic worth requires a functional balance between the aims of the biobanks, the altruism involved in donations and the notion of public good.[23] Biobanking as a system enables the transfer of biospecimens from the donor to the repository with altruistic motives or in the interest of research, the result of which may be beneficial to the patient or for others suffering from a similar situation as the donor. However difficulties arises where the potential use to which a donated sample extend beyond those that were originally conceived. In this context there arises two interrelated tensions one relating to the legal ownership over such genetic resources and the other relating to IPR where it applies.

The traditional concept of 'Ownership' refers to an exercise of complete dominion over things or claims[24] and gives the 'Owner' a '*jus in rem*'. 'Ownership' rights have often found an uncomfortable equation with HBMs used in research and has sought distinction from the common law notions of property.[25] When ownership is challenged, it is not challenged on the grounds that IP ought to be a public good, but rather to what degree it can be property.[26]

In the context of the discussions over tissue samples taken by research entities like for instance the biobanks, the purpose of the biobank often determines the creation and use of the resources and consequently the nature and conceptualization of ownership may vary. There is a lack of consensus as to how these concepts need to be governed.[27] While some writers consider the discussion of ownership meaningless in the context of genomic research[28] others consider it as the base for recognizing

22. E. Katz, Nature as subject: Human obligation and natural community. Rowman and Littlefield, 1997.
23. C. Waldby, Biobanking in Singapore: Post-developmental state, experimental Population. New Genetics and Society 2009; 28(3): 253–265.
24. Blacks law dictionary online http://thelawdictionary.org/ownership/.
25. I. Goold, 'Sounds suspiciously like property treatment: does human tissue fit within the common law concept of property?' *UTS Law Rw.* 2005; 3: 7.
26. TM Horbulyk, Intellectual Property Rights and Technological Innovation in Agriculture, *Technological Forecasting and Social Change* 43: 259–270.
27. N. Hawkins et al., 'Ownership of biomedical information in biobanks', in G. Pascuzzi et al., 'Comparative issues in the governance of research biobanks', Springer, 2013.
28. *Ibid.*, at p. 84.

different models governance.[29] Much of the literature on the property-related issue over samples held by biobanks and its research uses tends to mix up the notions of patent ownership with the discussions on ownership of the tissue samples per se.

The concept of ownership over tissues has been under the purview of national legislation and have been viewed through the lens of property laws. Accordingly, different jurisdictions have had differing justifications for fixing or excluding property rights in the context of biological materials. The English common law followed the '*work* and *skill*' test in determining the exceptions to the rule that human body and its separated body parts lacked proprietary status.[30] In other words where sufficient amount of skill and labour invested in procuring and preserving body parts could lead to limited possessory rights devoid of commercial usages. This approach was an influence from an Australian High court decision.[31] In *R v Kelly*,[32] the exception, recognized to confer on the right-holder the simple right to continue possessing the body part, while making it possible for the state to prosecute for its theft. However it did not offer any rights to sell, transfer or profit from such processed human biological parts. Thus while corpses cannot be owned under common law, those charged with their disposal such as hospitals, families and public or religious authorities were restricted by certain duties and endowed with certain powers not alignable to the ownership privileges.[33] The common law generally assumes that once tissue is separated from the living body, it has been abandoned by its original 'owner', or that it is always '*res nullius*', no one's thing or belonging to no one when removed.[34] While these common law traditions focused on penal prosecutions pertaining to HBMs taken from corpse and they did not make any distinction as to samples taken from live human bodies spite of having an opportunity in the Diane blood case.[35] In this case, the Court of Appeal refused to examine the legality of the sperm taken from an unconscious spouse without express consent in the interest of the appellant's wish to conceive a child from her husband. Instead the cases focused on the ethical implications of posthumous conception without consent while allowing the applicant to seek such conception elsewhere other than in the UK.

The debate on ownership of body parts is extensive and its reference herein serves to bring out the distinctiveness in the discussions over the concept of ownership per se and the exploitation of the research results. In other words the question as to whether the tissues can be a property per se is different from the question as to how to protect the research results of an invention, where for instance, the samples used arise from a biorepository. Patent law protects the functionality as disclosed from the

29. A. Turner, Biobank economics and the commercialization problem, *Spontaneous Generations: A Journal for the History and Philosophy of Science*. 2013; 7(1): 69–80.
30. I. Goold et al., Persons parts and property, how should we regulate human tissue in the 21st century?, Hart Publishing 2014.
31. *Doodeward v Spence* [1908] HCA 45; (1908) 6 CLR 406 (31 July 1908); *see also Yearworth and others v North Bristol NHS Trust* [2009] EWCA Civ 37.
32. [1999] 2 WLR 384.
33. D. Dickenson, Property in the body feminist perspectives, Cambridge University Press 2009; *See also Haynes Case* (1614) 77 ER 1389.
34. *Ibid.*, note 414.
35. *R v Human Fertilization and Embryology Authority*, [1997] 2 All ER 687.

technical disclosure and thus does not concern itself with the proprietary rights of tissues or cells.[36] Protection of biotechnological innovations or results from public research faces an unease in relation to the privateering of public benefits. It is beyond doubt that biobanks are aimed at public benefit. However, the dilemma over perforation of IPR in the sector is predominantly on account of the ethical concern that has surrounds the patenting of biotechnological invention and to a greater extent the legal uncertainties surrounding the ownership of samples.[37] To illustrate these difficulties, some of these internationally acclaimed cases will be discussed herein which highlight the public scepticism over the protection of genetic resources.

A noted case is that of *Moore v Regents of the University of California,*[38] where the question was whether Moore the patient whose spleen samples were used by his doctor in his own research, retained any property rights in the Mo cell line which was derived from Moore's spleen. The Mo cell line was subsequently patented by the doctor without appropriate consent for the use of the excised body part. The Supreme Court of California rejected Moore's claim for conversion thereby dissuading any property-related claims in the sample taken from Moore during his surgery.

Yet another most noted case is that of HeLa cells which are the most widely used model cell line for studying human cellular and molecular biology. It was the first cell line established in culture. Its application as a model organism has contributed to the characterization of important biological processes and more than 70,000 publications and 11,000 patent applications.[39] The cell line originates from a cervical cancer tumour of a patient named Henrietta Lacks, who later died of her cancer in 1951[40] and hardly knew that her cell lines may become immortal after all. This key example is highly illustrative of the concerns that may arise in the context of biobanks and patenting of HBMs. In a fairly recent case, a Canadian court ruled that, 'excised human tissue may indeed be personal property but it does not form part of the person from whom it came because it belongs to hospitals as part of the medical record'.[41] This does not however mean the donors do not have a say in how their samples ought to be used. In *Gudmundsdóttir v the State of Iceland,*[42] the Icelandic Supreme Court held that the daughter of a deceased man could prevent his health information from being entered into the Health Sector Database.[43] The ECtHR, in its decision in *Elberte v Latvia,* held that by taking tissues without proper assessment of consent and not informing the wife

36. P.A. Andanda, Human tissue related inventions: Ownership and intellectual property rights in international collaborative research in developing countries, *Journal of Medical Ethics* 2008; 34:171–179.
37. Bioethics and Patent Law: The Cases of Moore and the Hagahai People, WIPO Magazine 2006; *see also* T. Caulfield et al., A review of the key issues associated with commercialization of biobanks, *Journal of Biosciences*. 2014; 94–110.
38. 51 Cal. 3d 120; 271 Cal. Rptr. 146.
39. http://hamptonroads.com/2010/05/cancer-cells-killed-henrietta-lacks-then-made-her-immortal (last accessed on 8 December 2014). *See also* Jonathan J.M. Landry et al., The genomic and transcriptomic landscape of a HeLa cell line, G3 1 August 2013; 3(8): 1213–1224.
40. R. Skloot, The Immortal Life of Henrietta Lacks, Broadway Books 2011.
41. *Piljak Estate v Abraham*, 2014 ONSC 2893 (CanLII).
42. No. 151/2003.
43. R. Gertz, An analysis of the Icelandic supreme court judgment on the Health Sector Database Act. *SCRIPT-ed* ½. 2004: 241–258.

of the deceased (who was one of his closest relatives) she was unable to exercise the right to express consent to the removal of her husband's tissue.[44] This act by the Latvian Forensic authorities was a violation of her privacy and respect for dignity under the relevant provisions of the European Human Rights Convention. Hence the interrelated concepts of privacy and autonomy are unified a more fundamental level by the fact that each reflects a valued aspect of the human personality and is visible in the context of physical samples.[45] The court however did not touch upon the property rights instead focused on the rights of patients and relatives which were established under the national laws

This stands in line with the analogy taken in *Google Spain SL, Google Inc. v Agencia Española de Protección de Datos, Mario Costeja González,*[46] wherein the European Court of Justice held that an individual may require to remove any information pertaining to him even if 'those rights override, the economic interest of the operator'.[47] This implies that while '*jus in rem*' governs ownership rights over excised biological samples, yet there exists '*jus in personam*' in respect of the individual's right over the use of his biological samples.[48] This has in fact been the basis for the issue of various types of 'informed consent' originally mooted by Convention on Human Rights and Biomedicine.[49]

The above discussion offers two important inferences in the context of biobanking. First, the donor may choose the use of her samples through a FIC. The right of self-determination of the body is a fundamental right in itself.[50] This right along with the right of the relatives where such consent may not be obtained forms an undeterred right. Second, health researchers will be able to achieve the goals of medical research only if their research falls in line with standardized norms of consent and respect for privacy. The complexity of the biomedical research is such that once donated on the basis of informed consent (irrespective of the type of consent) following a standard protocol, a donor may not be able to make further claims in respect of the use of sample in research, perhaps even leading to an IP right. While a request for withdrawal of samples or data is possible in the light of the data privacy laws.[51] Samples sometimes fall under 'special data' category the processing of which is necessary for scientific or research purposes.[52] Where the data subject gives their explicit consent for the collection of these categories of data by signing an informed consent it will clearly state what data is being collected and why. Such special data category negates the subject's

44. *Elberte v Latvia,* Application No. 61243/08 [2015] ECHR 1.
45. The European Group on Ethics in Science and New Technologies to the European Commission recognizes the same connection between personal health data and personality; *see* Opinion of the EGE, Ethical Issues of Healthcare in the Information Society (Opinion No. 13, July 1999).
46. C-131/12.
47. *Supra* note 46 at paras 81–97.
48. *Ibid.*, 22 at 108.
49. Article 5. Convention for the Protection of Human Rights and Dignity of the Human Being with regard to the Application of Biology and Medicine: Convention on Human Rights and Biomedicine, Oviedo, 4.IV.1997.
50. Article 5. Universal Declaration on the Human Genome and Human Rights, 1997.
51. *See* GDPR and the protection of biomedical data under Chapter 2.
52. Article 9, GDPR, Regulation (EU) 2016/679.

right to erasure, or portability, as such data cannot be removed from the dataset without an audit trail as well as that changing the statistical trial outcome.[53] Apart from such practical difficulties it may not also be possible for the donor to make a claim on the sample as such[54] or any IP related to such samples.[55] Thus, property rights over human biological samples though not equivocally carved out in the legal paradigm, still finds an ethical undertone in favour of the innate rights of the donor to her samples. Needless to say, that rather than the proprietary rights over samples balancing the public scepticism may often be difficult at the cost of even dissolving the biobank both in terms of its structure and functional possibilities. For instance the failure of the Icelandic cohort involving the private company deCode is a living example in Europe which points to the lack of the Iceland government to address the various concerns of the public relating to the uses of the samples taken from the Icelanders. This means that while there may no longer be proprietary rights post donation of tissues, there may still be limited possessory right akin to the moral rights[56] under the law of copyrights, unless completely abandoned by the donor. In addition the '*use*', '*exchange*' and '*transfer*' of biomedical data including big genomic data to researchers outside the facility or even across borders can be a big challenge in the light of the ever permeating concern for ownership over genetic resources. As noted in the judgment of the Court of Justice of the European Union (CJEU), in *Maximillian Schrems v Data Protection Commissione*,[57] the protection of the 'privacy' and the fundamental rights of individuals while transmitting the samples across international borders through appropriate safeguards such as 'Informed Consent' and standard contractual clauses are major considerations for biobanks.[58]

[B] Treatment of HBMs under Patent Law: A Two-Way Approach

Biobanks can be part of academic medical institutions or pharmaceutical and biotechnology companies, delivering biological materials to researchers. Biobanks store and

53. *See* R. Neethu et al., Clinical trials data transparency & GDPR compliance: What does it imply for data sharing and open innovation?. *Science & Public Policy*, 2019 special issue.
54. Withdrawal and destruction of samples under the supervision of the relevant ethics committees may still be possible. However it may not be possible to remove the data analysis that has already been done using such samples. *See* more for this point, K. Melham et al., The evolution of withdrawal: Negotiating research relationships in biobanking. *Life Sciences, Society and Policy*. 2014; 10: 16. PMC. Web. 12 December 2016.
55. *Moore v Regents of the University of California*, 51 Cal. 3d 120; 271 Cal. Rptr. 146.
56. Under copyright law moral rights means preserving the integrity of the work bars the work from alteration, distortion, or mutilation. Anything else that may detract from the artist's relationship with the work even after it leaves the artist's possession or ownership may bring these moral rights into play. Moral rights are distinct from any economic rights tied to copyrights. Even if an artist has assigned his or her copyright rights to a work to a third party, he or she still maintains the moral rights to the work. For e.g., withdrawal of samples from Estonian Genomic Institute by donors of Russian origin to protest a political decision by the Government of Estonia, (insight offered in a personal interview to the author); *see also*: N. Hawkins, 'Intellectual property and biobanks' in D. Macalzoni, (eds) 'Ethics, law and governance of biobanking', First ed. 2015.
57. Case C-362/14, available at: http://curia.europa.eu/juris/liste.jsf?num=C-362/14 (last acce ssed on 13 January 2014).
58. Case C-362/14 paras 95–96.

preserve samples from donors that give their consent and use the samples for research purposes for which such consent was given. They are very relevant components in the biomedical research cycle leading to resourceful results that may be protected by patent rights. Therefore in order to understand the implications of patent law in the context of biobanks, it is essential to examine how the HBMs are treated under patent law

This understanding involves two important questions of contemporary significance. They are:

(1) can HBMs be subject to patent rights? The answer to that question depends on the discussion in Europe as to what are inventions that would be granted a patent right; and the second question is
(2) does patent law honour ethical obligations such as FIC for research?

Related to these questions the contextual discussion also raises questions on the rights of biobanks in relation to the samples. Thus it can be questioned: can biobanks have any patent rights with regard to the samples? what would be the nature of such rights if for instance, a biobank supplies sample to a researcher? who owns the patent rights? What role actual or potential is played by patents in context of biomedical research in general and biobanking in particular? what impact does it have?

A part of the answer to these complex questions lies in a legal understanding the functional assessment of biotechnological innovations involving human samples along with an impact assessment on the patentability question of HBMs. The first one is purely a legal assessment while the second is in fact a moral assessment.

[1] Patentability of HBMs in Europe: A Technical *Assessment*

A functionality assessment seeks to examine the principles on which the European patent system is founded. In the context of biotechnical inventions, the Biotechnology Directive sets the legal framework.[59] The directive stipulates that 'biological material which is isolated from its natural environment or produced by means of a technical process even if it previously occurred in nature' shall also be patentable.[60] The concerns over harmonization in the area of biotech patent are well expressed in recitals 8 and 9 of the directive. It states that, while a separate body of law for the area may not be ideal yet the national patent law being the basis of the patentability need adaptation in certain respects considering the technological advancement in the field of biotechnology.[61] This is considered essential by the directive because certain concepts in national laws based upon international patent and plant variety conventions have created uncertainty regarding the protection of biotechnological inventions.[62] The

59. Directive 98/44/EC of the European Parliament and of the Council of 6 July 1998 on the legal protection of biotechnological inventions.
60. Article 3(2), Directive 98/44/EC.
61. Recital 8, Directive 98/44/EC.
62. Recital 9, Directive 98/44/EC.

directive was thus, brought about on many accounts particularly to fill the void in the law for gene patents. The Trade-related aspects of Intellectual Property Rights (TRIPS) through its principle of non-discrimination provides that 'patents shall be available for any inventions whether a product or a process, in all fields of technology, provided they are new involve an inventive step and are capable of industrial application'.[63] This approach seeks to protect all kinds of innovation thereby encouraging technological progress. Nevertheless, every new technological advance is viewed through the same lens of the framework of national and international patent laws without distinguishing between different types of technologies.[64] Under the TRIPS Agreement there are two steps involved in the assessment of patentability namely that:

(1) It must be an invention.
(2) It must satisfy the criterion of patentability namely, novelty, inventiveness and industrial applicability.

The very same provisions are also reflected in Article 52 of the European Patent Convention (EPC). Paragraph (2) of Article 52 enumerates a list of subject matter, which will not be regarded as patentable inventions as such. This means that any 'invention', to be a patentable invention must satisfy the criteria related to patentability such as (a) its newness (b) the non-obviousness of it and (c) weather it is capable of industrial application. Such an assessment requires addressing the nature of a patentable invention. However, so far there is no generally accepted definition of the term invention.[65] The traveux préparatoires to the EPC reveal that the working committee on the EPC did not find a comfortable solution in attempting to define the term invention both in its positive as well as in its negative sense.[66] The matter was finally resolved with the realization that an absence of a definition did not in the past give rise to any problems in the national law.[67] The present Article 52(2) of EPC[68] provides that discoveries, scientific theories and mathematical methods *as such* are not patentable.[69] This is in fact the starting point where the controversies depart regarding patentability. This is so because in determining if an invention falls within the scope of patentability or not the legislators ignored the difficult question of whether the application is in fact an invention instead they tried to allay their fears by indulging in technical nature

63. Article 27 of the TRIPS, Agreement on Trade-Related Aspects of Intellectual Property Rights. The TRIPS Agreement is Annex 1C of the Marrakesh Agreement Establishing the World Trade Organization, signed in Marrakesh, Morocco on 15 April 1994.
64. D.L. Burk and M.A. Lemley, 'Policy levers in patent law', *University of Minnesota Law School Public Law & Legal Theory Research Paper Series*, Research Paper No. 03-11(2003) Lemely and Burk observes that while the object is promotion of advance technology, the patent statute creates a general set of legal rules that govern a wide variety of technologies and does not distinguish between different technologies in setting and applying legal standards.
65. J. Pila, On the European requirement for an invention, OUP 2010.
66. Travaux Préparatoires EPC 1973, https://www.epo.org/law-practice/legal-texts/archive/epc1973/traveaux.html (last accessed on 7 March 2016).
67. *Ibid.*, at p. 5.
68. European Patent Convention, 1973 of 5 October 1973 as currently revised.
69. Article 52(2)(a) and (3), EPC, 1973.

assessment.[70] The EPC Implementing Regulations also hint at the technical character of an invention, in prescribing that the description shall specify the technical field to which the invention relates[71] along with a description of the invention as claimed in such terms that the technical problem, even if not expressly stated as such, can be understood.[72] Further, the claims shall define the matter for which protection is sought in terms of the technical features of the invention.[73] This is also applicable in the case of 'discoveries' which is an important part of the present discussion because only inventions are patentable and not discoveries. The practical application of an idea or discovery leads to patentability irrespective of whether it is the discovery, object of discovery, or process of discovery that proves to be useful and practical. Therefore it is the technical application of the discovery which must create a novelty and inventiveness.[74] Thus under the EPC the technical character determines the distinction between discovery and invention.[75] The fine line between invention and discovery was assessed in the relaxin case, T 0272/95.

The Relaxin Case

The application involved the gene coding for the unexpected second form of human relaxin H2, and the synthetic form produced through cloning technology. The other claims included further DNA fragments encoding H2-relaxin and the processes for the production of the fragments. Although relaxin as a hormone was known to assist in female caesareans, research revealed a second form of human insulin, the existence of which had not previously been known. The structure of human relaxin was found to differ from other species, such that only human relaxin could be used for the medical purpose envisaged.[76] Thus it involved a significant medical use. However it was opposed by two applicant groups who claimed that apart from being objectionable under the 'morality' clause it was a claim for a discovery and not an invention in the real sense of the term.

The Opposition Division

The Opposition Division concluded, under Article 53(a) EPC, that an 'invention concerning a human gene was not an exception to patentability because it would not be universally regarded as outrageous'.[77] Further, it did not amount to patenting life because DNA as such was not life but one of the many chemical entities participating in biological processes, *no offence to human dignity had occurred as the woman who*

70. Bently & Sherman, at p. 397.
71. Rule 42(1)(a) EPC Implementing Regulation, 1973.
72. Rule 42(1)(c) EPC Implementing Regulation, 1973.
73. Rule 43(1) EPC Implementing Regulation, 1973.
74. A. FariasEisner, Patenting human genes violates laws of nature, impedes patient care, stifles research, and inhibits long-term business opportunities. *Northwestern Journal of International Law & Business*. 2014; 35.
75. C. Pamp, Intellectual property in science, Jure AB 2010.
76. http://www.wipo.int/wipo_magazine/en/2006/02/article_0009.html.
77. Howard Florey/Relaxin; Oppositions by Fraktion der Grünen im Europäischen Parlament; Lannoye; EPO 6/1995 388.

donated tissue was asked for her consent and her self-determination was not affected by the exploitation of the claimed molecules.[78] The DNA fragments which were new in the sense of having no previously recognized existence were not to be considered as discoveries and hence were not unpatentable.[79]

Appeal Before the Technical Board of Appeal, EPO

On appeal to the decision given by the opposition division an engaging argument was put forward by the opponents. They argued that it constituted a fundamental violation of a person's rights if an invention was derived from his/her body and no consent had been obtained for the specific exploitation which was intended for the invention. As to the nature of the application being a discovery, it was stated that the applicants had simply obtained a code book from the donors (the genetic material) and 'cracked the code' (discovered the number and sequence of human relaxin genes). That was no more than a discovery of the characteristics of a substance which had existed in nature probably for many thousand years.[80]

Outcome of the Appeal

Though the claims were directly or indirectly related to DNA's encoding the human protein it was isolated by a technical process and hence qualified for patentability. Thus, an element isolated from the human body or otherwise produced by means of a technical process including the sequence or a partial sequence of a gene may constitute a patentable invention, even if the structure of that element is identical to that of a natural element.[81]

The EU Biotechnology Directive, which came into force in 1998, pending the final conclusion of the relaxin case, offered to protect HBMs, isolated from the natural environment through a technical process.[82] Thus, patent law is no longer restricted to inanimate objects but also accessible for living materials including human genetic materials.[83] Following the directive 'biological materials' are regarded as an 'invention'. It therefore elevates biotechnological inventions above the status of other types of technology. Hence the countries are no longer required to examine the biotechnology patent as to the question of invention but assuming that it is one the states are required to proceed on the examination of the newness, non-obviousness and industrial applicability of it though it might in fact be a discovery in the real sense of the term.[84] Thus by a legal fiction biotechnological inventions i.e., either a product or a

78. *Ibid.*
79. Technical Board of Appeal in Howard Florey/Relaxin case http://www.epo.org/law-practice/case-law- appeals/recent/t950272eu2.html.
80. *Ibid.*, at para. XII p. 5.
81. Rule 23(e)(2) EPC.
82. Article 3(2), European Biotechnology Directive 98/44/EC 1998 and Rule 27 (a) EPC implementing Regulations.
83. *Infra* note 88.
84. *Infra* note 88.See also A. Hellstadius, A quest for clarity, reconstructing standards for the patent law morality exclusion, Stockholm University 2015.

process which is not capable of fulfilling the traditional patent three-step criterion would be accorded patent rights.

In ***International Stem Cell Corporation v Comptroller General of Patents***[85] it was observed in relation to Article 5(1) of the Directive that: '*while the human body at the various stages of its formation and the simple discovery of one of its elements are not patentable, an element isolated from the human body or otherwise produced by means of a technical process can be patented*'. The distinction recalls one of the basic principles of patent law that 'only inventions and not discoveries are patentable'.[86]

The EPO examination guidelines offers certain clarity on the patentability of genetic materials by following the line of arguments put forward in the relaxin:[87]

> If a new property of a known material or article is found out, that is mere discovery and unpatentable because discovery as such has no technical effect and is therefore not an invention within the meaning of Art. 52 (1). If, however, that property is put to practical use, then this constitutes an invention which may be patentable. For example, the discovery that a particular known material is able to withstand mechanical shock would not be patentable, but a railway sleeper made from that material could well be patentable. *To find a previously unrecognised substance occurring in nature is also mere discovery and therefore unpatentable. However, if a substance found in nature can be shown to produce a technical effect, it may be patentable.* An example of such a case is that of a substance occurring in nature which is found to have an antibiotic effect. In addition, if a microorganism is discovered to exist in nature and to produce an antibiotic, the microorganism itself may also be patentable as one aspect of the invention. *Similarly, a gene which is discovered to exist in nature may be patentable if a technical effect is revealed,* e.g. its use in making a certain polypeptide or in gene therapy.

This seeks to clarify the position taken in the relaxin case by adopting the theory of isolation for determining the patentability of an application containing human biological element. The adoption of the doctrine of isolation has lifted isolated biological material per se to the level of an invention which the directive had hoped to avoid.[88] This in turn could mean that both natural and artificial parts could be legitimately dealt with as though they represent two different substances objectively distinct from one another.[89]

[2] 'Whole Contents Approach'

The isolation of a biological material through a technical process by itself is not enough to assess the patentability of an invention. There is a need to asses other aspects of the invention like for instance if it is excluded from patentability and if it truly satisfies the novelty, inventiveness and utility criteria. Method claims in biobank techniques could

85. Case C-364/13, July 2014 paras 51–52.
86. *Ibid.*
87. EPO Examination Guidelines, November 2015, http://www.epo.org/law-practice/legal-texts/html/guidelines/e/index.htm.
88. T. Sommer, Can law make Life (too) simple? From gene patents to the patenting of environmentally sound technologies, DJOF Publishing Copenhagen 2013.
89. *Ibid.*, at p. 253.

be put to test in this respect. A whole content approach to an invention under EPC is used in a different discussion both in terms of novelty[90] assessment with respect to the prior art as well as complete disclosure of the application in question. The whole contents approach to novelty is based on the legal fiction that the earlier application as a whole (the complete disclosure) forms part of the prior art.[91] The whole content approach has also been used in the assessment of given inventions as a whole. In the Warf case[92] the enlarged Board of Appeal in considering the exceptions to patentability under the Implementing Regulations observed that, '*What needs to be looked at is not just the explicit wording of the claims but the technical teaching of the application as a whole as to how the invention is to be performed.*'[93]

This interpretation has been taken up in the discussions of plant production patents namely Brocolli I[94] and Tomato I[95] wherein it was held that the essence or character of the invention must be considered as a whole. The mere addition of a technical step to an otherwise non-technical process does not ipso facto change the essence or character of that process.[96] This applies even if the process comprises human intervention, including the provision of technical means, serving to enable or assist the performance of the process steps or if other technical steps relating to the preparation of the plant or animal or its further treatment are present in the claim before or after the crossing and selection steps.[97] In T 1199/08[98] the invention for which patentability was sought for was a method for the cryopreservation of sex-selected bovine sperm which comprised of the following claims:

(a) obtaining a bovine sperm sample;
(b) adding an initial extender and sex-selecting sperm by flow cytometry;
(c) cooling said selected sperm sample;
(d) isolating by centrifugation sperm from said selected cool sperm to produce isolated cool sperm;
(e) adding final extender to said cool isolated sperm to produce a cool suspension of sperm, wherein the final extender comprises a cryoprotectant and Tris(hydroxymethyl)aminomethane; and
(f) Freezing said suspension of sperm.

Thus the claims were directed to the biobanking technique of cryopreservation of selected sperm cells. However it was opposed by Greenpeace and others[99] on the grounds of non-patentability (under Article 53(a), 53(b) and 53(c) EPC) and also lack

90. *See* T 0167/84 (Fuel injector valve) of 20 January 1987.
91. C. Keussen, Position Paper of the Patentanwaltskammer concerning the Availability of Earlier Applications as Prior Art (Art. 8(2) Draft SPLT).
92. *Infra* 154 (G 0002/06 (Use of embryos/WARF) of 25 November 2008).
93. Rule 23d, Implementing Regulations, 1973.
94. G 2/07 Broccoli/Plant Bioscience OJ EPO 2012.
95. G 1/08 Tomatoes/State of Israel OJ EPO 2012.
96. *Ibid.*, note 473.
97. EPC Guidelines for examination, 2014 (point. 5.4.2).
98. T 1199/08 (Selected sperm/XY) of 3 May 2012.
99. Monsanto and Beyer Hiltrud.

of complete enabling disclosure. The method claim was entirely a non-biological process and relied on sex- selection by flow cytometry. While the use of the sperm was used in artificial insemination for the production of an animal it was not considered to be an essentially biological process as the method was not claimed in the application. While so it was contented that the selection step was decisive for the ultimate and inescapable result namely the production of animals. It was contented that a correct application of finding its exclusion under Article 53(b) EPC is to take not just the claims but the whole teaching of the application. Thus by following a whole content approach the application was at best a careful draft that seemingly avoided the biological process of creating an animal.

However, the board rejected the argument that the 'whole contents approach' developed in G 2/06 should be taken into consideration for a correct assessment of whether the claim in question would fall under the prohibition of Article 53(b) EPC. It was the opinion of the board that the process of the claims neither comprises of steps for breeding of animals nor any of the additional steps involved crossing unlike the plant breeding cases which were raised by the opponents. Thus it was decided that a claim to a method which allowed for the long-term preservation of sex-selected sperm did not qualify as an essentially biological process for the production of animals. Therefore, in line with the parallel reasoning developed in G 2/07 regarding processes for the production of plants.

[C] The Ethical Criterion: FIC and the Pre-patent Research

FIC is essential for the collection, storage, processing and use of samples in biomedical research. It is one of the fundamental ethical principles which every researcher needs to adhere to. The principle of free consent and self-determination with regard to one's own life has been internationally accepted starting with the Nuremberg code[100] to the WMA Helsinki Declaration on Ethical Principles for Medical Research Involving Human Subjects (1964), the European Convention for the Protection of Human Rights and Fundamental, Convention of Human Rights and Biomedicine.[101] Informed consent means that the person involved should have legal capacity to give consent and should be able to exercise free power of choice, without the intervention to make informed choices regarding their health and well-being and also how their genetic materials or information may be used or exploited. Under the Oviedo Convention:

- An intervention in the health field may only be carried out after the person concerned has given free and informed consent to it.
- This person shall beforehand be given appropriate information as to the purpose and nature of the intervention as well as on its consequences and risks.

100. First principle of the Nuremberg code provides for the voluntary consent of the human subject https://encyclopedia.ushmm.org/content/en/article/the-nuremberg-code.
101. Oviedo 1997.

- The person concerned may freely withdraw consent at any time.[102]

Thus, the goal of informed consent is to enable competent individuals to decide for themselves whether to participate in research.[103] However, obtaining consent involves a comprehensive process of ensuring an individual's decision.[104] Valid consent can be critical for protecting the rights and welfare of individuals whose biospecimens are used in research and for maintaining public trust in the research.[105] Article 22 of the Oviedo Convention also provides that during an intervention where any part of a human body is removed for storage and used for a purpose other than that for which it was removed, it can only done in conformity with appropriate information and consent procedures. Further the Taipei Declaration on health databases and biobanks, endorses that the collection, storage and use of data and biological materials by biobanks from individuals capable of giving consent must be voluntary.[106] The charter of fundamental rights of EU provides that, everyone has the right to physical and metal integrity.[107] In particular, it stipulates that the free and informed consent must be honoured as per law.[108] This obligation is emphasized in the donations of tissues,[109] clinical trials regulation,[110] organs,[111] General Data Protection Regulation (GDPR).[112] However within the realms of biotech patentability this is differently dealt with. The Biotech Directive offered a justification in terms of the use of biological samples. Recital (26) of the directive reads thus:

> if an invention is based on biological material of human origin or if it uses such material, where a patent application is filed, the person from whose body the material is taken must have had an opportunity of expressing free and informed consent thereto, in accordance with national law.

The provision was a realization from the council that patentability assessments cannot keep itself away from bioethical questions related to new and intimate technologies. More importantly the recital also follows another provision under the directive i.e., Rectial 16, which requires that '*patent law must be applied so as to respect*

102. Article 5, Convention for the Protection of Human Rights and Dignity of the Human Being with regard to the Application of Biology and Medicine: Convention on Human Rights and Biomedicine, Oviedo, 4.IV.1997.
103. L.M. Beskow et al., Informed consent for biobanking: Consensus-based guidelines for adequate comprehension. *Genetics in Medicine: Official Journal of the American College of Medical Genetics* 2014; 17(3): 226–33.
104. *Ibid.*
105. E.J. Emanuel and J. Menikoff, Reforming the regulations governing research with human subjects. *The New England Journal of Medicine.* 2011; 365(12): 1145–1150.
106. Article 11, Taipei Declaration on Ethical considerations regarding health databases and biobanks, Adopted by the fifty-third WMA General Assembly, Washington, DC, USA, October 2002 and revised by the sixty-seventh WMA General Assembly, Taipei, Taiwan, October 2016.
107. Article 3, Charter of Fundamental Rights of the European Union, OJ C 326, 26.10.2012.
108. *Ibid.*
109. Tissues and Cells Directive (2004/23/EC).
110. Regulation (EU) No. 536/2014 of the European Parliament and of the Council of 16 April 2014.
111. Directive 2010/53/EU/2010 on standards of quality and safety of human organs intended for transplantation.
112. General Data Protection Regulation (EU) 2016/679, deals in consent for processing of data.

the fundamental principles safeguarding the dignity and integrity of the person'.[113] Significant progress in the treatment of diseases is possible due to the existence of medicinal products derived from elements isolated from the human body or otherwise produced. Consequently, it is stipulated by the directive that research aimed at obtaining and isolating such elements valuable to medicinal production should be encouraged by means of the patent system.[114] With such obligations for respecting human dignity and FIC, raised by the Biotech Directive one may assume that its enforcement will be ensured through the provisions of IP law. However, it has been stipulated that the scope of the declarations in favour of human dignity simply reinforce the demand that human rights should be respected without offering anything new to the discourse.[115] Therefore, it is essential to understand the implication of this ethical requirement in patent law and to examine how informed consent is addressed under procedure and practice of patent law.

[1] Informed Consent under EPC

Under the EPC, Article 53 holds the repute of being a key element of distinction in the European Patent jurisprudence.[116] This is because this provision of law makes it clear that morality is a matter to be regarded with respect to innovations.[117] The full text of the provision reads:

> European patents shall not be granted in respect of:
>
> (a) *Inventions the commercial exploitation of which would be contrary to 'ordre public' or morality; such exploitation shall not be deemed to be so contrary merely because it is prohibited by law or regulation in some or all of the Contracting States;*
>
> (b) *Plant or animal varieties or essentially biological processes for the production of plants or animals; this provision shall not apply to microbiological processes or the products thereof;*
>
> (c) *methods for treatment of the human or animal body by surgery or therapy and diagnostic methods practised on the human or animal body; this provision shall not apply to products, in particular substances or compositions, for use in any of these methods.*

113. Rectial 16 of the Biotech Directive 98/44/EC, also provides whereas it is important to assert the principle that the human body, at any stage in its formation or development, including germ cells, and the simple discovery of one of its elements or one of its products, including the sequence or partial sequence of a human gene, cannot be patented; whereas these principles are in line with the criteria of patentability proper to patent law, whereby a mere discovery cannot be patented.
114. Recital 17 of the Biotech Directive 98/44/EC.
115. R. Brownsword, Bioethics today, bioethics tomorrow: Stem cell research and the dignitarian alliance. *Notre Dame Journal of Law, Ethics & Public Policy*. 2012; 17(1): (15–51), 42 and Plomer, 207.
116. R. Cook-Deegan and C. Heaney, Patents in genomics and human genetics. *Annual Review of Genomics and Human Genetics*. 2010; 11: 383–425. PMC.Web. 7 March 2016.
117. Dr O. Mills, Biotechnological inventions: Moral restraints and patent law, Ashgate Publishing, Ltd., 28 February 2013.

Individuals have substantial social rights in any modern society and their normative force calls for a different kind of protection independent of the national laws. States have a duty to protect such rights and freedom of individuals. The exceptions to IPR such as the one provided under Article 53 are technical exceptions provided by law and have their underlying rationale based on ethical, social and developmental concerns.[118] The traditional rationale for granting patents on commercial innovations was to serve the utilitarian function of welfare maximization by providing a necessary incentive for innovative activity and its disclosure to the public. There are grave doubts about whether these objectives are being met in the case of patents that encompass genetic sequences. These doubts are shared both by scholars and by those involved in science, biotechnology and the health industries, who argue that too many patents, some of dubious quality and validity, are posing unnecessary constraints on competition, follow-on research and downstream innovation.[119] Assimilation of new technologies arising in unanticipated ways has thus always posed difficulties. This standard cut off exemption was said to be an effective means wherein a Member State may refuse to grant patent in the higher interest of the public.[120] This provision originally offered under TRIPS was effectively adopted under the EPC under Article 53(3). Under EPC the patent rights derived are still a bundle of rights from each national jurisdiction,[121] hence the bundle also involves with it a diversity of public opinions which the provision hopes to balance. But, the effectiveness of this approach has greatly been doubted in respect to Unitary Patent System which is currently evolving.[122] Though the content of the provision is vague the intended purpose of the protection under EPC is to deny protection to inventions likely to induce riot or public disorder, or to lead to criminal or other generally offensive behaviour.[123] Some of the examples offered by the examination guidelines tend to throw some light on this like *incitement to riot* or *acts of disorder*; *incitement to criminal acts*; *racial, religious* or *similar discriminatory propaganda*; and *grossly obscene* matter. The concept of *morality* is related to the belief that some behaviour is right and acceptable whereas other behaviour is wrong, this belief being founded on the totality of the accepted norms which are deeply rooted in a particular culture. For the purposes of the EPC, the culture in question is the culture inherent in European society and civilization. Accordingly, under Article 53(a) EPC, inventions the exploitation of which is not in conformity with the conventionally-accepted standards of conduct pertaining to this culture are to be excluded from

118. *Supra* note 116.
119. B. Amani and R.J. Coombe, The human genome diversity project: The politics of patents at the intersection of race, religion, and research ethics. *Law & Policy*. 2005; 27: 152.
120. G.H.C Bodenhausen, Guide to application of the Paris Convention for the protection of industrial property, as revised at Stockholm in 1976, WIPO publication No. 611(E) BIRPI 1969, Reprinted 1991.
121. According to Recital 39 of the Biotech Directive one should when assessing ordre public and morality take into account i.a. 'ethical or moral principles recognized in a Member State'.
122. *See* for more discussions on the point, C. Peterson, T. Riss and J. Schovsbo, The Unified Patent Court (UPC) in action – How will the design of the UPC affect patent law? Kluwer in 'transitions in European patent law – influences of the unitary patent package', 2015.
123. EPC Examination Guideline 2014.

patentability as being contrary to morality.[124] Some authors have suggested that the provision of patent law is not an appropriate mechanism to regulate biotechnological inventions and any attempt to deny patentability based on moral obligation is rather misplaced.[125] However decision to offer patent is a distinct function independent of ethical nature of research but the provision offers an opportunity that while making a decision on patentability the individual and the collective social security remains unaffected.[126]

The approach under the EPC differs from its counterpart provision under TRIPS. Under TRIPS a 'necessity' test requires the members to offer an assessment of the necessity in preventing the commercial exploitation of such invention.[127] Further, such exclusion must not be made merely because it is prohibited by law. While one approach tends to examine what is offensive the other requires examining the necessity, which gave rise to such an objection. The objective of both these provisions is twofold, namely to assess the 'necessity' or 'abhorrence' of the said application for patentability in the eyes of the public and second to ensure that inventions are not avoided from a patent protection merely because it is prohibited by law or regulation in some or all of the Contracting States. This is so because a product could still be manufactured under a European patent for export to States in which its use is not prohibited.[128] Thus, it is a matter of an 'impact assessment' rather than a strict examination of the technical frontiers behind the said invention in question. With respect to the biotech inventions the 'Implementing Regulations to the Convention on the Grant of European patents', commonly known as the 'Implementing Regulations' offers some explanation. The function of the Implementing Regulations is 'to determine in more detail how the Articles should be applied'.

Rule 28 of the Implementing Regulation gives examples from the field of biotechnology that potentially give rise to an objection under the 'Ordre Public' and morality clause.[129] The enlarged Board of Appeal in Warf case noted that the correct approach to Rule 28(c) of EPC is to identify the claimed monopoly and ask whether that monopoly embraces the exceptions mentioned under the provision.[130] As can be seen from the provision of the EPC, the moral obligation requirement stands as the only aperture for assessing the ethical foundations behind an invention. There exists no specific provisions under EPC that requires adherence to FIC just like Recital 26 of the Biotech Directive. However, the implementing regulation stipulates that the directive

124. T 0356/93 (Plant cells) of 21 February 1995.
125. M. Oliver, Biotechnological inventions: Moral restrains and patent law, Ashgate, 11.
126. Å. Hellstadius, A quest for clarity: Reconstructing standards for the patent law morality exclusion, Stockholms universitet 2015.
127. *Ibid.*
128. *Supra* note 126.
129. Under Art. 53(a), European patents shall not be granted in respect of biotechnological inventions which, in particular, concern the following: (a) processes for cloning human beings; (b) processes for modifying the germ line genetic identity of human beings; (c) [29]uses of human embryos for industrial or commercial purposes; (d) processes for modifying the genetic identity of animals which are likely to cause them suffering without any substantial medical benefit to man or animal, and also animals resulting from such processes.
130. G 0002/06.

shall be a supplementary means of interpretation with regard to questions of general patentability.[131]

[2] Informed Consent under the Biotech Directive

The moral exemption also finds itself well placed in the Biotech Directive under Article 6. It offers two-step exclusion just as its counterpart in the convention. While inventions contrary to *ordre* public and morality may be eliminated, there could be specific instances in the context of biotechnological inventions which are regarded standard examples to such exclusions. The actual text of the provision reads:

1. Inventions shall be considered unpatentable where their commercial exploitation would be contrary to ordre public or morality; however, exploitation shall not be deemed to be so contrary merely because it is prohibited by law or regulation.
2. On the basis of paragraph 1, the following, in particular, shall be considered unpatentable:
   (a) processes for cloning human beings;
   (b) processes for modifying the germ line genetic identity of human beings;
   (c) uses of human embryos for industrial or commercial purposes;
   (d) processes for modifying the genetic identity of animals which are likely to cause them suffering without any substantial medical benefit to man or animal, and also animals resulting from such processes.

While the above list offers a limited certainty on patent standards and as an interpretative tool, yet is not conclusive in itself and has been contested in different situations.[132] In T 0019/90 (Onco-Mouse) it was observed that the exclusion serves in 'providing a proper balance between the interest of inventors in this field in obtaining reasonable protection for their efforts and society's interest in excluding certain categories'.

One such essential issue which has been contested but found little attention of the lawmakers is the issue of 'consent' in biomedical research leading to patentable invention. Often biobanks follow different approaches to securing consent from the research participants. For instance the UK biobank offers an informed consent with the possibility of re-contacting the donors if the research is new or to seek new information of their possible involvement in a study that requires new information.[133] On the contrary, certain other biobanks like for instance the Danish National Biobank has an opt-out procedure for consent[134] or some other may require explicit consent or implicit consent. The differences in approach often change the equations of research use of such samples. The question then is whether it is possible to patent a research result

131. Rule 26, Implementing Regulations to the Convention on the Grant of European Patents of 5 October 1973.
132. For example The plea for assessing the usefulness of the invention in relation to the environment T 19/90 Onco-mouse case.
133. UK Biobank http://www.ukbiobank.ac.uk/all-faqs/ (last accessed on 27 March 2016).
134. J.H. Solbakk, S. Holm and B. Hofmann, The ethics of research biobanking, Springer Science & Business Media, 31 July 2009.

when the consent is not adequate as per the national bodies assessing a patent. What if the samples put into such research do not have consent? Can the patent law seek to address the pre-patent research? Some of these questions have found way into European patentability discussions under the Ordre public and morality clause. The earliest discussion that touched upon the issue was the Howard Florey case[135] discussed in the previous section. The opponents asserted that isolating the naturally occurring relaxin hormone from pregnant women and securing a patent right over it amounts to 'slavery and dismemberment of women' and their bodies. The proprietors pointed out that the *mRNA taken from the tissues of pregnant women where in fact donated by such women within the framework of gynaecological operations and its use was perfectly moral. Further many lifesaving substances such as blood clotting factors are isolated in this way and are patented moreover the use for other purposes of parts of the human body during the course of an intervention is explicitly approved by Article 13 of the draft Bioethics convention of the council of Europe*[136] *provided there are appropriate information and consent procedures.*[137] Based on this the Technical Board of Appeal was also of the opinion that human dignity was not violated in the case. Though there was not much of a discussion on the consent and its ethical impacts for the assessment of '*Ordre Public* and *Morality*', the arguments of the case sought to clarify that European Patents would be granted only to those inventions which are not regarded as outrageous and has been the result of research following the appropriate ethical procedures as prescribed by the Council of Europe.

Subsequently the Biotech Directive provided for FIC under Recital 26. In addition, Recital 38 to the directive states that although the directive offers certain exclusions from patentability so as to provide courts and patent offices with a general guide as to the interpretation of 'ordre public and morality', yet this list is not exhaustive. Therefore, all processes the use of which offends against human dignity are also excluded from patentability.[138] While these recitals including Recital 26 astoundingly offers a higher pedestal to ethics within patent law it is of weak legal value. A 'Recital' in an EU Directive has no binding force whatsoever on EC-member countries and the terms used are extremely feeble.[139] For instance, while Recital 26 FIC it is not clear whether such consent has to be obtained only for the use of the material in research or

135. *Supra* note 73.
136. Article 13 -Information for research participants. The persons being asked to participate in a research project shall be given adequate information in a comprehensible form. This information shall be documented. The information shall cover the purpose, overall plan, possible risks and benefits of the research project, and include the opinion of the ethics committee. In addition, they shall be informed of the rights and safeguards prescribed by law for their protection, and in particular of their right to refuse consent or to withdraw consent at any time without prejudice to their right to medical care and without suffering any other detriment. http://www.iqb.es/leyes/protocolo%20al%20convenio%20de%20derechos%20humanos%20y%20biomedicina.pdf.
137. Opposition Division grounds for decision 18 January 1995.
138. Recital 38, Directive 98/44/EC.
139. NCCR-Trade Working Paper, 2007/36, Human Rights in Patent Procedure, Michelangelo Temmerman.

its proof needs to be offered at the filing of the patent application.[140] As to the second notion, it can be said with casting a doubt that a recital carries the value at best of a guide. The drafting history of the Biotech Directive offers to throw some light on why the requirement of consent was silently dropped from the substantive provisions and found place only in the recitals. The Belgian draft of the directive expanded the notion of ordre public and morality clause by excluding the patentability of inventions produced through means that are contrary to *Ordre public* and *Morality*. The legislation states that inventions produced in violation of human rights and informed consent or exported in violation of the Convention on Biological Diversity, shall not be patentable.[141] While the Belgian draft found an ethical voice in patent jurisprudence yet the commission was persuaded to exclude it owing to the concern that it may tend to violate the TRIPS provisions. While the TRIPS only permits the exclusion of patents on grounds of Public Ordre and Morality it does not permit an exclusion where the process of creating the invention violates these norms.[142] While the protection and enforcement of IPR should contribute to the promotion of technological innovation and to the transfer and dissemination of technology it should proceed in a manner conducive to social and economic welfare, and to a balance of rights and obligations.[143] TRIPS also offers considerable space for Member States to formulate or amend the laws in order to promote the public interest in sectors of vital importance to their socio-economic and technological development.[144] Thus creating economic norms with due consideration of social norms ought to have been given impetus at least through the Biotech Directive which lost this opportunity.

The Biotech Directive also entrusted the reigns of addressing the ethical issues raised during patentability discussions to the commission's Group on Ethics in science and technology which under Article 7, has the task of evaluating all ethical aspects of biotechnology. However, in reality it is a mere advisory body and does not provide specific authorization to individual patent applications like the ethics committees under the Clinical Trials Directive.[145]

The essence of Recital 26 is to ensure effective and transparent measures towards FIC in the context of pre-patent research. In many national jurisdictions, ensuring FIC is a part of procedural law. For instance the Danish Order on Patents and Supplementary Protection Certificates (SPCs), provides a procedural measure to ensure patent applications are accompanied by documents relating to FIC for the biological material used in the invention.[146] The original text of Danish order reads as follows:

140. T.K. Hervey, J.V. McHale, Health law and the European union, Cambridge University Press 2004.
141. Article 4(3) of the Belgian Draft of the Legislation.
142. E.R. Gold and A. Gallochat, The European biotech directive: Past as a prologue. *European Law Journal*. September 2001; 7(3): 331–336.
143. TRIPS, Art. 7.
144. TRIPS, Art. 8.
145. *Supra* note 140.
146. Order on Patents and Supplementary Protection Certificates, The Patent and Trademark Office Denmark (Order No. 25 of 18 January 2013), Chapter II, Art. 3(6), available at: http://www.dkpto.org/media/183780/the%20patent%20and%20trademark%20office%20order%202013%20no%20%2025.pdf (last accessed on 7 January 2019).

> If an invention relates to or makes use of a biological material of human origin, it shall appear from the patent application whether the person from whom the biological material originates has given his consent to the filing of the application. The information about consent shall not affect the examination and other processing of the patent application or the validity of the rights conferred by the granted patent.[147]

This means that while patentability of invention may not be affected by consent, yet it may have other liabilities under law.[148] The Swedish law on the point of consent in research is addressed under the ethical procedures for research. Under the act concerning the Ethical Review of Research Involving Humans, research involving the using of HBMs may only proceed with appropriate consent for such research.[149] While this is not a part of the substantive patent law, yet it tends to regulate the general pre-patent and other research environments with adequate sanctions in place for non-compliance.[150]

[3] Informed Consent in Patent Cases

Even after the adoption of the Biotech Directive the issue of consent with respect to pre-patent research and their redress under patent law were raised before the CJEU. In the case of *Kingdom of Netherlands v European Parliament and Council of the European Union*[151] it was contented by the Dutch side that, 'the patentability of isolated parts of the human body provided for by Article 5(2) of the directive reduces living human matter to a means to an end, undermining human dignity. Moreover, the absence of a provision requiring verification of the consent of the donor or recipient of products obtained by biotechnological means undermines the right to self-determination'.[152] The CJEU clarified the position thus:

> the right to human integrity, in so far as it encompasses, in the context of medicine and biology, the free and informed consent of the donor and recipient ....Reliance on this fundamental right is, however, clearly misplaced as against a directive which concerns only the grant of patents and whose scope does not therefore extend to activities before and after that grant, whether they involve research or the use of the patented products. *Furthermore the CJEU observed that* the grant of a patent does not preclude legal limitations or prohibitions applying to research into patentable products or the exploitation of patented products, as the fourteenth recital of the preamble to the directive points out. The purpose of the directive is

147. *Supra* note 146.
148. Under § 162 of The Danish Criminal Code Order No. 909 of 27 September 2005 (as amended by Act Nos. 1389 and 1400 of 21 December 2005), any person who otherwise makes an incorrect statement before any public authority or for the information of such authority concerning matters on which he is bound to give evidence shall be liable to a fine or to imprisonment for any term not exceeding four months.
149. SFS 2003:460, available at: http://www.codex.vr.se/en/manniska2.shtml (last accessed on 7 January 2019).
150. https://www.riksdagen.se/sv/dokument-lagar/dokument/svensk-forfattningssamling/lag-2003460-om-etikprovning-av-forskning-som_sfs-2003-460.
151. Case C-377/98 Judgment of the Court of 9 October 2001.
152. *Ibid.*

> not to replace the restrictive provisions which guarantee, outside the scope of the directive, compliance with certain ethical rules which include the right to self-determination by informed consent.[153] Thus while patent law by itself may not be allowed to modulate the consent issues, yet other restrictive provisions could resolve such issues for e.g., requiring an informed consent for all research as per Oviedo Convention.[154]

In *Evans v the United Kingdom*[155] the higher standard was set by Article 5 of the Oviedo Convention, which was applied by ECtHR. What the court postulated in the said case was that, when dealing with life and human health issues, the Oviedo Convention is to all intents and purposes a 'patient rights treaty'. 'Informed Consent' offers autonomy to patients to make choices as to matters affecting their health and well-being.

In *V.C. v Slovakia*[156] yet another landmark ruling from the ECtHR, in which it was observed that Article 5, paragraph 2, mentions the most important aspects of the information which should precede the intervention but it is not an exhaustive list; informed consent may imply, according to the circumstances, additional elements. In order for their consent to be valid the persons in question must have been informed about the relevant facts regarding the intervention being contemplated. Thus the donor of the samples ought to be informed about the relevant research for which her samples and purported taken for. However it is highly impossible to visualize in advance the nature of patents that may arise out of such research. Thus while a research endeavour always has the duty to secure informed consent of the donors or participants, this duty however does not extend to economic interests.

In *Greenberg case*[157] it was observed that seeking consent for ever research would be an unworkable proposition which would chill medical research as it would mandate that researchers constantly evaluate whether a disclosable event has occurred. Also this extra duty would give rise to a type of dead-hand control that research subjects could hold because they would be able to dictate how medical research progresses.[158] From an American patent landscape this makes perfect sense, however in Europe where the cultural of ethics is highly embedded in almost all spheres including economic frontiers there would be serious limitation to such proposition. Hence it is unsurprising that the issues of 'consent' and 'human dignity' in biomedical research have been raised frequently in patentability assessment. In G 0002/06[159] the ethical approach was resounded in relation to Article 6 of the Biotech Directive that one of the essential objectives of the whole directive to protect human dignity.[160] However, what was sounded in the discussions in relation to the definition of 'Human Embryo', in the

---

153. *Ibid.*, para. 80.
154. Convention for the Protection of Human Rights and Dignity of the Human Being with regard to the Application of Biology and Medicine: Convention on Human Rights and Biomedicine 1997.
155. ECHR 2007-I 353.
156. ECHR 2011-V 381.
157. *Greenberg v Miami Children's Hospital Research Institute*, 264 F. Supp. 2d 1064 (S.D. Fla. 2003).
158. *Ibid.*
159. Use of embryos/WARF [2009]EPOR 15(EBA).
160. *Ibid.*

Warf case was scaled down to a different interpretation in *Oliver Brüstle v Greenpeace*[161] particularly with regard to ethical issues. It was noted that patent for invention does not authorize the holder to implement that invention, but merely entitles him to prohibit third parties from exploiting it for industrial and commercial purposes; consequently, substantive patent law cannot serve to replace or render superfluous national, European or international law which may impose restrictions or prohibitions or which concerns the monitoring of research and of the use or commercialization of its results, notably from the point of view of the requirements of public health, safety, environmental protection, animal welfare, the preservation of genetic diversity and compliance with certain ethical standards.[162] However '*patent law must be applied so as to respect the fundamental principles safeguarding the dignity and integrity of the person*'; thus the human body, at any stage in its formation or development, including germ cells, and the simple discovery of one of its elements or one of its products, including the sequence or partial sequence of a human gene, cannot be patented.[163] The result of these landmark judgments has brought a sea change in European patent jurisprudence. Rather than a mere technical enquiry in which consideration of ethics have no role beyond the examination of an invention's outrageousness, patentability must take full account of human dignity as one of the values for biotechnological inventions.[164] The Brüstle case also seeks to examine pre-patent materials to a limited extend to ensure that they are not excluded from patentability. But such an examination suggested by the decision does go into the depths of the procedure related to the collection of such materials. Thus the issue of 'informed consent' or a lack of it may not be considered in the assessment of human dignity and integrity of the person for a patentability examination. This is clearer from a similar approach taken by the EPO in a very lengthy discussion in T 1213/05.[165] The contention raised by the opponents before the Board of Appeal was that no proof had been provided by appellant that the donors of the cells that had been critical to identify the BRCA1 gene had given a previous informed consent to the use of said cells. Such previous informed consent would have had to include an explicit consent to the commercial exploitation of the research results by patents as well as a benefit sharing agreement with the members whose cell donations of which had been essential in arriving at the claimed invention. In the absence of such proof, it had to be assumed that the initial obtaining of these research results involved severe ethical violations, and thus a violation of 'ordre public' or morality as referred to in Article 53(a) EPC.[166] In response to this opposition the Board of Appeal observed thus:

161. C-34/10, CJEU 2011.
162. Paragraph 14, C-34/10, CJEU 2011.
163. *Ibid.*, para. 32.
164. J Pila *Supra* note 23.
165. Breast and ovarian cancer/University of Utah of 27 September 2007.
166. Examination Guidelines 2014 Ed.: Although in general a medical claim directed to tests carried out on 'animals' should exclude from its scope the use of human beings as 'test animals' (e.g., by means of a disclaimer). In some infrequent cases, a claim may, in the light of the description, be interpreted as exclusively relating to a clinical trial of an experimental medicament carried out on human beings. It is assumed that, unless there is evidence to the contrary, such trials are

> *EPC contains no provision establishing a requirement for applicants to submit evidence of a previous informed consent or a benefit sharing agreement*. According to recital (26) of the Biotech Directive 'opportunity of expressing free and informed consent' ought to be made 'in accordance with national law'.[167]

The legislators have thus not provided for a procedure of verifying the informed consent in the framework of the grant of biotechnological patents under the EPC.[168] Although the requirement of consent to all potential uses of human material may be regarded as fundamental, patent law is not the appropriate framework for the imposition and monitoring of such a requirement.[169] It is interesting to note that in T 1213/05 case the opponents of the patent requested a reference to the enlarged Board of appeal as follows:

> In the case of patent applications which depend on donations of biological material of human origin in a critical way, is it necessary in view of Article 53(a) EPC that the previous informed consent of the donors of critical material is proven in the application proceedings by documents (or other means of proof)? If the answer to the question is 'yes':
>
> - Should the previous informed consent in view of Article 53(a) EPC include an explicit consent to the commercial exploitation of the donations with the aid of patents?
> - Should the informed consent include a benefit sharing agreement?

These questions were unanswered stating that no important point of law arises since the EPC neither provided for such provision as consent nor has there been uniformity of law with regard to the point.[170] It is thus clear from the above discussion that while FIC is vehemently advocated, it is not raised in the context of commercial exploitation and protection of results through IPR in inventions containing biological materials. The distinction of informed consent for research and informed consent for exploitation of the results of the research are not one and the same. As is clear Europe has been carefully sceptical about discussing consent issues relating to HBMs in the sphere of commercialization.

On the contrary, it seems that plant genetic materials are treated differently and so also research results of plant origin. The Convention on Biodiversity states that access to genetic resources shall be made only with prior informed consent.[171] Similarly, in Europe having regard to the Biodiversity convention and the Nagoya

---

performed under strictly controlled conditions and with informed consent of the patient concerned. In such cases, no objection under Art. 53(a) should be raised (*see* however G-II, 4.2.1.2).

167. *See* paras 48, 49, 50, 80 of T 1213/05.
168. *Ibid.*, para. 49.
169. Opinion of Advocate General Jacobs' delivered on 14 June 2001 in Case C-377/98 (document D175) in *Kingdom of the Netherlands v European Parliament and Council of the European Union*.
170. *Supra* note 155.
171. Article 15(5), Convention on Biological Diversity (CBD).

Protocol,[172] Regulation (EU) No. 511/2014[173] was formulated. Article 4 of this regulation states that in the absence of prior informed consent obtained in a timely manner and mutually agreed terms and an agreement with the provider country concerned, no exclusive rights of any kind will be claimed.[174] This differential treatment for plant and human materials by the European commission may be owing to the pressures on various quarters particularly the fact that EU being an economic entity may need to carefully balance its equations particularly in the front of exclusive patent rights. The downside of such differential treatment is the lack of clarity in the process leading to pre-patent research and a general mistrust in research and collaboration with private entities. The public attitude towards Biobank research in Europe demonstrated by a study commissioned by European commission re-emphasizes the need for FIC in all phases of research and the study went on to demonstrate that a vast majority of people across Europe considered consent as an essential feature for any new research conducted by the Biobanks.[175] Technological integration thus offers more and more anomalies for law to intervene in developing new direction for enhancing research.

With increased data-oriented research, the ethical bases particularly FIC and respect for human dignity need to be placed in a higher pedestal than ever before. Such discrepancies in law becomes increasingly visible and challenging with the changing research environments particularly in the context of PM which will be examined below.

§3.02 PATENTS, BIOBANKS AND PERSONALIZED HEALTHCARE INITIATIVES

The unravelling of human genome has paved the way to new possibilities in healthcare sector. This has enabled a movement from ineffective experimental administration of drugs to a more data-oriented model that is customized to the needs of the patients. Thus PM is as a new approach to the patient which is built on several pillars namely omics methods (proteomics, metabolomics and epigenomics), systems medicine, bioinformatics and biobanks.[176] PM involves a four 'P' characterization namely:

(1) personalization: by which it means individualization of genetic resources;
(2) predictiveness: foreseeability of risk factors involved;

172. The Nagoya Protocol on Access to Genetic Resources and the Fair and Equitable Sharing of Benefits Arising from Their Utilization to the Convention on Biological Diversity,the 'Nagoya Protocol' is an international treaty adopted on 29 October 2010 by the Parties to the Convention.
173. Regulation (EU) No. 511/2014of the European Parliament and of the Council of 16 April 2014 on compliance measures for users from the Nagoya Protocol on Access to Genetic Resources and the Fair and Equitable Sharing of Benefits Arising from their Utilization in the Union Text with EEA relevance.
174. *Ibid.*
175. Biobanks for Europe: A challenge for governance, 2012 http://bookshop.europa.eu/en/biobanks-for-europe-pbKINA25302/ (last accessed on 30 March 2016).
176. J. Kinkorová, Biobanks in the era of personalized medicine: Objectives, challenges, and innovation: Overview. *The EPMA Journal.* 2015; 7: 4. PMC. Web. 17 December 2016.

(3) preventiveness: the aim of the whole concept being prevention or reduction of risks; and
(4) participation: i.e., which calls for greater involvement of individuals in healthcare and related research.[177]

This technological revolution thus enables a tailored diagnosis and prognosis based on the genetic information of patients.[178] PM in its commonest perception aims to examine variations by demonstrating scientific links between biological patient characteristics, diagnoses and treatment options. Europe is moving beyond this phase to a level which examines genetic anomalies to data-driven PM. This new regime though data oriented is fundamentally based on genomic information and goes on to the next level of using larger sets of viable data[179] as the foundations for evolving relationship and treatment protocols for differing sets of patients.[180] Thus, large and rich dataset coupled with machine learning techniques enables many predictions based on complex and often implicit connections between patient information and expected treatment results.[181] While technology continues to lead, the implementation of PM requires a confluence of multiple factors. These factors include regulation, research and development, ethical principles of research, comparative effectiveness in research, health insurance models, patient participation and finally IP laws (*See* Figure 3.1). Full implementation of PM can only be achieved when all sectors converge towards the goal of adopting this new technological approach in different ways. The lure of PM anchors biobanks as institutions for storage, use and exchange of genetic information.[182] Besides the genetic information pools are resources for pharmaceutical innovation and clinical studies as well.

177. P. Sobradillo, F. Pozo and A. Agustí, P4 Medicine: The future around the corner. *Arch Bronconeumol*. 2011; 47(1): 35- 40.doi: 10.1016/j.arbres.2010.09.009.
178. J. Schovsbo et. al., Legal aspects of biobanking as key issues for personalized medicine and translational exploitation. *Personalized Medicine*. 2014; 11(5): 497–508.
179. Viable data refers to the quality of data with it carefully selected attributes enables predicting outcome for personalised medicine. *see*: S.I. Vizirianakis, Handbook of personalized medicine: Advances in nanotechnology, drug delivery, and therapy, CRC Press 2014, at p. 1422.
180. M. Aguirre et al., PerMed, shaping Europe's vision for personalised medicine, strategic research and innovation agenda (SRIA), June 2015.
181. W. Price Nicholson, Black-box medicine. *Harvard Journal of Law & Technolog*. 2015; 28: 419.
182. *Infra* note 188.

Figure 3.1 On Factors Affecting Personalized Health Care. Modified from PM Coalition: The Case for PM 4th Edition 2014[183]

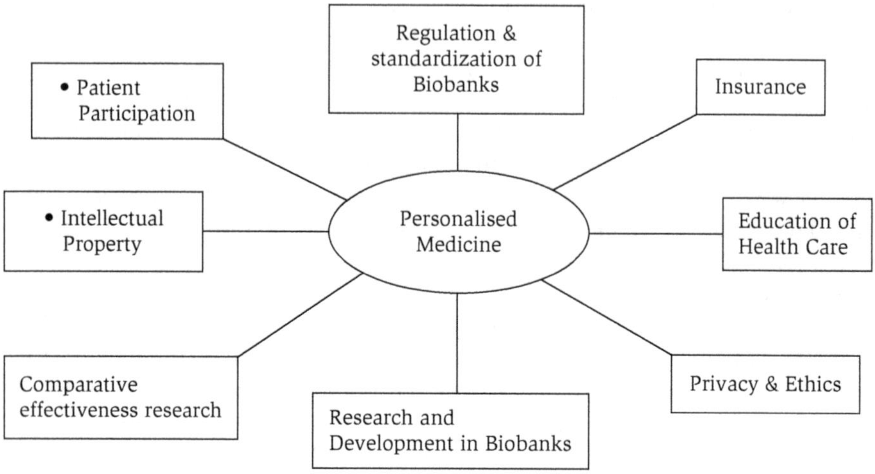

Hence, it becomes essential to consider the types of patent claims relating to personalized medical research within biobanks. The purpose of this examination is to throw light on the possibilities and challenges of patents for PM using biobank samples. The technical implication of helps to map the areas where patent law has a role to play. This enables biobanks to secure perspectives, which they may take into consideration in structuring their IP policies more effectively.

The patent eligible subject matter in medical research may extend from product claims i.e., over chemical compounds, proteins or compositions or their use, etc.[184] Apart from product patents on drugs or composition of substances[185] there could be other claims such as those relating to methods of testing, those relating to methods of treatment of different groups using known compositions and those related to novel dosage forms of the medicine. Thus medical diagnostic methods (methods of diagnosing a specific disease or affliction), methods of using a specific drug on a patient or on a defined subpopulation or a subgroup of *patients,* and methods of *dosage of a particular drug* are the main claims for patentability in personalized healthcare research.[186] While the first is partly covered by discourse above in relation to the biotechnological patents in Europe, there could also be certain apparatus claims used

183. Available at: http://personalizedmedicinecoalition.org/Resources/The_Case_for_Personalized_Medicine (last accessed on 18 December 2016).
184. In addition there could also be process claims like analytical methods, extraction process or hybrid claims like purpose-bound product claims for use of products in specific purposes. Report from the Commission to the Council and the European Parliament - Development and implications of patent law in the field of biotechnology and genetic engineering (SEC(2005) 943) /COM/2005/0312 final.
185. Article 53(c) and Art. 54(5), European Patent Convention, 1973.
186. Nuffield Council on Bioethics, Pharmacogenetics; Ethical issues (Nuffield council 2003).

in relation to diagnostic methods which will also be touched upon herein. The focus herein will primarily be on:

(a) diagnostic method claims in personalized healthcare;
(b) patient selection and categorization;
(c) dosage regime.

[A] Diagnostic Method Claims in Personalized Healthcare under EPC

Personalized healthcare initiatives aim to develop an evidence base on how to assess and integrate innovative diagnostics (including laboratory diagnostics and medical imaging) into health policy and practice.[187] At the same time there is also a focus on the discovery, validation and translation of biomarkers for risk prevention for diseases and also evolve new patient practice in the process.[188] The understanding and treatment of many diseases is assisted by the presence or absence of biomarkers that can be measured in body fluids like blood or urine.[189] Identifying biomarkers and their relationships to patient health outcomes is a resource-intensive process and it is argued by some writers that patents are often the driving force behind biomarker discovery.[190] To identify and validate biomarkers in pharma research requires excellent clinical materials. This requires biobanks to ensure their pre-analytical conditions are tightly controlled.[191] Apart from quality measures it is also essential for biobank-based research in biomarkers to concentrate on qualitative proofs which could ensure patentability for their biomarker. In this regard it is essential to understand how biomarker patents would be dealt with in Europe.

As mentioned above one of the aims of personalized care is assessing diagnostic methods which not only helps to define patient groups but also helps in the selections of drugs and even dosage regimes. With regard to patentability of diagnostic methods, the EPC, 1973, Article 52(4), regarded diagnostic methods practised on the human or animal body not to be an '*invention which are susceptible of industrial application*', over which a patent could be claimed. However the exclusion was later shifted to exception to patentability.[192] The exclusion of medical methods from patenting is based on the ethical and social reasons in order to ensuring provision of medical services for the public and the exercise of medical skills should not be restricted or hindered by

187. Personalized Medicine overview, Canadian institute of Health research.
188. Strategic Research and Innovation Agenda (SRIA) developed by the PerMed consortium. *See also* A. Liu and K. Pollard, Biobanking for personalized medicine, *Advances in Experimental Medicine and Biology*. 2015; 864: 55–68.
189. K. Strimbu and J.A. Tavel, What are biomarkers?' Current opinion in HIV and AIDS (2010);5(6): 463–466. PMC. Web. 19 December 2016.
190. A.S. Kesselheim and N. Shiu, The evolving role of biomarker patents in personalized medicine. *Clinical Pharmacology and Therapeutics*. Febuary 2014; 95(2).
191. *Ibid.*
192. Under Art. 53(c) by Amendment Act revising the European Patent Convention of 29 November 2000.

patents as a matter of principle.[193] Thus, methods for treatment of the human or animal body by surgery or therapy and diagnostic methods practised on the human or animal body shall not be patentable.[194] However, the provision does not apply to products, which are substances, or compositions, which are used in any of these methods of treatment.[195] In order to be patentable a claimed method must neither be a therapeutic nor a surgical nor a diagnostic one.

[1] Therapeutic Method

Therapeutic method cannot be patented if they include at least one feature defining a physical activity or an action that constitutes a method step for treatment of the human or animal body by therapy. The term therapy relates to the treatment of a disease in general or to a curative treatment in the narrow sense as well as the alleviation of the symptoms of pain and suffering and includes both curative and prophylactic.[196] In other words it must contain a therapeutic step to be non-patentable.[197] This often created issues with new pharmaceutical medicaments for medical purposes which were defeated by the protection under Article 53(c) of EPC. In rectifying this Swiss-type claims were devised which required the claims to drafted as 'Use of compound X for the manufacture of a medicament for the treatment of disease Y'.[198] However owing to certain limitations in its application it is now made obsolete through an order issued by the EPO.[199]

[2] Surgical Methods

The term 'surgery', encompasses an invasive step representing a substantial physical intervention on the body which requires professional medical expertise to be carried out and which entails a substantial health risk even when carried out with the required

193. CA/PL 7/99, Travaux preparatoires on Revision of the EPC: Art. 52(4) and 54(5), available at: http://www.epo.org/law-practice/legal-texts/epc/archive/documentation/travaux-preparatoires/plc-documents.html (Last accessed on 19 December 2016).
194. *Infra* note 196
195. Article 53(C) EPC,1973.
196. T 144/83 (OJ 1986, 301); G 5/83, OJ 1985, 64.
197. *See* T 81/84 (OJ 1988, 207); T 469/94; T 241/95 (OJ 2001, 103); T 1075/06.
198. G 0005/83 (Second medical indication) of 5 December 1984, The claim under Swiss-type had to be formulated thus 'Use of a substance or composition X for the manufacture of a medicament for therapeutic application Z'. While these types of claims were not literally provided under the European Patent Convention, they served to evade the limitation faced on account of therapeutic exclusion. The claim also suffered limitations for defining the second and further medical uses of substances. This apart a consistent problem with the claim was having to define the term 'manufacture'. If a patent merely teaches how the invention is to be used, it will be a use claim and hence excluded as a method of medical treatment. For more discussion on the point *see*: D. Armstrong, The arguments of law, policy and practice against Swiss-type patent claims', *Victoria University of Wellington Law Review*. 2001; 32(1): 201.
199. OJ EPO 2010, 514, Available at: https://www.epo.org/law-practice/legal-texts/official-journal/2016/etc/se4/p258.html (last accessed on 23 December 2016).

professional care.[200] In recent times the EPO has taken an open minded approach to the exclusion in considering that for a method to be regarded as a method for surgical treatment and as such excluded from patentability under Article 52(4) EPC, it is not necessary that the intervention be invasive or that tissues be penetrated.[201] This incorporates new technological developments in medical care systems.

[3] Diagnostic Method Claims

In G 0001/04[202] on a referral to the enlarged board,[203] it was held that in order to be excluded from patentability, the method is to include all steps relating to the claim namely:

(i) a diagnosis for curative purposes representing the deductive medical or veterinary decision phase which is a purely intellectual exercise i.e., an examination phase;

(ii) preceding steps which are constitutive for making that diagnosis, i.e., comparison of data sets and finding the deviation; and

(iii) finally the specific interactions with the human or animal body which occur when carrying out these preceding steps which are of a technical nature i.e., decision for curative purpose.[204] Besides it is also essential that all the steps must be present and must also be applied in human or animal body. The type or intensity of interaction with the human or animal body is not really relevant and whether the diagnostic method is excluded or not from patentability depends neither on the involvement of medical or veterinary staff, nor on the involvement of the patient himself or herself or any automated system, to perform the method.[205] Thus ex-vivo[206] diagnostic methods are also excluded from patentability whereas diagnostic methods carried out in vitro[207] are patentable in Europe. Also the reagents and other diagnostic method tools used for implementing diagnostic methods such as probes and primers, labelling or contrast agents, etc. are patentable.[208]

200. G 1/07.
201. T 5/04.
202. (Diagnostic methods) of 16 December 2005.
203. On 29 December 2003, the President of the EPO, making use of his power under Art. 112(1)(b) EPC, referred four questions of law to the enlarged Board of Appeal.
204. *Infra* note 206 Examination guidelines 2014.
205. G 0001/04 (Diagnostic methods) of 16 December 2005; *See also* G 1/04 and G 1/07.
206. Performed from biological fluids sampled from the body and then returned to the same body; as per the EPO examination guidelines an example of this would be: the treatment of blood for storage in a blood bank or diagnostic testing of blood samples is not excluded, whereas a treatment of blood by dialysis with the blood being returned to the same body would be excluded. Available at: http://www.epo.org/law-practice/legal-texts/html/guidelines/e/g_ii_4_2_1.htm (last accessed on 30 December 2016).
207. Performed outside the human or animal body in lab conditions.
208. *Supra* note 206.

[4] Genetic Diagnostic Methods

Biobanking is a strategic activity for research and innovation in biomedicine in a clinical context, which is essential for the procurement of high quality samples for translational research.[209] Pharmacogenomics studies, within biobank aim to identify a correlation between a genetic anomaly and the efficacy and safety of drugs.[210] This requires directional measures such as identifying the genetic mutation which also servers to identify the predisposition to particular types of diseases in different population sets and also identifying genes that effect response to drugs. The testing for specific genetic variants, usually in the form of Single Nucleotide Polymorphisms (SNPs)[211] gives rise to two important claims to diagnostic method; namely product claims for diagnostic kit tests and process claims for methods of diagnosis through genetic testing. Diagnostic apparatus and new products, substances or compositions, for use in these methods of treatment or diagnosis are patentable. Further inventions based on an element isolated from a human body or produced by other means are not excluded from patentability provided that the gene is sufficiently disclosed along with its functionality and has an inventive step.[212] In Europe there also seems to be an evolving discussion as the method claims involving technical steps in genetic testing.[213]

In G 001/04,[214] it was held that to determine if the claims involved a diagnostic test it was essential to follow certain steps which were discussed earlier. These method steps to be carried out prior to making a diagnosis as an intellectual exercise are related to examination, data gathering and comparison. If only one of the preceding steps which are constitutive for making such a diagnosis is lacking, there is no diagnostic method, but at best a method of data acquisition or data processing that can be used in a diagnostic method.[215] It was also observed by the enlarged Board of Appeal that:

> Intermediate findings of diagnostic relevance must not be confounded with diagnosis for curative purposes stricto sensu ..., which consists in attributing the detected deviation to a particular clinical picture. It follows that a method for obtaining such results or findings does not constitute a sufficient basis for denying patentability by virtue of Article 52(4) EPC.[216]

209. D. Mascalzoni (ed.), Ethics, law and governance of biobanking, the international library of ethics, law and technology 2014 at p. 18.
210. Amanda Odell-West, 'Exclusions in patent law as an Inderresct form of regulation for new health technologies in Europe', in Mark L. Flear ed., European Law and New Health Technologies, Oxford University Press, 2013, p. 162.
211. Single Nucleotide Polymorphism (SNP), A variation in the human genetic code of a single base, which may be associated with normal human variation or disease; *See*: https://ghr.nlm.nih.gov/primer/genomicresearch/snp.
212. *Monsanto Technology LLC v Cefetra BV and Others*, Case C-428/08, at paras 75–76
213. S. Sterckx and J. Cockbain, Guido Pennings, patenting medical diagnosis methods in Europe: Stanford University and time-lapse microscopy, *Reproductive BioMedicine Online.* 2016; doi: 10.1016/j.rbmo.2016.10.014.
214. *Infra* note 205, (Diagnostic methods) of 16.12.2005, *see* point 6.2.2.
215. *Ibid.*
216. *Ibid.*, point 6.2.3.

Thus in T 0146/07,[217] the claim related to a 'Non-invasive prenatal diagnosis';[218] the Board of Appeal, in upholding the patent, dealt with the claims only on the issue of sufficiency of disclosure and inventive step. The board did not deal with exclusions from patentability although the claim involved a prenatal diagnosis. This was perhaps on account of the fact that there were simply intermediate findings following certain steps which did not qualify as a diagnostic method within the purview of Article 52(4) of EPC, and requiring the steps to be performed on the body (which was not so in this case). Also it is not clear as to if the embryo would be treated as a human body or assessment of a medical condition alone without an actual cure in through the method would be considered as medical diagnosis. Clarification to some of the issues is awaited in an appeal pending before the enlarged Board of Appeal at the time of writing this book.[219]

The Myriad case in Europe also entailed a detailed analysis which is discussed below. In a more recent national case of *X ZR 141/13*,[220] the Bundesgerichtshof decided a case on the patentability of methods for detecting a biomarker (FLT 3). The presence of such mutations is associated with prognosis in acute myeloid leukaemia patients. A case for nullity of the patent was brought in against the Invivoscribe and Takara patent FLT 3. The patent, EP 959 132 B1, covers testing for internal tandem duplication mutations in the juxtamembrane region of FLT 3. In this case, the plaintiff of the nullity action argued that the claimed nucleic acid molecules merely related to a discovery and therefore constitutes non-patentable subject matter pursuant to Article 52(2) a. and (3) EPC.[221] A technical teaching which relates to the application of a discovery in order to achieve a technical effect represents patentable subject matter both according to European and German laws. This principle applies independent of whether there is 'an additional inventive contribution' (*'erfinderischer Überschuss'*), in addition to the discovered relationship according to the law of natures.[222] The court further states that the recognition of a physical, chemical or biological relationship, which represents the basis for the technical teaching has to be taken into account in the assessment of inventive step.[223] Thus a doctrine of technical action, which teaches the use of a discovery to produce a certain success, is patentable, independent of whether the

217. T 0146/07 (Prenatal diagnosis/ISIS) of 13 December 2011, ECLI:EP:BA:2011:T014607.20111213.
218. The claim was a detection method performed on a maternal serum or plasma sample from a pregnant female, which method comprises detecting the presence of a nucleic acid of foetal origin in the sample, wherein said nucleic acid is a paternally inherited sequence which is not possessed by said pregnant female. EP 0994963 or 'the 963 patent' as it was popularly called was also debated in USA in the case of *Sequenom, Inc. v Ariosa Diagnostics, Inc.* (2014–1139, 2014–1144), where the federal court held. The court acknowledged that the inventors' 'discovery regarding cffDNA may have been a significant contribution to the medical field' and that the maternal plasma was previously discarded as waste, but even 'valuable contributions can fall short of statutory patentable subject matter.'
219. T-0990/16. July 2016.
220. BGH, Urteil vom 19. Januar 2016 -X ZR 141/13 -BundespatentgerichtECLI:DE:BGH:2016:190116UXZR141.13.0.
221. *See*: http://www.ib-patent.de/news/landmark-decision-nucleic-acids-still-constitute-patentable-subject-matter germany-dr-tanja (last accessed on 31 December 2016).
222. Paragraph 50 of the judgment *Supra* note 220 .
223. *Ibid.*

doctrine contains an 'inventive surplus' beyond the purposive use of the revealed natural context.[224]

[B] Myriad Genetics in Europe (T 0080/05) and Implications for Genetic Testing in Europe

The claim before the EPO constituted a method for diagnosing a predisposition for breast and ovarian cancer in a human subject. Myriad Genetics discovered the BRCA1 gene in 1994 and the BRCA2 gene in 1995. Based on this they developed genetic test to identify the risk associated with breast and ovarian cancer. Its monopoly in the area led to opposition from different quarters. In 2009 the patent was opposed in US by a number of organizations and individuals along with the Association of Molecular Pathology. The dispute raises emotive issues relating to the ownership and control of genetic material by pharmaceutical companies. In its decision the US Supreme Court held that a naturally occurring DNA segment which is a product of nature and, as such, cannot be patented. However a complementary DNA i.e., an artificial product designed to mirror the coding parts of genes – is eligible for patent protection because it is not naturally occurring.[225]

Before the EPO

Though the patents belonging to Myriad were controversial for various reasons it had a different outcome in Europe. In the first instance oppositions were filed against the European patent on the isolated BRCA-1 gene by several stakeholders.[226] The opponents challenged the patent on the basis of the EPC's patentability criteria and contented that the claimed invention lacked novelty, inventive step and industrial application, and that the patent failed to disclose the invention sufficiently for a person skilled in the art to carry it out. The opposition proceedings led to the revocation of European Patent 699754[227] on multiple grounds, in the year 2004.[228] However the appeal focused more on the errors in filing and the issue of the priority date. Yet the Board of Appeal considered the claims 1–7 raised in the original request.[229] It is also interesting in the present context to take note of claims raised by Myriad particularly Claim 1 of the main request read as follows:

---

224. BGH, Judgment of 19 January 2016 – X ZR 141/13 – federal patents court at paras 50–53, available at: http://juris.bundesgerichtshof.de/cgi-bin/rechtsprechung/document.py?Gericht=bgh&Art=en&Datum=2016- 1&Seite=5&nr=74097&pos=157&anz=275&Blank=1.pdf%3E (last accessed on 31 December 2016) (Author's translation).
225. E. Barraclough, What Myriad means for biotech, WIPO Magazine, August 2013.
226. Opponents included Switzerland's Social Democratic Party; Greenpeace Germany; the French Institute Curie; Assistance Publique-Hôpitaux de Paris; the Belgian Society of Human Genetics; the Netherlands, represented by the Ministry of Health; and the Austrian Federal Ministry of Social Security.
227. Which covered a method for diagnosis.
228. http://www.epo.org/law-practice/case-law-appeals/pdf/t050080eu1.pdf.
229. T 1213/05 (Breast and ovarian cancer/University of Utah) of 27 September 2007, available at: http://www.epo.org/law-practice/case-law-appeals/recent/t051213eu1.html (last accessed on 9 March 2016).

An isolated nucleic acid which comprises a coding sequence for the human BRCA1 polypeptide, wherein said polypeptide

- has 1863 amino acids,
- has a molecular weight of 208 kilodaltons, and
- comprises the amino acid sequence of....................................

said coding sequence being comprised in a genomic DNA which is obtainable by:

(a) providing a human genomic library;
(b) screening the genomic library using a probe

selected from the group consisting of:

the following DNA sequence:.......................................

This method of assessment of the sequence against large genetic data sets was in fact to ensure accuracy of the results. Myriad did a complete sequence analysis of BRCA1 and BRCA2 requiring over 800 individual steps that are controlled by trained technicians with an interactive database and two to three weeks processing to complete each specimen submitted.[230] The methods of the patent in the suit were performed on a tissue sample of a human subject and related to a specific gene, namely the BRCA1 gene. The diagnostic methods make use of the knowledge of the open reading frame coding for the BRCA1 polypeptide, and identify frameshift mutations in the patient's sample.

It was argued by the opponents of the application that the methods of the patent in suit were based on the discovery of a mutation in the genome of a human, on the further discovery of a relationship that exists in nature between this mutation and a disease and on the purely mental act that a human having this mutation has a predisposition for the disease. The Board of Appeal referred to the relaxin case discussed above and noted that in accordance with the implementing Rule 23e(2) EPC 1973 (Rule 29(2) EPC) *an element isolated from the human body or otherwise produced by means of a technical process may constitute a patentable invention. This finding applies to claims relating to products, i.e. genes, and is a fortiori applicable to the method claims here at issue.*[231]

Thus the invention does not fall within the term discovery which is unpatentable. As to the diagnostic methods claim it involved a process of determination in a sample of a human subject in order to assess if there is a mutation. These features were considered as working steps of technical nature which preceded the steps for making a diagnosis per se which is an intellectual exercise. Hence it does not fall under excluded inventions such methods performing mental acts.[232] Thus the Myriad case in Europe, though not catching attention as its US counterpart, still offers significant implications both in resounding the relaxin approach of 'isolation' and also in recognizing that the methods developed by Myriad for the analysis of DNA using

230. Myriad Genetics, Inc. Press release.
231. T 0080/05 http://www.epo.org/law-practice/case-law-appeals/pdf/t050080eu1.pdf (last acce ssed on 9 March 2016).
232. Art. 52(2) (c) EPC.

genomic sample frame(like a genomic Library) would essentially be a 'technical process'.

[C] Patient Selection

Personalized healthcare as a new healthcare paradigm stresses on new methods of prediction and prevention as well as targeted medicines, more tailored to the particular genetic and physiological characteristics of each individual.[233] Though it seems to be not possible to give each individual a precise, individually tailored disease risk, it may be possible to stratify them into groups with different levels of risk. Such stratification might lead to screening targeted at the most 'at-risk' group.[234] In fact in the realm of PM, biomarkers evolve through a process of target identification or population selection, research based on the requirement of selection i.e., prognosis, risk progression or response to drug compositions and finally personalized therapy based on the population selection which was identified.[235] The Chronic myelogenous leukemia (CML) case study below is illustrative of this relationship.[236] Thus biomarkers may have a variety of prospects. Preventive biomarkers prospectively identify *individuals at increased risk* for developing disease. Diagnostic biomarkers identify the *presence of disease* at the earliest stage, before clinical manifestation. Prognostic biomarkers stratify risk of *disease progression* in patients undergoing definitive therapy. Predictive biomarkers identify patients most likely to *respond to specific interventions*. Therapeutic biomarkers provide a quantifiable measure of *response to therapy* in patients undergoing treatment.[237]

Case Study

CML, is a cancer of the white blood cells. It is a form of leukemia characterized by the increased and unregulated growth of predominantly myeloid cells in the bone marrow and the accumulation of these cells in the blood. In 1960, researchers identified an abnormally short chromosome in 95% of patients with CML. This genetic abnormality was found on chromosomes 9 and 22 and was named by the researchers the 'Philadelphia chromosome'. Understanding the phenomenon of this biomarker was seen as the key to curing CML. After another thirteen years of research, it was discovered that the Philadelphia chromosome is the result of two chromosomes swapping DNA. When these two chromosomes combine they create a cancer-causing gene known as BCR-ABL.

233. Medical profiling and online medicine: the ethics of 'personalised healthcare' in a consumer age Nuffield council of Bioethics 2006.
234. *Ibid.*
235. R.E. Hewitt, Biobanking: The foundation of personalized medicine, *Current Opinion in Oncology*. 2011; 23: 112, 119.
236. Available at: http://www.epo.org/learning-events/european-inventor/finalists/2009/zimmermann.html.
237. M. Herder, Patents & the progress of personalized medicine: Biomarkers research as lens, Annual Health Law 18 (2009): 187.

In such patients, this gene acts as the principle initial point in all of the physiological manifestations of the leukemia. For many years, the BCR-ABL was simply used as a biomarker to stratify a certain subtype of leukemia. However in 1994, Novartis set to refine and improve the inhibitor for clinical trials that began in 1999. Today, the compound now known as Glivec is being hailed as something of a wonder drug. Follow-up data show that Glivec therapy helped 98% of patients in chronic-phase CML stabilize their blood counts.

(*Courtesy EPO European Inventor of the Year 2009 in the category 'Industry': New Treatment for Chronic Myelogenous Leukaemia*)

Thus the ultimate goal of biomarker research (i.e., whether preventive diagnostic, prognostic) is to stratify patient populations and to understand how well they will respond to a particular course of drug therapy.[238] The EPC requires that an independent claim directed to medical use of a substance/composition which is based on the use of said product in the treatment of a different disease should be formulated as 'Product X for use in a method for treating Indication Y'.[239] While selection of a patient group on which the specific biomarker work the same formulation could be applied as 'Product X for use in a method for treating indication Y in patient with the biomarker Z'. While this seems uncomplicated, the new therapeutic applications on the same subject groups may pose some difficulties. For example diabetes in celiac patients, which means the claim, would be Product X for use in a method for treating indication diabetes in patient with the celiac biomarker 'While the use may be different the selection of patient groups may essentially be same. In T 0019/86,[240] the claim related to a vaccine (therapeutic application) to immunize offering protection against Aujeszky's disease in sero-positive piglets. There has been no new therapeutic application of the vaccine instead the known vaccine is being applied on a new class of pigs – sero-positive pigs – that are maternally immune. The question in the case was whether the application of the vaccine to this new class of pigs could be considered a new therapeutic application from which novelty for the claims can be derived. It was held by the Board of Appeal that '*a medical indication is incomplete if the subject to be treated is not identified; only a disclosure from which both the disease and the subject to be treated are clear represent a complete technical teaching.*'[241]

The therapeutic application of a vaccine, which is known for treatment of a particular class of animal (here sero-negative pigs), to a new and different class of the same animal (here sero-positive pigs), is a second medical use and was thus held patentable. So also classification of subjects into haemophilic and non-haemophilic for

238. *Supra* note 235.
239. Therapeutic uses pursuant to Art. 54(5), Examination Guidelines EPC, available at http://www.epo.org/law-practice/legal-texts/html/guidelines/e/g_vi_7_1_2.htm (last accessed on 22 December 2016).
240. (Pigs II) of 15 October 1987.
241. Paragraph 6. (Pigs II) of 15 October 1987.

claims related to a composition for use in the treatment of non-haemophilia mammals was held to be patentable.[242]

In T 233/96,[243] the claim was made to the use of adenosine as a pharmacological stressor in the preparation of a diagnostic agent to be given to '*a human who is unable to exercise adequately*'; the prior art revealed adenosine was already known to be used as a coronary vasodilator for patients with coronary artery disease. It was held by the Board of Appeal that if the use of a compound was known in the treatment or diagnosis of a disease of a particular group of subjects, the treatment or diagnosis of the same disease with the same compound could nevertheless represent a novel therapeutic or diagnostic application, provided that:

(a) it was carried out on a new group of subjects which was distinguished from the former by its physiological or pathological status (distinguishability);
(b) the group does not overlap with the group previously treated;
(c) the choice of the new group, if distinguishable from the known one, must not be arbitrary, which means that there must exist a functional relationship between the particular physiological or pathological status[244] of this new group and the therapeutic effect obtained. (functionality[245])

Thus the classification of humans who are unable to exercise adequately was held to be very vague overlapping as it embraces many of the situations in which a pharmacological stressor may be used, ranging from patients in an almost normal physiological condition, who might be only subjectively unable to exercise, to patients in a critical pathological condition, who are objectively incapable of exercise.[246] A different technical effect was also held to acceptable spite of an overlap in composition and disease treatment.[247] In the minutes of a meeting between EPI Biotech Committee

242. T 0893/90 – 3.3.2; The claim in the case related to a method of producing a pharmaceutical composition for controlling bleeding in non-hemophilic mammals characterized by forming a mixture of phospholipid vesicles and mammalian blood Factor Xa in a form suitable for administration, the phospholipid and Factor Xa being present in amounts and in proportions just sufficient to arrest bleeding, said mixture excluding other physiologically-active materials. The claims were opposed on the grounds that the same composition was also used in the treatment of haemophilia in mammals by the prior art.
243. T 0233/96 (Adrenaline/MEDCO RESEARCH) of 4 May 2000.
244. T 1399/04,the claim was 'pharmaceutical composition for treating patient having a HCV genotype type 1 infection and a viral load of greater than 2 million copies per ml of serum as measured by HCV-RNA quantitative PCR.'at least more than 50% overlapped with the patient group disclosed in the prior art.The patentee argued that the patient group according to present claims 1 to 3 is defined as being infected by a specific genotype of HCV, genotype 1,which is a pathological characteristic allowing to differentiate members of this group from all other HCV patients, and it is further defined by a viral load of greater than 2 million copies per ml of serum, which is a physiologically characterising feature. The boards of appeal, considered that the invention represents a new therapeutic application as the patient group concerned is distinguishable from the patient group by its physiological and pathological status.
245. Herein the peculiar feature identifying the new group of patients must have a real impact on the result of the treatment.
246. *Supra* note 243 Point 8.8 of Judgment.
247. T 836/01.

and EPO Directors[248] it was observed with regard to medical uses for subgroups of patients defined by a biomarker that:

> In the past such claims needed to contain an active diagnostic step in order to be considered novel. Based on more recent case law, the EPO has reviewed its internal harmonization notes. Claims in this area are now construed to implicitly include the selection (step) of patients as a limiting feature. For example, if a subgroup of patients to be treated is defined by allele X and the prior art does not disclose any test for that allele, the claim will be regarded as novel, even if the prior art discloses a large patient population which - albeit untested for - included patients with that allele.

However in an earlier meeting of the Biotech committee the observations were different. It was observed with regard to inventions in the area of pharmacogenomics:[249]

> cases which are based on a genetic marker to treat a disease, for example methylation profiles. It can involve a new patient group defined by an SNP. The EPO said that often the claims can lack novelty, as one patient will have inevitably been treated with the SNP, even if the art does not explicitly say so.

This shift from a stricter approach in the assessment of novelty of medical use claims that refer to treatment of a specific patient group, relates to a realization within the EPO on inventions within personalized healthcare initiatives. While patentability of an invention needs to be new, inventive and sufficiently disclosed, a selection patent is no different. Selection patents in biotechnology can cause difficulties, both in terms of their patentability and their enforceability.[250] The difficulties arise on account in defining the selection from the wider class and to substantiate the inventiveness of such selection. This also shifts the perspective towards claims involving presence or absence of specific biomarker. Thus use of Compound X in treating indication Y in patients with or without biomarker Z, the novelty of the invention rests on the compound X. However in the use of X in treatment of Y, where it is established that a biomarker Z appears in certain group of population, it will not be novelty defeating even if prior art consisted of a large patient population which including those with the biomarker Z(though not tested). However following the decisions discussed above it would be essential to demonstrate the therapeutic efficacy of the compound in the group so selected[251] or a new clinical situation.[252]

Downstream research within biobanks is based on population selection for specific study cohorts from a given population e.g., cardiovascular studies, neurological, or even health-oriented studies to assess the proximity to certain diseases. Building

248. Point 6 of Minutes of meeting of epi Biotech Committee with EPO Directors on 12 October 2015, available at: http://information.patentepi.com/1-16/meeting-epi-biotech-committee-epo/ (last accessed on 25 December 2016).
249. June 2012 issue of epi Information, June 2012 issue, available at: http://patentepi.com/en/epi-information/archived- issues.html (last accessed on 25 December 2016).
250. Question Q209, Selection Inventions – the Inventive Step Requirement, other Patentability Criteria and Scope of Protection, AIPPI.
251. *Supra* note 241.
252. T 1642/06.

population-based prospective patient cohorts within biobanks is extremely resource intensive.[253] The majority of the cost is incurred during patient identification, selection and obtaining informed consent. Participant selection for downstream investigator-initiated studies is based on study-specific eligibility.[254] Being such a cost consuming affair prospective study designs within biobanks must ensures that specimens are used in personalized healthcare research are clearly defined by incorporating the guidelines of distinguishability and functionality of therapeutic effect based on hypothesis sought to prove by such studies.[255]

[D] Dosage Regimes and Bio-repositories

Dosage regimes are an essential element of clinical cohorts within biobanks. The decision regarding drug administration, route, drug dose, dosing interval and treatment duration is called a dosage regime.[256] The question of assessment of dosage regimes often arise after the pharmaceutical product has been formulated and more information is known about the in vivo and pharmacokinetic properties of the medical agent is being assessed.[257] In some jurisdictions the dosage regime was not patentable because dosage inventions were considered to be simple medical methods whose protection may limit doctors' choices in clinical practice.[258] Also novel dosage inventions are considered to involve a process that does not enjoy the same scope of patent protection as new chemical entities despite their superior therapeutic potential.[259] In Europe earlier boards of appeal decisions have considered recognizing specific therapeutic uses as patentable in principle to be problematic where they differ from the prior art merely in terms of the dosage regime.[260] However the enlarged Board of Appeal in G 0002/08,[261] Where it is already known to use a medicament to treat an illness, Article 54(5) EPC does not exclude that this medicament be patented for use in a different treatment by therapy of the same illness. Such patenting is also not excluded where a dosage regime is the only feature claimed which is not comprised in the state of the art'.[262] This has currently given wider acceptance to the patenting of dosage regimes in Europe. However it is also essential herein to point out an observation made by the technical Board of Appeal in Kos Life Sciences:[263]

253. F. Karimi-Busheri, Biobanking in the 21st century, Springer International Publishing 2015.
254. *Ibid.*
255. Workshop to clarify the scope for stratification biomarkers and to identify bottlenecks in the discovery and the use of such biomarkers, European Commission, DG Research – Brussels, 10–11 June 2010.
256. Medical Dictionary.
257. S. Sorthose, Guide to EU pharmaceutical regulatory law. Sixth Edition, 2015.
258. E.D. Ventos, Patent protection for dosage regimes in Europe: A dissenting view. *Journal of Intellectual Property Law and Practice.* 2011; 6(4).
259. G 2/08.
260. *See* for instance T 584/97, T 317/95, T 56/97 and T 4/98.
261. Dosage regime/Abbott Respiratory, of 19 February 2010.
262. *Ibid.*, point 6.
263. T 1319/04 (OJ 2009, 36), Kos Life sciences was later renamed as Abbott Respiratory LLC, So the refeence here is to the Board of Appeal decision in the same case referred in *Supra* note 244.

> Considerations of public health, of medical confidentiality to preserve the physician/patient relationship, or of preserving the freedom of physicians to treat their patients in the best possible manner, have indeed at various times influenced the legislators in the Contracting States in considering whether it is allowable at all to patent pharmaceuticals let alone therapeutic methods. ... However these are considerations primarily for the legislator in laying down the law, and not primarily considerations for interpreting the law.

This concern raised by the technical board offers a guideline while discussing the issue of dosage studies. PM not only allows the possibility of finding new uses of a known drug, but also allows the correlation of drug dosage to specific patients with a particular genetic makeup. If a correlation can be made, then genetic testing may be used to reveal which patients are suitable to take the particular drug and at what dosage allowing for the elimination of unsuitable test subjects during clinical trials.[264] Pharmacogenomics thus promises advance individualized therapy, improving both drug safety and efficacy, in many medical disciplines.[265] Genome wide association studies are increasingly being applied to such pharmacogenomics studies giving great role for biobanks to play.[266] Also there is a growing emphasis on integrating electronic health records (EHRs) with pharmacogenomics studies which offers novel opportunities to bring functional genomics to the bedside in the area of pharmacotherapy.[267] e.g., The warfarin case study.[268]

Case Study: Warfarin

Warfarin is an anticoagulant normally used to prevent the formation of blood clots in the blood vessels and their migration elsewhere in the body. Warfarin was found to be effective and relatively safe for preventing thrombosis and thromboembolism in many disorders.

264. J.I-H Hsiao and W.-L. Wang, Dosage patenting in personalized medicine, *Boston College Intellectual Property & Technology Forum*. 2012.
265. D. Gurwitz and M. Pirmohammad, Pharmacogenomics: The importance of accurate phenotypes, *Pharmacogenomics*. 2010; 11(4): 469–470.
266. *Ibid.*
267. R.A. Wilke et al., The emerging role of electronic medical records in pharmacogenomics. *Nature: Clinical Pharmacology and Therapeutics*. March 2011; 89(3); A.H. Ramirez et al., Predicting warfarin dosage in European-Americans and African-Americans using DNA samples linked to an electronic health record. *Pharmacogenomics*. 2012; 13(4): 407–418. pgs.11.164; M.D. Ritchie et al., Robust replication of genotype-phenotype associations across multiple diseases in an electronic medical record. *The American Journal of Human Genetics*. 2010; 86(4): 560–572; D.M. Roden et al., Development of a large-scale de-identified DNA biobank to enable personalized medicine. *Clinical Pharmacology & Therapeutics*. 2008; 84(3): 362–369; S. Purcell et al., PLINK: A tool set for whole-genome association and population-based linkage analyses. *American Journal of Human Genetics*. 2007; 81(3): 559–575. C.A McCarty and R.A. Wilke. Biobanking and pharmacogenomics, pharmacogenomics. 2010; 11: 637–641; D. Chhieng et al., Use of natural language programming to extract medication from unstructured electronic medical records. AMIA Annual Symposium Proceedings. 2007; 908.
268. A.H. Ramirez et al., Predicting warfarin dosage in European-Americans and African-Americans using DNA samples linked to an electronic health record. *Pharmacogenomics*. 2012; 13(4): 407–418. pgs.11.164.

However its intake showed varying response in different categories of patients. In order to study the avoidance of dosing error researchers at the Vanderbilt University School of Medicine used Vanderbilt EHR-linked DNA repository, to identify European-Americans and African-Americans on stable warfarin therapy and evaluated the effect of fifteen pharmacogenetic variants on stable warfarin dose. The ideal starting dose of warfarin is influenced by age, gender, genes, indication for the drug, diet and other medications. It was found by the study that clinical and genetic information derived from studies in European ancestry populations reduced error in European-Americans more so than in African-Americans. The number of potential combinations of the genetic factors requires genome wide association studies using biorepositories as real-world resources for pharmacogenomic discovery and implementation of dosage regime suiting the patient.

The linking of health records enable large multi-institutional biobanks three main advantages namely, (i) retrospective assessment of previously known findings in a clinical practice-based setting, (ii) discovery of new associations in huge observational cohorts and (iii) providing real-time decision support.[269] It has been suggested that biobanks created with PM research in mind should, when possible, have access to donors' clinical data, including detailed disease- and drug-response phenotypes.[270] Pursuing such outcomes comes with challenges in Europe particularly given the possibilities of patentability over dosage regime. While the potential of such studies are invaluable, publicly funded biobanks must ensure that such dosing studies ensures medical confidentiality and are appropriately designed in consent requirements suited such studies.

269. R.A. Wilke et al., The emerging role of electronic medical records in pharmacogenomics. *Nature: Clinical Pharmacology and Therapeutics*. March 2011; 89(3).
270. *Ibid.*

Part III Genetic Databases, Data and Digitalization

CHAPTER 4

Regulating Human Genetic Databases in Europe

§4.01 INTRODUCTION

Regulation of genetic databases is considered essential to enable a standardization for researchers to enable sharing of data more effectively in an effort to enhance the understanding of various diseases.[1]

In this chapter an effort will be made to explore the concept of genetic data and databases from the perspective of commercial rights and IP paradigm. To this end this part deals with the Directive (96/9/EC) also commonly referred to as database directive. The subsequent chapters in this part will deal in copyright law in the context of genetic data and the commercial protection of data under the trade secret directive each of which will be separately examined. These chapters combined together will enable a legal and institutional understanding of 'genetic information' in its broad sense.

Profound changes in genetic research coupled with technological innovation have triggered data production.[2] It has been noted by the Commission that, Europe is the largest producer of scientific data in the world.[3] The surge towards digital transformation in Europe has strengthened a move towards advanced digital technologies within traditional sectors to seize opportunities within technologies such as the Internet, Big Data and artificial intelligence.[4] Digitalization provides biobanks with

1. J. Kaye, 'Regulating human genetic databases in Europe', in M. Häyry, R. Chadwick, V. Árnason and G. Árnason. 'The ethics and governance of human genetic databases: European perspectives', Cambridge Law, Medicine and Ethics. Cambridge University Press, 2007.
2. C. Auffray et al., Making sense of big data in health research: Towards an EU action plan. *Genome Medicine*. 2016; 8: 71. PMC. Web. 26 March 2017.
3. *See infra* note 6.
4. Digital Transformation in Europe: https://ec.europa.eu/growth/industry/policy/digital-transformation_en.

great opportunities to improve their performance, including: (1) better documentation of the life cycle, quality and scientific use of biosamples such as databases; (2) maintenance of appropriate use and access procedures (e.g., Cloud); and (3) better interoperability with other sources of donor related data (e.g., integration with medical records).[5] Nevertheless, there exists insufficient and fragmented infrastructure in place to deal with such data and to exploit 'Big Data' to its full potential.[6] By strengthening existing research infrastructure and improving data communication, it is hoped that scientific researchers would be able to achieve a great step in storing and sharing of data.[7] This process also calls for understanding the instrument of property that may protect such data including structures involved in its management.

This chapter shall deal with the concept of 'database' as is used in the database directive and its implications in the context of biobanks. This part will further look into the integration of information from wet data into digital databases with a view to understand the scope of protection over 'genetic information'.

§4.02 DATABASE RIGHTS IN EUROPE

'Big Data in health' encompasses high volume, high diversity biological, clinical, environmental and lifestyle information collected from single individuals to large cohorts, in relation to their health and wellness status, at one or several time points.[8] Biobanks serve as tools in the process of integrating medical, clinical and research information within a single unit to serve the ends of biomedical research. The accumulation of vast amounts of data from samples within biobanks and the possibility of linking such data to the donors of such samples have been concerns for biobanks in terms of privacy and security.[9] Adding to these concerns, it has become a 'real challenge' to make a strict distinction between physical and the information elements in respect to the HBMs. Socio-philosophical discourse addresses this challenge as *Informatization of the body*.[10] The collection of tissue and information consolidated into a database forms the essential tools that provide the raw materials for many aspects of modern genomic research.[11] But before going into the challenges of physical and information distinction of biobank databases, it is essential to understand what a database is under the database directive. The first part of this chapter examines three main points in relation to the database directive:

5. G. Jacobs et al., Biobanks in the era of digital medicine. *Clinical Pharmacology and Therapeutics*. 2017; 103(5): 761–762.
6. European Cloud Initiative, http://europa.eu/rapid/press-release_IP-16-1408_en.htm (last acce ssed on 14 July 2016).
7. *Ibid.*
8. *Supra* note 2.
9. D. Budimir et al., Ethical aspects of human biobanks: A systematic review. *Croatian Medical Journal*, 2011; 52(3): 262–279.
10. L.A. Bygrave, The body as data? Biobank regulation via the back door of data protection law. *Law, Innovation and Technology*. 2010; 2(1).
11. D. Chalmers and D. Nicol, Human genetic research databases and biobanks: Towards uniform terminology and Australian best practice, *Journal of Laboratory Medicine*. 2008; 15: 538.

(1) The definition of a database.
(2) Rights protected under the directive.
(3) The scope of protection extended by the directive over genetic databases.

An understanding of 'ownership' closely follows this examination over genetic databases. In particular to highlight the nature of rights over genetic databases. Such an examination is considered essential in the light of the concerns over increased privatizing of the (public) biobank domain.[12]

[A] Definition of a Database

A 'Database' is defined under the Directive (96/9/EC) as:

> a collection of independent works, data or other materials, which have been arranged in a systematic or methodical way, and have been made individually accessible by electronic or other means.[13]

Databases are of different types and varieties, some of them are protectable databases under the law, while others are not. A database may be protected under copyright law as a literary work or under the database right. At the international front, the Berne Convention[14] first recognized 'collections of literary or artistic works which by reason of the selection and arrangement of their contents constituted intellectual creations'. Thus, collections such as encyclopaedias and anthologies would be protected as such, without prejudice to the copyright in each of the works forming part of such collections.[15] Analogous to this Article 10(2) of the TRIPS Agreement[16] and Article 5 of the WCT (WIPO Copyright Treaty)[17] provide that 'copyright protection on compilations of data or other materials which by reason of the selection and arrangement' of their contents constitute an intellectual creation.[18] Thus under the copyright regime subsistence of a *creative element* in the selection and arrangement qualifies to be an 'intellectual creation'.[19] As can be noticed international instruments interchangeably use 'collection' and 'compilation' to refer to databases without clearly defining it. The use of 'in any form' and 'other form' used under TRIPS and WCT refers to both electronic as well as non-electronic databases while the Berne offers protection only for

12. E.S Dove and Y. Joly, The contested futures of biobanks and intellectual property. 2012; 11(1).
13. Article 1(2) of the Directive 96/9/EC.
14. Berne Convention for the Protection of Literary and Artistic Works, 1886.
15. Article 2(5) Berne Convention, 1886.
16. Trade Related Aspects of Intellectual Property Rights, 1996, The wordings of the provision are: '*Compilations of data or other material, whether in machine readable or other form, which by reason of the selection or arrangement of their contents constitute intellectual creations shall be protected as such. Such protection, which shall not extend to the data or material itself, shall be without prejudice to any copyright subsisting in the data or material itself.*'
17. WCT wording under the provision: '*Compilations of data or other material, in any form, which by reason of the selection or arrangement of their contents constitute intellectual creations, are protected as such. This protection does not extend to the data or the material itself and is without prejudice to any copyright subsisting in the data or material contained in the compilation.*'
18. TRIPS, 1996 and WCT WIPO Copyright Treaty, 20 December 1996.
19. *Infra* note 208.

the non-electronic databases.[20] Further, the scope of protection both under TRIPS and WCT shall not extend to the data or material itself. This implies that the copyright shall subsist only in the selection and arrangement, which involves the creative input. The 'originality' requirement under the copyright law offers to protect only those databases which constitute an intellectual creation by reason of the selection or arrangement of its contents. However absence of originality does not necessarily mean that such databases would be unprotected spite of investments being made to produce them. While internationally there is a dearth of regulation for protecting the investments over such non-original databases, in Europe such investments in databases are protected.[21] The Database Directive (96/9/EC) governs the rights over databases in Europe.[22] Historically the directive was intended to protect electronic database within Europe based on the principles relating to unfair competition.[23] The database directive offers two different forms of protection in database namely a) copyright and b) sui generis rights. The directive thus aims at harmonizing the treatment of database in terms of both their selection and arrangement and the investments that go into creating, verifying and presenting a database in European internal market. It aims to protect the freedom of natural and legal persons who provide database (online or otherwise) goods and services.[24] Modern technology makes it is much easier to copy the database so meticulously created by the marker of the database. Such database may however not suit the criterion of protection under copyright law. A sui generis system thus became the appropriate solution to protect the efforts that were put into creating such database. Under the recital to the directive the term 'database' has been given an extended connotation to include literary, artistic, musical or other collections of works or collections of other material such as texts, sound, images, numbers, facts and data.[25] Nevertheless, the scope of protection under the directive only covers collections of independent works, data or other materials which are systematically or methodically arranged and can be individually accessed and thus recording or an audiovisual, cinematographic, literary or musical work '*as such*' does not fall within the scope of this Directive.[26] While the recital gives an overview of the term, under Article 1(2) of the Directive to qualify as a database the data or materials:[27]

20. *Infra* note 23.
21. WIPO summary on existing legislation concerning intellectual property (IP) in non-original databases, 2002. Available at: http://www.wipo.int/copyright/en/activities/databases.html (last accessed on 7 November 2016).
22. Article 1(2), Directive 96/9/EC of the European Parliament and of the Council of 11 March 1996 on the legal protection of databases.
23. *See* point no. 5 COM(92) 24 final SYN393 (Traveaux Preparatory to the Directive), *see also* M.J. Davison, The legal protection of databases, Cambridge University Press online June 2009.
24. Recital 2, Directive 96/9/EC.
25. Recital 17, Directive 96/9/EC.
26. *Ibid.*
27. A. Beunen, Protection for databases: The European database directive and its effects in the Netherlands, France and the United Kingdom, Wolf Legal Publishers 2007, at pg 61.

(a) shall *be capable of separation* without losing their informative content;[28]
(b) *shall be organized according to specific criteria*, which means that only planned collections are covered;[29] and
(c) *shall be individually accessible by electronic or other means*.[30]

According to recital 21 of the Directive, 'it is not necessary for those materials to have been physically stored in an organised manner'. Thus, a collection of unorganized data fixed on a hard disk or other digital medium would qualify as a database if combined with database management software enabling retrieval of the data.[31] Further, not only an individual piece of information, but also a combination of pieces of information, can constitute 'independent material' within the meaning of Article 1(2) of Directive.[32] Thus the term 'database' as defined in Directive 96/9 offers a wide scope, unencumbered by considerations of a formal, technical or material nature.[33] While an attempt has been made in the directive to elaborate on database what is less clear is the definition of 'data' and 'other materials' as is referred to in the definition.[34] It has been argued that the term other 'materials' would mean subject matter that is neither work nor data, such as sound recordings, non-original photographs and other products protected by neighbouring rights.[35] Another interpretation deems that other materials' only includes non-copyright subject matter.[36] Thus the inclusion of matter under the term other materials is limitless so long as the item is fixed in a medium.[37]

28. Derclays in I.A Stamatoudi and P. Torremans. EU copyright law: A commentary, Edward Elgar Publishing, 2014 the author provides the example of a novel, it cannot be regarded as a database because if any of its chapters are separated the whole story will not be of any sense.
29. Paragraph 30 OPAP (Case C-444/02, *Fixtures Marketing Ltd v Organismos Prognostikon Agonon Podosfairou* (OP AP)[2004] ECR I-10365), It is not necessary for the systematic or methodical arrangement to be physically apparent, however the collection should be contained in a fixed base, of some sort, and include technical means such as electronic, electromagnetic or electro-optical processes, or other means, such as an index, a table of contents, or a particular plan or method of classification, to allow the retrieval of any independent material contained within it. *See also* C-203/02, *British Horseracing Board Ltd v William Hill Organisation Ltd* [2004] ECR I-10415 at para. 33, The nineteenth recital of the preamble to the directive, according to which the compilation of several recordings of musical performances on a CD does not represent a substantial enough investment to be eligible under the sui generis right, provides an additional argument in support of that interpretation.
30. *Supra* note 22 –the term database for the purpose of the Directive should mean not only independent data being stored within it but also which are individually retrievable or accessible by physical or electronic means. A collection of moving images together constituting a movie (film) is not a 'database'. Recital 17 expressly excludes 'a recording or an audiovisual, cinematographic, literary or musical work as such'. (P. Bernt Hugenholtz, The new database right: Early case law from Europe, available at www.ivir.nl/publicaties/download/fordham2001.pdf).
31. *See* P. Bernt Hugenholtz, *ibid.*, note 26.
32. *Fixtures Marketing*, C-444/02, EU:C:2004:697, para. 35, and also *Football Dataco and Others*, C-604/10, EU:C:2012:115, para. 26.
33. *See* C-490/14, also judgments in *Fixtures Marketing*, C-444/02, EU:C:2004:697, para. 20, and *Ryanair*, C- 30/14, EU:C:2015:10, para. 33.
34. *Infra* note 161.
35. *Supra* note 26.
36. Recitals 25–25, Directive 96/9/EC.
37. *Supra* note 25 para. 30 (OPAP).

This would imply that HBM could in fact be treated as falling within the term other materials.[38]

'Data' on the contrary has been considered as 'information' in the widest sense of the term.[39] The compliance to TRIPS was ensured through the accession of the word 'data' to the definition of database.[40] Derclays[41] classifies 'data' into two: (1) 'pure data' which has no understanding or meaning; and (2) 'intelligible data' (i.e., which is understandable as 'information'). This tends to question whether biobanks containing biological material could claim a protection of their physical collection as a database within the meaning of the directive. However the status of HBM is widely disputed.[42] Also it is still unclear as to the extent to which database and pure data interact (*see* discussion below on raw and wet data) Another point is that there could be subjective distinctions as to what is meant by 'pure' in different contexts.[43] For instance in the context of Genomic research, biomedical companies have always considered non profitable to deal in 'pure data' owing to such data being out freely in the public domain through the Public HGPs, thus sequencing data is often considered to be 'pure data'.[44] In OPAP,[45] the CJEU noted that the term database within the meaning of the directive, *is more specifically defined in terms of its function; the legal protection provided by the directive is intended to encourage the development of systems performing a function of 'storage' and 'processing' of information, according to the tenth and twelfth recitals.*[46] While the court sought to explain database without going into the definition of data, yet this could mean that data could be synonymous to information that has a functional utility from a subjective point of the person retrieving such data from the database.[47] The CJEU in this regard has noted that finding a principal use for the information may pose difficulties in fixing criterion for the assessment of the autonomous informative value of the materials making up a collection hence information value must be assessed from the point of each third party interested by the extracted material.[48] However there has been differences in viewpoints with regard to data discovered in nature According to some authors like Gaster[49] that data discovered in nature are not covered by the directive, but others[50] considers that the directive does not supply any grounds for such a view. It has also been opined that since data are man-made (or computer-generated)

38. *See* more in point 5 below in the discussion of physical database and raw data.
39. Explanatory memorandum, COM(92) 24 final, 13 May 1992.
40. V.H. Bouganim, The legal protection of databases from copyright to data right, 1999.
41. E. Derclaye, The legal protection of databases: A comparative analysis, Edward Elgar 2008 at p. 58.
42. *Infra* point 5 below.
43. N. Wilkof et al., Overlapping intellectual property rights, Oxford University Press 2012.
44. R. Razgaitis, Valuation and deal making of technology-based intellectual property: Principles, methods and tools, John Wiley & Sons 28 July 2009.
45. [2004] ECR I-10549; [2005] 1 C.M.L.R. 16.
46. Paragraphs 27 and 28 of Jugement.
47. *See* definition of data in Chapter 1.
48. *Freistaat Bayern v Verlag Esterbauer GmbH*, Case C-490/14 (2014) at paras 24–26.
49. J.-L. Gaster, Der Rechtsschutz von Datenbanken: Kommentar zur Richtlinie 96/9 EG;mit Erläuterungen zur Umsetzung in das deutsche und österreichische Recht, Köln-Berlin-Bonn-München: Heymanns Verlag 1999 cited in Beunen *infra* note 50 below.
50. A.C Beunen, Protection for databases: The European database directive and its effects in the Netherlands, France and the United Kingdom, Wolf Legal Publishers 2007.

representations, they do not include biological material belonging to nature. Further biological 'material' such as animals and human beings (living or dead), organs, biological samples from which genetic information can be derived cannot be called data though they can still be covered by the category of 'other materials'.[51] This proposition may not find grounds in the current scenario where labs have completed automated systems and Hamilton robotics that can retrieve dry data and wet data within a fraction of time. In this sense 'wet data' may also be viewed from a functional and an application sense. This offers the possibility that both data and samples may come within the purview of a database. This will be further examined scope of protection extended by the directive over genetic databases.

While the term 'data' as such is elusive from the directive, the CJEU had dealt with the nature of data from the point of its generation and exploitation.[52] This is deducible from discussion as to the scope of the rights offered by sui generis rights.

[B] Scope of Rights Protected under Sui Generis Rights

In respect of non-original databases the efforts that go into building such databases are offered protection. Article 7 of the Directive ensures protection qualitatively and/or quantitatively of any substantial investment in obtaining, verifying or presenting the contents of the database for the limited duration of the right. Further, the protection of databases under the directive shall be without prejudice to rights existing in respect of their contents.[53] The crux of the protection lies in the 'substantial investment' in either the obtaining, verification or presentation of the contents. Further such investment may be either qualitative and/or quantitative in nature which means the efforts may be quantified e.g., time or it could be an effort put into building a biobank which cannot be measured quantitatively such as energy or intellectual efforts.[54] Such 'substantial investment' can either be in the form of monetary funding or by efforts by human input or in the form of materials[55]

The aim of such protection being to prevent extraction and/or reutilisation of the *whole or of a substantial part*, evaluated qualitatively and/or quantitatively, of the contents of that database.[56]

The right to prohibit extraction and/or reutilization of all or a substantial part of the contents relates not only to the manufacture of a parasitical competing product but also to any user who, through his acts, causes significant detriment, evaluated qualitatively or quantitatively, to the investment.[57] Reorganization does not limit the application of sui generis rights for instance, taking out substantial parts of the contents of a database and reorganizing it into another database.[58]

51. *Ibid.*, at p. 65.
52. *British Horseracing Board Ltd v William Hill Organisation Ltd* (C-203/02) [2004] ECR I-10415.
53. Article 7(4), Directive 96/9/EC.
54. Recitals 39 and 40.
55. Recitals 7 and 40 of the directive.
56. Article 7(1), Directive 96/9/EC.
57. Recital 42 of preamble to the Directive 96/9/EC.
58. J. Pila and P. Torremans, European intellectual property law, OUP 2016.

The right provided for in Article 7 shall run for a period of fifteen years from the date of its completion.[59] However if there are any substantial change (evaluated qualitatively or quantitatively) to the contents of a database resulting in the accumulation of successive additions, deletions or alterations, would result in the database being considered to be a substantial new investment giving rise to an additional period of fifteen years from the date of new additions.[60] The most important discussion within the database directive is the consideration of 'substantial investment'. In other words what constitutes a substantial investment and whether any substantial investment in 'obtaining' data includes investments in the actual creation of such data.[61] This question was discussed by the CJEU in *British Horse Racing Board Ltd v William Hill Organisation Ltd.*[62]

[1] Standards for Assessment of Databases under the British Horseracing Case

British Horseracing Board (BHB) a governing authority for horseracing in the UK maintained a database containing, *inter alia*, extensive pre-race information. William Hill (WH), a leading bookmaker, repeatedly obtained information indirectly from BHB's and used it on its website. Those interested could use the site offered by WH to find out what horses were running in which races at which racecourses and what were the odds. The information taken by WH were limited and included the names of all the horses in the race, the date, time and/or name of the race and the name of the racecourse where the race will be held. BHB claimed that WH's use of the data infringed its database right contrary to the Database Directive 96/9/EC and Copyright and Rights in UK Databases Regulations 1997.[63] It was contented that each day's use by WH of racing data taken from them is an extraction or reutilization of a substantial part of the contents of the BHB database, contrary to Article 7(1) of the directive even if the individual extracts made by WH were not substantial. The UK high court held that the action of BHB and others was well founded. However, on appeal the court referred certain questions as to the interpretation of the directive to the CJEU. By its second and third questions, the referring court sought an interpretation of the concept of 'substantial investment' in the 'obtaining' and 'verification' of the contents of a database within the meaning of Article 7(1) of the directive. It was observed by the court that Article 7(1) of the directive reserves the protection of the sui generis right to databases which meet a specific criterion, namely to those which show that there has been qualitatively and/or quantitatively a substantial investment in the obtaining, verification or presentation of their contents. Referring to the ninth, tenth and twelfth recitals of the preamble to the directive, the court noted that, the '*purpose of the directive is to promote*

59. Article 10(1), Directive 96/9/EC.
60. Article 10(3), Directive 96/9/EC.
61. M.J. Davison, The legal protection of databases, Cambridge University Press, online June 2009 at p. 86. E. Derclaye, The legal protection of databases: A comparative analysis, Edward Elgar 2008 at pp. 100–102.
62. Case C-203/02.
63. The Copyright and Rights in Databases Regulations 1997 (S.I. 3032/1997).

and protect investment in data "storage" and "processing" systems which contribute to the development of an information market against a background of exponential growth in the amount of information generated and processed annually in all sectors of activity'.[64] Following this the court declared that the expression '*investment in … the obtaining, verification or presentation of the contents*' *of a database must be understood, generally, to refer to investment in the creation of that database as such … the resources used to seek out existing independent materials and collect them in the database, and not to the resources used for the creation as such of independent materials.*[65]

The purpose of the protection by the sui generis right provided for by the directive is to promote the establishment of storage and processing systems for existing information and not the creation of materials capable of being collected subsequently in a database.[66] The court also observed that the expression '*investment in … the … verification … of the contents*' of a database must be understood to refer to the resources used, with a view to *ensuring the reliability of the information contained in that database, to monitor the accuracy of the materials collected* when the database was created and during its operation. This meant that resources used for verification during the stage of creation of data or other materials which are subsequently collected in a database, are resources used in creating a database and cannot therefore be taken into account.[67] Following this the CJEU found that the resources deployed by BHB in the selection of the horses admitted to run in each race related to the creation of the data and not the database.[68] While the resources used to draw up a list of horses in a race and to carry out checks in that connection were essential to the database, yet it did not represent investment in the obtaining and verification of the contents of the database.

Following the British horse racing case, it is essential that the investment has to be in the obtaining, verification or presentation of the contents of the database. This is essentially different from the investment in the data in itself and it cannot be taken into account when considering whether the investment has been substantial.[69] This distinction is essentially based on an assumption of the work of creation and gathering essentially to be different. It has however been opined by J.Laddie that where in actual practice one person both creates the underlying data and gathers it together, as BHB does, it may be difficult to draw a sharp dividing line between the two activities'.[70]

The protection of sui generis rights provided for by Article 7(1) of the directive gives the maker of the database the right to prevent the unauthorized extraction and or reutilization of all or a substantial part of the contents of the database.[71] The same also

64. Paragraph 30, Case C-203/02.
65. Paragraph 31, Case C-203/02.
66. Case C-203/02 at paras 29–31.
67. Paragraph 34, *British Horseracing Board Ltd v William Hill Organisation Ltd* (C-203/02).
68. Paragraphs 38–41, *British Horseracing Board Ltd v William Hill Organisation Ltd* (C-203/02).
69. Paragraph 35 of *British Horce Racing v William Hill*, [2001] EWHC 517 (Patents).
70. Paragraphs 33 and 34 of *British Horce Racing v William Hill*, [2001] EWHC 517 (Patents).
71. Recital 41.

applies to repeated systematic use of insubstantial parts which unreasonably prejudices the interest of the database markers.[72] This provision is provided in line with the economic justification to offer protection to the maker of the database and to guarantee a return of investment employed in the creation and maintenance of the database.[73] It is essential to understand the meaning of the terms used under Article 7, to understand the scope of application of the directive.

[a] Extraction

The term '*extraction*' means the permanent or temporary transfer of all or a substantial part of the contents of a database to another medium by any means or in any form.[74] It thus covers not only the transfer to a data medium of the same type but also to one of another type. This may also include merely printing out data.[75] Furthermore, it has been opined by the advocate general that 'extraction' clearly cannot be construed as meaning that the extracted parts must then neither be in the database if the prohibition is to take effect; Nor, however, must 'extraction' be so widely construed as also to cover indirect transfer, rather direct transfer to another data medium is required.[76] They may not also imply a direct access to the database concerned, since extraction by a third party from a source other than the database concerned are liable, just as much as such acts carried out directly from that database prejudice the investment of the maker of the database.[77] In this sense, extraction may mean removal, duplication and copying of the contents of the database.[78] Examples of what includes within the purview of extraction can be exhaustive. It has been contemplated that extraction includes both removal and copying of the contents and thus broader than the concept of reproduction under copyright law.[79] The concept of 'reproduction' of works has been given an autonomous and uniform interpretation following the Infopaq case.[80] In *Infopaq International A/S v Danske Dagblades Forening,*[81] the CJEU, in preliminary ruling examined the concept of 'reproduction' under the law of copyright in finding that the use of extracts that are the results of a process of data capture undertaken by the media analysis company was not a temporary reproduction which was exempt under law.[82] Article 2 of the Information Society Directive provides that Member States shall provide for the exclusive right to authorize or prohibit direct or indirect, temporary or permanent reproduction by any

72. Article 7(5), Directive 96/9/EC.
73. Recital 48, Directive 96/9/EC.
74. Article 7(2)(a), Directive 96/9/EC.
75. Paragraphs 99–102, *British Horseracing Board Ltd v William Hill Organisation Ltd,* opinion of Advocate General, Stix- Hackl, delivered on 8 June 2004 (1).
76. *Ibid.,* para. 100 opinion of Advocate General Stix Hackl.
77. Paragraph 53 British Horse racing.
78. Derclays p. 104.
79. Citing Buydens (1998) in Derclays at pg 104.
80. Following the observations in *Football Association Premier League Ltd and Others v QC Leisure and Others* (C- 403/08) and *Karen Murphy v Media Protection Services Ltd* (C-429/08).
81. Case C-5/08.
82. Article 5 of Information Society Directive 2001/29/EC of the European Parliament and of the Council of 22 May 2001 on the harmonisation of certain aspects of copyright and related rights in the information society.

means and in any form, in whole or in part for the authors of their works. This exclusive right of 'reproduction' is subject to the exception under Article 5 of the Information Society Directive pertaining to certain acts of temporary reproduction.[83] In considering these provisions the CJEU in Infopaq case found that the protection conferred by Article 2 of Directive 2001/29 must be given a broad interpretation[84] to include reproduction of the original work including 'direct or indirect', 'temporary or permanent', 'by any means' and 'in any form' as used in the directive.[85] Accordingly, other provisions such as Article 2 and Article 5 of the Information Society Directive will apply to temporary or permanent extraction of electronic databases subject to copyright laws.[86] Though the act of '*reproduction*' under copyright law has been considered in the broadest sense of the tem, the essence of the right rests in some form of '*copying*' an original work.[87] On the contrary the term 'extraction' as per the dictionary meaning[88] would mean to draw forth, take or remove the contents of such databases. In this sense 'extraction' of a database can be viewed from two dimensions. One in the sense of an electronic database in which case extraction would mean the acts of removal and or copying of the electronic contents including temporary copies in the machine memory and in the other sense the physical removal of the contents and making copies of its contents. Nevertheless, Article 9 of the database directive offers certain exemptions for lawful user of databases, including extraction for private purposes in the context of non-electronic databases. While extraction may also involve 'removal' it however not mean that parts must then no longer be in the database if the prohibition is to take effect.[89]

[b] Reutilization

The term reutilization means any form of making available to the public all or a substantial part of the contents of a database by the distribution of copies, by renting, by online or other forms of transmission.[90] The term 'reutilization' may involve an act of extraction from the database before making it available to the public.[91] On the contrary it is possible that an act of reutilization may exist without an extraction[92] e.g., third party use of the database. In the context of text and data mining, when data analysis is made on the basis of data and information held by a database, such analysis

83. Recital 33 Information Society Directive and Art. 5, which are transient or incidental reproductions, forming an integral and an essential part of a technological process and carried out for the sole purpose of enabling either efficient transmission in a network between third parties by an intermediary, or a lawful use of a work.
84. Paragraphs 43–45 of Judgment in Inforpak case.
85. *Ibid.*
86. Recitals 57, 58 of Directive 96/9/EC.
87. *Interlego AG v Tyco Industries Inc* (1989)AC 217 AT 265.
88. Meriams Websters.
89. Paragraph 100, *British Horseracing Board Ltd v William Hill Organisation Ltd*, opinion of Advocate General, Stix-Hackl, delivered on 8 June 2004 (1).
90. Article 7(2), Directive 96/9/EC.
91. Case C-304/07 *Directmedia Publishing* [2008] ECR I-7565, para. 28.
92. Derclays at p.105.

will involve extraction of all or substantial parts of the content of the database but it does not normally amount to reutilization.[93]

The concept of extraction is considered to be more of private act, while reutilization implies a more public and commercial activity.[94] However, it has also been opined that the specific use of the term 'reutilization' instead of re-exploitation, is expressive of non-commercial private users too who may make available to the public. This is clearly visible in the exception clause under Article 9(a) and (b) which offer only the right of extraction for private use and educational use and not the right of reutilization. This means private, educational and scientific uses cannot transmit the extracted materials to others or make it available to public. The first sale of a copy of a database within the community by the right-holder or with his consent shall exhaust the right to control resale of that copy within the community; It has thus been interpreted that the sending by one person, by means of a web server located in Member State A, of data previously uploaded by that person from a database protected by the sui generis right under that directive to the computer of another person located in Member State B, at that person's request, for the purpose of storage in that computer's memory and display on its screen, constitutes an act of 'reutilization' of the data by the person sending it.[95] It has been observed that the principle of exhaustion does not allow the reproduction of data. It follows from forty-third recital of the preamble to the directive states that 'in the case of online transmission, the right to prohibit reutilization is not exhausted either as regards the database or as regards a material copy of the database or of part thereof made by the addressee of the transmission with the consent of the right-holder'.[96]

[c] Quantitative and Qualitative

The sui generis rights rests on two focal points: (1) quantitative or qualitative 'substantial investment'; and (2) quantitatively or qualitatively evaluated substantial 'extraction' or reutilization. However there is no definition of what is qualitative or quantitative. While the words are enhanced by the term 'substantial', it has also not been defined in the directive. The exploratory memorandum of the proposal for the directive considers that '*no fixed limits can be placed in this Directive as to the volume of materials which can be used*'.[97] Thus it is left to the database maker to demonstrate that the extraction or reutilization was to the detriment of her own database. It was observed in the British Horse racing case, that the reference to 'a *substantial* part' in the definition of the concepts of extraction and reutilization gives rise to a confusion given that, under Article 7(5) of the directive, extraction or reutilization may also concern an insubstantial part of a database. However, reference to the substantial nature of the

93. EU commission paper: Jean -paul Trialle et al., 'study on the legal framework of text and data mining', March 2014.
94. *Ibid.*
95. Case C-173/11 at para. 47.
96. Paragraphs 58–59, *British Horse Racing v William Hill.*
97. Proposal for a Council Directive on the legal protection of databases. COM(92) 24 final, 13 May 1992.

extracted or reutilized part does not concern the definition of those concepts as such but must be understood to refer to one of the conditions for the application of the sui generis right laid down by Article 7(1) of the directive.[98] Thus the assessment, in qualitative terms, of whether the part at issue is substantial, must, like the assessment in quantitative terms, refer to the investment in the creation of the database and the prejudice caused to that investment by the act of extracting or reutilizing that part.[99] Thus it may be understood that nature of the information, efforts involved in collection in relation to the investment made could be qualitative considerations, while the size and amount of information extracted or reutilized which causes a financial detriment to the making of the database can be a quantitative consideration.

[2] Changing Scope of Sui Generis Protection

The database directive prohibits extraction and/or reutilization not only of the whole of a database protected by the sui generis right but also of a *substantial part, evaluated qualitatively or quantitatively, of its contents.*[100] Further, repeated and systematic extraction and/or reutilization of *insubstantial parts of the contents* of the database implying acts which conflict with a normal exploitation of that database or which unreasonably prejudice the legitimate interests of the maker of the database are also prohibited. This implies that the database directive prevents the extraction /reutilization (whole, substantial or insubstantial) with reference to the actual 'content' of the database. However according to CJEU the forty-second recital of the preamble to the directive, that provision is intended to prevent a situation in which a user 'through his acts, causes significant detriment, evaluated qualitatively or quantitatively, to the investment'. It appears from that recital that the assessment, in qualitative terms, of whether the part at issue is substantial, must, like the assessment in quantitative terms, refer to the investment in the creation of the database and the prejudice caused to that investment by the act of extracting or reutilizing that part.[101] While this approach was followed in the CJEU in British Horse racing case, it left the question of what it meant by extraction and reutilization of the actual 'contents' of the database from the purview of assessment. Though this question was unanswered in the case by CJEU, it led to more complexities than it aimed to resolve.

In **Fixtures Marketing case,**[102] this tension was revealed when the court observed 'a *wide interpretation various aspects of the directive* demonstrate that the term database within the meaning thereof is more specifically defined in terms of its function'.[103] The 'extraction', 'reutilization' of contents must be understood broadly, as extending to any act, not authorized by the maker of the database protected by the sui generis right, of distribution to the public of the whole or a part of the contents of

98. Paragraph 50 *British Horse Racing v William Hill.*
99. Paragraph 69 *British Horse Racing v William Hill.*
100. Article 7(1).
101. Paragraph 69 British Horse racing.
102. C-444/02, *see supra* note 28.
103. Paragraph 27 OPAP.

the database.[104] The substantial extraction or reutilization of the contents would suggest the protection of the 'contents' in preventing such acts which are prohibited by the database directive. This challenge in understanding the scope of protection is visible from more recent cases in the area.

In *Directmedia Publishing GmbH v Albert-Ludwigs-Universität Freiburg*[105] an anthology based on a list of verse titles drawn up by Mr Knoop, which was in fact a collection of verses from 1720 to 1933. It was published under a project of the Albrecht-Ludwigs-Universität Freiburg. Directmedia marketed a CD-ROM, 1,000 poems everyone should have. Of the poems on that CD-ROM, 876 date from the period between 1720 and 1900, and these were also mentioned in the list of Mr Knoop. Directmedia used the list of verse titles drawn up by Mr Knoop as a guide to select the poems which were to appear on its 'CD-ROM'. Directmedia critically examined each poem selected by Mr Knoop and ultimately omitted to include in the marketed medium some poems that figured in that list whilst adding others. The referring court raised the question whether using the contents of a database in such circumstances constitutes an 'extraction' within the meaning of Article 7(2)(a) of Directive 96/9. The CJEU held that transfer of material from a protected database to another database following an on-screen consultation of the first database and an individual assessment of the material contained in that first database is capable of constituting an 'extraction', within the meaning of Article 7 of Directive 96/9.[106]

In Innoweb BV v Wegener ICT Media BV and Wegener Mediaventions BV,[107] a website (AutoTrack) of Wegener provided access to an online collection of car ads, together with a list, updated daily, of second hand cars. This website search engine enabled the user to carry out a targeted search for a vehicle on the basis of various criteria. 'Innoweb' another company provided a meta search engine dedicated to car sales called 'GasPedaal'. A 'meta search engine' uses search engines from other websites, transferring queries from its users to those other search engines. Being a meta search engine it is subject specific and is programmed in such a way that it is dedicated to specific subject matter. By means of the GasPedaal meta search engine it is possible to search through the AutoTrack collection on the basis of different criteria. This included not only the make, the model, the mileage, the year of manufacture, the price, but also other vehicle characteristics, such as the colour, the shape of the chassis, the type of carburant used, the number of doors and the transmission in real time. On the view that Innoweb compromises its sui generis right in relation to its database, Wegener brought an action claiming that Innoweb should be ordered to desist from infringing Wegener's database rights. While there was some success at the first instance, the Court of Appeal was doubtful that the Wegener's collection of advertisements was a database and if there was a substantial extraction and reutilization of the database. Hence the matter was referred to the CJEU to assess if the activity of a meta search engine amounted to 'extraction or reutilization of whole or a substantial part of

104. *Football Dataco Ltd v Sportradar GmbH*, Case C-173/11 para. 20.
105. Case C-304/07.
106. Paragraphs 56–60.
107. Case C-202/12, [2013] ECJ.

the contents of a database covered by its service'. It was held that although the meta search engine was not the manufacture of a competing product, yet it had the effect of providing the end user with a form of access to that database and to that information which is different from the access route intended by the database maker. Hence a dedicated meta search engine that regularly crawls through a sui generis protected database reutilizes the whole or a substantial part of that database.[108]

Both Direct Media[109] and Innoweb[110] (discussed above) clearly offer a wider interpretation of the scope of protection. While the protection under Article 7 of Directive 96/9 does not cover consultation of a database.[111] Thus if the database maker makes the contents of that database accessible to third parties, even if he does so for a consideration, his sui generis right does not enable him to prevent such third parties from consulting that database for information purposes.[112] However, the above-mentioned cases reveal that if such consultation amounts to 'extraction' or 'reutilization' of the contents then such acts can be prevented by the database maker.

The 'information value' of such database seeks an empirical assessment of the given data collection. Thus extracting and recopying a poem into another database was considered to be acts that were detrimental to the value of the database. The effect of these changing scenarios as it unfolds through these case laws is that the scope of protection of sui generis rights also seems to encompass the protection of 'data' involved within such collection.

As is apparent from Recital 38 to Directive 96/9, the increasing use of digital recording technology exposes the database maker to the risk that the contents of his database may be copied and rearranged electronically, without his authorization, to produce a database of identical content, which however, does not infringe any copyright in the arrangement of his database. This admittedly resounds that sui generis rights protects the 'data' contained within such collection are also protected by the directive.

[3] Concept of Autonomous Informative Value and Legal Protection for Databases in Any Form

Article 1 of the database directive offers the legal protection of databases in any form. The CJEU has been expanding the notion of database under Directive 96/9 with the aim of further protecting investments in EU's information market. In *Freistaat Bayern case*, topographical maps were given protection under the database directive. This case is interesting to the present context as it demonstrates that an individual element or data contained in a map may be subject to the database rights.

108. Paragraphs 46–49; *See also* P. Hugenholtz, Something completely different: Europe's sui generis database right (book chapter) chapter 9, pp. 205–222, 2016, (In: The Internet and the Emerging Importance of New Forms of Intellectual Property, S. Frankel and D. Gervais (eds), Information Law Series, Vol. 37, Kluwer Law International 2016.).
109. *Supra* note 91.
110. *Supra* note 93.
111. *see* The British Horseracing Board and Others, para. 54, and Directmedia Publishing, para. 51.
112. Paragraph 46 Case C-202/12 (Innoweb).

In *Freistaat Bayern v Verlag Esterbauer GmbH*[113] a reference for preliminary ruling was made before the CJEU. The context of a dispute was between the land of Bavaria, the official makers of the topographical map and the publishing house Esterbauer who were alleged to have extracted and utilized the original map. It was alleged that Esterbauer made use of the topographic maps and the underlying data and extracted information from it (e.g., the location and type of a building). They produced new maps with this information and highlighted bike trails, primarily aimed at bikers and hikers. The application by land of Bavaria was upheld by the Court of First Instance. Esterbauer appealed against the decision before the higher regional court which set aside the judgment in part. On an appeal before the Bundesgerichtshof (Federal Court of Justice), doubts were raised on the ability of a topographic map to be a database and hence the proceedings were stayed and questions were referred to the CJEU for a preliminary ruling. The appeal expressed doubts on the scope of Article 1 of the Database Directive, which provided that the directive concerns the legal protection of databases in *any form*, and the term 'database' shall mean a collection of *independent works*, *data* or *other materials* arranged in a systematic or methodical way and individually accessible by electronic or other means.[114]

The question referred to the court was: whether Article 1(2) of Directive 96/9 must be interpreted as meaning that geographical data extracted from a topographic map in order that a third party may produce and market another map, retain, after extraction, sufficient informative value to be held to be 'independent materials' of a 'database' within the meaning of that provision.[115] In other words, the court had to consider whether the information on topographical map would constitute 'independent information' for the purposes of the directive.

It was argued by Verlag Esterbauer that the topographic map was made up of two pieces of information namely, the 'geographical coordinates point', that is to say, the numbered code corresponding to a certain coordinates point of the two-dimensional grid network and, on the other, the 'signature', that is to say, the numbered code used by the map producer to designate a unique feature, such as a church. Once this has been extracted, the information value is practically reduced to zero. However, the court based on settled case law on the point in affirmed that not only an individual piece of information, but also a combination of pieces of information can constitute 'independent material' within the meaning of Article 1(2) of Directive 96/9.[116] Therefore, topographic maps, such as the one at issue in the main proceedings, serve as basic products, which are then used to make sub-products through selective extraction of material from those maps. For instance, Verlag Esterbauer used scanning techniques to extract geographical information about tracks appropriate for cyclists, mountain bikers and inline skaters from the Land of Bavaria's topographic maps. Thus a greater combination of information, such as the geographical information about tracks appropriate for cyclists, mountain bikers and inline skaters, can be 'independent material'

113. Case C-490/14.
114. Article 1(2) Directive 96/9 EC.
115. Paragraph 11 of the Judgment.
116. Paragraphs 19–20 of the Judgment in Case C-490/14.

within the meaning of that provision, provided however that the extraction of that information from the topographic map concerned does not affect the value of their informative content. The court observed that value of material from a collection will tend to increase by being arranged in it and it's extraction from that collection will tend to result in a corresponding decline in value but will not affect its classification as an 'independent material' within the meaning of Article 1(2) of Directive 96/9. Thus a decline in the informative value of material linked to its being extracted from the collection of which it forms a part does not necessarily rule out the possibility that that material may come within the definition of 'independent materials' within the meaning of Article 1(2) of Directive 96/9, provided that that material retains autonomous informative value.[117]

Further the court noted that, *the autonomous informative value of material which has been extracted from a collection must be assessed in the light of the value of the information not for a typical user of the collection concerned, but for each third party interested by the extracted material.*[118] This assessment followed the difficulty in determining the principle intended user of such collection.[119] On this basis, it was held that Article 1(2) of Directive 96/9/EC on the legal protection of databases must be interpreted as meaning that geographical information extracted from a topographic map by a third party so that that information may be used to produce and market another map, retains, following its extraction, sufficient informative value to be classified as 'independent materials' of a 'database' within the meaning of that provision.[120]

The assessment of 'autonomous informative value' in this case essentially amounted to an assessment of the content of the database, which in the present case constituted the topographical data. It can be thus, assumed that if 'autonomous informative value' is deducible from the content of such database there may not be a need to emphasize the 'individual accessibility'.[121]

[4] Protection of Contents Through Protection of Investment

The broadening approach to the protection of database requires an understanding of the relationship between a database and its contents. This will also enable an understanding of how Big Data could be standardized in the context of biobanks. Article 7(1) of the Directive 96/9 aims to protect the substantial investment in the

117. Paragraphs 23–24, Case C-490/14.
118. Paragraph 27 of Judgment in Case C-490/14.
119. Paragraph 26 of Judgment, in Case C-490/14 it was also observed that the difficulties involved in determining a principal intended use or typical user of a collection..., the application of such a criterion for the assessment of the autonomous informative value of the materials making up a collection would run counter to the intention of the EU legislature to give broad scope to the definition of the term 'database'.
120. Paragraph 30, Case C-490/14.
121. Discussions in the IP fraternity seems to consider this being ignored by the ECJ: http://ipkitten.blogspot.dk/2015/11/c-49014-verlag-esterbauer-get-off-my-map.html.

obtaining, verification or presentation of the contents of the database and this object is fulfilled by preventing 'extraction' or 'reutilization' of the contents.

The history of the directive also reveals some of these tensions starting from the formulation of the proposal for the directive.[122] The preliminary proposal for the directive offered limited protection to the contents of the database where such contents are not protected by copyright. This proposal, was aimed at regulating the parasitic behaviour of competitors and to create a climate in which investment in data processing can be stimulated and protected against misappropriation.[123]

While no exclusive right were considered with respect to the information for the creator of the database, if the creator of such database was the sole source of such information, then there were possibilities to license akin to copyright.[124] Again in the amended proposal[125] forwarded by the commission the right of the owner to prevent extraction or reutilization of the database did not apply to the contents of a database where they are works already protected by copyright or neighbouring rights.[126] In the common position document adopted by the council, it was held that the council '*sees no valid reason for the sui generis right not to apply to the contents of a database consisting of works already protected by copyright or of objects protected by other rights; this could lead to anomalies where a database consisted, for example, partly of works protected by copyright and partly of other material protected by no other right.*[127] The Council has therefore provided for the sui generis right to apply irrespective of the eligibility of the contents of the database for protection by copyright or by other rights. The common position thus specified that, '*protection under the sui generis right is without prejudice to copyright or to other rights existing in respect of works or other material forming part of the contents of the database*'.[128]

However as seen from a number of examples the protection offered by the directive for the substantial investment in obtaining, verifying and presenting is integrated with the contents included in such database.[129] The proposal for the directive on the contrary observed that, if the contents of a database are already protected by copyright or neighbouring rights, no cumulation can occur since the right to prevent unfair extraction cannot apply.[130] In these circumstances the proposal considers that the normal idea/expression dichotomy doctrine should apply, such that, the ideas contained in the works incorporated into a database remain accessible whereas the expression of these ideas is protected under copyright. This does not apply

122. Proposal for a Council Directive on the legal protection of databases, OJ No C 156, 23. 6. 1992.
123. Point 3.2.8 of Proposal for a Council Directive on the legal protection of databases, OJ No C 156, 23. 6. 1992.
124. *Ibid.*
125. Amended proposal for a Council Directive on the legal protection of databases. COM(93) 464 final, 4 October 1993.
126. Article 10(2), Amended proposal for a Council Directive on the legal protection of databases. COM(93) 464 final, 4 October 1993, at p. 25.
127. Common Position (EC) No. 20/95 adopted by the Council on 10 July 1995 with a view to adopting Directive 95/ /EC of the European Parliament and of the Council of ... on the legal protection of databases.
128. *Ibid.*, at p. 27.
129. *Supra* note 41 at p. 100.
130. *Supra* note 122.

where the works, which form the contents of the database, are themselves databases containing unprotected works or materials. Thus where the database forms the sole source of the data (i.e., where no copyright subsists in the content or the content is not a matter of copyright) then it could seek protection of its contents from extraction or re utilization under the sui generis rights.[131] On the contrary, compilations involving copyrighted elements would solely be protected based on the nature of 'substantial investment' in such database, while the content would be protected based on the copyright involved in them.[132]

[5] Non-electronic Database, Physical and Material Objects

The European Council adopted the database directive after it passed through several phases. In its first proposal[133] and the amended version,[134] the definition of 'database' was restricted to electronic databases. Thus 'database' was defined as,

> a collection of works or materials arranged, stored and accessed by electronic means, and the electronic materials necessary for the operation of the database such as its thesaurus, index or system for obtaining or presenting information; it shall not apply to any computer programme used in the making or operation of the database.[135]

While electronic databases were subject to protection as per the proposal, the non-electronic databases were protected Article 2(5) of the Berne Convention[136] i.e., protection only for the selection and arrangement. However, when the directive was finalized it offered protection to databases in 'any form'. Also the definition of 'databases' included independent works, data or other materials arranged in a systematic or methodical way and individually accessible by *electronic or other means.*[137] The extension of the scope of the directive to non-electronic or paper databases was considered based on the TRIPS obligation, piracy and the commissions' own efforts in avoiding a divergent approached towards electronic and non-electronic databases.[138] Article 10(2) of TRIPS[139] requires that compilations, machine readable or otherwise

131. *Ibid.*, p. 43 point 2.5 of proposal.
132. *Supra* note 122 at point 2.5.
133. *Supra* note 122.
134. *Supra* note 125.
135. *Supra* notes 133, 134.
136. Article 2(5) of the Berne Convention, collections of literary or artistic works such as encyclopaedias and anthologies which, by reason of the selection and arrangement of their contents, constitute intellectual creations shall be protected as such, without prejudice to the copyright in each of the works forming part of such collections.
137. Article 1(2) of Directive 96/9 EC.
138. M. Powell, The European union's database directive: An international antidote to the side effects of feist?, 20 *Fordham International Law Journal*. 1996; 1215. Available at: http://ir.lawnet.fordham.edu/ilj/vol20/iss4/6.
139. Article 10(2). Compilations of data or other material, whether in machine readable or other form, which by reason of the selection or arrangement of their contents constitute intellectual creations shall be protected as such. Such protection, which shall not extend to the data or material itself, shall be without prejudice to any copyright subsisting in the data or material itself.

had to be offered protection based on the selection and arrangement. This paved way for equal treatment of electronic and non-electronic databases both under copyright over database and over sui generis rights. Recital 17 of the Directive considers a database to include literary, artistic, musical or other collections of works or collections of other material such as texts, sound, images, numbers, facts and data. Further materials necessary for the operation or consultation of certain databases such as thesaurus and indexation systems are also included within the directive. While the recognition of non-electronic databases is pretty much clear in the directive and the travaux prėparatoires, there have been doubts regarding the protection of physical objects. The directive defines 'database' as 'a collection of independent works, data or other materials'.[140] The other conditions are, a 'systemic arrangement' and 'individual accessibility'. Apart from this the recitals 17, 23 of the directive also considers the elements constituting the database including exclusion of computer program. Nevertheless, none of them apparently exclude physical objects from its purview. Hugenholtz points out that the explanatory memorandum describes the contents of the database as '"information" in the widest sense of that term', making it clear that the notion of database does not encompass collections of physical objects, such as stamps, books or butterflies.[141] The explanatory memorandum of the proposal for the directive also contained a rather ambiguous sentence that the term database '*is not intended to include three-dimensional objects or the mere stockage of quantities of works or materials in electronic form*'.[142] Based on this many writers[143] have suggested an exclusion of physical objects within the purview of the directive. However it should not be overlooked that the initial proposal did not involve non-electronic database and hence the reference to 'three-dimensional objects', 'stockage of works' and 'materials' ought to be treated *ejusdem generis*[144] with the word 'electronic form'. Further no other preparatory documents post the initial proposal consider physical objects in three dimensions.

Another argument is that a database cannot be a collection of mere physical objects; instead, it must be a collection of data.[145] This argument stems from the aims of the directive in boosting the database industry in the information society. Recital 9 of the directive provides that the database as an industry is useful not only to the information society but also in other fields as well which uses data and databases in

140. Article 1(2) of the Directive 96/9 EC.
141. Hugenholtz, P. Something Completely Different: Europe's Sui Generis Database Right (Book Chapter)Chapter 9, pp. 205–222, 2016, (In: The Internet and the Emerging Importance of New Forms of Intellectual Property, S. Frankel and D. Gervais (eds), Information Law Series, Vol. 37, Kluwer Law International 2016).
142. Paragraph 1.1 p. 41: proposal for a Council Directive on the legal protection of databases. COM(92) 24 final, 13 May 1992.
143. Derclays at p. 59; Hugenholtz and Robin Elizabeth (R.E. Herr, Is the sui generis right a failed experiment?, DJØF Publishing 2008) consider this possibility, however other researchers like Bygrave, Lee A., The Data Difficulty in Database Protection (20 June 2012). University of Oslo Faculty of Law Research Paper No. 2012–18.) considers that it would still be possible to protect three-dimensional objects.
144. The rule of construction that, when particular words used in an instrument or statutes are followed by general words, the latter should be interpreted as being limited to the same.
145. Derclays at p. 59.

multiple ways.[146] This may well be the reason for broadening the approach towards including databases in any form in the common position and in the directive distinct from the initial proposal. The question however remains as to how distinct are physical objects in forming a database?

Information represents a state of awareness (consciousness) and the physical manifestations they form.[147] Information is thus, data that has been processed into a form that is meaningful to the recipient (*See* discussion as to raw data below). Envisioning 'data' alone to constitute a database as perceived in the proposal for the directive, would imply only meaningful data or information under its purview. This would be rather misleading to exclude 'physical objects' merely on the grounds of having no information value. There is at least a strong analytical philosophy from the twentieth century that 'sense-data' are facts of perception. According to sense-data theorists,[148] one perceives an external object, one infers, and on the basis of the sense-data one directly apprehends and in this way physical object contributes to empirical knowledge. Moore points out that these facts, while also preserving some widely held beliefs that are thought to constitute knowledge.[149] He gives the example of coins. The fact that the coins really are round; that they have an inside and a lower side, even though these are not presently seen; that the quarter is really larger than the penny; and that the coins exist when we are not looking at them. Though this philosophy has been subject to criticism, it has been the foundation for subsequent approaches in the twenty-first century mainly theories of perception and spatial perception.[150] Although a collection with three-dimensional material may in principle qualify as a database, it has been argued that it still needs to satisfy the three requirements in the definition of database particularly the requirement of a systematic or methodical arrangement, which is not always met in respect of collections of three-dimensional material.[151] Corollary to this it has also been contemplated that a collection to qualify as a database, it must be fixed on a solid medium of some sort.[152]

Such an arguments has some footing from Recital 13 which states that the 'Directive protects collections, sometimes called "compilations", of works, data or other materials which are arranged, stored and accessed by means which include electronic, electromagnetic or electro-optical processes or analogous processes'. Further Recital 21 of the directive while requiring a systematic arrangement also considers that it is not necessary for those materials to have been physically stored in an

---

146. Recital 9, Directive 96/9, EC: Whereas databases are a vital tool in the development of an information market within the community; whereas this tool will also be of use in many other fields.
147. A. Debons et al., Information science: An integrated view, G.K. Hall 1988. *See* C. Zins, Conceptual approaches for defining data, information, and knowledge. *Journal of the American society for information science and technology*. 2007; 58(4): 479–493.
148. Analytic philosophy arose in the early decades of the twentieth century, with Bertrand Russell and G.E. Moore leading the way. *See* G. Hatfield, 'Perception and sense-data', in M. Beaney (First Ed.) 'The oxford handbook of the history of analytic philosophy, 2013.
149. G.E. Moor, Some judgments of perception, *Proceedings of the Aristotelian Society*. 1918–1919; 19: 1–29.
150. *Ibid.*, at p. 132.
151. *Supra* note 50 at p. 63.
152. J. Axhamn, Databasskydd, PhD thesis Stockholms universitet 2016.

organized manner. In OPAP[153] this point was considered and the CJEU observed that '*Classification of a collection as a database requires that the independent materials making up that collection be systematically or methodically arranged and individually accessible in one way or another. While it is not necessary for the systematic or methodical arrangement to be physically apparent, according to the 21st recital; that condition implies that the collection should be contained in a fixed base, of some sort, and include technical means such as electronic, electromagnetic or electro-optical processes, in the terms of the 13th recital of the preamble to the directive, or other means, such as an index, a table of contents, or a particular plan or method of classification, to allow the retrieval of any independent material contained within it.*' This means that independent data or materials must essentially be structured (even though not in an organized manner) following a plan or classification or electronic methods which could enable the retrieval of the data or material, constituting the collection.[154] Besides the CJEU in OPAP also considered that not only an individual piece of information, but also a combination of pieces of information can constitute 'independent material' within the meaning of Article 1(2) of Directive 96/9.[155] Thus, for instance the compilation of dates, times and names of teams relating to the various fixtures in a football league can be considered to be an independent material.[156] Similarly, as seen in *Freistaat Bayern v Verlag Esterbauer GmbH*[157], two pieces of information consisting of the geographical coordinate points (the numbered code) corresponding to a certain coordinate point of the two-dimensional grid network and the numbered code used by the map producer to designate a unique feature on the map, could be joined together.[158] This clearly implies that in structuring a database of physical objects it may be essential to have a plan or methodical arrangement even though they are not placed or stored in a similar fashion. The arrangement of physical objects could thus, be supported by information or other data pertaining to the physical object and could be bound in a catalogue in a physical medium or an electronic medium. To illustrate this we may consider some examples:

(a) X arranges stones she collected from a river based on their shape and colour on her shelf.
(b) X arranges stones[159] she collected from different sources and arranges them on shelf based on information pertaining to each of them (such as origin, period, nature, texture, colour, size, weight, etc.) she also writes a numbered list corresponding to each one of them for the ease of reference.

153. *Supra* note 32.
154. Paragraph 53 of the judgment.
155. Paragraph 35 OPAP.
156. *Ibid.*
157. Case C-490/14.
158. Case C-490/14 *Freistaat Bayern v Verlag Esterbauer GmbH.*
159. For example Building Stones Database, available at: http://www.bgs.ac.uk/mineralsUK/buildingStones/resources.html.

In the two above-mentioned scenarios one can clearly distinguish how a physical object (which is 'stone' in both the cases), is converted into 'information' arranged in systematic way creating autonomous value for the content. In the first example there is a rather loose arrangement of the physical object which though independent material, neither qualifies the criterion of systematic arrangement nor individual accessibility because if one takes up the stones for examination it may tend to shift places than originally placed owing to lack of an order. On the contrary the second example of the same physical object is efficiently displayed into systemic information content which may be individually accessible. The numbering attached to the stones are such that even if they are arranged randomly there is an essential reference point to its arrangement, which also ensures traceability. Nevertheless, if the collection B has to secure protection under the database directive, the 'substantial investment' in obtaining, verifying or presenting the contents must be proved among others. The discussion on physical objects translates into an interesting discourse in context by examining the concept of 'raw data' which will be discussed in the next section.

[C] Genetic Databases Raw Data and Biological Data

While the definition of database under the directive is broad enough to include 'works', 'data' and 'other materials', yet it suffers from definitional clarity as discussed elsewhere in this book. These often create hurdles in assessing the nature and scope of the database. In furthering the enquiry the question that will be explored herein is, considering that physical object may be protected under the database directive, would that be any different when the data is obtained from nature?. Such an enquiry also enables one understand the nature of rights that emerge in structuring such data into a database.

Raw data[160] has been defined as data which has not been analysed including values of the variables as they were recorded.[161] In science such data is defined as data that are collected during a research study and recorded or measured using an apparatus.[162] Raw data in scientific studies thus take on two forms depending on the study namely *observational data* and *measurement data.*[163] Raw data are considered important because these data have not been interpreted except perhaps at the most basic level of the observer making an observation or measurer taking a measurement.[164] However, raw data helps the scientific community to extract valid information from such data. There are three major arguments in relation to sui generis rights

160. Raw data is also sometimes referred to as primary data and pure data in certain context. e.g., Algorithmic information, biological materials, space data.
161. J. Nicholson, Raw data. The concise Oxford dictionary of mathematics, 2014.
162. F.G. von der Dunk and M.M.T.A. Brus, The international space station commercial utilisation from a European legal perspective, Brill – Nijhoff; 1st Edition, 2006, at p. 100.
163. D.J. Mazur, Full disclosure of the 'raw data' of research on humans: Citizens' rights, product manufacturers' obligations and the quality of the scientific database, philosophy compass, Blackwell Publishing Ltd 2011.
164. *Ibid.*

(following the discussion of the definition of database under §4.02[A] above) with regard to 'raw data' containing database which will be discussed herein.

[1] Discovered in Nature

It has been argued that data discovered in nature are as such not protected under the database directive.[165] A prominent reason for such an argument to arise is the changing concept of data itself. The twenty-first century scientific research particularly in the context of molecular biology witnesses a high interoperability of wet biology with computer technology. The process and progress of scientific research have resulted in a 'data mirage' whereby it has become difficult to separate material data (wet data) from other data (dry data) secured through technical means. Against this background it had been considered difficult to consider the 'information status' of materials obtained from nature such as biological materials.[166]

Recital 46 of the Directive which considers that 'the right to prevent unauthorized extraction and/or reutilization of the whole or a substantial part of works, data or materials from a database should not give rise to the creation of a new right in the works, data or materials themselves'. Notwithstanding, it is clear from the history of the directive that the database may contain 'data' protected by copyright as well as those without a copyright protection. Bovenberg considers that 'it would be at odds with the text and objectives of the directive to suggest (whether or not based on Recital 46) that collection of data 'discovered in nature' could not amount to a protected database'.[167] On the contrary Visser[168] suggests that raw data falls from tree-like ripe apples giving it no protection. However as per other observers even if data may not exist in the state of nature it may still serve as a data medium hence, data may have an embodiment with significant natural elements.[169] This in many ways follows the sense-value theorist in assessing the value of data obtained from nature. Further, such data may involve specific functional criteria for assessment based on the study for which such data is being collected. Thus, raw data can be regarded as information being processed by some technical process in response to a specific set of criteria or purpose, which will be put to use in such purpose.[170] For example biological sample of obese human male aged below 30. Supposing the aim of using the raw data may be to

165. J.-L. Gaster, Der Rechtsschutz von Datenbanken: Kommentar zur Richtlinie 96/9 EG;mit Erläuterungen zur Umsetzung in das deutsche und österreichische Recht, Köln-Berlin-Bonn-München: Heymanns Verlag 1999. As cited in F.G. von der Dunk et.al *see* note 145 above at pg 101.
166. National Research Council (US) Committee on Frontiers at the Interface of Computing and Biology; J.C. Wooley and H.S. Lin (eds). Catalyzing inquiry at the interface of computing and biology, National Academies Press 2005. 3, On the Nature of Biological Data.
167. J.A. Bovernberg, Should genomic companies set up Database in EU? The EU database directive revisited, *European Intellectual Property Review*. 2001; 364.
168. Cited from *Supra* note 167, D. Visser, 'Database right and the spin-off theory', in Snijder and Weatherills (eds) 'E-Commerce law', Kluwer International, 2003.
169. L.A. Bygrave, The data difficulty in database protection, 20 June 2012. University of Oslo Faculty of Law Research Paper No. 2012-18.
170. *See* for e.g., the argument in the contact of Data protection and human tissues in, H. Widdows et al., The governance of genetic information who decides?, Cambridge University Press 2009.

study obesity or type 2 diabetes based on the genetic constitution. The preliminary information for collection is set on certain basic outlines which create a distinction from fallen apples or leaves or stones lying around.

[2] Independence

In order to qualify for a sui generis protection the database must be *independent* works, data or other materials arranged in a *systematic* or methodical way and *individually accessible* by electronic or other means. It is clear from the definition of biobanks, that they have a systematic framework following set standards of organization with individual accessibility. As for its criteria of independence there seems to be a divergence of opinion. Since the information is not directly available from biological samples without closer analysis it has been the opinion of some observers that they do not qualify for a database protection under the directive.[171] It has thus been argued that while certain biological samples like viruses or bacteria may be capable of an autonomous informative value this may not be the case with genetic sequences from tissue samples.[172] Other commentators have considered that while DNA sequences are partial and their 'meanings' or functions unknown, they may be considered independent, given that genomes have been described as 'books of life', it has been suggested that sequences with a known function are 'chapters' or 'paragraphs' of an entire genome.[173] This would amount to treatment of the genetic information as a 'work'. For example Celera genomics considers DNA sequences and their annotation as copyrighted works.[174] Genetic information can be viewed in two ways:[175]

(1) **As a sequencing data**: Sequence data, such as those associated with the DNA of various species, have grown enormously with the development of automated sequencing technology. Sequence data generally consist of text strings indicating appropriate bases.[176] This is the type of data which most writers have in their analysis. Thus the chemical composition expressed as TCAAG could be one way to view biological data.

(2) **As a high-dimensional omics data:**[177] Modern genomic research is not limited in its outlook to individual elements but comparing the behaviour of

171. L.A. Bygrave, The data difficulty in database protection, *European Intellectual Property Review*. 2013; 35(1), 25–33
172. *Ibid.*
173. *Infra* note 174.
174. A cited in J.A. Bovenberg. Nijhoff law speciais: Property rights in blood, genes and data: Naturally yours?. *Brill* 2005; 1; *See also* D.J.G. Visser, A database from space: The legal protection of data created or collected in outer space under the 1996, EU database directive', in 'Frans Gerhard von der Dunk, Marcel M. T. a. Brus, The international space station: Commercial utilisation from a European legal perspective', Martinus Nijhoff Publishers, 2006.
175. Biological data may come in many types, Sequences, graphs, high-dimensional data, geometric information, scalar data, patterns, etc. *supra* note 151 above. However the contextual discus sion calls for consideration of two important forms in which the argument proceeds.
176. *Supra* note 174.
177. F. Karimi-Busheri, Biobanking in the 21st century, Springer 2015 at p. 97.

various biological units, data points that might be associated with the behaviour of an individual unit. This involves larger collections of biological information from multiple subjects (i.e., donors). Such comparison as generally applied in genome wide studies offers inputs on the various anomalies affecting different species. In this sense genetic information sought from individual participants such as within a biobank would be treated as independent pertaining to the 'data subject'.

In addition, there is no explicit requirement that the database be created exclusively or primarily for the purpose of retrieval and use of individual datum or information.[178] Further with the changing technological paradigms such as microarrays, splicing technology,[179] etc. it would be harder to consider the argument of lack of independent nature of genetic material. Traditionally, genes have been analysed individually but with the microarray technology the DNA microarrays measure differences in DNA sequence between individuals and the expression of thousands of genes, which can be analysed simultaneously. Such comparative analysis can reveal abnormalities such as chromosomal insertions and deletions or abnormal chromosomal numbers.[180] Thus, the criterion of 'independence' may relate to the dimension viewed in any enquiry.

[3] Obtaining or Collecting the Content

Another point of objection in relation to raw data is based on whether the data was obtained or collected. Only the resources used to seek out existing independent materials and collect them in the database, and not to the resources used for the creation as such of independent materials will be considered for protection under the directive. Whether raw data is created or collected has been subject to wider differences among the academia. In the context of astronomical data obtained through space technologies, Visser[181] points out that if recording of data (i.e., by some technical means) is labelled as creating then no database rights would exist in a raw collection.

178. M.J. Davison, The legal protection of databases, Cambridge University Press, online June 2009 at pp. 70–71.

179. RNA splicing, involves the removal or 'splicing out' of certain sequences referred to as intervening sequences, or introns. The final mRNA thus consists of the remaining sequences, called exons, which are connected to one another through the splicing process. RNA splicing was initially discovered in the 1970s, overturning years of thought in the field of gene expression. S. Clancy, RNA splicing: Introns, exons and spliceosome. *Nature Education*. 2008; 1: 31; A term **used** to refer to the process by which the DNA of an organism is cut and a **gene**, perhaps from another organism, is inserted. (*See* **genetic** engineering and recombinant DNA.) **Gene splicing** is often **used** in industry to allow single-celled organisms to produce useful products, such as human insulin. (dictionary.com).

180. D.B. Kell. The virtual human: Towards a global systems biology of multiscale, distributed biochemical network models. *Iubmb Life*. 2007; 59: 689–695.

181. D.J.G Visser, 'A database from space: The legal protection of data created or collected in outer space under the 1996, EU database directive', in Frans Gerhard von der Dunk, Marcel M. T. a. Brus, 'The international space station: Commercial utilisation from a European legal perspective', Martinus Nijhoff Publishers, 2006.

Data recoded by some instrumental means represent data of pre-existing natural phenomenon and in this sense they cannot be strictly considered as created. Visser also point out that the observation by the CJEU in the British horse racing case pointed out to the fact that in football matches or horse racing events the organizers of such events not only create the facts but also the data regarding the matches to be played or the race to be run. Visser distinguishes this in the context of astronomical data as they are at best collected from nature as pre-existing data. In the context of biological materials, they have been referred to as collections from time immemorial e.g., Taxidermy collection in a natural history museum. This is because, such biological materials have been considered to be collected from nature. So also seeking blood or tissue from a donor is often referred to as 'collecting' and not creating. This is exactly why the principle of consent for collection of sample was formulated to seek the altruism of the donor in offering his or her samples to the study for which the consent was sought. While raw data may be further processed for the purpose of formulating it into a database, it cannot be strictly considered as being created instead it amounts to fixation into a suitable 'medium'.[182]

Perhaps one of the more sensible explanations in trying to avoid raw data is that monopolistic power may be exercised over the generation and use of 'raw data'. Thomas[183] observes that raw observational data is of paramount importance in research activities, but it is doubtful whether the raw data has any significant practical application in the industries. While it is still a matter of policy the directive per se does not distinguish between types of data so long as the conditions under the directive are fulfilled.

[4] Status of Biological Material as 'Information'

The above analysis demonstrates that sui generis rights protect both physical and electronic databases including those involving 'material elements'. One constrain involved in discussion of genomic research is the difficulties in conceiving of a multidimensional view of genetic resource.[184] This is also witnessed in the discussion revolving patentability of biological materials and its storage (*see* the status of biological material under Chapter 3). In the same vein, biological materials as information or rather the status of biological materials as 'data' is one of the looming questions in the context of protecting biological databases.

Historically, the discussion on the status of biological materials arose from the need to process personal data relating to individuals. In the earlier directive 'personal data' was defined as 'any information relating to an identified or identifiable natural person'('data subject'); an identifiable person is one who can be identified, directly or

182. Paragraph 30 OPAP.
183. T. Riis, Economic impact of the protection of unoriginal databases in developing, countries and countries in transition. LEFIC Working Paper. Copenhagen: Copenhagen business school centre for law, Economics and Financial Institutions, 2002–2003.
184. M. Macilotti, The legal status of human Biological material and its consequence, Rev Der Gen H 34/2011: 119–140.

indirectly, in particular by reference to an identification number or to one or more factors specific.[185] This meant specific information or coded data pertaining to human material without considering the biological material in itself.[186] Thus, as noted by Bygrave, the law and policy on data protection have generally tended to operate on the assumption that a distinction exists between data/information on the one hand, and, on the other, the persons to which the data/information can be linked.[187] These limitations in addressing HBMs and understanding its nature have been gaining attention in the contemporaneous time with the growth of health databases and biobanks. The result of this development is the change in both perspective and approaches to genetic material. The General Data Protection Regulation for instance, considers 'personal data' as any information relating to an identified or identifiable natural person ('data subject') who can be identified, directly or indirectly, in particular by reference to an identifier such as a name, an identification number, location data, an online identifier or to one or more factors specific to the *physical,* physiological, ***genetic***, mental, economic, cultural or social identity of that natural person.[188] In the same line Recital 35 of the regulation personal data concerning health should include all data pertaining to the health status of a data subject ... including information derived from the testing or examination of a body part or bodily substance, including from genetic data and biological samples.

In the same line the Recommendation CM/Rec(2016)6 of the Committee of Ministers to Member States on research on biological materials of human origin[189] (*see* Chapter 2) also considers braiding of samples with data. Article 2(3) of this recommendation points out thus:

> When obtained, stored or used, biological materials of human origin may be accompanied by associated personal data. Where in this recommendation provisions make reference to biological materials of human origin, these extend, where relevant, also to associated personal data.[190]

185. Directive 95/46/EC of the European Parliament and of the Council of 24 October 1995 on the protection of individuals with regard to the processing of personal data and on the free movement of such data.
186. W.G. Urgessa, The feasibility of applying EU data protection law to biological materials: Challenging data as exclusively informational, *Journal of Intellectual Property, Information Technology and Electronic Commerce Law*. 2016; 7, 96 para. 1.
187. L. Bygrave, The body as data? Bio-bank regulation via the "back door" of data protection law, *Law, Innovation and Technology*. 2010; 2(1): 1–25.
188. Article 4(1), Regulation (EU) 2016/679 of the European Parliament and of the Council of 27 April 2016 on the protection of natural persons with regard to the processing of personal data and on the free movement of such data, and repealing Directive 95/46/EC (General Data Protection Regulation) (Text with EEA relevance).
189. Adopted by the Committee of Ministers on 11 May 2016 at the 1256th meeting of the Ministers' Deputies.
190. *See also* Art. 3(1)(i) & (ii), Recommendation CM/Rec(2016)6 of the Committee of Ministers to Member States on research on biological materials of human origin where it defines identifiable and non-identifiable biological materials of human origin.

This shift in approach demonstrates the difficulties in dividing data from the medium in which it generates, particularly from a governance point of view.[191] This data-sample integration has been of particular interest in biometric identification,[192] forensic database, synthetic biology and biobanking.[193] Following the genetic studies and research-based technologies for use in medical research and other streams such as criminal investigation, biological materials have been considered to be extremely resourceful. As a scholar notes that the informational dimension of HBM arises from the fact that even after its removal from the body of the donor, it continues to share the information about the donor either actually or potentially.[194] Hence, it was not surprising that European Convention of Human Rights (ECHR) noted that fingerprints, DNA profiles and cellular samples constituted personal data.[195] Many commentators have argued that the term data is not limited to metaphysical elements but is also inclusive of the source of information; hence grounds that it must be interpreted before information can be gathered from it has no valid standing.[196] In fact this intertwining of 'source' and 'information' is what gives strength to the arguments such as 'book of life',[197] 'blue print of life'[198] in a genetic reductionist sense.[199] The special status of 'genetic data' has also been acknowledged by UNESCO's International Declaration on Human Genetic Data.[200] Under this declaration it has been held that human genetic data have a special status because:

(i) they can be predictive of genetic predispositions concerning individuals;
(ii) they may have a significant impact on the family, including offspring, extending over generations, and in some instances on the whole group to which the person concerned belongs;
(iii) they may contain information the significance of which is not necessarily known at the time of the collection of the biological samples;
(iv) they may have cultural significance for persons or groups.[201]

The declaration considers the special status based on identifiability and its potential consequences. The Committee of Ministers' Recommendation, No. R (97) 5

191. The collection, linking and use of data in biomedical research and health care: ethical issues, Nuffield council of Bioethics, February 2015.
192. E.J. Kindt, Privacy and data protection issues of biometric applications, a comparative legal analysis, Springer 2013.
193. *Supra* note 187.
194. *Supra* note 171.
195. *S. and Marper v The United kingdom*, 25 BHRC 557, [2009] Crim LR 355, (2009) 48 EHRR 50, [2008] ECHR 1581, 48 EHRR 50 at para. 68.
196. *see* Matteo Macilotti, *supra* note 184; ALRC, 'Essentially yours', para. 8.29, see also M. Taylor, Genetic data and the law, Cambridge University Press 2012
197. *Supra* note 160.
198. J.A. Bovenberg, Property rights in blood, genes and data: Naturally yours?, Martinus Nijhoff Publisher 2006.
199. Nelkin and Lindee. 'The DNA mystique, the gene as a cultural icon', W.H. Freeman and co NY. The writers define reductionism as the reduction of self to a molecular entity, they consider that the media and scientific hype with such terminological hype is more or less commercially motivated.
200. 16 October 2003.
201. Article 4 of the UNESCO Declaration on Human genetic data.

on the protection of medical data applicable to the collection and automatic processing of medical data also considers the nature of genetic data in Europe.[202] According to this recommendation, genetic data means 'all data, of whatever type, concerning the hereditary characteristics of an individual or concerning the patterns of inheritance of such characteristics within a related group of individuals'. It also refers to all data on the carrying of any genetic information (genes) in an individual or genetic line relating to any aspect of health or disease, whether present as identifiable characteristics or not.[203] This clearly demonstrates that 'data' in the context of HBM is inclusive of the material i.e., genes also involved. However, it would not amount to rights over the body as such.[204] The question of the status of biological material is complex and intersects at multiple layers with in different legal and governance regimes.[205] While processing of biological materials secures greater attention in view of personal data, little has been considered in the context of sui generis rights which makes this enquiry all the more essential. The objective of database directive is to afford an appropriate and uniform level of protection of databases as a means to secure the remuneration of the maker of the database. This is in fact different from data protection, which relates to protection of individuals with regard to the processing of personal data.[206] Further, the data contained in a databases may also relate to other laws such as data protection law, copyright, rights related to copyright, any other rights or obligations subsisting in the data, works or other materials incorporated into a database; patent rights, trademarks, design rights, the protection of national treasures, laws on restrictive practices and unfair competition, trade secrets, security, confidentiality, access to public documents and the law of contract.[207] This means other obligation relating to 'data', 'works' or 'other materials' may apply to the database apart from those provide in the directive. In this sense, the status of biological materials under other legal obligations may apply to the database containing biological samples.

Subjective distinctions in the treatment of the concept of a database under the directive requires focus over the subjective elements dealt with the directive itself. Interestingly much of the literature tends to focus on the concept of 'data' while tending to ignore the concept of 'information' and 'content'.[208] In considering the fact that sui generis rights tends to protect the substantial investment in collecting verifying and presenting the 'contents' of such a database and not personal data per se, the term

202. Adopted by the Committee of Ministers on 13 February 1997 at the 584th meeting of the Ministers' Deputies.
203. Article 1 of the Committee of Ministers' Recommendation No. R (97) 5.
204. K. Greasley, 'Property rights in the human body: Commodification and objectification', in I. Goold et. al. (eds), 'Persons, parts and property: How should we regulate human Tissue in the 21st century?', Bloomsbury Publishing, 25 September 2014, pp. 68–69.
205. *Supra* note 178; it has also been noted by the Working Party (the European advisory body on data protection established under Art. 29 of the European Data Protection Directive) acknowl edged the need to attend carefully to the legal status of tissues and the range of data subjects' rights they engage.
206. Recital 48 of the Database Directive 96/9/EC.
207. Article 13 of Directive 96/9/EC.
208. For instance Derclays in 144–145, Bygrave (2010) considers the problematic issue of defining 'data' which according to the writers have been a major difficulty in assessing the scope of the database directive.

'content' needs attention. As pointed out earlier the database directive is thin on definitions of 'data', 'information' and 'content'. 'data' is synonymous with information under the proposal to the directive.[209] In the same document, it has also been observed that 'data' is an accumulation of facts, statistics, information, names and addresses constituting the raw material of such database.[210] Information on the other hand means data which has been interpreted and analysed and may also be inclusive of the source from which such data arises.[211] Content on the other hand is contextualized data. Context situates data within a system of values, concepts, sources and utterances.[212] The term content is used in a broad sense to include data, information, works and other materials.[213] In addition, it is to be noted that the directive does not address the issues of the protection of contents because of the diversity in protection regimes of different works incorporated into the database. The contents may however be protected by other rights or subject to prior obligations, in such cases there may be combination with those rights but not conflicting with those prior rights.[214] This would imply that in the absence of a copyright in the contents of the database, sui generis rights might prevent copying of the content.[215]

The status of such a physical database collection involving HBM will also be subject to the Recommendation CM/Rec(2016)6,[216] which thought not binding under Article 288 of Treaty on the Functioning of the European Union (TFEU), has to be complied with.[217] This would imply non-profiting from sale of such material while ensuring a balance of interest for ethically oriented research outcomes.[218]

Considering, the above discussion that genetic materials have the status of data and following CJEU's dictum that pieces of information can be combined to be a database within the meaning of the directive[219] it would be easier to consider that biobanks both in their physical sense and in the bioinformatics sense constitute a database within the directive. While the biological samples and human genomic data exist in nature even before they are extracted, yet it is only through human effort that

209. Page 19 of Proposal for the directive.
210. Page 25, of proposal, Proposal for a Council Directive on the legal protection of databases. COM(92) 24 final, 13 May 1992.
211. M. Taylor, Genetic data and the law, Chapter 7, Cambridge University Press 2012; *see also* Chapter 3 of the same document at p. 41.
212. S. Abel and R.A. Bailie, The language of content strategy, XML press 2014.
213. *See* point 3.2 the relationship between protection of database and its contents in the Proposal for a Council Directive on the legal protection of databases. COM(92) 24 final, 13 May 1992.
214. Part 2 point 8.1. of the Proposal for a Council Directive on the legal protection of databases. COM(92) 24 final, 13 May 1992.
215. *See supra* note 120.
216. Recommendation CM/Rec(2016)6, of the Committee of Ministers to Member States on research on biological materials of human origin(Adopted by the Committee of Ministers on 11 May 2016, at the 1256th meeting of the Ministers' Deputies).
217. Article 2(1) on the scope of the recommendation provides that it applies to the obtaining of biological materials of human origin for storage for future research purposes. Also other conventions such as the Oviedo convention along with Additional Protocol to the Convention on Human Rights and Biomedicine, concerning Biomedical Research, Treaty No. 195, Strasbourg, 25/01/2005, may also apply in the governance of such sample collection.
218. Article 6 and Art. 21 of the Recommendation.
219. *Supra* note 28.

it is translated into an intelligible form to be processed as data preserved through a biobank.[220] This has been the reason behind the argument that such data are 'created'.[221] In spite of such a view the discourse from patent law offers differing view to the creation argument in relation to biological materials. In the case of *Association for Molecular Pathology v Myriad Genetics,*[222] where the US Supreme Court dealt the issue regarding the patentability of two genetic sequences linked to breast and ovarian cancer the court ruled that: *'a naturally occurring DNA segment is a product of nature and not patent eligible merely because it has been isolated, but cDNA is patent eligible because it is not naturally occurring'.*[223] This gives great impetus to the argument that human biological samples collected from patients to be stored in a biobank database consists of collected and not created materials. In Europe, the biotechnology directive, which governs the law relating to biotech inventions, provides additional support to this view (*See* Chapter 3 on Patentability issues).[224] According to the biotech directive an element isolated from the human body or otherwise produced by means of a technical process, including the sequence or partial sequence of a gene, may constitute a patentable invention, even if the structure of that element is identical to that of a natural element.[225] This would mean that biological materials from the state of nature would be treated at par with those technically processed. Considering this line of discussions in the context of databases involving biological materials there would be ample scope to qualify genetic materials as 'data' under the directive.[226]

[5] Biobanks and Bioinformatics Databases

At the outset the creation of a biobank/genomic database involves recruitment of the relevant group of research participants from whom the samples are collected. Upon such recruitment the next step is the collection, identification and processing of both the samples and the data belonging to the participants of the study. The physical samples would be arranged based on standard protocol of such biobanks. The data obtained from these samples at the first instance may be raw or pure which offers light on the basic genetic constituents of the samples. The scope of protection under other IP rights such as patents for this data is limited as much of them are already in the public domain. A data set of human genome alone is not subject to copyright owing to the lack of creativity and originality on the part of the researcher in formulating such data. Hence, such data would be at best genetic data that goes along with the physical collection. Since sui generis database rights apply without prejudice to rights existing in respect of their contents it would be still possible to protect such databases.[227]

220. *Supra* note 18.
221. *Ibid.*
222. 569 US 12–398.
223. *Supra* note 222.
224. Directive 98/44/EC on the legal protection of Biotechnological inventions, 6 July 1998.
225. Article 5(2), Directive 98/44/EC.
226. *Supra* note 152 at p. 78.
227. Article 7(4), Directive 96/9 EC.

Integrating primary data with IT to manage biological information is called bioinformatics.[228] Bioinformatics helps in understanding various biological process and is innate to modern life science research[229]

Bioinformatics databases can be classified into: (1) primary databases consist of gene-related data (i.e., including nucleic acid, proteins sequences, with information about features of the nucleic acid, amino acid sequences and biochemical reactions, metabolic pathway, etc.) and (2) secondary databases, on the contrary, are created based on primary databases and derived from the information of primary databases.[230] The primary databases record mainly experimental results while secondary database is derived from the information from the primary databases.[231] Other data can be derived from the primary data.[232] For instance data relating to phenotype or other sequence related information like SNPs[233] or SAPs.[234] Deriving such data may involve a long process wherein the sequences must be compared to multiple versions of the same sequence to find the single nucleotide differences.[235] Use of big-genomic data is increasingly being used for the creation of intelligent databases with sophisticated computational analysis in order to interpret data and manage all associated information.[236] Such intelligent databases are being used in storing data generated by intelligent robots using artificial intelligence and involves a process of selection, processing, transformation data mining and evaluation to create new knowledge.[237]

Such databases involves the efforts of AI programmers, researchers or the scientists in supplying predefined parameters and data for the functioning of such systems. Such skills along with creative intellectual efforts may qualify for a copyright protection although it is a subject of debate.[238] There is an ongoing discussion in EU on creating a producers right with regard to the data. Offering such a right is aimed at clarifying the legal situation and giving more choice to the data producer, by opening

228. H. Liu, J. Li and L. Wong, Use of extreme patient samples for outcome prediction from gene expression data, 2005; *see* K. Raza, Application of datamining in bioinformatics. *Indian Journal of Computer Science and Engineering.* 1(2): 114–118.
229. M. Chow, Intellectual property strategy in bioinformatics, *Journal of Intellectual Property Rights*. March 2003; 8: 130–137.
230. J. Chang and X. Zhu, Bioinformatics databases: Intellectual property strategy. *Journal of intellectual property rights*. November 2010; 15: 447–454.
231. *Ibid* note 230.
232. It has also been noted that at times certain data can include both primary and secondary characteristics and would be based on the mode of data integration. Source EMBL-EBI, European Molecular biology laboratory.
233. Single nucleotide polymorphisms (SNPs) are one type of genomic DNA variations in a population.
234. Single amino-acid polymorphisms (SAPs) derived from non-synonymous SNPs represent protein variations in a population. *See* Jia-Rui Wu,Rong Zeng Molecular basis for population variation: From SNPs to SAPs, FEBS Letters, 31 August 2012, 586(18): 2841–2845.
235. Central Dogma of molecular biology by Crick F. in 1958, available at https://profiles.nlm.nih.gov/ps/access/scbcch.pdf (last accessed on 1 August 2016).
236. Technopedia definition of intelligent databases, *see* https://www.techopedia.com/definition/14703/intelligent-database.
237. S.J. Russell and P. Norvig, Artificial intelligence A modern approach, Pearson Publisher, 3rd Edition, 2009.
238. R.K. Hariis and S.S. Rosenfield, Copyright protection for genetic databases, *Jurimetrics*. Winter 2005; 45(2): 225–250, American Bar Association.

up the possibility for users to utilize their data and thereby contribute to unlocking machine-generated data.[239] This approach has not found many takers for fear of creating increased monopolistic behaviour among data producers.[240] In the context of databases the concept of the producer of the database raises two relevant questions in relation to AI generated databases. On the one hand, if a computer program generates a database it could be contended that there is no producer or 'creator' as defined in the database directive. On the other hand it can still be argued that the database directive focuses on the investment, hence the person who invested in the database could be the owner of such database. In this sense, it may still be possible that databases drawn through AI could be protected.[241] In the context of health databases, this creates additional ethical challenges raising concerns on monopoly over such databases. Derived bioinformatics and analytical databases are of great importance to the biobanks. It may involve data analysed from primary data, studies by other researchers and their results or data mined from other primary or secondary databases.[242]

The spin-off nature of bioinformatics databases may also be problematic from the point of database rights within EU. In seeking an assessment of created and collected with regard to databases the CJEU considers the spin-off doctrine.[243] According to the spin-off doctrine, the database right accrues only in investment that is directly attributable to the production of the database.[244] Following the decision of CJEU in the British horse racing case investments in *obtaining verifying presenting must......... be understood to refer to the resources used to seek out existing independent materials and collect them in the database, and not to the resources used for the creation as such of independent materials.*[245] If however the creator of the database is also the creator of the materials constituting the database, protection under the directive could be obtained provided the substantial investment is proved by such maker.[246] Another problem pointed by a scholar is that bioinfomatic database is built from integrating sequential data contributed from several contributors over a period of time, this may cause concerns of multiple claims of 'substantial' investment.[247] The directive covers this issue under Recital 41 where it provides that the maker of a database (and thus the

239. Communication from the Commission to the European Parliament, The Council, The European Economic and Social Committee and the Committee of the Regions: 'Building A European data economy'{SWD(2017) 2 final}.
240. J. Drexl et al., Position statement of the Max Planck institute for innovation and competition of 26 April 2017 on the European commission's 'public consultation on building the European data economy' (26 April 2017). Max Planck Institute for Innovation & Competition Research Paper No. 17-08. Available at SSRN: https://ssrn.com/abstract=2959924 or http://dx.doi.org/10.2139/ssrn.2959924.
241. M. Koščík and M. Myška, Data protection and codes of conduct in collaborative research. *International Review of Law, Computers & Technology.* 2018; 32(1): 141-154.
242. M.J. Zvelebil and J.O. Baum, Understanding bioinformatics. *Garland Science,* 2008; 54.
243. M.J. Davison and P.B. Hugenholtz, Football fixtures, horse races and spin-offs: The ECJ domesticates the database right. *European Intellectual Property Review* 2005; (3).
244. *Ibid.*
245. Case C-203/02 (*British Horse Racing Board Ltd v William Hill Organisation Ltd*) *see* paras 31-35.
246. Paragraph 45 of OPAP.
247. M. Madhavan, Copyright versus database right protection in the UK: The bioinfomatic bone of contention, *Journal of World Intellectual Property.* January 2006; 9(1): 61-90.

holder of the database right) is the person who takes the initiative to make the investments and bears the risks.[248] It explicitly excludes subcontractors, a status that might apply *inter alia* to annotation staff. This however is not the case with collaborators or external publicly funded research teams submitting multiple sequences or even genomes may not consider themselves subcontractors and may therefore, wish to retain a database right with respect to their submission.[249] The nature of ownership in such cases could be questionable. Often research within university settings may work on specific projects for years and in the course may develop their own findings or that of the group which they may evolve into databases. In such cases the nature of employment and the source of resources used for creating the database may guide the ascertainment of ownership rights over them.[250]

Funding arrangements are also crucial for deciding the substantial investments made in the context of databases. While publicly funded biobanking institutions may receive monetary support with regard to their database; database from other cohorts developed in collaboration within the biobanks may find it difficult to seek protection under the database directive. At best it would be seen as inconvenient and less sustainable to seek sui generis protection in relation collaborative databases as pointed out many biobanks in Europe.[251]

Under such circumstance secondary bioinformatics databases may benefit greatly based on contractual agreement rather than sui generis rights. In *Ryanair Ltd v PR Aviation BV*,[252] the applicability of Directive 96/9 to databases that did not fall under the category of copyright nor sui generis rights was considered. It was held by the CJEU that, the Directive 96/9 must be interpreted as meaning that it is not applicable to a database, which is not protected either by copyright or by the sui generis right under that directive. The directive do not preclude the author of such a database from laying down contractual limitations on its use by third parties, without prejudice to the applicable national law.[253] In contractual agreements relating to databases which do not fall within the category of the directive, care should be taken to ensure the contract is clear and intelligible to the users.[254] This will however be dealt with in detail the next section.

[D] Contractual Agreements and Licensing Arrangements for Biobank Databases

Having discussed the nature and scope of the database rights it is also important to touch upon the issue of contracts and licensing arrangements with regard to database to appreciate its practicalities and feasibility in the context of biobank databases. This

248. *Supra* note 198.
249. *Ibid.*
250. W.D. Streitz et al., Material transfer agreements: A university perspective. *Plant Physiology*. September 2003; 133: 10–13.
251. Based on interviews conducted by the author.
252. Case C-30/14.
253. Paragraphs 43–45.
254. *Pearson v Bär Software*, 22 November 2016, the Court of Appeal of Amsterdam.

is essential from the point of view of biobanks as substantial amount of investment and efforts go into creating it and at the same time biobank databases may be multifarious in types and dynamic in structuring based on the needs of the biobank.[255] Also as pointed out in the context of bioinformatics databases, there may be differing segments of database within a biobank. One relating to the primary and other secondary databases based on the types of cohorts or collaborative research that functions within a biobank. In such instances there may be multiple contributors for the HBMs (physical databases) as well as the data. For example, researchers from other facilities placing samples for biobank storage or the employees within the biobank extracting data or samples for specific cohorts within biobank related research activities. Although these may form a part of the biobank's database they may still be individually a different database. In examining the contractual arrangements, it may be pertinent to visit certain scenarios as follows.

[1] Lawful Users

The sui generis rights protect extraction and reutilization of whole or substantial parts of the database. Under Article 8 of the directive a lawful users of a database may not however be prevented from extracting or reutilizing insubstantial parts of the contents or part of the database where the user has been required to access only part of such database.[256] This comes with an obligation that a lawful user may not perform acts which conflict with normal exploitation of such databases to which an access was lawfully provided.[257] Further a lawful user of a database have been granted an exception where such user can extract or reutilize substantial part of the contents for:

(a) private purpose in case of non-electronic database; and
(b) case of extraction for the purposes of illustration for teaching or scientific research, as long as the source is indicated and to the extent justified by the non-commercial purpose to be achieved.[258] The provision under Article 8 is made indispensable under Article 15 of the directive which states that 'any contractual provision contrary to Article 8 is null and void'. The term 'insubstantial' is equated with small or any part which does not fulfil the definition of a substantial part, evaluated both quantitatively and qualitatively, falls within the definition of an insubstantial part of the contents of a database.[259]

255. Biobank Graz.SOP_IT_Entwicklung_BB.
256. Article 8(1) Directive 96/9 EC.
257. Article 8(2) Directive 96/9 EC.
258. Article 9(1)(a), (b) Directive 96/9 EC.
259. Paragraph 73 of Case C-203/02 (*British Horse Racing Board Ltd v William Hill Organisation Ltd*).

This would mean that when a lawful user[260] is granted an access lawfully to the limited contents or parts of the contents of the database, she shall not be restricted in her usage of such parts of the contents of the database. In the context of biobanks, where a lawful access has been provided to the sample and its associated data, the researcher would be free to exploit it in an ethical manner. Often MTAs (which is a contractual arrangement between the researcher and the biobank) requires return of research results or return of remaining samples upon the end of the project for which such samples and data were sought or other restrictions on its use and exploitation.[261] While such requirements are considered essential in the interest of responsible research by contributing researches it may not be feasible in the light of the above provisions under the database directive.[262] This would equally be the case with any 'data use arrangements' which the lawful users may need to comply. For example, the UK biobank contemplates that if a researcher creates separate datasets as a result of their use of the data belonging to the UK biobank then *such generated datasets will be owned by the researchers and/or their institutions subject to the requirement to grant a non-exclusive licence back to UK Biobank for its use on an irrevocable, perpetual, worldwide, fully paid-up, royalty-free, fully sublicensable basis.*[263] Such limitation stands contrary to exploitation of the insubstantial or parts of the contents database that was offered to the lawful user upon payment of the requisite fees for such access. Databases not covered by the directive may apply contractual limitation following the decision of the CJEU in Ryanair. Thus non-protected databases may enjoy full freedom to contract.[264]

Another limitation would be in respect to clauses requiring return of samples post the research project. This could pose limitations for the right of lawful extraction in the context of scientific research.[265] The term 'scientific research' within the meaning of this directive covers both the natural sciences and the human sciences.[266] Thus giving impetus to the argument in favour of lawful users rights in relation to databases within genomic research.

[2] Employee Usage

Employees are considered to be lawful users of database if they have sought a subscription to the use of such database.[267] However in the context of biobanks there

260. The term lawful user is not defined in the directive but it is interpreted to include a licensee or an acquired user of a database *see* for more discussion in Derclays pp. 120–126.
261. MTAs collected during the study under NDA.
262. *See* for instance: S.M. Wolf et al., Managing incidental findings and research results in genomic research involving biobanks and archived data sets. *Genetics in Medicine.* 2012; 14: 361–384.
263. B8.4: http://www.ukbiobank.ac.uk/wp-content/uploads/2012/09/Access-Procedures-2011.pdf (last accessed on 25 March 2017).
264. *See* for more discussion on the point: M. Borghi et al., Contractual restrictions on lawful use of information: Sole-source databases protected by the back door?, *European Intellectual Property Review.* 2015; 37(8): 505–514.
265. *Supra* note 242.
266. Recital 36 of the Directive.
267. *Supra* note 244.

may different ways in which employees may be involved with the use of the contents in a database. As noted above the databases may not have a singular storage structure and this may vary in relation to new projects or the requirement to sort different genetic resources from different sources. In such cases too there exist as an extraction which may however be well within the terms of employment. Any other uses not within the terms of usage under a contract or an SOP for the management of such databases by employees would be treated as an act of unauthorized extraction of such database.[268] The directive leaves the arrangements applicable to databases created by employees to the discretion of the Member States.[269] However, the directive does not prevent Member States from stipulating in their legislation that where a database is created by an employee in the execution of his duties or following the instructions given by his employer, the employer exclusively shall be entitled to exercise all economic rights in the database so created, unless otherwise provided by contract.[270]

[3] Access to Databases

It has been generally considered that access as such is not a part of the sui generis rights.[271] The directive is silent about the modes of accessing physical or electronic databases. However, the directive considers that once the right-holder has chosen to make available a copy of the database to a user(whether by an online service or by other means of distribution) that lawful user must be able to access and use the database for the purposes and in the way set out in the agreement with the right-holder. This is the case even if such access and use necessitate performance of otherwise restricted acts.[272] This implies other contractual arrangements in parallel to the terms of protection offered by the directive.[273]

The philosophical imperative and the directive's purpose is visible under Article 16, which, requires the commission to verify the application of the sui generis right, including Articles 8 and 9, particularly whether the application of this right has led to abuse of a dominant position or other interference with free competition which would justify appropriate measures being taken, including the establishment of non-voluntary licensing arrangements. This implies equitable measures for lawful users and the database owners in any contractual arrangements between the two. Similar approach was also acknowledged by the HUGO (in statement on Human genomic databases, 2002, recommendation 1to 6) that researchers, institutions and commercial entities 'have a right to a fair return for intellectual and financial contributions to

268. For example the heist in a gene bank in Sardinia leading to the theft of both physical materials and data sparked controversies on the security and control over genetic resources. http://www.nature.com/news/dna-heist-that wasn- t-sparks-data-questions-1.20620.
269. Recital 29.
270. *Ibid.*
271. L.V. Armesto and P. Laurent, The intellectual property of medical data: Copyrights to patients' records and database rights to biobank?, The protection of medical data: challenges of the 21st century, (2008).
272. Recital 34.
273. Derclays at p. 174.

databases but fees should not restrict the free flow of scientific information and equitable access'.[274] However, the problem of overridability cannot be ignored. Electronic databases such as those for genetic databases or bioinformatics databases may involve different access regimes. Click wrap, subscription model or open access models have been suggested and many have also been put in practice.[275] Biobanks may however be 'user' and 'purpose' specific in its approach along with provision under data protection of donor information who contributed their samples to such biobanks. Researchers may thus be granted only a limited licences to use the data and samples to conduct the approved research project for a particular period of time.[276] Besides Biobanks are rich in resources and may be distinct in terms of the uniqueness of their sample and information collection thus functioning as a sole-source database.[277] Such overridability can exist where the exceptions under the database directive are ignored particularly 'substantial extraction and reutilization for educational and scientific research purposes'.[278] Nevertheless, the distinction of HBM and databases involving such materials calls for special consideration or frame work for its creation, operation and discontinuance.[279] The OECD guidelines on genetic databases requires that such database operators much 'ensure that access to and uses of HBM and data are in line with those described in the research protocols, consistent with the participant's informed consent and respect the privacy of the participant and confidentiality of the HBMs and data'.[280] The OECD guidelines also notes that depending on the nature of the resource, the data/sample provider and the end user, access agreements may impose restrictions on the data, materials to be provided or access fees or other arrangements as to its use and exploitation.[281] In reducing overridability in such special databases it has been suggested that differential fees or access modes apply for researchers and universities distinct from commercial entities in the fair access and use of such databases.[282] Many of the biobanks (such as Biobank Graz, the UK biobank, etc.) have also implemented them in practice to ensure balancing the rights of the users and the holders of genomic databases.

[E] Public Sector Database

Public sector is the single largest source and producer of information. It is produced and collected by public bodies in multifarious ways.[283] One of the principal aims of the establishment of an internal market is the creation of conditions conducive to the

274. Stratum WP7: Final Report. May 2013.
275. *Supra* note 219.
276. For example UK Biobank access procedure.
277. D. De Beer, 'Is open-sourced biotechnology possible?' in M. Wynants and J. Cornelis (eds) 'How open is the future? economic, social & cultural scenarios' 2005.
278. Derclays at pg 183(also http://www.serci.org/2005/derclaye.pdf).
279. OECD Guidelines on Human Biobanks and Genetic Research Databases, 2009.
280. Point 60 OECD Guidelines on Human Biobanks and Genetic Research Databases, 2009, at pg 37.
281. Point 66.
282. *Supra* note 257.
283. Citizens Awareness 'A cloud of Public Sector & Public Advertising', 2013.

development of community-wide services. Public sector information is an important primary material for digital content products and services.[284] The directive does not specifically state anything in this respect.[285] However, the question as to whether public sector databases can secure protection under the directive is indeed a relevant one particularly with 'open data initiative'[286] and digital integration efforts by the commission are underway. On the contrary there are also other contentions like the use of tax payer's money.[287] In *Compass-Datenbank GmbH v Republik Österreich.*[288] Compass-Datenbank, a limited liability company established under Austrian law provided a database containing economic data for the purposes of providing information services. It also set up an electronic version of that database based on a card index system the content of which was checked, corrected and supplemented after searching in the Firmenbuch which was the central journal for entries in the companies register of the Republik Österreich. The information services thus provided by the said database were based on information contained in the Firmenbuch, supplemented by information resulting from searches carried out by Compass-Datenbank's own editorial services and by other information, such as that emanating from Chambers of Commerce. In 2001, Austria brought before the Handelsgericht Wien, an action seeking, *inter alia*, to prevent Compass-Datenbank from using the Firmenbuch data, including storage, reproduction or transmission of that data to third parties. While the Austrian court ordered Compass-Datenbank to refrain, on a provisional basis, from using the Firmenbuch database, yet another case was filed by the Datenbank against this decision. A reference for preliminary ruling was made before the CJEU by the Court of Appeal in that case. The question before the CJEU was in essence whether the activity of a public authority consisting of storing data in a database (which was protected by sui generis rights) and permitting interested persons to search for data and provide them with printouts thereof for payment, while prohibiting any other use of that data, constituted an economic activity of the public authority within the meaning of Article 102 TFEU.[289] The CJEU observed that:

284. Directive 2003/98/EC of the European Parliament and of the Council of 17 November 2003 on the reutilization of public sector information.
285. E. Derclaye, 'Does the directive on the re-use of public sector information affect the State's database sui generis right?' in J. Gaster, E. Schweighofer and P. Sint (eds) 2008.
286. Brussels, 12.12.2011, COM(2011) 882 final available at https://ec.europa.eu/digital-single-market/en/open-data (last accessed on 30 July 2016).
287. E. Derclaye, 'Does the directive on the re-use of public sector information affect the state's database sui generis right?', in J. Gaster, E. Schweighofer and P. Sint (eds), 'Knowledge rights - legal, societal and related technological aspects'. Austrian Computer Society, 2008.
288. Case C-138/11, 2012.
289. Article 102, Treaty on the Functioning of the European Union, 2007, (ex Art. 82 TEC) Any abuse by one or more undertakings of a dominant position within the internal market or in a substantial part of it shall be prohibited as incompatible with the internal market in so far as it may affect trade between Member States. Such abuse may, in particular, consist in: (a) directly or indirectly imposing unfair purchase or selling prices or other unfair trading conditions; (b) limiting production, markets or technical development to the prejudice of consumers; (c) applying dissimilar conditions to equivalent transactions with other trading parties, thereby placing them at a competitive disadvantage;(d) making the conclusion of contracts subject to acceptance by the other parties of supplementary obligations which, by their nature or according to commercial usage, have no connection with the subject of such contracts.

> an undertaking is any entity engaged in an economic activity, irrespective of its legal status and the way in which it is financed.[290] A public entity may be regarded as an undertaking in relation to only part of its activities, if the activities which form that part must be classified as economic activities. Activities which fell within the exercise of public powers were not of an economic nature. Thus a data collection activity in relation to undertakings, on the basis of a statutory obligation on those undertakings to disclose the data and powers of enforcement related thereto, falls within the exercise of public powers. As a result, such an activity is not an economic activity.[291] Equally, an activity consisting in the maintenance and making available to the public of the data thus collected, whether by a simple search or by means of the supply of print-outs, in accordance with the applicable national legislation, also does not constitute an economic activity, since the maintenance of a database containing such data and making that data available to the public are activities which cannot be separated from the activity of collection of the data. The collection of the data would be rendered largely useless in the absence of the maintenance of a database which stores the data for the purpose of consultation by the public.[292]

This would essentially mean an assessment of distinction between 'public function' and 'economic undertaking'. However CJEU also held in the case that a public entity which creates a database and which then relies on IPR, and in particular the above-mentioned sui generis right, with the aim of protecting the data stored therein, does not act, by reason of that fact alone, as an undertaking. Such an entity is not obliged to authorize free use of the data which it collects and make available to the public. A public authority may legitimately consider that it is necessary, or even mandatory in the light of provisions of its national law, to prohibit the reutilization of data appearing in a database in order to protect or respect the interest of the companies and other legal entities which makes the disclosures required by law before such public authorities. In such cases, the authorities may have a duty to ensure that no reuse of the information is made beyond that database.[293] The European commission has adopted the directive on the reuse of public sector information (Directive 2003/98/EC, known as the 'PSI Directive').[294] It was further revised by Directive 2013/37/EU.[295] The purpose of the measure is to serve as a general framework for the conditions governing reuse of public sector documents is needed in order to ensure fair, proportionate and non-discriminatory conditions for the reuse of such information. Public sector bodies in its role and function collects, produces, reproduces and disseminates information in the course of their public tasks. Use of such documents for other reasons constitutes a reuse.[296] The directive however neither regulates or controls the public sector bodies in

290. Paragraph 35 of the Judgment.
291. Paragraphs 38–40 of the Judgment *see also* Case C-113/07 P *SELEX Sistemi Integrati v Commission* [2009] ECR I-2207, para. 72.
292. Paragraph 41 of Judgment.
293. Paragraph 47 of Judgment.
294. Revision entered into force on 31 December 2003. Avaliable at: https://ec.europa.eu/digital-single market/en/european-legislation-reuse-public-sector-information (last accessed on 30 July 2016).
295. Entered into force on 17 July 2013.
296. Recital 8, Directive 2013/37/EU.

the reuse of their information nor does it interfere with IPR[297] or database rights under the database directive. Further, it does not require public bodies to permit a reuse of information. Instead what it does is that it spells out the conditions within which public sector bodies can exercise their IPR in the internal information market if such public bodies choose to allow the reuse of documents to third parties.[298] Thus it seems that databases in the public sector may opt to choose a sui generis protection in order to regulate their databases which are not distinctly within public functions. Even if they fall under the category of public function, the need to protect the information donors can well be a reason for limiting access rights to such databases.

In the context of biobanks there has been a similar discussion as to the *nature of such intuitions* for the purposes of value-added tax (VAT) exemptions which was discussed in a case.[299] In this case the biobank was authorized by the competent health authorities to handle cord stem cells. The question submitted for reference before the CJEU was whether the collection, transportation, analysis and storage of cord blood, with a view to the possible use of the stem cells in it for the purposes of future autologous medical treatment, can be covered by the exemption from VAT.[300] An exemption was provided under the relevant law for duly recognized establishment 'closely related' to hospital and medical care undertaken by bodies governed by public law.[301] In answering the said question the CJEU looked into the nature of the biobanking authority and held that the exemption does not cover activities such as those at issue as they were only potentially related to hospital activity.[302] Thus the nature of funding, nature of the establishment, its governance and standardization framework may be essential factors in determining the nature of investment for public sector databases.

297. It does not include industrial property rights like Patents.
298. Recital 24, Directive 2013/37/EU.
299. *CopyGene A/S v Skatteministeriet*, Case C-262/08, 10/06/2010.
300. Article 13A(1)(b) of the Sixth Directive: hospital and medical care and closely related activities undertaken by bodies governed by public law or, under social conditions comparable to those applicable to bodies governed by public law, by hospitals, centres for medical treatment or diagnosis and other duly recognized establishments of a similar nature.
301. Article 13A(1)(b) of Sixth Council Directive 77/388/EEC of 17 May 1977 on the harmonisation of the laws of the Member States relating to turnover taxes.
302. Paragraphs 78–81 of the Judgment in *CopyGene A/S v Skatteministeriet*, Case C-262/08, 10/06/2010.

CHAPTER 5

Copyrights Within Genetic Database and Biobanks

§5.01 INTRODUCTION

Copyright defined as the right of an author to the productions of his mental exertions may be classed among the species of property acquired by occupancy and being founded on labour and invention.[1] The concept of copyright has evolved from a mere right of production to preventing others from copying the author's works in an attempt to recognize the creative efforts of the author.[2] The distinction in approaches to copyright law namely the Anglo-Saxon copyright law and the civil law traditions (droit d'auteur) have deeply contributed in evolving the area of law.[3] While there exists a conceptual difference between the two streams with one viewing copyright profoundly on economic and the other viewing works as an extension of author's personality, yet it is considered essential to avoid the problem of free riding. In the absence of copyright protection, the market price of a book or other expressive work will eventually be bid down to the marginal cost of copying, with the result that the work may not be produced in the first place because the author and publisher may not be able to recover their costs of creating it.[4] Thus, copyright incentivizes creativity and tends to identify itself with literary, musical or artistic works. In this sense, Bob Dylan's recordings[5] or

1. W.A. Copinger, The law of copyright, Stevens and Haynes 1870.
2. V.H. Bouganim, The legal protection of databases from copyright to data right, 1999 (Doctoral dissertation, University of London, unpublished thesis).
3. R. McGinnis, Originality and intellectual property in the French and English Enlightenment, Routledge, 2009.
4. W. Lades and R.A. Posner, The economic structure of intellectual property law, Harvard University Press, 2003, Chapter 2 at p. 40.
5. http://www.nytimes.com/2013/12/12/arts/music/european-copyright-laws-lead-to-rare-music-releases.html.

JK Rowling's[6] wizard stories or Walt Disney's film production or Edvard Munch's painting scream[7] may be some of the prominent examples that one may picturize with the use of the term 'copyright'. It may thus seem fanciful to consider copyrights particularly in discussing biobanks. However copyright's importance within biomedical research information increasingly permeates the discussions within biobanks as well. The changing legal and technological structures in EU along with a call for sharing of research data have been the driving force for new approaches within biomedical research.[8] Most importantly digital technologies have changed the way 'works' and 'other protected subject matter' are being treated, produced, distributed and exploited.[9] For instance, data sets forming a part of Big Data may owe great value to research. They are often created by technological process although involving human intervention; however its eligibility for being protected as a copyrighted work is debatable and challenge indeed for law.[10] So also such changing technological structures also offers thrust to new uses, new actors and business models e.g., genomic cloud sharing offering opportunities for researchers to access protected content via the cloud. Such changes in biotechnological research and sharing paradigm calls for an understanding of whether the European copyright offers to protect the 'data' in the context biobanks. In attempting to answer this thought, it must also be realized that data comes in differing forms within biomedical research particularly involving biobanks. In this regard, the data created during the primary and secondary activities of the biobank would be analysed in the light of the copyright law.

[A] The Criterion for Seeking Copyright in Europe

Efforts for legal harmonization began with the treaty of Rome.[11] However in terms of copyright law in EU Harmonization began in early 1980s with the single EC treaty on European communities. Further the EC Treaty (Treaty establishing the European Community (TEC))[12] made an exception to the flow of goods and services where necessary for the protection of IP, including copyright and related rights giving an impetus to harmonization efforts.[13] In 1991, directives were designed to harmonize the copyrights within the national law of Member States.[14] The information society directive was passed in 2001which harmonizes the rights of reproduction, distribution,

6. http://newsvote.bbc.co.uk/mpapps/pagetools/print/news.bbc.co.uk/1/hi/entertainment/arts/2846105.stm.
7. http://www.museumsyndicate.com/artist.php?artist = 15.
8. C. Auffray et al., Making sense of big data in health research: Towards an EU action plan. *Genome Medicine.* (2016); 8: 71. PMC. Web. 16 April 2017.
9. COM(2016) 593 final, 2016/0280 (COD), 'proposal for copyright in EU digital single market', Brussels, 14 September 2016.
10. T. Hoeren, Big data and the ownership in data: Recent developments in Europe, *European Intellectual Property Review*. 2014; 36(12): 751.
11. 1 January 1958.
12. Treaty of Maastricht, 1992.
13. The European Concern with Copyright and Related Rights, in Bernt Hugenholtz, Harmonizing European Copyright Law, Kluwer Law International, 2009.
14. First Directive harmonising copyright within Europe was on computer programs Directive 91/250/EEC.

communication to the public, the legal protection of anti-copying devices and rights management systems within the EU.[15] The international and regional harmonization has contributed to extensive minimum standards of copyright protection for literary and artistic works.[16] Based on the principle of territoriality the national rules govern copyright subject matter within a given Member State in Europe.[17] Irrespective of the national variations in Europe in the scope of the rights granted under copyright law it offers to protect 'works' that are 'original' in nature.[18]

[1] Work

Copyright offers to protect expression of a work and not the ideas involved in it.[19] Works include literary, dramatic, artistic, musical works and films. Every production in the literary,[20] scientific and artistic domain, whatever may be the mode or form of its expression, such as books, pamphlets and other writings; lectures, addresses, sermons ... dramatic or dramatico-musical works, choreographic works, musical compositions, works of drawing, painting, architecture, sculpture, engraving and lithography; photographic works to which are assimilated works expressed by a process analogous to photography; works of applied art; illustrations, maps, plans, sketches and three-dimensional works relative to geography, topography, architecture or science qualifies as a work for protection as a work.[21] Nevertheless, national laws may prescribe certain criteria for inclusion or exclusion of works. For instance, various countries impose restrictive criteria before a 'compilation'[22] can seek copyright.[23] Further irrespective of the nature of the expression (i.e., as a literary, dramatic or musical), a work could be protected as a copyright only when it is fixed in some material form.[24]

[2] Originality

The most important criterion for a work seeking copyright protection is that it must be original in its expression. This also means that translations, adaptations, arrangements

15. http://europa.eu/rapid/press-release_IP-01-528_en.htm?locale = en.
16. P. Goldstein and P.B. Hugenholtz, International copyright, principles, law, and practice, Oxford University Press 2013, at pp. 14–16.
17. *See* for more discussions A. Kur and T. Dreier, European intellectual property law, Edward Elgar 2013 at p. 12.
18. *Ibid.*, at p. 4.
19. 9(2), Art.TRIPS.
20. *See* Literary value of words and phrases e.g., *Exxon corporation v Exon Insurance Consultants* [1982] ch 119, Case C-5/08 *Infopak Internation A/S v Danske Dablades Forening* [2009] ECDR 16. Words considered in isolation are not the intellectual creation of the author who employs them.
21. Article 2 Berne Convention.
22. A compilation relates to a collection of items in a written form and is protected if they possess sufficient originality. They are different from databases which contain independent works literary, artistic or other collections and seek protection for their selection and arrangement or for the investments as a sui generis rights as discussed in point 4.3 above.
23. M.J. Davison, The legal protection of databases, Cambridge University Press 2009, pp. 10–49.
24. Article 2(2), Berne Convention.

of music and other alterations of a literary or artistic work shall be protected as original works.[25] Originality does not impose aesthetic quality or intellectual ability to be demonstrated in the expression but it is sufficient that it forms a creative expression of the relationship between the author and the work.[26]

In EU concept of 'originality' became more visible in its efforts to bring harmonization in different subjective areas such as computer programs, photographs and database rights. The result was different considering differing technical standards under consideration.[27] While the EU legislature has not deemed it necessary to adopt a harmonized understanding of originality for subject matter (other than for computer programs, databases and photographs) the CJEU has acted proactively towards the actual harmonization of copyright, by adopting an EU-wide notion of originality.[28]

The CJEU in the Infopaq decision while discussing the issue of infringement of the right of reproduction and exception to copyright law, the court also considered originality under the Information society directive.[29] Infopaq, a firm which, by means of a 'data capture process', drew up summaries of articles from Danish newspapers and send them by e-mail to its customers, on the basis of agreed subject criteria. Danske Dagblades Forening ('DDF'), an association of Danish daily newspaper publishers, formally required Infopaq to request this consent, in accordance with the copyright rules. Infopaq, disputing DDF's claim, applied to the competent courts for relief. The case was brought before the Højesteret, which referred questions to the Court of Justice concerning the interpretation of Directive 2001/29/EC on the harmonization of certain aspects of copyright and related rights in the information society. The CJEU considered that that the directive applied only if a work was original in the sense of the author's own intellectual creations. The data capture process used by Infopaq allowed for the reproduction of multiple extracts of protected works. That process reproduces an extract of eleven words each time a search word appears in the relevant work and, moreover, often operates using a number of search words because some clients ask Infopaq to draw up summaries based on a number of criteria. The cumulative effect of such extracts may lead to the reconstitution of lengthy fragments which are liable to reflect the originality of the work in question, with the result that they contain a number of elements which are such as to express the intellectual creation of the author of that work.[30] Further it was also observed 'regarding the elements of such works covered by the protection, it should be observed that they consist of words which, considered in isolation, are not as such an intellectual creation of the author who employs them. It is only through the choice, sequence and combination of those words that the author may express his creativity in an original manner and achieve a result

25. Article 2(3), Berne Convention.
26. A. Dietz, The artist's right of integrity under copyright law: A comparative approach, *IIC*. 1994; 25: 177 at 182.
27. European commission staff working paper on the review of the EC legal framework in the field of copyright and related rights, SEC (2004) 995.
28. L. Rosati, Originality in the EU copyright law full harmonization through case law, Edward Elgar 2013.
29. C-5/08 infopak internation A/Sv. Danske Dablades Forening [2009] ECDR 16 para 37.
30. *Ibid.*, paras 48–49.

which is an intellectual creation'.[31] Thus 'originality' in the case was cemented in the sense that it is its 'author's own intellectual creation'.[32] In the *Painer case*[33] where the question related to the protection offered to photographs taken by Mrs Painer and was subsequently used by the media in relation to a criminal investigation. The news papers published the photographs Painer had taken of the abducted girl without indicating the name of the photographer, or indicating a name other than Painer's as the photographer. Furthermore, several of those publications had also released a portrait (a photofit), created by computer from the contested photographs.[34] It thus became very difficult to assess the intellectual creativity in such adapted photofit images. Hence, the Austrian court stayed the proceedings and raised four questions to the CJEU. One of the main question related to the 'originality' with respect of photographs. The CJEU held that an intellectual creation is an author's own, if it reflects the author's personality that is say that the author was able to express his creative abilities in the production of the work by making free and creative choices.[35] Thus, the author's ability to exercise creative choices and to express creativity or personal touch offers the key to identifying the concept of originality in a work.[36] As regards a portrait photograph, the photographer can make free and creative choices in several ways and at various points in its production. In the preparation phase, the photographer can choose the background, the subject's pose and the lighting. When taking a portrait photograph, he can choose the framing, the angle of view and the atmosphere created. Finally, when selecting the snapshot, the photographer may choose from a variety of developing techniques the one he wishes to adopt or, where appropriate, use computer software. By making such choices, the author of a portrait photograph can stamp the work created with his 'personal touch'.[37] From this one can get a basic sense of how creativity is construed and rewarded under the copyright law. With this perspective we can move to the discussion of copyrights over genetic databases and data.

[B] Copyright Law, Genetic Data and Ownership

Technological integration has led biomedical research to be more data driven than ever before.[38] Vast amounts of data are generated in research and analysis. This magnanimity of data can also help in refining information which may help researchers in

31. C-5/08 infopak internation A/Sv. Danske Dablades Forening [2009] ECDR 16 para. 45.
32. *Ibid.*, para. 37.
33. *Eva-Maria Painer v Standard VerlagsGmbH and Others*, C-145/10 paras 88–96 and paras 107–108.
34. *Ibid.*, paras 33–34.
35. *Ibid.*, paras 88–89.
36. *Ibid.*, *see also*, C. Waelde, et al., Contemporary intellectual property law and policy, OUP, 4th ed, 2016 at p. 58 point 2.45.
37. *Supra* note 33, paras 90–92.
38. J. Luo et al., Big data application in biomedical research and health care: A literature review. *Biomedical Informatics Insights.* 19 January 2016; 8(1–10).

translation outcomes or for epidemiological or clinical research.[39] While it can be agreed that biobanks as defined in the first chapter involves in its simplest sense samples and data. 'Data' is commonly understood as 'information' in the broadest sense of the term.[40] However, the scope of 'data' as envisioned initially by the biobanks has become much broader. In the earlier definition of a biobank found in the Council of Europe recommendation on research on biological material of human origin,[41] biobank was defined as consisting of biological materials and associated personal data which may be linked to genealogical, medical and lifestyle data.[42] In the present scenario of biological Big Data research, Biobank data constitute a 'universal language' for all biobank bases research activities.[43] In any biobank the value and utility of a biospecimen or biological resource apart from its innate quality, is determined by the quality of the associated and attributed information.[44] A biobank's richness as a research resource in enhanced by not only the existence of sensitive personal data but also other kinds of analysis and derived data as well. Each type of data being integrally different in its formulation and nature, it would be hard to generalize an assessment of copyright over biobank data in general. Irrespective of the differences in the type of data found within a biobank, individual data may well be protected by copyright if it is fixed as a work and suffices the standard of originality as discussed above.

The concept of 'data ownership' on the contrary proceeds with the notion of control over intangible assets derived through IPR.[45] The CJEU in C-128/11[46] was of the view that even though copyright licences may govern the data (i.e., the software in this case) yet it may also be governed by the sale of goods indicating the existence of possible ownership rights over data as well.[47] Although the commission proposed an initiative to address the issue of data ownership in the context of the Big Data research, it was subsequently delayed to offer an understanding of the full potential of data within Big Data economy.[48] The persistence of the CJEU's decision and lack of clarity on the issue of data ownership according to an author has opened the door for a discussion on ownership in intangible assets.[49] Yet what is less clear is the relationship between property in data and the ownership in the medium where the data are

39. T.D. Wade. Traits and types of health data repositories. *Health Information Science and Systems.* 2014; 2: 4. PMC. Web. 29 March 2017.
40. Leebygrave (2012).
41. Recommendation Rec(2006)4 of the Committee of Ministers to Member States on research on biological materials of human origin, 2006.
42. *See* Biobanks For Europe A challenge for Governance, 2010.
43. S.Y. Nussbeck, et al., '*Life in data*' – outcome of a multi-disciplinary, interactive biobanking conference session on sample data. *Biopreservation and Biobanking*, 2016; 14(1): 56–64.
44. That is information used to describe, annotate and authenticate the biospecimen as well as the data that provide a record of the processing and pre-analytical variables to which it has been exposed *see* note 43; http://www.ukbiobank.ac.uk/wp-content/uploads/2013/10/ukbiobank-data-management.pdf.
45. *Infra* note 46.
46. *UsedSoft GmbH v Oracle International Corp.*, Case C-128/11, 3 July 2012 *see* paras 82–84.
47. T. Horen, Big data and the ownership in data: Recent developments in Europe, *European Intellectual Property Review*. 2014; 36(12): 715.
48. Commission Staff Working Document on the free flow of data and emerging issues of the European data economy (SWD (2017) 2/1).
49. *Supra* note 40.

stored.[50] In this regard it also become even more essential for biomedical research to understand the various possibilities of copyright protection over data including commercial data in the context of such research and its interference with individual rights such as privacy.[51] In this regard, the ensuing discussion will consider the data and its storage from the primary activities of the biobank namely databases, sequencing data in relation to its other related activities the data derived from medical records, study cohorts and the data developed and shared through the biobank cloud will be analysed (See fig 5.1)

Figure 5.1 Copyright Analysis over Biobank Data

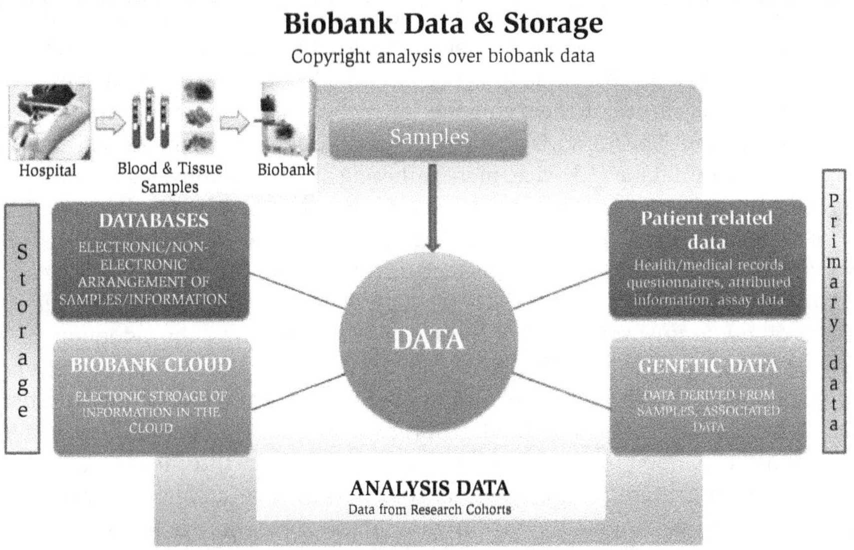

[C] Copyright in Database in Europe

The structure of a database may be subject to copyright if it suffices the conditions of originality. Under the international conventions like Berne,[52] WCT[53] and TRIPS[54] original and creative databases enjoy copyright protection as literary works. While so there exists a difference in approach in these conventions in relation to the scope of copyright protection over databases. Under the Berne Convention for instance protection of database is offered only to 'Collections of literary or artistic works' which

50. *Ibid.*
51. G. Malgieri, Property and intellectual ownership of consumer information: A new taxonomy for personal data. *Yale Law Journal.* 2013; 123(2): 266.
52. Article 2(5) of the Berne Convention, 1886.
53. Article 5, WIPO Copyright Treaty, 1996.
54. Article 10(2) Trade Related Aspects of Intellectual Property Rights, 1994.

constituted 'intellectual creations' both in terms of their 'selection and arrangement'.[55] This means that most of the general databases may not fit within its scope.[56] On the contrary under TRIPS and WCT compilations of 'data or other material' can form the content of the database. Further either the original 'selection ***or*** arrangement' could be regarded as sufficient to consider the database for protection.[57]

In Europe, Directive 96/9/EC deals with copyright protection of databases apart from the sui generis rights that was discussed in the previous part. Under the directive, a database covered by copyright the selection or arrangement of their contents, which constitute the author's own intellectual creation, shall be protected as copyright.[58] In addition, a database for the purposes of the directive includes 'a collection of independent works, data or other materials arranged in a systematic or methodical way and individually accessible by electronic or other means'.[59] This means that there must be sufficient 'originality' in the collections which are not just limited to 'works' but includes independent works, data or other materials which are arranged in a systematic or methodical way and individually accessible by electronic or other means.[60] The selection or arrangement of their contents must be the result of the author's own intellectual creation. The author's creative choices must be visible in the selection and arrangement of the database. Hence, mere gathering of information does not qualify for the protection under the copyright provisions under Chapter II of the directive. It has been provided by recital 16 of the Database Directive that '*no criterion other than originality in the sense of the author's intellectual creation should be applied to determine the eligibility of the database for copyright protection, and in particular no aesthetic or qualitative criteria should be applied*'.[61] Prior to the adoption of the directive, the national laws in different Member States differed with respect to the level of 'originality' which was used to determine whether a database was protectable or not under copyright law.[62] The threshold of 'originality' for the copyright protection of compilations in common law jurisdictions was lower than the threshold of 'originality' that prevailed elsewhere in the community. The directive attempts to establish a uniform threshold of 'originality' for 'original' databases which is the author's own intellectual creation.[63] This criterion of originality for all works is 'free and creative choices' which the author exercises in relation to the work.[64] This is a subjective

55. M. Walter and S. von Lewinski, European copyright law, a commentary, Oxford University Press 2010 at p. 704.
56. *Ibid.*
57. *Ibid.*
58. Article 3, Directive 96/9/EC.
59. Article 1(2), Directive 96/9/EC.
60. Derclays in I.A. Stamatoudi and P. Torremans, EU copyright law: A commentary, Edward Elgar Publishing 2014.
61. *See* recitals 15, 16 and preamble of Directive 96/9/EC.
62. DG Internal Market and services working paper: First evaluation of Directive 96/9/EC, 12 December, 2005 on the legal protection of databases at p. 7.
63. *Ibid.*
64. E. Derclaye, Assessing the impact and reception of the court of justice of the European union case law on UK copyright law: What does the future hold? Revue Internationale du Droit d'auteur. 2014 (240): 5–117. ISSN 0035-3515.

assessment rather than an objective one as creativity depends on choice and arrangement of its creator.[65] The copyright protection of databases provided for by this directive does not extend to their contents and shall be without prejudice to any rights subsisting in those contents themselves.[66] Separate copyright may subsist in the works which are brought together to form the database and in the selection or arrangement of the works themselves; However no additional copyright can be gained by the inclusion of an unprotected work into the database unlike the sui generis rights.[67]

In *Football Dataco & Others v Yahoo UK,*[68] where the claimant (Football Dataco) argued that the creation of the fixture lists of the English and Scottish football leagues were protected by copyright as databases because the person who makes them invested a lot of skill and labour into them and not merely following the golden rules required in making such databases. The high court of England and Wales and the Court of Appeal accepted the claim of copyrights in such database. However a reference was made to the CJEU on certain points of law (under Article 3 of the directive) i.e., what is meant by 'databases which, by reason of the selection or arrangement of their contents, constitute the author's own intellectual creation' and in particular:

(a) should the intellectual effort and skill of creating data be excluded;
(b) does 'selection or arrangement' include adding important significance to a pre-existing item of data (as in fixing the date of a football match); and
(c) does 'author's own intellectual creation' require more than significant labour and skill from the author, if so what?

In response to the question a preliminary ruling was given by the CJEU that the directive's concepts of 'selection' and 'arrangement' refer to the 'selection and arrangement of the data through which the author of the database gives the database its structure'. Selection and arrangement do not extend to the creation of the data contained in the database. Therefore, the intellectual effort and skill expanded in creating data are not relevant in order to assess the eligibility of the database that contains them for copyright protection.[69] Further it was also observed that as regards the setting up of a database, that criterion of originality is satisfied when, through the selection or arrangement of the data which it contains, its author expresses his creative ability in an original manner by making free and creative choices and thus stamps his 'personal touch'.[70] Thus even though the setting up of the database required significant labour and skill of its author, it cannot as such justify the protection of it by copyright under Directive 96/9, if that labour and that skill do not express any originality in the selection or arrangement of that data.[71]

65. *Ibid.*
66. Article 3(2), Directive 96/9/EC.
67. Proposal for a Council Directive on the legal protection of databases. COM(92) 24 final, 13 May 1992 at p. 42.
68. Case C-604/10, March 2012.
69. Paragraphs 32 and 33 of the Judgment in Case C-604/10.
70. Paragraph 38 of the judgment in *Football Dataco & Others v Yahoo UK! & Others*, Case C-604/10.
71. Paragraph 42 of the Judgment in *Football Dataco & Others v Yahoo UK! & Others*, Case C-604/10.

It may thus seem that whether a database qualifies for protection under copyright law or database rights depends on the sufficiency of effort put into selection or arrangement of the collection.[72] This means that when a database is dictated by technical considerations, rules or constraints which leave no room for creative freedom then it cannot be considered original for the purposes of a copyright protection.[73] The copyright protection also entails with it all protection to the author of the database both moral and economical for the same term[74] of protection procured under the traditional copyright law.[75]

[D] Big Data Research and Genomic Databases

Biomedical data sets may also be aligned as a database for longitudinal or other types of detection studies.[76] Formulating such informational databases involves a highly complicated, expensive, time-consuming and intricate process of accessing, collecting, storing, analysing and interpreting biological samples.[77] While the creations of databases are distinct from ethical and legal arguments yet they are inseparable from it.[78] For example collecting a sample requires that the rights of donors are adhered to; likewise storage and use require respect to privacy rights. Within this sphere of complexity copyrights have been considered to be most malleable and amenable to the concerns of genetic research.[79] While the above analysis seeks to clarify the European position, two questions that still arises within the context of biobank databases are:

(1) Whether the selection and arrangement of the samples be considered to be copyrightable as a databases?
(2) Whether the selection and arrangement of the data amount to a work protectable by copyright?

Copyright in databases has been considered to be really 'thin' in the sense that the nature of the subject matter being protected involves the expression of author's intellectual creation which may often be difficult to deduce.[80] Thus, the creative elements may involve the selection of the fields, the categories of input along with the ease of access to the collection. That being said copyright offers distinct possibilities

72. *Ibid.*
73. Derclays in I.A Stamatoudi, P. Torremans, EU copyright law: A commentary, Edward Elgar Publishing 2014.
74. Recital 25 The term of copyright is already governed by Council Directive 93/98/EEC.
75. Articles 4, 5, 6 and recital 28 of the Directive 96/9/EC.
76. J. Galli et al., The biobanking analysis resource catalogue (BARCdb): A new research tool for the analysis of Biobank samples. *Nucleic Acids Research.* 2015; 43(Database issue): D1158–D1162. PMC. Web. 31 August 2017.
77. H. Gottweis and G. Lauss, Biobank governance: Heterogeneous modes of ordering and democratization. *Journal of Community Genetics.* 2012; 3(2): 61–72. PMC. Web. 30 March 2017.
78. *Ibid.*
79. G. Wei, An introduction to genetic engineering, life sciences and the law, NUS Press 2002; *see also* P. Bernt Hugenholtz, Implementing the European database directive, *IVIR*.
80. T. Dreier and G.W. Karnell, Originality of the copyrighted work: A European perspective, *Journal of the Copyright Society of the USA.* Summer, 1992; 39(4): 289–302.

over sui generis rights. One of the major distinctions is that, sui generis rights offers to protect only the investment in collecting verifying and presenting the contents. Copyright in databases on the contrary protects the 'structure' of the database, that involves the creative elements constituting 'selection' and of 'arrangement' of contents of data, through which the author of the database gives the database its structure.[81] In this sense attention must be paid either to the selection or arrangement of the sample and the data in the biobank. The criterion of selection relates to independent materials following the definition of databases under Article 1(2) of the Directive 96/9/EC.[82] Apart from being independent the content of the database may also consist of 'other materials'.[83] Further irrespective of the nature of the contents, the arrangement must relate to contents as provided under Article 3(1) of the directive such that they are individually accessible.[84]

In the context of biobanks storage and preservation of biological samples are often for one or more purpose. For instance a population based biobank may have samples relating to the population, specific cohorts based on such populations or other collaborative study cohorts with external research participants, in other case for instance larger research biobanks such as Graz or integrated IBBL[85] holds different types of samples varying from hospital residues, cohorts or samples belonging various partners across Europe. These are often systematically arranged following the database management criteria of the biobank which is often devised based on its need. Further, each of the samples are independent and belonging to different contributors. So also, the primary information or the 'data' derived from such samples will also belong to different contributors and they are arranged within biobanks in a codified and anonymized form. Although being independent the selection or arrangement must reflect the author's own intellectual creation.[86] Conducting epidemiological or pathological analysis with diverse samples require diverse structures to conduct complex analytical studies.[87] This creates a need to constantly design databases to suit the needs of scientific exploration irrespective of the database management systems or platforms that are used in the process.[88] So also biobank practices have shown that physical storage of samples involves different decisions to ensure the quality of such resource. Examples of such decisions include but are not limited to intended exploration, purpose, size of aliquots,[89] pre-analytic factors and analytic factors,[90] ease of access,

81. Case C 604/10, March 2012.
82. M. Walter and S. von Lewinski, European copyright law, a commentary, Oxford University Press 2010, at pg 704.
83. Article 1(2), Directive 96/9/EC.
84. *Supra* note 83.
85. Integrated Biobank Luxembourg.
86. Article 3(1), Directive 96/9/EC.
87. *See* C. Voegele, et al., A sample storage management system for biobanks. *Bioinformatics*. 2010; 26 (21): 2798–2800. doi: 10.1093/bioinformatics/btq502.
88. Also as evidenced by the author in the biobank visits.
89. A portion of a larger whole, especially a sample taken for chemical analysis or other treatment (source Wikipaedia).
90. Pre-analytic factors refer to collection, processing and storage variations that influence biospecimen integrity prior to its removal from the human research participant and carry through to the

use, etc.[91] Such intellectual choices as exemplified by the court in Painer case[92] are essential in the very structure of the biobank. Hence it would be plausible to say that a selection or arrangement of an independent 'data' or 'samples' constituting a biobank database structure could be subject of a copyright.

Adaptation to changing institutional needs and technical updating of the facilities or inclusion of new functions is the effort of the database administrator or the project manager.[93] While the personnel of a biobank may be responsible for the selection, arrangement of the database, they may well be within contractual clauses governing their work unless the laws of Member State in which the biobank is situated provides otherwise.[94] In general, however the copyright in such database schema[95] rest with the author of the work if it is the result of 'author's own intellectual creation'.[96]

[1] Ownership of Rights in Databases

The ownership of the database shall vest in a natural person or group of natural persons who created the database or, the legal person designated as the right-holder by the legislation of a Member State.[97] Under Article 4 of the Directive 96/9/EC, the author of a database shall be a natural person or a group of natural persons who created the base or, where the legislation of a Member States so permits, the legal person designated as the 'right-holder' by that legislation will be designated as the author. Where collective works are recognized by the legislation of a Member State, the economic rights shall be owned by the persons holding the copyright. In respect of a joint authorship of a database the exclusive rights shall be owned jointly.

The author of the database shall have the exclusive right to carry out or to authorize:[98]

(a) temporary or permanent reproduction by any means and in any form, in whole or in part;
(b) translation, adaptation, arrangement and any other alteration;
(c) any form of distribution to the public of the database or of copies thereof;[99]
(d) any communication, display or performance to the public;

---

point at which a biological specimen is ready for testing. Analytic factors refer to those variations that affect performance of a particular testing procedure.

91. P. Hainaut et al., Biobanking of human biospecimens, principles and practice, Springer 2017.
92. Case C-145/10 *Eva-Maria Painer v Standard VerlagsGmbH and Others.*
93. G. Wiederhold, Databases in healthcare, *Stanford Computer Science Department*, Report No. STAN-CS-80-790.
94. *Infra* note 97
95. A database schema is the skeleton structure that represents the logical view of the entire database. It defines how the data is organized and how the relations among them are associated. It formulates all the constraints that are to be applied on the data. https://www.tutorialspoint.com/dbms/dbms_data_schemas.htm.
96. Case C-5/08.
97. Article 4, Directive 96/9/EC.
98. Article 5, Directive 96/9/EC.
99. As per Art. 5(c), The first sale in the community of a copy of the database by the right-holder or with his consent shall exhaust the right to control resale of that copy within the community.

(e) any reproduction, distribution, communication, display or performance to the public.

Thus the owner of copyright in the database has the exclusive right to reproduce, translate, adapt or arrange the database, or to distribute, communicate, display or perform the database to the public. The owner of the database also has the same rights in respect of any translation, adaptation or arrangement of such database. Exceptions have however been provided for under Article 6 of the directive for private and educational uses similar to those under traditional copyright law. Yet, it does not provide for copyright of online databases. Thus unauthorized copying for private purposes of an online database is prohibited.[100]

One of the concerns for databases including genomic databases is the issue of ownership particularly within an employment relationship. The initial proposal for the database directive[101] included a provision on database created in the course of employment which read:

> 'where a database is created by an employee in the execution of his duties or following the instructions given by his employer, the employer exclusively shall be entitled to exercise all economic rights in the database so created, unless otherwise provided by contract'.[102]

However, this provision was rejected in order to avoid a presumption of exclusive entitlement of the employer in the exercise of the database.[103] Eventual the Council left the matter to be governed by National laws through recital 29. Under recital 29 'the arrangements applicable to databases created by employees are left to the discretion of the Member States'. Further, the recital also provided that the Directive did not prevent Member States from stipulating in their legislation that where a database is created by an employee in the execution of his duties or following the instructions given by his employer, the employer exclusively shall be entitled to exercise all economic rights in the database so created, unless otherwise provided by contract.[104] However, this position on databases created in the course of employment has been criticized for leaving it open to differing national legislations.[105] In some European Member States databases created in the course of employment strictly belongs to the employer unless otherwise agreed upon,[106] in other states the creator is regarded as the sole author of

100. DG Internal Market and services working paper: First evaluation of Directive 96/9/EC, 12 December 2005 on the legal protection of databases.
101. First proposal (COM(92) 24 final).
102. Article 3(4), (COM(92) 24 final).
103. *Supra* note 102.
104. Recital 29, Directive 96/9/EC.
105. A. Quaedvlieg, 'Authorship and ownership: Authors, entrepreneurs and rights', in Tatiana-Eleni Synodinou (eds) 'Codification of European copyright law. challenges and perspectives', Information Law Series 29. Kluwer Law International, 2012, 197–232.
106. For example. Belgium.

the database and employers may need to have specific contracts to deal with such databases.[107]

[E] Sequencing Data and Genetically Engineered Genetic Code

Copyright criterion does not apply homogenously to all biomedical information. While specific categories like databases, software, literary or artistic works, etc. have been addressed in law, others need to be examined under specific criteria of copyright law to appreciate if it could qualify as an original work that could be copyrighted. One such category, which so far has been limited to academic discussions, is the use of copyright to protect genetic sequence.[108] Between 1970s and 1980s there were similar tensions revolving the computer programs as to whether it must be patented or copyrighted.[109] Such discussions resulted in the acceptance for copyright protection for computer programs while offering patent protection for the invention using computer software or software-related inventions.[110] For example the US Copyright Act, 1976[111] and the UK Copyright, Designs and Patents Act 1988[112] and the EU Computer Program Directive 1991. These changes brought in greater impetus to the copyright discussion in the context of biotechnology which was also facing similar complexities owing to the differing judicial opinions and the innate nature of the subject matter.[113] The impetus for such a discussion also arises from Article 2 section 1 of the Berne Convention for the protection of literary and artistic works which also expressly includes scientific

107. For example. France, UK and Germany; *See* more in White Paper – Data ownership in the context of the European data economy: proposal for a new right, 6 February 2017.
108. T.D. Kiley, Learning to live with the living invention. *APLA Quarterly Journal*. 1980; 7: 20; I. Kayton, Copyright in genetically engineered works, *The George Washington Law Review*. 1982; 50: 191–218.
109. R.A Jordan, On the scope of protection for computer programs under copyright. (Computer programs: The patent/copyright interface), *AIPLA Quarterly Journal*. Summer, 1989; 17(3): 199–214.
110. Article 52 EPC, 1973; *See also* J.G. Silva's article, Copyright protection of biotechnology works: Into the dustbin of history?. Intellectual Property and Technical Forum. 2000 B.C. 012801.
111. Through the amendment in 1980, the definition of 'computer program' was added to section 101 of the US Copyright Act, 1976.
112. Article 3(1)(b) protects computer program and its preparatory design material as literary works.
113. For example. In USA, in the context of computer programs there have been a string of judicial decisions like *Gottschalk v Benson*, 409 US 63 was a United States Supreme Court case in which the court ruled that a process claim directed to a numerical algorithm, as such, was not patentable, however later in *Diamond v Diehr*, 450 US 175 (1981), the Supreme Court held that mere presence of a software element did not make an otherwise patent-eligible machine or process patent ineligible; likewise biotechnology and patentability has witnessed contrasting views in the same jurisdiction like for instance in the case of *Diamond v Chakrabarty*, 447 US 303, while considering the patentability of genetically modified organisms the US Supreme Court considered that 'anything under the sun can be patentable', however in the more recent *Association for Molecular Pathology v Myriad Genetics* 133 S.Ct. 2107, DNA isolated from its natural state cannot be patented however complementary DNA (cDNA) is a synthetic creation not normally present in nature and may be patentable.

productions.[114] While scientific productions are admitted in principle such that books, articles, lectures and pictorial presentations, etc. which could get copyright protection, it is still uncertain if scientific findings, discoveries and other substantive material including genetic are offered any protection at all.[115] The academic discourse over the subject widely differs in its outlook in this respect. Further there has only been a handful of meaningful discussions in regard to genetic copyright from the European jurisdiction.[116] However, the general discussion on the topic will be touched upon herein to offer some insights for current biomedical research in Europe and which will enable an understanding of whether sequencing of DNA from a human biological sample could be treated as a copyrightable work. There are mainly three approaches in literature considering copyright protection over genetic sequences which will be discussed herein.

[1] The Literary Approach

The literary approach considers genetic sequence to be protected as an original literary work.[117] Literary work includes works in literary, scientific and artistic domain in which ever mode it is expressed.[118] The Berne Convention offers various examples of such expressions such as compositions with or without words; cinematographic works to which are assimilated works expressed by a process analogous to cinematography; works of drawing, painting, including three-dimensional works in science.[119] While this may seem broad, yet intellectual creations expressed in differing forms seeks protection irrespective of their quality or style.[120] Genetic sequences are expressed as 'A', 'T', 'G' and 'C'[121] which denotes the nucleotides of the DNA giving it a match to a literary work.[122] While single words per se may not attract a copyright protection, its use as part of sentence or publication or communicating to the reader would be considered as an expression of the author's intellectual creation.[123] Through the choice, sequence and combination of those words that the author may express his

114. G. Schricker, 'Protection of scientific creations under patent and copyright law', in Liber Amicorum Joseph Straus, 'Patents and technological progress in a globalized world'. *Competition and Tax Law*. 2009; 6 of the series MPI Studies on Intellectual Property, at pp. 59–65.
115. *Infra* note 117.
116. The Modern Law of Copyright and Designs by Laddie, Prescott and Vitoria, Butterworths (2nd edn); A. Speck, Genetic copyright. *European Intellectual Property Review*. 1995; 17(4): 171–173; S. Hird and M. Peeters, UK protection for recombinant DNA – exploring the options. *European Intellectual Property Review*. 1991; 13(9): 334–339; J. Stanley and D.C. Ince, Copyright law in biotechnology: A view from the formalist camp, *European Intellectual Property Review*. 1997; 19(3): 142–148.
117. The Modern Law of Copyright and Designs by Laddie, Prescott and Vitoria, Butterworths (2nd edn); A. Speck, Genetic copyright, *European Intellectual Property Review*. 1995; 17(4): 171–173.
118. Article 2(1) Berne Convention, 1886.
119. *Ibid.*
120. R. Tomkowicz, Intellectual property overlaps: Theory, strategies, and solutions, Routledge 2011.
121. Fundamental components of a DNA namely Adenine, Thymine, Guanine and Cytosine.
122. *Infra* note 125
123. Case C-5/08 *Infopak A/S v Danske Dagblades Forening* (2009) ECDR 16.

creativity in an original manner and achieve a result, which is an intellectual creation.[124] In this sense it is considered that a biologist involved in arranging genes in a plasmid or a synthetic biologist creating string of nucleotides are considered to be creating works which may qualify as 'original literary' for the purpose of a copyright protection.[125] This would mean that 'literary works' encompasses sequences of their nucleotide bases and any written representation in this respect.[126] However, critics of this approach consider that DNA are genetic material available in the state of nature and mere presentation of facts do not qualify as an original literary work.[127] Speck on the contrary considers that the originality resides in the finding out of the sequence and presenting it in a form (or language) that can be understood by a section of the public. Thus, what is not original is the actual sequence of amino acids or nucleic acids that existed before the work on the elucidation began.[128] In this sense elucidation and recording of genetic sequence is also seen as a translation of a literary work.[129] While this viewpoint is limited to those sequences derived naturally it does not explain the 'literary work' in itself from which such translation has been made.

[2] The Compilation Approach

Compilations of pre-existing works or collective works[130] as they are also referred are protected by copyright. Under the Berne Convention,[131] TRIPS Agreement[132] and under the WCT,[133] databases which constitute creative compilations enjoy protection under copyright as literary works if the selection and arrangement is original. Compilations are protected in different parts of the world in varying ways.[134] The compilation

124. C-5/08 *Infopak internation A/Sv. Danske Dablades Forening* [2009] ECDR, para. 45.
125. A. Torrence, DNA copyright, *Valparaiso University Law Review*. 2011–2012; 46(1).
126. D.L. Burke, Copyrightability of recombinant DNS sequences, *Jurimetrics*. (Summer 1989); 29(4): 469–532.
127. *Supra* note 387 quoting the Canadian decision in *CCH Canadian Ltd v Law Society of Upper Canada*, [2004] 1 S.C.R. 339, 2004 SCC 13 at para. 22 where concerns were raised that 'sweat of the brow' doctrine improperly extends copyright over facts. Thus if copyright is offered to genetic material it would just be a fact taken from nature thought it may involve skill or labour to decipher the same.
128. A. Speck, Genetic copyright, *European Intellectual Property Review*. 1995; 17(4): 171–173.
129. *Ibid.*
130. Developed by French courts by the usage 'oeuvres collections' in reference to dictionaries and other such works; *see* Mascarade case Tribunal of first instance Siena, 19th March, 1935 cited in P. Kamina, Film copyright in the European union, Cambridge University Press 2016.
131. Article 2(5) Berne Convention, 1971, 'Collections of literary or artistic works such as encyclopaedias and anthologies which, by reason of the selection and arrangement of their contents, constitute intellectual creations shall be protected as such, without prejudice to the copyright in each of the works forming part of such collections'.
132. Article 10 of TRIPS, 1994.
133. Article 5 of WCT, 1996.
134. For instance in UK a compilation may be protected as a copyright or in terms of their investments as a sui generis right, in USA on the other hand the copyright in a compilation of data extends only to the selection, coordination or arrangement of the materials or data, in Europe a compilation whose selection and arrangement selection of the contents which constitute the author's own intellectual creation is protected as a copyright. In France it is referred by the concept of 'æuvres collectives, which as a collective work presupposes the

approach to copyright over DNA sequence views the arrangement of various bits of DNA or its combination with other materials (e.g., combining with a plasmid to develop new resultant materials) constitutes a compilation.[135] The advantage of this approach is that it enables ignoring originality of individual components while focusing on the selection and arrangement, which involves the creative freedom of scientist working in the field. This approach also helps incorporate scientific tinkering of genetic materials specially with rapidly advancing technologies such as gene editing such as CRISPER/Cas 9[136] tool in which the biologist can select a target sequence for gene editing. Such tailoring of bits of DNA into host cells could amount to creating a compilation of pre-existing materials.[137]

In Europe, however the approach to copyrightability of a compilation is based on the concept of 'originality' (defined as author's own intellectual creation[138]) in the selection and arrangement. The 'author's own.' means that the author was able to express his creative abilities in the production of the work by making free and creative choices.[139] This would imply that irrespective of a work involving technical expertise of professionals, it would be enough if such person used her knowledge and skills in making her free and creative choice in developing such work. Even so, genetic sequencing may offer limitation in securing author's 'personal touch'.[140] Further it will not also be able to suffice the criterion of independence. This has also been further clarified under Recital 17 of the database directive in terms of the examples.[141] While 'A', 'T', 'G', 'C' though representing the independent amino acid combinations, yet the genetic information as such is not retrievable from them individually as they are interdependent combinations which formulated the information and hence by itself cannot constitute a database.[142]

creation and publication to take place in special ways involving a conjoint venture (*see* for more Silke Von Leweinski paras 8.1.70–71).

135. *Supra* note 125.
136. CRISPER (clustered regularly interspaced short palindromic repeats) is a genome editing tool naturally-occurring as an ancient defence mechanism found in a wide range of bacteria. It enables gene editing to be far more precise and flexible and is considered to be a magic wand in curing and preventing may genetic disease. *See* https://innovativegenomics.org/blog/how-to-make-a-guide-rna-for-cas9/ (last accessed on 16 May 2017).
137. *Ibid.*
138. Case C-5/08 *Infopak Internation A/S v Danske Dablades Forening* [2009] ECDR 16.
139. Case C-145/10 *Eva-Maria Painer v Standard VerlagsGmbH and Others*, at para. 89; *see also* E. Rosati, Originality in the EU copyright law full harmonization through case law, Edward Elgar 2013.
140. *Ibid.*
141. Recital 17, Directive 96/9/EC: Whereas the term 'database' should be understood to include literary, artistic, musical or other collections of works or collections of other material such as texts, sound, images, numbers, facts and data; whereas it should cover collections of independent works, data or other materials which are systematically or methodically arranged and can be individually accessed; whereas this means that a recording or an audiovisual, cinematographic, literary or musical work as such does not fall within the scope of this directive.
142. Grutzmacher, Databanken 172 as cited by Silke Von Lewinski at pg 697.

[3] *Software Approach*

Under this approach, genetic sequencing is compared to computer programs. The preamble to the council directive on computer programs defines the term 'computer program' to include programs in any form, including those which are incorporated into hardware and also includes preparatory design work leading to the development of a computer program provided that the nature of the preparatory work is such that a computer program can result from it at a later stage.[143] In this sense, computer programs include those instructions, which give raise to a technical result and are expressions protected by copyright.[144] Likewise, the DNA sequence acts as a program to produce specific proteins and is readable through a cell.[145] While such similarities exist between DNA sequence and computer programs doubts have been raised on the scope of protection of the sequencing code within the cell and on paper as human readable computer program.[146] In Europe following the decision of the CJEU in SAS[147] and Bezpenostní softwarová asociace case[148] it is clear that the forms of expression of a computer program and the preparatory design work capable of leading, respectively, to the reproduction or the subsequent creation of such a program is protected by copyright. Nevertheless its functionality may not be protected as such.[149] This means that both machine readable and human readable programs can claim copyright in Europe provided it involves 'the author's intellectual creation'. Attempts were made in the USA to copyright engineered genetic codes as a part of an academic experiment by Holman and his team without much success.[150] So also, the courts in US do not appear to have ever addressed the question as in Europe.[151]

143. Council Directive of 14 May 1991 on the legal protection of computer programs (91/250/EEC).
144. *SAS Institute Inc v World Programming Ltd*, C-406/10, May 2012.
145. *Supra* note 379.
146. D. Smith, Copyright protection for the intellectual property rights to recombinant deoxyribonucleic acid: A proposal. *St. Mary's Law Journal*. 1987–1988; 19: 1083.
147. Case C-406/10, *SAS Institute Inc v World Programming Inc*, 2 May 2012, at para. 37.
148. *Bezpečnostní softwarová asociace – Svaz softwarové ochrany v Ministerstvo kultury*, paras 37–41.
149. In Case C-406/10, *SAS Institute Inc v World Programming Inc*, 2 May 2012, at para. 39 it was observed by the CJEU that neither the functionality of a computer program nor the programming language and the format of data files used in a computer program in order to exploit certain of its functions constitute a form of expression of that program.
150. Christopher M Holman, Charting the Contours of a Copyright Regime Optimized for Engineered Genetic Code Oklahoma Law Review (2016).
151. C.M. Holman, Are engineered genetic sequences copyrightable?: The US copyright office addresses a matter of first impression, Biotechnology Law Report, 2016; Although in USA and in Europe the question of genetic copyright never came up before the court, it was however discussed a higher court in the Indian Jurisdiction in the case of *Emergent Genetics India Pvt. Ltd v Shailendra Shivam and ors, Nos. 388/2004, 1267/2004&1268/2004 in CS (OS) 50/2004, August 2, 2011 (HC (Ind))*, the claim of genetic copyright was however turned down in this case *see* for more discussion: https://indiankanoon.org/doc/183763759/ (last accessed on 10 September 2017). *See* for more discussion on the point: R. Neethu, Genetic Copyright in the era of Biobanks and Synthetic Biology. *European Intellectual Property Review*. 2018.

[4] Genetic Copyright and Biomedical Research in Europe

The relevance of genetic copyright to biobanks is implicit in the essence of copyright protection for the author and her creative works.[152] Biobanks stores different biological materials along with differing types of information attached to the samples. Biobanks serve as resources for identifying groups of population or patient groups which tend to offer valuable genetic information for the study, assessment and treatment for diseases.[153] For instance identifying polymorphism involves categorizing patient groups for the assessment of various factors relating to the disease and response of individuals towards particular treatments enabling scientist to create new biomarkers with the use of such resources.[154] This in fact creates value for genetic resources and which often tends to increase exponentially over time owing to added data sets[155] e.g., from study cohorts. Commercialization in such scenario involving patents for instance tends to exclude other from making using or selling the gene over which patent exits besides protecting the working knowledge of the innovation which is most likely to be inferred from data contributed from different groups or from specific donors in case of distinct samples. This may not only limit sharing and access to resources but often tends to ignore the wishes of the donors who may have contributed the samples to a noble cause. In this sense copyright law offers greater degree of flexibilities to incorporate ethical legal concerns that often revolve around the use of genetic resources;[156] for instance offering a creative licensing for the genetic materials belonging to a particular study such as the Framingham cohort offered valuable information in terms of heart studies. Chris Holman[157] notes that copyright offers possibilities for identify the owner of the copyright and its licensing status and recommends the formation of registries with copyrighted sequences which may also be licensed as a database. Patent registrations and prosecutions can often be costly for biobanks which are already under siege for stability in maintaining their resources. Ensuring efficiency, sustainability of bio-resources along with recognition of such resources in other research activities requires a reward for the valuable resources that was built with time and efforts.[158] Copyright offers these possibilities for biobanks in many ways as is discussed in this chapter. Besides new forms and formats of copyright material and the changing nature of information has always been an interest to the EU. It has been suggested in the report of the commission Contribution of Copyright and Related Rights to the European

152. I.A Stamatoudi and P. Torremans, EU copyright law: A commentary, Edward Elgar Publishing 2014; 14–16.
153. A.C. Thomson et al., Biobanks for genomics and genomics for biobanks, *Comparative and Functional Genomics.* 2003; 4: 628–634.
154. *Ibid.*
155. L. Mabile, BRIF as a tool for improving bioresource sharing in biomedical research, *Nature Precedings*, 4 November 2011.
156. *See* D. Hogle, Copyright for innovative biotechnological research: An attractive alternative to patent and trademark law. *High Technology Law Journal.* Spring, 1989; 5(1): 75–127.
157. C. Holman, Copyright protection of DNA sequences: Market implications (Part 2), *GQ Life Sciences Blog.*
158. *Infra* note 159

Economy[159] that the commission and Member States must continue to ensure that new forms are recognized and that an appropriate copyright enforcement mechanisms and processes are in place so that the community benefits economically from such new industries or activities.[160] This gives impetus to exploring the possibilities over genetic copyright in Europe.

[5] Patient-Generated Health Data: Questionnaires and Medical Records

In addressing the data held within biobanks it would be relevant to touch upon the various types of data held within a biobank along with the rights and control over such information. Often data created for systematic usage of samples by a researcher within a biobank could automatically be the subject of a copyright. This is so because unlike other IPR copyright applies to the author's intellectual creation without the need for any separate registration.[161] Patient-generated health data or patient-related information are created, recorded, gathered or inferred by or from patients or their designees to help address a health concern.[162] Such information may also be collected from donors of samples who participate in the biobank or its specific cohorts.

Research biobanks invariably seek information from the participants in the form of questionnaires along with the samples collected from such donors. These may include information as to the physical measurements or lifestyle or other factors of participants.[163] Also, specific cohorts may also offer questionnaires for participants for seeking genealogical information from them. Thus, there may exists copyright in such questionnaires.[164] Nevertheless, not all questionnaire may be subject of a copyright. Copyright law aims to protect author's intellectual creations in which the author may have exercised her own free and creative choices.[165] Thus, works which necessarily are modification of pre-existing works, even if newly generated may not involve a creative effort and thus may not be able to seek copyright.[166] Copyright over questionnaire entails with it the economic rights arising from copyright including the right of reproduction and making adaptations of the work. The Berne Convention also states that translations, adaptations, arrangements of music and other alterations of a literary or artistic work shall be protected as original works.[167] Copyright in such adaptation or translation is also independent of the copyright that subsists in such works.[168] This

159. Contribution of Copyright and Related Rights to the European Economy, 20th October 2003, European Commission Directorate General – Internal Market.
160. *Ibid.*, at p. 18.
161. J. Pila and P. Torrenmans, European intellectual property law, OUP 2016, at p. 325.
162. M. Shapiro et al., Patient-generated health data (white paper). 2012Apr [cited 1 September 2014].
163. OECD, Creation and Governance of Human Genetic Research Databases, 2006.
164. S. Pathmasiri et al., Intellectual property rights in publicly funded biobanks: Much Ado about nothing?'. *Nature Biotechnology*.2011; 319.
165. *Painer v Standard VerlagsGmbH*, C-145/10.
166. European Commission, Report on the responses to the Public Consultation on the Review of the EU Copyright Rules, 2013.
167. Article 2(3) of Berne Convention for protection of Literary and artistic works, 1886.
168. *Ibid.*

means that even though the author of a questionnaire may generally be the author of such translation or adaptation, it is possible to license the same.[169] While this may seemingly be considered to be of lesser importance, interesting issues have been reported in the past on copyright issues related to health outcome measures such as Asthma Quality of Life Questionnaire.[170] The questionnaire developed a research group were adapted for another research by a different group without acknowledgment.[171] Scientific researchers have also advocated for the maintenance of the scientific integrity of the copyrighted instrument which will ensure that researcher of study cohorts use the correct version of such works and also abide by appropriate licensing arrangements from the rightful owner of such works.[172] Often such questionnaires may be valuable to biobanks in securing patient-reported outcomes which may offer important information regarding the health-related quality of life of biobank participants or more generally of a given population.[173]

Apart from these some biobanks particularly population biobanks may incorporate additional information from the medical records which may be linked to the biobanks. For example, population biobanks like UK biobank or research-oriented biobanks such as biobank Graz holding population collections for research studies. There also exists diversity in the amount of and procedure involved is securing the data collected from medical records.[174] For instance, it has been reported that while the UK biobank collects data from National Health Service (NHS), Estonian biobank bank on the contrary gathers a description of the state of health from the questionnaires and health records prepared by a processor of information appointed for the purpose.[175] This implies that there could be different modalities involved in collection of data[176] and differing types of data within biobanks that could qualify as a 'work' under a copyright regime.[177] In a report prepared for the commission on EHRs it was observed

169. T. Dreier and P.B. Hugenholtz, Concise European copyright law, Kluwer Law International 2006.
170. A.C. Patient-reported outcomes instruments: Bridging the gap between international copyright laws and common practice for developers and users – a case example. *Quality of Life Research* 2009; 18(10): 1281–1283.
171. *Ibid.*
172. D.A Revicki and C.E Schwartz. Intellectual property rights and good research practice. *Quality of Life Research* 2009; 18(10): 1279–1280.
173. C. Petersen and P. DeMuro, Legal and regulatory considerations associated with use of patient-generated health data from social media and mobile health (mHealth) devices. *Applied Clinical Informatics*. 2015; 6(1): 16–26. http://doi.org/10.4338/ACI-2014-09-R-0082; *see also* an example of a study under: Z. Ul-Haq, et al., Association between physical and mental health-related quality of life and adverse outcomes; a retrospective cohort study of 5,272 Scottish adults. *BMC Public Health*. 2014; 14: 1197. http://doi.org/10.1186/1471-2458-14-1197.
174. *Supra* note 173.
175. *Ibid.*
176. K. Beier et al., The ethical and legal regulation of human tissue and biobank research in Europe, proceedings of Tiss. EU project, Universitätsverlag Göttingen 2011.
177. The concept of work in itself is broad. Under Art. 2(1) of the Berne Convention, The expression 'literary and artistic works' shall include every production in the literary, scientific and artistic domain, whatever may be the mode or form of its expression.

that data may be the object of IPR.[178] Although the discussion did not go into the issues of ownership per se, it was acknowledged that issues such as ownership required a much more sophisticated and nuanced approach.[179] The method of securing patients health information, the conditions of access and usage all determine the rights of ownership and control over informational resources. It has been noted by a commentator that even though medical data relates to patients and may involve privacy rules, nonetheless the information is 'created', sorted and structured by a medical professional.[180] This may however be of different nature like those recorded by a doctor or a medical practitioner during an examination of a patient, diagnostic information, test results, virtual recordings or a brief patient history compiled for certain purposes.[181] Each of these may qualify as a copyrightable work provided they satisfy the test of copyright originality. Usually the entry in the consultation notes consists of only a few words describing the names of the patient or her social security number, the medical conditions, medications as well as physiological and pathological data. Offering a right over such records may often be faced with the lack of originality and independent intellectual effort.[182]

The copyright ownership vests with the creator of the work. Thus, where a medical practitioner creates the records she may be legally considered as the creator of the work. On the contrary when developed or filed by a health personnel such as an administrator or like the Estonian biobank where a description is created by a staff of a biobank such person will be considered the author of such work. This is however subject to employer-employee contracts that may govern the transfer of rights in such works. In this sense it may be easier for publicly funded institutions to control the use and access to sensitive information contained in the work. Further as discussed above it has to be remembered that copyright protects the expression of information and not the information in itself. This would mean that it would be possible to extract information from medical records without infringing any copyright.[183] However, nature of application of copyright in particular patient-related information has to be assessed on a case-to-case basis.

178. EU Health Programme, Overview of the national laws on electronic health records in the EU Member States and their interaction with the provision of cross-border eHealth services. Final report and recommendations, 23 July 2014.

179. *Ibid.*

180. L. Vilches Armesto and P. Laurent, The intellectual property of medical data: Copyrights to patients'records and database rights to biobank?, *Dans La protection des donnnées médicales: les défis du XXIe siècle = The protection of medical data: Challenges of the 21st century.* Anthemis, 2008; 153–185.

181. *Ibid.*, at p. 155.

182. For example the *Judgment by the Federal Court of Australia in Primary Health Care v Commissioner of Taxation* [2010] FCA 419, found that in some cases there is no copyright in health records at all. *See also* M. Worsman, Copyright in health records, *Mondaq Business Briefing*, 18 November 2010.

183. *Infra* note 186.see also B. Campbell et al., Extracting information from hospital records: what patients think about consent, *Quality and Safety in Health Care*, 16(6): 404–408.

[6] Copyright and Privacy: Implications for Biobanks

With the above discussion on the automatic application of copyright law to documents that are created, a question that arises is the relationship between copyright and privacy. This question though seemingly simple has many dimensions (particularly with respect to digital rights management systems[184]) which the current work do not find necessary to deal in its full length. Hence, the focus will be limited on genetic information pertinent to biobank data and its processing.

Biobanks are often confronted with differing dimensions of privacy such as data anonymization and sharing.[185] At the same time, stakeholders including biobanks themselves are concerned about questions of ownership and control of medical information.[186] The digital paradigm and development of creative platforms for sharing of information have made these questions even more relevant.[187] In the sphere of biobanking, this has led to a fundamental debate over management of genetic information and more importantly ensuring confidentiality of patient information.[188] These concerns also accelerate with changing approaches to the governance of such information. On the one hand publicly funded biobanks have been engaged in the process of collection and storage of human biological samples, as well as personal information which are also mostly linked to the medical records of individual donors.[189] On the other hand there is a growing impetus to offering patients more control and access to their own health information.[190] For instance the Swedish implementation of its patient accessible EHRs[191] and NHS wales offering data management systems for patients to access and regulate the health records concerning their own health information.[192] These evolving trends pose many challenges for research cohorts particularly managing different regulatory processes across each data.[193] The existence of copyright in a given work does not modify the nature of data or affect the data

184. For instance *see* Lee A. Bygrave, The technologisation of copyright: Implications for privacy and related interests, *European Intellectual Property Review*. 2002; 24(2): 51–57.
185. M.G. Hansson, Ethics and biobanks, *British Journal of Cancer*. 13 January 2009; 100(1): 8–12.
186. N. Hawkins et al., 'Ownership of biomedical information in biobanks', in G. Pascuzzi and U. Izzo, 'Comparative issues in the governance of research biobanks, property, privacy, intellectual property and the role of technology, Springer 2013.
187. *Ibid.*
188. H. Gottweis, Biobanks in comparative perspective, Routledge; *See also* H.T Greely. Informed consent and other ethical issues in human population genetics. *Annual Review of Genetics*.2001; 35: 785–800; H.T Greely. Human genomics research: New challenges for research ethics. *Perspectives in Biology and Medicine* 2001; 44: 221–29.
189. Biobanks and the Public: Governing Biomedical Research Resources in Europe, A Report from the BBMRI Project.
190. I. Passarani, Patient access to electronic health records, Report of the eHealth Stakeholder Group, VERSION June 2013.
191. S. Armstrong, Patient access to health records: Striving for the Swedish ideal, *BMJ* 2017; 357: j2069 doi: 10.1136/bmj.j2069.
192. M. Limb, Patients in wales to take control of medical records, BMJ 2017;357:j2982 doi: 10.1136/bmj.j2982 (Published 2017 June 20).
193. L. Adamska et al., Challenges of linking to routine healthcare records in UK Biobank. *Trials* 2015 16(Suppl 2):O68.

protection rules.[194] Fundamentally, both sets of rights are aimed essentially at regulating the flow of information in order to preserve certain values and interests.[195] However there still exist tensions over exclusivity of rights. Copyright concerns itself with the rights over authorship in a given work including the right of communicating the work to public. Privacy on the contrary concerns itself with the processing of personal information including the transmission or use of such information.[196] However, copyright and privacy may also overlap where an unauthorized access of the work is made.[197] Even so, each applies in its own distinct juridical standpoint.[198] While IP law does not offer a legal basis for participants' ownership of biomedical information[199] it does not limit the rules of data privacy from applying. Thus the communication of a work containing personal information must ensure the rightful authorization from the patient or the participant whose medical information is contained in such work.[200] There is ample support to this from the decision of highest court in Europe.[201] An interesting example relevant in context is the case of Mrs Bodil Lindqvist[202] who had published the names, jobs, hobbies, telephone numbers, family circumstances, etc. of her colleagues in a blog written by her. While writing the blog was a part of her creative effort and perhaps even subject to a copyright, it did not offer her the right to use the personal information of her colleagues without their relevant consent. Thus it was not surprising when the Court of Justice of EU ruled that the data protection rules and freedom of expression must be balanced against each other, and the regime of the data protection directive provides in itself multiple mechanisms allowing a balancing of the different fundamental rights to be carried out.[203] In the same vein extensive information entered into medical records on people's health, may contain, personal information. Information of this kind can relate to some of the most intimately private affairs of the person concerned. This entitles the patients to object, modify or secure copy of the information pertaining to themselves or those affecting their family members.[204] The General Data Protection Regulation (2016)[205] recognizes this right

194. *Infra* note 195
195. L. Bygrave, 'Data protection v Copyright' in Dan Jerker B. Svantesson & Stanley Greenstein internationalisation of law in the digital information society: Nordic yearbook of law and informatics'. 2010–2012, First edition, first impression.
196. A. Drassinower, 'Copyright infringement as compelled speech', in A. Lever 'New frontiers in the philosophy of intellectual property', Cambridge University Press, 2012.
197. *Ibid.*
198. *Ibid.*
199. *Supra* note 184.
200. *Supra* note 188.
201. C-275/06, Promusicae, 29.1.2008, S. and *Marper v The United Kingdom* [2008] ECHR 1581 (2008); *Van der Velden v the Netherlands* (dec.) (No. 29514/05, ECHR 2006-XV; *see also* Nuffield Council on Bioethics: The forensic use of bioinformation: ethical issues, 2007.
202. Case C 101/01-Lindqvist.
203. Paragraphs 82–87 and 90 of Case C 101/01-Lindqvist; for more decisions *see* Laraine Laudati, summaries of the EU court of decisions relating to data protection 200–2001, 28 January 2016 (Prepared for OLAF and DPO).
204. *Ragnhildur Guðmundsdóttir v The State of Iceland*, No. 151/2003 Icelandic Supreme Court.
205. Regulation (EU) 2016/679 of the European Parliament and of the Council of 27 April 2016 on the protection of natural persons with regard to the processing of personal data and on the free movement of such data, and repealing Directive 95/46/EC (General Data Protection Regulation).

when it provides in the recital that 'a data subject should have the right of access to personal data which have been collected concerning him or her, and to exercise that right easily and at reasonable intervals, in order to be aware of, and verify, the lawfulness of the processing'. This includes the right for data subjects to have access to data concerning their health, for example the data in their medical records containing information such as diagnoses, examination results, assessments by treating physicians and any treatment or interventions provided and the like. Further this right should not adversely affect the rights or freedoms of others, including trade secrets or IP and in particular the copyright protecting the software.[206] Further privacy and data protection are core values of the EU, recognized in Article 8 ECHR and Articles 7 and 8 of the EU Charter of Fundamental Rights, which must be respected in all the policies, and rules adopted by the EU pursuant to Article 16 of the TFEU.[207] Thus any use of genetic information contained in a work subject to copyright could not be used to the detriment of patients' rights. While so copyright in sensitive information containing work could enable publicly funded biobanks as protective custodians of information.[208]

[F] Biobank Cloud and Copyright

One of the interesting developments of the contemporary genomic era is the quantum leap in the wave of data from genomic information to Big Data.[209] This shift has implication in the context of copyright laws as well which will be discussed herein. This is summarized appropriately in a EU background paper on the review of copyright law thus:

> *The digital economy has been a major driver of growth in the past two decades ... The emergence of new business models capitalising on the potential of the internet to deliver content represents a challenge and an opportunity for the creative industries, authors and artists as well as the other actors in the digital economy.*[210]

Biobanks have already entered the area of 'Big Data' and are increasingly turning into large data centre facilities or 'cloud' environments.[211] One of the reasons for this shift is the pressure of sustenance, decrease in sequencing costs and limitation in stabilizing commercially with traditional sample storage alone.[212] At the same enabling such a shift comes with many challenges distinct to the digital environment. Some of these legal and ethical challenges have been identified as those relating to data security,

206. Recital 63, Regulation (EU) 2016/679.
207. Opinion of the European Data Protection Supervisor on the current negotiations by the European Union of an Anti Counterfeiting Trade Agreement (ACTA), 2010/C 147/01.
208. R. Brownsword, 'Rights, responsibility and stewardship: Beyond consent'. In H. Widdows and C. Mullen (eds), 'The governance of genetic information: Who decides?' Cambridge Law, Medicine and Ethics, Cambridge University, 2009, pp. 99–125.
209. *Infra* note 428.
210. European Commission, Orientation Debate on Content in the Digital Economy (2012).
211. *Ibid.*
212. Attacking the Biobank Bottleneck, Biobank cloud initiative supported by the European Commission's Seventh Framework Programme (FP7).

confidentiality, transfer and accountability.[213] But a lesser explored challenge is that of copyright infringement which will be addressed herein.

Cloud computing is the term used to refer to the ability to access information through a remote bank of servers rather than from a local computer. Information stored in the cloud can be accessed from the nearest bank of servers, which reduces the bandwidth used.[214] Cloud computing represents a further industrialization with its multifarious uses. For instance consumers can use cloud services to store information (e.g., pictures or files in dropbox), organizations, including public sector can use cloud services to successively replace internally run data centres and information and communication technology (ICT) departments or companies can use cloud services to scale up their services to the customers because they can do so without investing in and building physical infrastructures.[215] Genomic cloud computing can be defined as a scalable service where genetic sequence information is stored and processed virtually (i.e., in the 'cloud') usually via networked, large-scale data centres accessible remotely through various clients and platforms over the Internet.[216] In contrast to the traditional the traditional lab information management system such as LIMS[217] cloud-based technology is considered more cost-effective and flexible. Hence, cloud technology is being floated as an alternative that provides the opportunity to small and medium-sized biobanks to automate their operations in a cost-effective manner with ease to collaborate with other research cohorts (*see* Figure 5.2).[218] By this it is also anticipated that cloud-based solutions could offer the advantage of heightened security, rapid scalability, dynamic allocation of services, which can create a collaborative environment between different research groups by using a shared environment on a 'pay-as-you-go' basis.[219]

213. *Infra* note 214
214. European Commission. Unleashing the potential of cloud computing. COM(2012)529 final; *see also* P. Ollier, The cloud and copyright explained, Managing intellectual property, June 2011.
215. *Supra* note 214.
216. E.S. Dove et al., Genomic cloud computing: legal and ethical points to consider, *European Journal of Human Genetics* 2014; 1–8; *See also* L.D Stein. The case for cloud computing in genome informatics. *Genome Biology* 2010; 11: 207.
217. Laboratory Information Management Systems (LIMS)- sometimes referred to as a laboratory information system (LIS) or laboratory management system (LMS), is a software-based laboratory and information management system with features that support a modern laboratory's operations. Key features include – but are not limited to – workflow and data tracking support, flexible architecture, and data exchange interfaces, which fully 'support its use in regulated environments; *see* Laboratory Information Management: So what is a LIMS?'. *Sapio Sciences*. 28 July 2010; A. McLelland. What is a LIMS – a laboratory toy, or a critical IT component?. *Royal Society of Chemistry*, 1998.
218. S. Paul et al., The state of cloud-based biospecimen and biobank data management tools, *Biopreservation and Biobanking* 15(2): 2017.
219. *Ibid.*

Figure 5.2 Data Integration in the Cloud

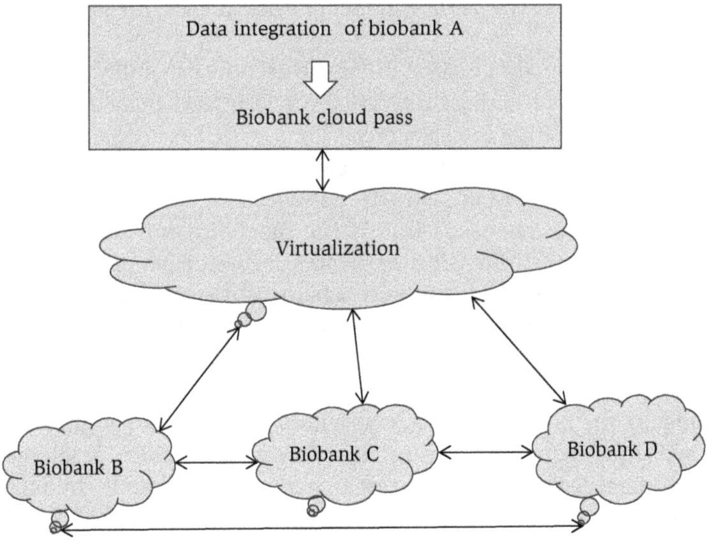

Biobank data integration in the cloud

There are different types of cloud platforms. Generally they have classified these in four main deployment model types namely:[220]

(1) *Public cloud infrastructure*: it is provisioned for open use by the general public and may also be developed for commercial cloud. Commercial cloud infrastructures enable customers to build, manage and scale an infrastructure based on their needs.[221]
(2) *Community cloud infrastructure*: is developed for exclusive use by a specific community of consumers from organizations that have shared concerns (e.g., mission, security requirements, and policy and compliance considerations). It may be owned, managed or operated by one or more organizations in the community, a third party or a combination of both.
(3) *Hybrid cloud infrastructure*: The hybrid cloud infrastructure comprises of two or more distinct cloud infrastructures (private, community or public) that remain unique entities, but are bound together by standardized or proprietary technology that enables data and application portability.
(4) *Private cloud infrastructure*: is developed for use by a single organization. It is for exclusive uses and may be operated by the organization or third party or in combination. This type as per the author offers the best safeguards for healthcare organizations.

220. J.J.M Seddon and W.L Currie. Cloud computing and trans-border health data: unpacking US and EU healthcare regulation and compliance. *Health Policy and Technology* 2013; 2: 229–241.
221. *Supra* note 216.

The type of platform is generally based on the use and the form of service such infrastructures aim to provide.[222] While there exist differing types of deployment models as discussed above the service model in general is of three types namely:

(1) *Software-as-a-Service* ('SaaS'): offers the user the capability to use the provider's applications running on a cloud infrastructure. Such an application can be downloaded from a web server.[223]
(2) *Platform-as-a-Service* ('PaaS'): the capabilities offered to the consumers are deployed in the cloud infrastructure itself.[224]
(3) *Infrastructure-as-a-Service* ('IaaS'): The capability provided to the consumer in this type is a provision of processing, storage, networks and other fundamental computing resources where the consumer is able to deploy and run arbitrary software, which can include operating systems and applications.[225]

Traditionally the biobank data stored within the biobank's digital environment were processed as per request from researchers following an ethical assessment of such research. Such data derived from the researchers or by research conducted by the scientific staff within the biobanks were then entered back into the system.[226] The cloud initiative within biobanks now offers the users a possibility to create a virtual infrastructure to store and process their data within the cloud itself.[227] Thus sharing, processing storage and reuse of data can happen within the same platform.[228] Further clouds offer novel research opportunities in genomics in facilitating cohort studies to be carried out at unprecedented scale by enabling computer processing with superior pace and throughput, allowing researchers to address questions that could not be addressed by normal study cohorts.[229]

The European biobank cloud initiatives have been expanding its cloud service approach in two forms namely as a 'SaaS' and 'PaaS'. The first one is through an open source system, which is merely software for bioinformatics analysis without any services. In this version it is not possible to connect to other Biobank Cloud users, and

222. A. Bessani et. al., 'BiobankCloud: A platform for the secure storage, sharing, and processing of large biomedical data sets,' in 1st International Workshop on Data Management and Analytics for Medicine and Healthcare, DMAH 2015 and Workshop on Big-Graphs Online Querying, Big-O(Q) 2015 held in conjunction with 41st International Conference on Very Large Data Bases, VLDB 2015, 2016, pp. 89–105.
223. P. Mell and T. Grance, The NIST definition of cloud computing, US national institute of standards and technology, 2009; The European Commission Staff Working Document (SWD(2012) 271 final) also follows the same definition and classification of cloud as in the NIST document.
224. *Id*
225. *Id.*
226. L.D. Stein, The case for cloud computing in genome informatics, *Stein Genome Biology* 2010; 11: 207.
227. V. Vielmo Cogo et al., From data Islands to sharing data in the cloud: The evolution of data integration in biological data repositories. *Communications and Innovations Gazette*, 2016.
228. V. Marx. Biology: The big challenges of big data. *Nature*, 2013; 498(7453): 255–260.
229. M. Gábor et al., Computing patient data in the cloud: Practical and legal considerations for genetics and genomics research in Europe and internationally. *Genome Medicine*. 2017; 9: 58.

thus not possible to share any data via the software. Further, this version does not require any prior authorization and can be downloaded for use by any researcher online.[230] The first platform uses a standard software licence agreement. The downloading of the software itself does not entail any processing of personal data and therefore the Biobank Cloud consortium does not assume the role of a processor vis-à-vis the person downloading the software.[231] The commercial version is through a formal institutional structure such as BBMRI-ERIC that has implemented the Biobank Cloud platform, including all the services for data storage, analysis and metadata sharing. The biobank cloud project hopes that the collaboration of industrial partners with research organizations can only enable full version of Biobank Cloud platform. With such aims at hand, the use and access of this platform will require users to fulfil the terms and conditions of use of the platform, as set out in the controller-processor agreement.[232] By this a balance is sought between the interests of patients along with the concerns involved in medical research particularly those of consent and maintaining standards of ethics. The BBMRI also coordinates with European life-sciences Infrastructure for biological Information (ELIXIR), an intergovernmental organization that brings together life science resources from across Europe. These resources include databases, software tools, training materials, cloud storage and supercomputers.[233] ELIXIR and BBMRI coordinates in developing framework of shared services between different infrastructures to enhance the efficiency, productivity and impact of European biomedical research and its translation into medicine e.g., CORBEL project. So also a comprehensive 'rare disease data linkage plan' for selected biobanks and registries within the rare disease community was established in association with registries under BBMRI to link rare disease data resources for research purposes.[234] This apart there are also other cloud-based biobanking platforms such as Base Space from Illumina, which enables their clients to directly connect their sequencing machines with the cloud.[235] Another example is the E-Bio Grid, which is a Dutch cloud infrastructure for life sciences which several simple to complex programs for enabling genomic research via the cloud.[236] The European Clinical Research Infrastructures Network is also engaged in a cloud-based initiative to pool the data from research biobanks to make a meaningful association of such data to clinical studies.[237] These examples demonstrate the immense efforts being carried out within different institutions in Europe in the area of biobanking cloud which aims on building more data bridges for research resources

230. Biobank cloud project: Scalable, Secure Storage Biobank, Regulatory and Ethical Requirements for Biobanking Data Storage and Analysis (WP1) recommends the usage of GitHub: https://github.com/.
231. *Ibid.*
232. *Ibid.*, note 231.
233. https://www.elixir-europe.org/about-us.
234. ELIXIR Annual Report 2016, https://www.elixireurope.org/system/files/elixir_annual_report_layout_v16_digital_singles.pdf (last accessed on 21 July 2017); http://www.elixir-finland.org/wp-content/uploads/2013/04/WWW.BBMRI-leaflet_EN.pdf.
235. https://blog.basespace.illumina.com/about/.
236. *Supra* note 230.
237. http://www.ecrin.org/node/926.

rather than being data islands in themselves.[238] Such an understanding not only helps biomedical research but also offers researchers the ease to collaborate easily within different sectors of health research. However, copyright issues are sparsely addressed within a discussion on biobank cloud. The reason for a lean examination is often on account of the fact that developers of such cloud technologies often leave out contracts to be drafted by legal departments which may be limited in its approach to the intricacies of new technologies while trying to offer a general stand for all. For instance, the terms of use of a cloud initiative acknowledges that there could be 'data subject to third-party rights such as copyright' and 'it is the responsibility of the uses to ensure that such third-party rights are not infringed'. The service provider itself could neither comment on the validity of their claims nor grant unrestricted permission regarding the use of the data.[239] Such static language often occurs in terms of use or electronic license agreements. This is so because an electronic licence constructed with a rights expression language, may have difficulty in adequately representing and implementing legal rights and relationships central to copyright law.[240] Further the existence of different legal arrangements which do not exactly cater to the needs of cloud computing makes analysis of legal issues with cloud a less straightforward exercise.[241] While so an optimistic view considers that the cloud just like the cyber-space is not an abstraction but is a technology operated by means of computers and communication facilities that are owned, operated and used by identifiable persons or legal entities, in one country or in another.[242] In this sense national laws and international treaties apply to this phenomenon just like in relation to any other technologies. Thus, copyright in respect of information stored in a cloud is an essential part of understanding the data contained within a genomic cloud.

The issues of copyright in the cloud vary based on how the cloud is being used, the nature of access arrangement involved, the nature of control over such resources and the type of copyright materials are stored in the cloud.[243] Copyright in the context of commercial cloud platforms for sharing of genetic and research data will be discussed herein.

[1] Identifying Copyright Ownership

One of the major challenges in the development of any type of cloud whether it is for sharing files, music or genomic information, is the uncertainty over the ownership of

238. *Supra* note 230, V.V. Cogo et al., From data Islands to sharing data in the cloud: the evolution of data integration in biological data repositories. *Communications and Innovations Gazette*, 2016.
239. https://www.elixir-europe.org/legal/terms-of-use.
240. A. Cunningham, Rights expression on digital communications networks: Some implications for copyright, *International Journal of Law and Information Technology* Spring 2005, 13(1): 1–38.
241. C. Millard, Cloud computing law, Oxford Scholarship Online, January 2014.
242. M.J. Ficsor, The WIPO 'internet treaties' and copyright in the 'cloud', copyright and related rights in the 'cloud' environment, *ALAI* 2012 Congress, 16–18 October 2012.
243. K. Kariyawasam and C. Talagala, Cloud computing and the future of copyright law, *European Intellectual Property Review*. 2017; 39(2): 102–116; *See also* Storing Content in the Cloud: Copyright Law Issues, copyrightlaws.com.

such information.[244] Digitizing content or formulating metadata does not imply the rights over the data in itself. Instead, this depends upon whether such content is created by a user or a creator outside the cloud or created inside a cloud.[245]

[a] Content Created Outside the Cloud

Works created outside the cloud by an author or a creator, when placed in the cloud would carry the same status as it was before it was placed;[246] Authors of literary and artistic works have the exclusive right of authorizing the reproduction of works,[247] in any manner or form.[248] So also, the authors of literary or artistic works shall enjoy the exclusive right of authorizing adaptations,[249] arrangements and other alterations of their works.[250] So also making a work available to the public is an act restricted under copyright law in respect of literary, dramatic, musical and artistic works.[251] Transmitting a work through the Internet is an act of 'making such work available and as such only the owner of the work or its licensee is entitled to transmit a work'.[252] Accordingly the ownership of works placed in cloud depend on if the provider or a user of a cloud created such work outside the cloud. If created by the user or the provider then the question of copyright ownership over such work may be straightforward provided it is the result of their own intellectual creation.[253] On the contrary where the work placed in a cloud belongs to a third party other than the user or the provider then it becomes

244. *Supra* note 230.
245. *Ibid.*
246. *Ibid.*
247. Reproduction of a work amounts to copying of a work subject to copyright without permission from the relevant copyright owner. Reproduction could be applied in two senses (1) Similarity of the work and (2) Exact copying e.g., Storing the work in a different medium such as an electronic version.
248. Article 9, Berne Convention, for the Protection of Literary and Artistic Works, of 9 September 1886.; *See also* Art. 2, Directive 2001/29/EC of the European Parliament and of the Council of 22 May 2001 on the harmonization of certain aspects of copyright and related rights in the information society, which states that, Member States shall provide for the exclusive right to authorise or prohibit direct or indirect, temporary or permanent reproduction by any means and in any form, in whole or in part for authors, of their works.
249. Adaptation is usually understood as the transformation of a work into another form of expression that is not tantamount to a simple reproduction, e.g., making a film out of a novel, although 'there is an unclear dividing line between what amounts to a reproduction of a work and what amounts to an adaptation of a work'(Copinger & Skone James on Copyright, 16th Edition 2013).
250. Article 12, Berne Convention, for the Protection of Literary and Artistic Works, of 9 September 1886.
251. Article 3(1), Directive 2001/29/EC of the European Parliament and of the Council of 22 May 2001 on the harmonization of certain aspects of copyright and related rights in the information society, states that authors with the exclusive right to authorise or prohibit any communication to the public of their works, by wire or wireless means, including the making available to the public of their works in such a way that members of the public may access them from a place and at a time individually chosen by them.
252. C. Waelde, et al., Contemporary intellectual property law and policy, OUP 4th ed, 2016 at pg 156, point 4.59.
253. C-5/08 *Infopaq International A/S v Danske Dagblades Forening*, judgment of, 16 July 2009.

essential to examine the basis for use of such work including any licensing arrangement or conditions of use of such work. Such specific arrangement for IP is intended in particular to ensure the right-holders concerned protection of the right to exploit commercially the marketing or the making available of the protected subject matter, by the grant of licences in return for payment of remuneration.[254]

[b] Content Created Inside the Cloud

In the course of uploading or processing of contents, the users as well as providers of the cloud may develop IPR within the cloud. These may be a database right for developing a certain arrangement for individual works within the cloud.[255] In such case the rights relating to sui generis databases in Europe discussed in the earlier chapter applies. If the protected work of another author is quoted, adapted or remixed within the cloud to be shared in the cloud, the legal eligibility of such works to be a parody or a transformative use will depend upon the traditional copyright limitations offered to that effect.[256] If on the contrary the content is the result of a collaborative effort by the provider and the user within a cloud, such work may be subject to join authorship if the contribution of each of the parties cannot be sufficiently identified.[257] Further, where the provider develops meta data about the user for the benefit of third parties, such data relating to specific users may be categorized as personal data or may be subject to confidentiality being an information created or used by a user.[258] It has been suggested that such unauthorized access or reuse of information without the consent of the owner could affect the trust involved in the cloud structures.[259] It therefore requires that service terms should address the creation of ownership and use of such data including the consent needed for aggregation of information by the providers themselves.[260]

[2] Addressing Infringement

The transient nature of the digital environment has always been a challenge in addressing the nature of infringement involved.[261] The nature of infringement of copyright in a cloud depends upon the type of platform, the type of content and of

254. Joined Cases C-403/08 and C-429/08, *Football Association Premier League Ltd and Others v QC Leisure and Others* (C-403/08) and *Karen Murphy v Media Protection Services Ltd* (C-429/08). At para. 107.
255. A. Cunningham, Rights expression on digital communication networks: Some implications for copyright, *International Journal of Law and Information Technology* 2005; 13(1): 1–38.
256. M. Senftleben, Breathing space for cloud-based business models exploring the matrix of copyright limitations, safe harbours and injunctions, 4 (2013) *Journal on Intellectual Property, Information Technology and Electronic Commerce Law* 2, para. 87.
257. *Ibid.*
258. *Supra* note 230.
259. S. Paul, A. Gade, and S. Mallipeddi, The state of cloud-based biospecimen and biobank data management tools, *Biopreservation and Biobanking*; 2017; 15(2)
260. Intellectual property in the cloud, A& O report, May 2013.
261. M.A. Melzer,'Copyright enforcement in the cloud', *Fordham Intellectual Property, Media and Entertainment Law Journal.* 2011; 21: 403, 404.

course the question of ownership over such content. Apart from creating, processing or storing information in a cloud distributing or sharing of copyright materials via a cloud could also be problematic without the rightful licence. The user or the provider of a cloud could be held liable for a copyright infringement depending on the circumstances of a case. Individual user making copies of pre-existing works for commercial uses may be liable for infringing the economic and moral rights of the authors of such work. The right of reproduction and communication to the public as set out in the *InfoSoc Directive*[262] *can well be infringed by user-generated content shared via a cloud.*[263] However, user generated law is not fully harmonized in EU though efforts seem to be currently on the way to regulate it under copyright law.[264] An exception to individual infringement is provided in the case of private non-commercial fair use of a copyrighted work on condition that the right-holders receive fair compensation.[265] In *Padawan SL v SGAE*[266] 'fair compensation' was held to be autonomous concept of union law which compensates for the harm suffered by the author from the reproduction of the author's protected work without her authorization. This in turn implies the individual's obligation with regard to use of copyrighted works even when used for private purposes.[267] However, given the practical difficulties in identifying private users, a 'private copying levy'[268] may be established chargeable to the persons who offers the digital equipment device or platform.[269]

The cloud service provider could also be liable for distribution of copyrighted material illegally via the cloud e.g., Distributing copyrighted works or offering links to such information.[270]

262. Articles 2 and 3 of Directive 2001/29/EC of the European Parliament and of the Council of 22 May 2001 on the harmonisation of certain aspects of copyright and related rights in the information society.
263. A.G. Monteleone, 'User-generated-content and copyright: The European union approach' WIPO Academy, University of Turin and ITC-ILO - Master of Laws in IP - Research Papers Collection - 2015-2016. The article defines user-generated content or UGC includes all and various kinds of media content generally available online (but not necessarily), irrespective of the content, that it is original and/or an adaptation of pre-existing material; *see also* D. Gervais, The tangled web of UGC: Making Copyright sense of user-generated content, 11 *Vanderbilt Journal of Entertainment & Technology Law*, 2008–2009, 841 ff.
264. http://www.europarl.europa.eu/oeil/popups/ficheprocedure.do?lang=en&reference=2016/0280(COD); *see* the news on vote on the proposal for an exception on User generated law: http://www.completemusicupdate.com/article/music-industry-welcomes-eu-committee-votes-on-safe-harbour-reform/ (last accessed on 17 July 2017).
265. Article 5(2)(b), Directive 2001/29/EC of the European Parliament and of the Council of 22 May 2001 on the harmonisation of certain aspects of copyright and related rights in the information society.
266. C-467/08, *Padawan SL v SGAE*, judgment of 21 October 2010.
267. *Ibid.*
268. For more on the topic: R. Ghafele, Counting the costs of expanding copyright levies to cloud computing, *European Intellectual Property Review*. 2017; 39(6): 350–358.
269. *Ibid.*, para. 46 of Judgment.
270. *See* Judgment in Case C-160/15, *GS Media BV v Sanoma Media Netherlands BV, Playboy Enterprises International Inc.,Britt Geertruida Dekker,* the CJEU observed with reference to the posting of hyperlinks for profit, that it can be expected that the person who posted such a link carries out the necessary checks to ensure that the work concerned is not illegally published on the website to which those hyperlinks lead, so that it must be presumed that that posting has occurred with the full knowledge of the protected nature of that work and the possible lack of

The liability of the providers for copyright infringement in relation to its users is usually determined on contractual relationship between the cloud provider and the user.[271] However offering a platform or merely offering provision of physical facilities for enabling or making a communication does not in itself amount to communication of a work and hence an infringement by a cloud service provider.[272]

In *SGAE v Rafael Hotels SL*[273] a copyright collection society contented that the provision of television sets with broadcast signals within hotel rooms violated copyright by public communication. The CJEU observed that while the mere provision of physical facilities, such as television sets, does not as such, constitute, a communication, the installation of such facilities may nevertheless make public access to broadcast works technically possible. Therefore, if, by means of television sets thus installed, the hotel distributes the signal to customers staying in its rooms, then communication to the public takes place, irrespective of the technique used to transmit the signal.[274] Thus, while offering a cloud service itself may not be infringing, the cloud providers could still be held liable where a facility or mechanism allows the users of such facilities to violate a copyright. In the recent years, European courts have been considering differing aspects of data sharing in the digital environment.[275] In *Case C-610/15*[276] involving a dispute between a Dutch anti-piracy group Stichtin Brein against two Internet service providers, in the issue of copyright infringement by the providers in offering file sharing platform pirate bay, the court observed that the operators of the online sharing platform cannot be considered 'to be making a mere provision' of physical facilities for enabling or making a communication, within the meaning of recital 27 of Directive 2001/29. The making available and management of an online sharing platform, such as that at issue in the main proceedings, must be considered to be an act of communication.[277] Thus, making available and managing an online platform for sharing copyright-protected works may constitute an infringement of copyright. However it appears from this decision that the courts will also make a factual assessment of the knowledge of the provider in assessing a copyright infringement.[278] The nature of technology and its consequent technicality has been well

consent to publication on the Internet by the copyright-holder. In such circumstances, and in so far as that rebuttable presumption is not rebutted, the act of posting a hyperlink to a work which was illegally placed on the Internet constitutes a 'communication to the public'.

271. *Supra* note 241.
272. Recital 27, Directive 2001/29/EC of the European Parliament and of the Council of 22 May 2001 on the harmonisation of certain aspects of copyright and related rights in the information society.
273. C-306/05 *SGAE v Rafael Hotels SL*, [2006] ECR 1-11519.
274. *Ibid.*, paras 46–47.
275. C-279/13 *C More Entertainment AB v Sandberg* [2015] EDRC15(March 2015); C-466/12 *Svenson v Retriver Sverige* AB [2014] EDCR 9 (February, 2014); *Dramatico v BskyB* [2012] ECDR 14(ch); *Twenty Century Fox v Newzbin* [2010] EDCR 8; *Nils Svensson and Others v Retriever Sverige AB*, C-466/12.
276. *Stichtin Brein v Ziggo BV, XS4ALL Internet BV*, CJEU 14 June 2017.
277. *Ibid.*, paras 38–39.
278. *Ibid.*, para. 36.

regarded under the European copyright law. For instance under the Information Society Directive:[279]

> Temporary acts of reproduction...., which are transient or incidental [and] an integral and essential part of a technological process and whose sole purpose is to enable:
>
> (a) a transmission in a network between third parties by an intermediary, or
> (b) a lawful use of a work or other subject-matter to be made, and which have no independent economic significance, shall be exempted from the reproduction right.

Further the E-commerce Directive also offers a safe harbour[280] provision for hosting which provides that where an information society service consists of storage of information provided by a recipient of the service, the service provider is not liable for the information stored at the request of a recipient of the service, if the provider does not have actual knowledge of illegal activity or information or upon obtaining such knowledge or awareness, acts expeditiously to remove or to disable access to the information. While this posits to lessen the burden for service providers a due diligence is expected in the conduct of services to ensure that it does not violate IPR particularly copyright.[281] The exemptions from liability under the E-Commerce Directive cover only cases in which the activity of the information society service provider is 'of a mere technical, automatic and passive nature', which implies that that service provider 'has neither knowledge of nor control over the information which is transmitted or stored'.[282] Accordingly, it was held in *Google France* joined Cases (C-236/08 to C-238/08),[283] that, in order to establish the liability of a service provider it is necessary

279. Article 5(1), Directive 2001/29/EC of the European Parliament and of the Council of 22 May 2001 on the harmonization of certain aspects of copyright and related rights in the information society.
280. Originally the safe harbour provisions can be traced to the WIPO Internet treaties, 1996, which requires Member States to provide immunity or safe harbours to limit the liability of ISPs for the acts of their users or subscribers.In in 2000 the European Commission adopted in the E-Commerce Directive a set of provisions commonly referred to as safe harbour provisions granting immunity to intermediaries from liability incurred in the supply of three types of services: mere conduit, caching and hosting. Recital 40, 43 of E-Commerce Directive. *See also* Commission Proposal for a European Parliament and Council Directive on certain legal aspects of electronic commerce in the internal market, 18 November 1998, COM(1998) 586 final.
281. *L'Oréal SA and Others v eBay International AG and Others*, (Case C-324/09, 12 July 2011) with regard to the safe harbour hosting and the liability of a service provider, the CJEU noted that '*in order for the provider of an information society service to be denied entitlement to the exemption from liability provided for in Article 14 of Directive 2000/31, for it to have been aware of facts or circumstances on the basis of which a diligent economic operator should have identified the illegality in question*'. *See also* I ZR 80/ (12 15 August 2013) Rapidshare decision by Bundesgerichtshof.
282. *Google France SARL and Google Inc v Louis Vuitton Malletier SA* (C-236/08), *Google France SARL v Viaticum SA and Luteciel SARL* (C-237/08) and *Google France SARL v Centre national de recherche en relations humaines (CNRRH) SARL and Others* (C-238/08), EU:C:2010:159.; *See also* recital 42, Directive 2000/31/EC of the European Parliament and of the Council of 8 June 2000 on certain legal aspects of information society services, in particular electronic commerce, in the Internal Market ('Directive on electronic commerce').
283. *Ibid.*

to examine whether the role played by that service provider is neutral, in the sense that its conduct is merely technical, automatic and passive, pointing to a lack of knowledge or control of the data which it stores.[284] This would require that platform provider availing itself of the immunity following from the safe harbour for hosting is under an obligation to promptly take action once sufficiently substantiated information about infringing content is received through a standard measure of notice and take down.[285] In addition, it also gives an obligation for cloud providers to assess its knowledge of the nature of data being stored or shared through the cloud.

[3] Sharing of Genomic Information and Research Data Through a Cloud

The technological leap from a Moore's Law[286] conceived computer application to the cloud has been enormous. The implications cloud computing has offered to genomic research is also immense considering the fact that under a fixed cost the genome sequencing capacity is growing rapidly than storage capacity.[287] Cloud-based tools provide biobanks with easy access to biospecimen data for real-time sharing with clinicians. Another major benefit realized by biobanks by implementing cloud-based applications is unlimited data storage on the cloud and automatic backups for protecting any data loss in the face of natural calamities.[288]

Data sharing and collaborative research within biobanks are aimed to be more effective with the possibilities of the cloud.[289] This also means that genomic data will also increase rapidly. Regulating the growing Big Data with the genomic cloud also implies the requisite optimization at different levels.[290] As discussed above clouds not only vary in their type but also may serve differing functional purposes. For the field of genomics a key feature of cloud computing is the ability of service providers and their customers to store large datasets in the cloud.[291] These datasets, which take the form of a virtual disk image,[292] are capable to store the entire data archive belonging to a genomic biobank.[293] The distinction with regard to genomic information unlike others is the presence of diversity in the nature of data itself which may involve sensitive or

284. *Ibid.*, paras 113–114 of the Judgment.
285. *Infra* note 230.
286. In 1965, Intel co-founder Gordon Moore published a paper which observed that the number of transistors on an integrated circuit was doubling every two years. He predicted that at this pace it would lead to computers becoming embedded in homes, cars and communication systems. http://www.digitaltonto.com/2016/moores-law- will-soon-end-but-progress-doesnt-have-to/.
287. P.E. Verissimo and A. Bessani, 'E-biobanking: What have you done to my cell samples?,' security & privacy, *IEEE*. November-December 2013; 11(6): 62, 65.
288. S. Paul et al., The state of cloud-based biospecimen and biobank data management tools, *Biopreservation and Biobanking*. 2017; 15.
289. D1.3 Legal and Ethical Framework in the BiobankCLoud, Biobank cloud Paas.
290. D. Holdsworth, 'The ethics of 21st century bioinformatics: Ethical implications of the vanishing distinction between biological information and other information', in A.K. Thomson and R.F. Chadwick, 'Geneti information, acquisition, acces and control', Kulwer Academic, 1999.
291. *Supra* note 230.
292. Virtual hard disk (VHD) is a disk image file format for storing the complete contents of a hard drive.(http://searchvirtualdesktop.techtarget.com/definition/virtual-hard-disk-VHD).
293. Izzo, M., et al., A digital repository with an extensible data model for biobanking and genomic analysis management. BMC genomics, 2014, 15 Suppl 3(Suppl 3), S3.

personal data. Health-related data are subject to patient confidentiality and can be processed only as a personal data following the General Data Protection Regulation[294] and other international principles that have been agree upon by sovereign states.[295] However, in genomic research there are also other types of data involved apart from patient's health data which will be addressed herein (hence the issue of regulating personal health data in the cloud is not considered herein). Generally, a genomic cloud may encompass three different types of data namely:

(1) non-sharable (or protected data/reference data which may involve patient data);
(2) protected but having authorized access (e.g., research data or other scientific data) or those data which is managed for sharing and offered for access;
(3) open data or data which the general public may access in general(includes data within public domain including works which are offered for the public domain).[296] While all categories of data are valuable resources for biomedical research, from a legal standpoint there are differing concerns which may emerge while placing such data in a digital environment. For instance where a patient's health record is concerned, security and protection of personal data would be the primary concern; on the contrary where the question of research data arises the nature of its ownership including IPR appears to dominate the front. A primary reason for this diversity of legal approach to data is the fragmentation of different legal regimes which apply to digital information.[297] This has been a matter of concern and has often been raised by stakeholders of the cloud.[298] In addition, a lack of a harmonized regulatory framework for the governance of a digital single market for cloud computing in Europe makes matters more complex.[299] Thus, data location, data content, data security, cloud providers liability, etc. are primary matters of concern while addressing the current issues within the cloud. This heterogeneity in legal approaches governing biomedical data in a cloud environment brings forth two major challenges for governance of such platform from a copyright

294. Regulation (EU) 2016/679 of the European Parliament and of the Council of 27 April 2016 on the protection of natural persons with regard to the processing of personal data and on the free movement of such data.
295. For example, US HIPAA similar to the EU data protection regulation, UNESCO International Declaration on Human Genetic Data (2003), the Guidelines on Human Biobanks and Genetic Research Databases (2009). The Council of Europe has enacted an Additional Protocol to the Convention on Human Rights and Biomedicine, concerning Genetic Testing for Health Purposes (2008).
296. D1.4 Disclosure model, http://www.biobankcloud.com/sites/default/files/deliverables/2015/D1.4-final.pdf.
297. Study on Online Platforms – Contrasting perceptions of European stakeholders: A qualitative analysis of the European Commission's Public Consultation on the Regulatory Environment for Platforms, https://ec.europa.eu/digital-single-market/en/news/results-public-consultation-regulatory-environment-platforms- online-intermediaries-data-and.
298. *Ibid.*
299. J.J.M. Seddona and W.L. Currie, Cloud computing and trans-border health data: Unpacking US and EU healthcare regulation and compliance, *Health Policy and Technology*. 2013; 2: 229–241.

perspective(particularly for research data and publications), namely ensuring the protection of copyrighted information within a cloud environment, and the responsible management (including sharing) of biomedical data and other resources in the cloud. To this end data sharing with in a genomic cloud should invariably ensure the scientific use of data and biospecimens following national and international biomedical convention or approaches.[300] However, such a responsible scientific use of resources also involves respect for different IPR, which are also essential in the context of biomedical research.[301] Often protection of IPR are an essential concern for researchers who are involved in such research and who may also be authors of data over which they have invested years of effort.[302] It has been suggested in the international charter of principles for sharing biospecimens and data, developed by RD-Connect by a group of experts working in the field that sharing of genomic data must among other principles involve the attribution of intellectual contribution.[303] According to the charter a scientific use of data required that:

(a) Proper attribution and IP should be accorded as appropriate.
(b) The sharing of data and biospecimens should follow criteria for the acknowledgement of intellectual contributions and originality through rules of authorship and IPR.
(c) The sharing of data and bio-resources must be done in a way that protects proprietary information and addresses the interests of institutions and third-party funders. These parties may have legitimate proprietary interests associated with data collected by researchers. The intellectual investment of investigators involved in the creation and maintenance of data registries and bio-repositories is often substantial, and should be appropriately acknowledged.[304]

Interestingly these principles have also been offered in guidance for the biobank cloud pass project as a case study in the legal and ethical implications of the cloud.[305] While this approach is essentially focused on a responsible use of biomedical information, it offers little in terms of the actualities to be worked out for copyright protection within a genomic cloud. From the discussion above the two main copyright concerns in cloud identified were ownership and the accountability of platform providers in the sharing of data. Authorship rights tend to define the initial owners of copyright which will be the authors or more likely the employers or assignees of those authors.[306] This

300. D. Mascalzoni et.al, International charter of principles for sharing bio-specimens and data. *European Journal of Human Genetics*, 2015; 23(6): 721–728.
301. Donna M. Gitter, 'The challenges of achieving open source sharing of biobanks', in G. Pascuzzi et. al. 'Comparative issues in the governance of research biobanks', Springer 2013, at p. 165.
302. *Ibid.*
303. http://rd-connect.eu/platform/ethics/sharing-bio-specimens-and-data/ (last accessed on 24 July 2017).
304. *Ibid.*
305. *Supra* note 296.
306. C. Reed, 'Information in the cloud: Ownership, control and accountability', in A.S.Y. Cheung and R.H. Weber (eds), 'Privacy and legal issues in cloud computing', Edward Elgar 2015.

in turn will also be the case where the information is being placed in the cloud by service providers, third-party software houses and database proprietors.[307]

The ownership over a copyrighted work may, however, be transferred through a formal assignment or can even be licensed out to a third party. It is also possible to offer a work to the public domain in which case no further rights may be claimed in such regards. However, in either case the author of a work is entitled to an inalienable moral right to attribution (paternity) and to object to a derogatory treatment of the work prejudicial to the author's honour and reputation.[308] This right has been internationally acknowledged by the Berne Convention on literary and artistic works and also by other national laws in Europe.[309] Thus the mere attribution of authorship as suggested under the Charter on Sharing of Biomedical Data[310] is only a partial reflection of copyright's moral right. Further, it may also lead to an associated problem particularly in scientific research called '*attribution stacking*' particularly in the context of data sets derived from cloud databases which may involve different authorship or if shared from another interoperable database may require similar acknowledgment.[311] If a dataset are at the end of a long chain of derivations, or if large teams of contributors were involved, the list of credits may also be too large to offer attribution.[312]

In considering the lawful use of a work, it may often be difficult for larger sharing platforms to ensure the copyright of each data being shared. There exists a possibility of a genomic IP clearing house which can serve as a resource centre for both the users and provider in addressing copyright concerns including seeing the agreement with research groups for sharing of their data in the interest of collaborative research. Nelson points out that the creation of the legal and technical infrastructure to accommodate researchers' data sharing concerns is a huge task, and requires serious public investment to mitigate such concerns.[313] Thus, creation of such a clearing house by a public research infrastructure such as BBMRI-ERIC could create more confidence among researchers to share their data over cloud environments as well which is normally considered a huge challenge.[314] Another essential element for genomic cloud providers is to consider the various technical measures to prevent or limit the reproduction of data or research resourced shared through the cloud. The making or

307. *Ibid.*
308. Articles 6*bis*, Berne Convention for the protection of literary and artistic work, 1886.
309. For example, France, Germany and UK. The information society Directive acknowledges the application of Moral rights of the authors thought it does not per se deal in them. Recital 19 of the directive reads thus: (19) The moral rights of right-holders should be exercised according to the legislation of the Member States and the provisions of the Berne Convention for the Protection of Literary and Artistic Works, of the WIPO Copyright Treaty and of the WIPO Performances and Phonograms Treaty. Such moral rights remain outside the scope of this Directive.(Directive 2001/29/EC of the European Parliament and of the Council of 22 May 2001 on the harmonization of certain aspects of copyright and related rights in the information society).
310. *Supra* note 303.
311. *See* https://data.research.cornell.edu/content/intellectual-property.
312. http://www.dcc.ac.uk/resources/how-guides/license-research-data#fn11x0-bk.
313. B. Nelson, Empty archives, *Nature*. 2009; 461: 160–163.
314. *Supra* note 301 on the challenges of fostering a culture of sharing data among researchers.

digital copies of copyrighted works can be regulated using the digital rights management technologies (DRMs).[315] A variety of technologies are employed to realize these functions e.g., encryption for access control.[316] The Information Society Directive[317] recognizes its application and also its protection against any anti-circumvention efforts including devices that try to circumvent digital rights management of copyrighted works. DRMs are considered an excellent solution for cloud-related copyright concerns and the ease of its incorporation into the cloud.[318] Further the practicalities of ensuring privacy of data is also accorded by DRMs which restrict the ability of third parties to duplicate and further exploit personal data complied with in certain registries.[319]

The genomic cloud initiatives could consider the following approaches while sharing or archiving data or works in the cloud:

(a) Respect for IPR while sharing/archiving of protected data including copyright over works created by an author or joint authors.
(b) Providers of a genomic cloud who offers copyrighted research materials or scientific data must ensure that the such scientific data or research materials have been lent or purchased or adequate permission for its use have been secured. The provider must also offer sufficient clarity as to the copyrightability of databases held within the cloud.
(c) Any user placing or sharing scientific or other information in the cloud must also ensure that relevant permissions are sought and granted before sharing of such resources.
(d) Clearing copyright: user-sharing resources via a cloud much approach the designated clearing house when in doubt regarding the rights over such data.
(e) Fair uses: educating researchers on what could be regarded as a fair use is also essential. Many jurisdictions offer fair reuse of copyrighted information for the purpose of quotation, parody, news reporting, private study, etc.[320] (Fair use will be explained in detail in the next part)

315. It is referred under the Information Society Directive (Art. 6) as 'technological measures' which means any technology, device or component that, in the normal course of its operation, is designed to prevent or restrict acts, in respect of works or other subject matter, which are not authorised by the right-holder of any copyright or any right related to copyright as provided for by law or the sui generis right.
316. Other examples include steganography (digital watermarking for authentication of RMI) and electronic agents (e.g., web spiders/bots for monitoring usage of digital works). *See* E. Bekker and Others (eds), Digital rights management: Technological, economic, legal and political aspects, Springer 2003;*see also* L. Bygrave, 'Data protection v copyright' in D.J.B. Svantesson and S. Greenstein (eds) 'Internationalisation of law in the digital information society: Nordic yearbook of law and informatics' 2010–2012, First edition, first impression.
317. Article 6, Directive 2001/29/EC of the European Parliament and of the Council of 22 May 2001 on the harmonisation of certain aspects of copyright and related rights in the information society.
318. http://www.pcworld.com/article/218620/is_drm_the_answer_to_cloud_security.html.
319. *Supra* note 316, Eberhard Bekker et al., At pp. 418–419.
320. UK Copyright, Designs and Patents Act 1988.

(f) Service agreements with different collaborators must envision indemnity for parties involved in the cloud under mutually agreeable terms.[321] This must also involve an effective notice and take down policy to qualify for the safe harbor protections under E-commerce Directive.

In 2015 the EU Commission released its Digital Single Market Strategy which presented steps towards the realization of a connected digital single market to generate additional growth in Europe in the course of its mandate.[322] Several fronts were aimed to be addressed under this strategy including copyright and IP in the digital environment. On this basis, the EU Commission launched a public consultation on platforms and online intermediaries.[323] In this one of the major concern for stakeholders was the uncertainty in dealing with copyright including the role and responsibility of platform providers.[324] This bears the responsibility on public cloud providers to identify sector specific issues in relation to the application of copyright with such cloud. In this respect biobank cloud providers must clarify the nature of data or information being shared in the cloud and be specific in their data sharing agreements or service agreements about handling copyright as related to the nature of information being shared.

§5.02 COPYRIGHT FAIR USE AND CHALLENGES FOR BIG DATA IN PERSONALISED MEDICINE

The use and exploitation of big data for scientific research requires reproduction, adaptation and even text and data mining. Scientific research flourishes with use and reuse of information contained in works that may be subject to copyright. This strengthens the need for flexibilities that are particularly significant to the development of scientific research and development. While offering extensive protection to works of author's or copyrightable works as discussed in the previous parts, a balance between protection of creation and use of works has been achieved through flexibilities and fair uses within copyrights. The need for fair uses arises because of the fact that rigorous structure impedes not only cultural, social and economic progress, but also undermines the social legitimacy of copyright law.[325] At the international level the Berne Convention contains provisions granting latitude to members states in limiting the author's rights. These consist of three types and include limitations,[326] immunities and

321. *See* Negotiating Cloud Contracts: Looking at Clouds from both sides now http://www.cloudlegal.ccls.qmul.ac.uk/Research/index.html.
322. Communication from the Commission to the European Parliament, the Council, the European Economic and Social Committee and the Committee of the Regions, A digital single market strategy for Europe, COM(2015) 192 final.
323. European Commission, Public consultation on the regulatory environment for platforms, online intermediaries, data and cloud computing and the collaborative economy, 24 September 2015, available at http://ec.europa.eu/newsroom/dae/document.cfm?doc_id = 10932.
324. *Ibid.*
325. B. Hugenholtz and M.R.F. Senftleben, Fair use in Europe: In search of flexibilities, November 2011.
326. Reproduction of official texts of a legislative, administrative and legal nature (Art. 2(4)), news of the day (Art. 2(8)), and speeches delivered in the course of legal proceedings (Arts 2*bis*(1)) etc. for which can be used without permission as they do not fall under protection.

compulsory licensing.[327] Immunities from infringement or provision of permitted uses under the convention includes use of copyright works for the purpose of quotation, teaching or research, reporting current events, etc.[328] Compulsory licensing enables the use of protected works under special circumstances without the consent of the author of the work (11bis, 13 and appendix of the convention). The Berne Convention also provides that such exceptions and limitations must meet the 'three-step test' and be confined: (1) to certain special cases; (2) which do not conflict with normal exploitation of the work; and (3) do not unreasonably prejudice the legitimate interests of the right-holder.[329] These have also been resounded under Article 13 of TRIPS Agreement in an effort to harmonize economic rights with social requirements. In Europe, these flexibilities have been adopted through Article 5 of the Information Society Directive[330] which offers a list of limitations and exceptions for Member States to choose and apply. Predominantly, these include exceptions to reproduction rights in certain cases, use for the sole purpose of illustration for teaching or scientific research, uses, for the benefit of people with a disability, different types of uses such as for criticism or parody, making available certain works for private study or by educational establishments or museums, or by archives, which are not for direct or indirect economic or commercial advantage.[331]

The Information Society Directive requires that certain exceptions are offered for cases such as educational and scientific purposes, for the benefit of public institutions such as libraries and archives.[332] So also, the directive provides that in applying the exception or limitation for non-commercial educational and scientific research purposes, the non-commercial nature of the activity in question should be determined by that activity as such and not the organizational structure and the means of funding of the establishment.[333] While these seem to fairly strengthen the outlook towards scientific research, yet Article 5(5) of the directive resounds the Bern convention and cautions that the exceptions and limitations can only be applied in certain special cases which do not conflict with a normal exploitation of the work or other subject matter and do not unreasonably prejudice the legitimate interests of the right-holder.[334] The justification for a three-step examination was addressed in the *Infopak decision*, and was regarded to be essential for legal certainty for authors with regard to the protection of their works.[335] This however means that the European fair use with a scientific

327. S. Ricketson, WIPO Study on limitation and exception to copyright and related rights in the Digital environment, SCCR/9/7, 5 April 2003.
328. *See* Arts, 9, 10 and 10*bis* of Berne Convention, 1886.
329. Article 9(2), Berne Convention, 1886.
330. Directive 2001/29/EC of the European Parliament and of the Council of 22 May 2001 on the harmonisation of certain aspects of copyright and related rights in the information society.
331. Article 5, Directive 2001/29/EC.
332. Recital 34, Directive 2001/29/EC.
333. Recital 44, Directive 2001/29/EC.
334. *Ibid.*
335. Case C5/08, *Infopaq International A/S v Danske Dagblades Forening*, 16 July 2009 para. 58. The inclusion of this caution of a tree-step test further ensures that the obligations under Berne and its sister agreement WCT, 1996 are met.

research is fairly limited in terms of scope and application.[336] Despite the limited scope for fair uses under the law, scientific practice particularly data-oriented research rely heavily on understanding different types of data from varied number of sources found within the information landscape. This is increasingly seen as a conceivable change in the contemporary scientific research particularly within biobanks where there is an increasing need for analytics and exploitation of larger data resources. This is particularly essential for the development of data-oriented personalised medicine (PM) which rigorously seeks genotypic and phenotypic data particularly for classification of patient groups and pharmaceogenetic applications for drug selection, dosing or interactions. At the same time the need for improving an understanding of varied types of data is also one of the foremost challenges of PM. Text and data mining have increasingly become synonymous with Big Data analytics particularly for PM research.[337] Text and data mining refers to the performance of extensive automated searches of publisher's content, with and attempt to discover new and previously unknown information by applying techniques from information retrieval.[338] One of the key elements of data and text mining is linking of extracted information to form new facts or new hypothesis for further experimentation.[339] The text mining involves identification of specific entities in surface text such as diseases, genes, or relational terms and the deep normalization of these entities to standardized ontologies. Text mining, though related to data mining is often limited to the exploration of interesting patterns in the unstructured textual data of various types of documents.[340] Text and data mining are both essential tools for biomedical research particularly situated within biobanks. Biomedical research situated within biobanks is as an author puts it 'drowning in data yet starving for knowledge'.[341] This reflects the importance of data mining particularly for biomedical advancement including PM. By integrating participant data (Including health records) along with data relating to samples biobank databases constitute a computable collection of fine-grained longitudinal phenotypic profiles, facilitating cohort-wide

336. J. Griffiths, The 'three-step test' in European copyright law: Problems and solutions, *Intellectual Property Law Quarterly*. 2009; 489; M. Senftleben, The international three-step test: A model provision for EC fair use legislation. *Journal of Intellectual Property, Information Technology and Electronic Commerce Law* 1 (2010): 67, para. 1; T. Cook, Exceptions and limitations in European union copyright law, *Journal of Intellectual Property Rights*, May 2012: 243–245; J.H. Reichman and R.L. Okediji, When copyright law and science collide: Empowering digitally integrated research methods on a global scale, *Minnesota Law Review*. 1 July 2012; 96(4):1362–1480.
337. M. Truyens and P. Van Eecke, Legal aspects of text mining, computer law & security review. 2014; 30: 153–170.; see also E. Estape et al., Translation in data mining to advance personalized medicine for health equity. *Intelligent Information Management* (2016); 8(1): 9–16.
338. Definition of UK national centre for Text Mining and the international association of scientific, technical and medical publishers. For more on the definition *see* J.P. Triaille et al., Study on the legal frame work of text and data mining, Report for European Commission.
339. M.A. Hearst, What is text mining?, *SIMS*, UC Berkeley 2003.
340. Simmons M., A. Singhal and Z. Lu, Text mining for precision medicine: bringing structure to EHRs and biomedical literature to understand genes and health. *Advances in Experimental Medicine and Biology* (2016); 939: 139–166.
341. A. Holzinger and I. Jurisica (eds), Knowledge discovery and data mining, *LNCS* 2014; 8401: 1–18.

investigations and knowledge discovery on an unprecedented scale.[342] In addition access to biomedical literature enables relationship extraction through semantic identification which ultimately helps in data curation and adds value to data.[343] (see Figure 5.3).

Figure 5.3 Data Mining and Copyright Interface for PM

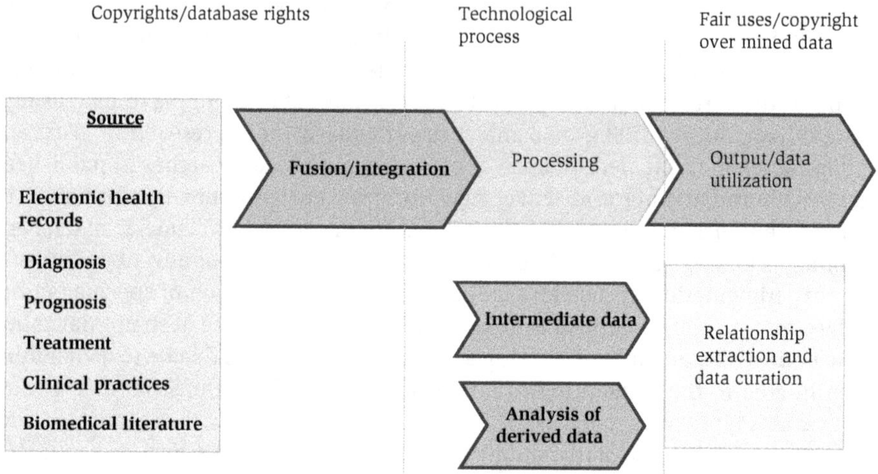

While this appears to be core to big data research, yet it has important implications for copyright law. Data or text may be subject to copyright so also databases containing such data may be subject to protection. Processing such larger texts or data often facilitates the creation of new data or data derived from the existing ones. Data analysis includes reproduction of works including selection arrangement of works, adaptation of works into different formats or even translation of such works in deducing the informational data.[344] The data so analysed may be used in evolving new results or new applications that may further new research.[345] However arriving at this requires differing technological processing of data with the end result that it may often be extremely difficult to identify individual contributions including the copyright-holders of such data.[346] Thus in dealing with this one has to invariably consider the limitations and exceptions offered by copyright law. With regard to reproduction of a copyright work, Article 5(1) of the Information society Directive provides that:

342. Peter B. Jensen, Lars J. Jensen and S. Brunak, Mining electronic health records: Towards better research applications and clinical care, *Nature Genetics*, June 2012; 13.

343. *Ibid.*

344. *Supra* note 338.

345. N. Korn, Professor Charles Oppenheim and Charles Duncan, IPR and licensing issues in Derived Data, May 2007.

346. *See* for general information on the scale of processing and data mining: A. Holzinger, Machine learning for health informatics: Sate of the art and future challenges, Springer 2016; *see also* Hargreaves, Supporting document T to the hargreaves report e text mining and data analytics in call for evidence responses, May 2011.

'*temporary acts of reproduction which are transient or incidental and an integral and essential part of a technological process* and whose sole purpose is to enable:

(a) *a transmission in a network* between third parties by an intermediary, or
(b) a lawful use of a work or other subject-matter which have *no independent economic significance*, shall be exempted from the reproduction right'.

In *Infopak II*[347] it was held that the conditions are cumulative in the sense that non-compliance with any one of them will lead to the act of reproduction not being exempted, pursuant to Article 5(1) of Directive 2001/29, from the reproduction right provided under the directive. In the context of data mining the extraction of data flows through a process as in Figure 5.3 above. As a first step, it involves identifying a source which may be created, sought from third parties or from an independent publisher of the data.[348] Often data may also be integrated from several other independent sources. The processing stage may require advanced approaches, for example to merge data sets of different resolutions or data types (vector and raster), or to analyse data using techniques, both quantitative and qualitative.[349] Processing further involves the derivation of preliminary data and its further analysis to secure the derived data. While this is enabled through a technological process, it also involves making copies of works while the final analysis of derived data proceeds.[350] Further, the sole purpose of such mining may not be for transmission in a network even though it may be a lawful use. Most importantly, the essence of data mining is seeking valuable derived data which can be commercially useful in different ways.[351] In this sense data mining per se do not meet the exceptions and limitations offered under the Information Society Directive. It has hence been argued that a European approach to fair use is frustrating the purposes of digital economy which it seeks to achieve. Such uses require agreement of the rights holders if they fall outside the pre-established and closed list of categories for permissible exceptions provided by the Information Society Directive.[352] This also tends to hamper innovation when unduly rigid applications of copyright law enable rights holders to block potentially important new technologies.[353] Hargreaves report from UK has offered multiple examples from biomedical research which has significantly benefited from text and data mining. One of the interesting conclusions it draws is the requisite for open access and flexibility for scientific researchers to deal in a reuse of data for the purposes of their research. Even though the current copyright regime in Europe is not fully equipped to handle the use and exploitation of Big Data, yet things are not as dark as it seems.

At the time of writing this piece, the European Commission passed its proposal for a copyright exception that would permit researchers to conduct analysis on a

347. Case C-302/10 at para. 26.
348. *Supra* note 345.
349. *Supra* note 338.
350. *Ibid.*
351. *Supra* note 337.
352. *Supra* 346, see Art. 5 Directive 2001/29/EC.
353. *Ibid.*

large-scale scientific data to which they have lawful access.[354] This exemption for text and data mining is aimed through a directive that makes amendments to both the database directive and information society directive to adjust the copyright laws to the digital age.[355] Under the directive the commission has identified three major areas of the digital single market namely digital and cross-border uses in the field of education, the field of scientific research, and preservation of cultural heritage in which text and data mining exception is seen to be effective and useful.[356] 'Text and data mining' under the new directive have been defined to include 'any automated analytical technique aiming to analyse text and data in digital form in order to generate information such as patterns, trends and correlations'.[357] The directive makes reproductions and extractions made by research organizations in order to carry out text and data mining of works legal provided they have a lawful access. Further, any contractual provisions limiting this right to text and data mining shall be unenforceable as per the new directive.[358] While this seemingly offers greater thrust to long-standing claims for increased fair use in Europe, it may still have more limitations that can affect text and data mining in effective ways. The new directive while limiting contractual clauses over the fair use of text and data mining does not limit any measures which are used to ensure the security and integrity of the networks and databases where the works or other subject matter are hosted. Such technology protection measures (TPMs) or DRM tools (Digital rights management) possess legal protection under the information society directive against the circumvention carried out with wilful knowledge.[359] Combinations of contractual and technical measures are frequently used to create insurmountable hurdles for researchers engaging in text and data mining.[360] Even in the absence of limitations from contractual clauses TPMs may limit not only access to protected materials but a whole lot of other data and materials that may not be even subject to an intellectual property rights.[361] Besides the new directive stipulates that the exception or limitation should only apply where the work or other subject matter is accessed lawfully by the beneficiary, including when it has been made available to the public online, and insofar as the right holders have not reserved an appropriate manner to make reproductions and extractions for text and data mining. In the case of content

354. https://www.consilium.europa.eu/en/press/press-releases/2019/04/15/eu-adjusts-copyright-rules-to-the-digital-age/ (15 April 2019).
355. Directive of the European Parliament and of the Council on copyright and related rights in the Digital Single Market and amending Directives96/9/EC and2001/29/EC (2016/0280 (COD), 2 April 2019.
356. *Ibid.*
357. See *Supra* note 355 and Art. 2, Proposal for a Directive of the European Parliament and of the Council on copyright in the Digital Single Market – COM(2016)593.
358. Article 7, Directive of the European Parliament and of the Council on copyright and related rights in the Digital Single Market and amending Directives96/9/EC and2001/29/EC (2016/0280 (COD), 2 April 2019.
359. Article 6(1), Information Society Directive, Directive 2001/29/EC.
360. Geiger, Christophe and Frosio, Giancarlo and Bulayenko, Oleksandr, The Exception for Text and Data Mining (TDM) in the Proposed Directive on Copyright in the Digital Single Market - Legal Aspects (2 March 2018). Centre for International Intellectual Property Studies (CEIPI) Research Paper No. 2018-02.
361. *Ibid.*

that has been made publicly available online, it should only be considered appropriate to reserve those rights by the use of machine readable means, including metadata and terms and conditions of a website or a service.[362] However where such data is not machine readable TPMs along with electronic contracts enable publishers to protect data and information delivered online without offer much support in the interest of research or public interest purposes.[363] These significant changes, particularly the exception for data mining can offer a great deal terms of data mining for personalized healthcare. At the same time its effectiveness may be limited where TPMs are involved or where reservations are made in the mining of such data.[364] Nevertheless it is hoped that time will reveal how these fair use exceptions brought about by the new copyright directive will condition the needs of new research environments such as data mining for PM.

362. http://www.europarl.europa.eu/sides/getDoc.do?pubRef=-//EP//TEXT+TA+P8-TA-2019-0231+0+DOC+XML+V0//EN.
363. J. Reichman et al., A reverse notice and takedown regime to enable public interest uses of technically protected copyright works, 22 *Berkely Technology Law Journal* 2007; 981; See also G. Westkamp, Cod, copying, competition: the subversive force of para-copyright and the need for unfair competition based assessment of the DRM laws after INFOPAKQ, 58 *Journal Copright Society USA* 2011; 601, 627–643.
364. E.S. Estape, M.H. Mays and E.A. Sternke. Translation in data mining to advance personalized medicine for health equity. *Intelligent Information Management*. 2016; 8(1): 9–16. http://doi.org/10.4236/iim.2016.81002.

CHAPTER 6

Protection of 'Genetic Data': Trade Secrets Law and Public Research

§6.01 INTRODUCTION

Impediments involved in current genomic research are multifarious. On the one hand the developments in genomic research challenge the governance frameworks and established models for consent giving rise to concerns for participants about their rights to privacy and protection of personal information.[1] On the other hand the researchers also face challenges in managing issues of sustainability of their research, maintaining the legal parameters of privacy and consent along with balancing their innovative freedoms. Researchers often collect samples and phenotypic information from biobank participants with the intent of storing them within biobanks for future research purposes which is often not completely clear at the time of collection of such samples or data. This has often led to a growing critique as to the extent of informed consent[2] and the nature of use of these resources.[3] It has also been considered that even where that subjects' identities can be protected through confidentiality or anonymity, these same safeguards increasingly conflict with the practical needs of genomic research, which requires broad and deep DNA datasets.[4] Research into the possible genetic bases of diseases demands detailed phenotypic and environmental data including information about the people whose DNA was donated in order to seek correlations and infer

1. J.E. Lunshof et al., From genetic privacy to open consent. *Nature Biotech.* May 2008; 9.
2. D. Hallinan and M. Friedewald, Open consent, biobanking and data protection law: Can open consent be 'informed' under the forthcoming data protection regulation? *Life Sciences, Society and Policy,* 2015; 11(1).
3. T. Caulfield et al., DNA databanks and consent: A suggested policy option involving an authorization model. *BMC Medical Ethics.* 2003; 4(1).
4. J.M. Conley et al., A trade secret model for genomic biobanking. *The Journal of Law, Medicine & Ethics: A Journal of the American Society of Law, Medicine & Ethics.* 2012; 40(3): 612–629.

causation.[5] Dissemination of sensitive data, though in the interest of greater good can cause harm to the patient or donor in different ways. There are multitude instances of such non-material harm or injury. For example in a case before the CJEU Case T-881/16 *HJ v EMA*, the applicant claims that the dissemination of that sensitive data pertaining to him, which were made public and accessible to any member of staff of the European Medicines Agency has caused a real and non-material harm to the applicant.[6] Likewise, the non-consented use of human tissues and other body parts which rocked the NHS[7] are examples which have altered the faith of research participants in the use and exploitation of HBMs and related information for biobanking research. These have resulted in several reform proposals calling for new ethical paradigms for research involving biobanks that respect both public interest and protect the rights of the human subjects.[8] The trade secret approach is one such model that aims to use trade secret licensing as a legal and governance method to address the concerns of ethical use of resources within biobanks.[9] While the trade secret approach is considered by some scholars as an alternative mechanism to deal with the concerns of biobanks, yet there are two different focuses to viewing this approach:

(1) One being the concern over consent and privacy as discussed above (from the perspective of the patients or donors).
(2) The other being the concerns of protecting innovation within a patent paradigm (i.e., from the point of view of the researchers or scientific task force including public research entities working in the area of biomedical research).[10]

In appreciating both the above angles to trade secret approach it would be essential to understand what trade secret stands for and how it influences the European context particularly in protecting the biomedical information.

Trade secrets are conceptually seen as a deviant anomaly, which is viewed in some jurisdictions like US as a distinct form of IP that falls somewhere between copyright and patent law.[11] In Europe, the assessment of policy reveals that the law of trade secrets has a distinct identity as against IP laws.[12] The nature of trade secret law has also been the subject of intense debates as to the functional basis of trade secrets as a relational obligation, a tortious liability, a measure of unfair competition law and

5. E.C. Hayden, Secrets of the human genome disclosed. *Nature*. 2011; 478: 17.
6. http://eur-lex.europa.eu/legal-content/EN/TXT/HTML/?uri = CELEX:62016TN0881&from = EN; *see also Alcock v Chief Constable of south Yorkshire police* (1992) 1 AC 310(HL).
7. *See* C. Lenk, et al., Biobanks and tissue research: The public, the patient and the regulation, Springer Science & Business Media, 2011, at pp. 20–23.
8. M.A Rothstein, Expanding the ethical analysis of biobanks. *Journal of Law, Medicine & Ethics*. 2005; 33: 89–101.
9. *Supra* note 4.
10. Recital 1, EU Directive 2016/943 on the protection of undisclosed know-how and business information (trade secrets) against their unlawful acquisition, use and disclosure.
11. J.H. Reichman, Legal hybrids between the patent and copyright paradigms. *Columbia Law Review*. 1994; 94: 2432–2558.
12. Recital 39, Directive (EU) 2016/943.

so on.[13] Such differing views converge on trade secret law's development within a sense of discomfort in relation to the traditional IPR.

The EU Directive (EU) 2016/943 forms the law of trade secret in Europe.[14] Under this directive a trade secret is defined as information, which meets certain requirements namely that:

(a) it is secret in the sense that it is not readily accessible to persons within the circles that normally deal with such kind of information;
(b) it has commercial value because it is secret;[15]
(c) reasonable steps have been taken by the person lawfully in control of the information, to keep it secret.[16]

This definition is derived from Article 39 of the TRIPS Agreement on protection of undisclosed information, which in turn places reliance on principles of unfair competition under Articles 10*bis* of the Paris Convention.[17] Thus, importance of trade secret is that it enables the protection of a valuable piece of information for an enterprise, which would be treated as confidential. This in fact gives the enterprise a competitive advantage over other competitive interests.[18] At the same time, trade secrets can also be strategic in protecting information for a shorter or a longer period of time.[19] The directive offers protection against the unlawful acquisition, use and disclosure of trade secrets. The acquisition of a trade secret without the consent of the trade secret holder shall be considered unlawful, whenever carried out by an unauthorized access, appropriation of, or copying of any documents, objects, materials, substances or electronic files, lawfully under the control of the trade secret holder.[20] It may also be regarded as dishonest if under the circumstances, is considered contrary to 'honest commercial practices'.[21] The CJEU in a different scenario has interpreted the notion of 'honest practice', as *a duty to act fairly in relation to the legitimate interests of the owner*

13. M. Schultz and D. Lippoldt, 'Approaches to protection of undisclosed information (trade secrets): Background paper', OECD Trade Policy Papers, 2014, No. 162, OECD Publishing.
14. Adopted on 8 June 2016. Directive (EU) 2016/943 of the European Parliament and the Council on the protection of undisclosed know-how and business information (trade secrets) against their unlawful acquisition, use and disclosure.
15. *Faccenda Chicken v Fowler ChD* [1984] ICR 589.
16. Article 1(2), Directive (EU) 2016/943.
17. Paris Convention for the Protection of Industrial Property of 20 March 1883, which requires that: Arts 10*bis* Unfair Competition, (1) The countries of the Union are bound to assure to nationals of such countries effective protection against unfair competition. *See also* L.C. Paul, Torremans, The road towards the harmonisation of trade secrets law in the European union, *Revista La Propiedad Inmaterial*, No. 20, Julio-Diciembre De 2015.
18. http://ec.europa.eu/growth/industry/intellectual-property/trade-secrets_en; *see also* M. Sch ultz and D. Lippoldt, 'Approaches to protection of undisclosed information (trade secrets): Background paper', OECD Trade Policy Papers, 2014, No. 162, OECD Publishing.
19. *Ibid.*
20. Article 4(2)(a), Directive (EU) 2016/943.
21. Article 4(2)(b), Directive (EU) 2016/943.

of such right.[22] However, under the directive, an acquisition of a trade secret shall be considered lawful if it was the result of an independent discovery or creation, observation, study, disassembly or testing of a product or object that has been made available to the public or that is lawfully in the possession of the acquirer of the information such as a worker for the concern.[23] Reverse engineering of a lawfully acquired trade secret which was one of the concerns prior to the creation of the directive owing to lack of clarity in the law is now addressed through the new directive.[24] Further, the recital also provides that reverse engineering of a lawfully acquired product should be considered as a lawful means of acquiring information, except when otherwise contractually agreed.[25] Thus, any practice, which, under the circumstances, is in conformity with honest commercial practices, would be regarded as lawful.[26] Where the acquisition, use or disclosure was aimed to excise the freedom of expression or for revealing misconduct or protecting legitimate interests then it would qualify as an exception to the application of the measures in trade secret infringement.[27] The trade secret directive thus visualizes a mechanism, which while enabling the enterprises to protect information as a secret would also be legally obliged to divulge such secret for public policy objectives if such need arises.[28] In matters of public interest such as health, environment or safety of consumers, such public interests prevail over private interest.[29] The approaches to applying a trade secret theory in the context of biobanking would have to be regarded in this light in appreciating its applicability in Europe.

[A] Modelling Trade Secret Law as an Alternative to Issues of Consent

This approach works with the realization the traditional concept of informed consent is illusory and that different approaches to the ethics of genetic sample collections are needed.[30] The proponents of this approach R. Mitchell et al. considers that DNA is unique and deeply personal as it is capable of revealing a great deal about the individual who is its source.[31] By making major investments and efforts to recruit the subjects to contribute their DNA and associated information, the biobank serves as an

22. Case C 228/03, *the Gillette Company and Gillette Group Finland Oy v LA-Laboratories Oy*, the Court of Justice of the European Union has interpreted the notion of 'honest practice' in relation to Directive 89/104/EEC on the approximation of the laws of the Member States relating to trade mark.
23. Article 3(1), Directive (EU) 2016/943.
24. A. Ohly, Reverse engineering: Unfair competition or catalyst for innovation?, Patents and Technological Progress in a Globalised world: Liber, Joseph Straus, ed., pp. 535–552, Berlin, Springer, 2009.
25. Recital 16, Directive (EU) 2016/943.
26. *Ibid.*
27. Article 5, Directive (EU) 2016/943.
28. *Supra* note 22.
29. *Ibid.*
30. R. Mitchell et al., A trade secret model for genomic biobanking, *The Journal of Law Medicine & Ethics.* September 2012.
31. *Supra* note 30.

institution in the 'business' of biomedical research.[32] Further, genetic information so gathered has value precisely because it was not generally known. This according to the scholars of the approach satisfies the basic elements of the definition of a trade secret. In offering a trade secret licensing model this approach differs from informed consent in two distinct ways. First, unlike the informed consent, which does not offer any monetary compensation owing to fears over economic exploitation, the trade secret model is based on giving people something in return for their participation. This according to the proponents need not be monetary but a confidence to the patients or donors of the use of such resources in biomedical research leading to the development of new products useful to the community. Second, the trade secret model does not require conversing directly with each participant, as informed consent generally does. Informed consent becomes meaningless when it is solely used for protecting the researchers. Conversely there is a need to treats subjects as autonomous, competent agents, not vulnerable people in need of protection.[33] The trade secret model thus offers to recognize the contributions of the participants towards the noble cause of research rather than treat them as raw materials of such research.[34] Therefore, under the trade secret approach, the contributor retains legal ownership of the information embodied in the specimen (not the specimen itself) and sets the conditions under which such information can be used.[35] It has also been suggested that personal privacy rights including the ability to control public disclosure of private facts about an individual such as genomic information could also supplement legal approaches such as the trade secret model.[36]

The trade secret model has however been criticized on the following points:

(i) While trade secrets bank on its value based on the information being kept a secret, the value of genomic information particularly those related to rare to serious diseases may benefit from data sharing. Sharing data and research information offers the possibilities to appreciate the nature of the disease or its treatment in better or more ways than one.[37]

(ii) Lack of a practical prospective for the model in disease research biobanks owing to the difficulty involved in accurately tracking and implementing the diverse licensing preferences of multiple research participants with respect to the research uses of biospecimens.[38]

(iii) Considering value for the biomedical information and gain offered to the participants implies a sense of business which is not the case with biomedical samples collected from altruistic donors.[39]

(iv) Trade secret information, by definition, must confer an economic benefit on the holder, deriving specifically from the fact that the information is not

32. *Ibid.*
33. *Supra* note 30.
34. *Ibid.*
35. *Ibid.*
36. J.H. Matsuura, Trade-secret model: Privacy rights, *Science*. 16 September 2011; 333.
37. C.J. Weil and C. Compton, Trade-secret model: Potential pitfalls, *Science*. 2011; 333.
38. *Ibid.*
39. E.S. Dove, et al., Trade-secret model: Legal limitations, *Science*. 333 (6049): 1575, 2011.

generally known.[40] Further trade secrets presuppose that the holder knows the confidential information, which is generally not the case when the donors or patients donate their samples.[41]

In a response to the above criticism which also published in science, the proponents of the trade secret model argued that, researchers working in the genomic or biomedical research are not just altruistically motivated but also monetarily motivated. Seeking patents to protect innovation was one such commercial effort by researchers. In contrast, the trade secret model offered an opportunity for individuals to be actual partners, rather than simply 'subjects,' in biobank research.[42] Further, it was also argued that the conflation of concept of 'value' and 'secret' were misinterpreted. The information sought to be protected must have economic value to its proprietor, and it must not be generally known. The avid interest of medical science in obtaining DNA samples was conclusive evidence that a person's genetic information has economic value so also it could be maintained as a secret in the sense that the donor can choose whether to divulge the information for research or not.[43]

[B] Modelling a Trade Secret Approach to the Concerns of Patent Paradigm

While the above approach sought to alter the issues of consent with the panacea of trade secret law, there seems to be a developing approach to trade secret law from within the biomedical research sector with a need to find a better mechanism to protect the research results. The protection of intangible assets is as crucial both for businesses and for non-commercial research bodies, and is necessary for the EU's competitiveness in promoting innovation and in encouraging collaborative research or cross-border cooperation.[44] This is also the case with biomedical research where the advancement of research to the delivery of medical care use of IPR particularly patents to achieve the goal of improving the quality of healthcare.[45] While patents are more often the preferred route for researchers within biomedical research, yet it has become less popular owing to the immense expenditure involved in securing patents, maintaining it and dealing with litigation process as it arises in the course of an infringement action. For example it was reported that maintaining Gentech's antibody patent in a single litigation against another pharmaceutical company cost USD 237 million.[46] Thus, the

40. *Ibid.*
41. *Ibid.*
42. R. Mitchell et al., Response, *Science*. 333 (6049): 1575, 2011.
43. *Ibid.*
44. Proposal for a Directive of the European Parliament and of the Council on the protection of undisclosed know-how and business information (trade secrets) against their unlawful acquisition, use and disclosure COM(2013) 813 final – 2013/0402 (COD).
45. R.M. Patino, Moving research to patient applications through commercialization: Understanding and evaluating the role of intellectual property. *Journal of the American Association for Laboratory Animal Science*. 2010; 49(2): 147–154.
46. E. Waltz, Genentech's cabilly victory (NEWS) Nature Biotechnology, April, 2009, Vol. 27(4), p. 307.

equation of win or loss in such patent battles can be the same. Besides these innate monetary issues associated with patents, it has been less popular in other fronts.[47] Patents have also been considered as impeding medical innovation in different ways.[48] Biotechnological research particularly in Europe has undergone seismic shift through patent conflicts and decisions. These have developed concerns over funding for translational research in European startups and companies and equally among the scientific fraternity in particular.[49] For instance, the implications of the CJEU's decision for human embryonic stem cell research and commercialization in Europe have been widely debated in the light of the Brüstle case[50] giving concerns not only for research but also the feasibility over maintenance of patent rights in hESC research.[51] In this respect there has been an increasing reliance on secrecy with respect to biomedical research.[52] Finding alternative models to some of the concerns raised by the limitations of patenting have led to a trade secret discussion in the field of biotechnology.[53] Trade secret protection differs from patent protection in the sense that patents prohibits any unauthorized use of the patented invention, on the contrary trade secret is protected only against access or use in violation of a duty of confidentiality or if it was obtained through improper means.[54] Trade secret can be supplemental to or alternative to patents. Trade secret protection can arise if the concern or the enterprise with such valuable information takes sufficient measures to maintain it a secret. Thus, it does not require for formal application process unlike patents.[55] So also unlike patents which may expire after a standard period including regulatory extensions, the trade secret may be maintained as long as reasonable steps are in place to maintain such information a secret.[56] Legal protection for trade secrets applies to a wide variety of commercially relevant information such as extraction or manufacturing processes, product development plans, industrial techniques, formulas, customer lists, marketing strategies, genetic engineering techniques, software used in biological process, genomic information and the like.[57] This approach does not consider the sample donor to

47. T. Seldon, Beyond patents: Effective intellectual property strategy in biotechnology, *Innovation, Management Policy and Practice.* 2011; 13:1, 55–61, (2011).
48. For instance it is argued that apart from the maintenance cost or cost of seeking patents, it is often used by commercial entities as a means of return on their investments. This is claimed as an incentive toward innovation and reinvestment into further R&D. However patents also tend to stifle biomedical research, by preventing researchers from accessing patented materials. Further Patents have also been blamed for impeding medical care by raising prices of essential medicines i.e., the results of biomedical research- *see* E.R. Gold et al., Are patents impeding medical care and innovation?. *PLoS Medicine* 2010; 7(1): e1000208.
49. Nature biotechnology, Editorial, 'Tilting toward secrecy', volume 29 number 12 December 2011.
50. Judgment of the Court (Grand Chamber) of 18 October 2011, *Oliver Brüstle v Greenpeace*, European Court Reports 2011 I-09821.
51. *Supra* note 7.
52. *Ibid.*
53. Holman Christopher M.Biotechnology Law Report. April 2016, 35(2): 45–54. *See also* T. Seldon, Beyond patents: Effective intellectual property strategy in biotechnology, *Innovation, Management Policy and Practice.* 2011; 13(1): 55–61; N. Moran, The rise of trade secrets in biotechnology, *Science Business.* 26 June 2008.
54. *Supra* note 44.
55. *Ibid.*
56. *Supra* note 49.
57. *Supra* note 36.

possess any trade secret unlike the previous approach. Instead, it considers that information derived from biomedical research may be protected under trade secret law as opposed to patents. Thus genomic research entities, pharmaceutical companies or other similar entities could possess trade secret as opposed to patenting research results. Nevertheless, the critics of this approach argue that trade secret protection of genomic data is inappropriate because it impedes the free flow of information that is necessary to advance PM.[58] Critics have also cautioned that removing the ability to protect IP with patents could result in companies deciding to protect the information by the use of trade secrets which may prove counterproductive to the advancement of genomic research in general.[59]

From the above discussion, it appears that none of the two approaches seems to be fully conclusive especially in the context of biomedical research involving biobanks. The first approach, in seeking to value the donors wrecks the essential principle of Europe Convention on Human Rights and Biomedicine[60] on prohibition of financial gains from human body parts. Even though approach considers that such benefits need not be monetary, yet by offering ownership rights over the trade secret to the donors and in considering their genomic information to be of value, the approach tends to defeat the essence of the principle. So also, the participants of a biobank neither discover their genetic information nor may they be aware of what their genes may hold for them. Applying a trade secret law with rights held by participants of a biobank does not seem appropriate as to the principles of trade secret law as well as bioethics.

The second approach while being more feasible, questions the possibilities for sharing of resources within the biomedical fraternity, which has been advocating open sharing, and free flow of data in the interest of research.[61] However, contrary to the general conception of trade secret laws being restrictive in nature, a distinguished scholar Mark Lemley points out that they can promote inventions and at the same time its eventual disclosure.[62] Trade secret laws confer an exclusive right on the possessor of valuable information not generally known to or readily ascertainable by competitors. In this sense it offers the hallmark of an intellectual property right which is offered both by patents as well as copyrights.[63] When it comes to disclosure, it appears that trade secret is a secret not to be divulged. Patents and copyright on the other hand encourages disclosure of the invention or the publication of the work or its communication to the public. While trade secret at sight appears to limit disclosure paradoxically, however, it actually encourages broader disclosure and use of information by

58. R. Cook-Deegan et al., The next controversy in genetic testing: Clinical data as trade secrets?, European Journal of Human Genetics. June 2013; 21(6): 585–588.
59. A.F. Konski, Genetic data, patents, and trade secrets, *Personalized Medicine Bulletin*. 9 November 2012.
60. Council of Europe Convention on Human Rights and Biomedicine (1997) Art. 21 – Prohibition of financial gain http://conve ntions.coe.int/Treaty/en/Treaties/Html/164.ht.
61. HUGO Ethics Committee – Statement on Human Genomic Databases, Eubios *Journal of Asian and International Bioethics* 6 (1995) 59–60; see also A.M. Capron, et al., Ethical issues in governing biobanks: Global perspectives, Ashgate Publishing Ltd. 2013.
62. M.A. Lemley, 'The surprising virtues of treating trade secrets as IP rights', *Stanford Law Review*. 2008; 61: 118.
63. *Supra* note 62.

creating a gradual perforation flow of information between business partners or to new employees.[64] Trade secret owners may choose to license such information or not, however realistically it may not be feasible for concerns engaged in enhancing commercial relationships to keep information secret. Trade secrecy laws penalize the misuse of licensed proprietary knowledge; however in practice, initially restrictively shared trade secrets, will 'leak' out and diffuse to the public at large in the long run.[65] Thus essentially what trade secrets offer is an edge for creators or developers of information over their competitors for an uncertain period of time until such diffusion occurs.[66] Thus trade secrets can be completely kept confidential by the owner of such information or selectively shared. In either event a certain period of control over information can be ensured for researchers just like patents but without its limitation.[67]

[C] Publicly Funded Biobank Research and Trade Secret Law

Management of IP within the sphere of biotechnology offers opposing choices which need a careful weighing. In addressing the possibilities of trade secret law within biobank-based research the question is how far it is possible to maintain genomic information (including databases) a secret particularly in the context of publicly funded biobanks. This question embarks not only a legal enquiry but also a factual one about the emerging research environments within which such a discourse proceeds.

Trade secrets exhibit different contours within law with elements of confidentiality, contract, of tort, of property, or even of criminal law.[68] So much so that it has been debated by scholars around the globe whether to consider it an intellectual property right as such.[69] Irrespective of the consensus on this question it would be fairly safe to say that trade secret law offers good opportunity to protect investment in innovation as such.[70] This has been considered as major reason for its increased

64. *Ibid.*
65. G. Van Overwalle, 'Uncorking trade secrets: Sparking the interaction between trade secrecy and open biotechnology', in Rochelle C. Dreyfuss and Katherine J. Strandburg (eds), 'The law and theory of trade secrecy: A handbook of contemporary research', Edward Elgar Publishing Ltd, 2011 at p. 246.
66. *Supra* note 62.
67. A.K. Rai, Regulating scientific research: Intellectual property rights and the norms of science, *Northwestern University Law Review.* 1999 Fall; 94(1): 77–152.
68. *Supra* note 65.
69. I.H. Reichman, Charting the collapse of the patent-copyright dichotomy: Premises for a restructured international intellectual property system, 13 *Cardozo Arts & Entertainment Law Journal.* 1995; 475, 504–517; J.H. Reichman, Legal hybrids between the patent and copyright paradigms, *Columbia Law Review* (1994); 94: 2432, 2504–2557 P. Samuelson and S. Scotchmer, The law and economics of reverse engineering, *Yale Law Journal.* 2002; 888: 1575; M.A. Lemley, The surprising virtues of treating trade secrets as intellectual property rights, *Stanford Law Review* 61: 311, 315 ~ 353; J.H. Reichman, How trade secrecy law generates a natural semi-commons of innovative know-how, in Rochelle C. Dreyfuss and Katherine J. Strandburg (eds), 'The law and theory of trade secrecy: A handbook of contemporary research, Edward Elgar Publishing Ltd, 2011.
70. *Supra* note 65.

application.[71] In a study published by the EU Intellectual Property Office (EUIPO) it was found that over 52% of the companies preferred trade Secrets to patents to protect innovation.[72] In a sector-wise analysis it was revealed that in scientific research and development alone 79.3% of usage of trade secrets.[73] The study also involved projects which functioned under a public funding and also public sector-based collaborations. It was also reported by the study that those with collaborative partnerships tended to use trade secret more vigorously along with other IPR such as patents. This indicates that the propensity to use trade secret in research and development is essentially in line with changing paradigms of research, to ensure a lead-time in recouping the investments that go into such research. The current research environment with university-based or publicly funded research institutions is also increasingly becoming collaborative such that research is getting more intertwined with private sector. This is particularly the case within EU since the Lisbon agenda[74] which has demanded a focused on improving research and innovation in EU including the environment for private research investment in partnerships within universities and other public research organizations.[75] This urge for integrated research environments have also been highlighted under the European strategy 2020.[76]

European universities and publicly funded or autonomous research institutions within EU not only cater to basic research or education but are also engaged in collaborative research across borders with multiple partners including industrial partners in an effort to achieve global standards in research.[77] Thus, universities are no longer limited in outlook with regard to neither their research nor their outreach. However, such changing outlook of publicly funded research has its own challenges. Given the needs of commercial oriented research, it is essential to incorporate the needs of such collaboration coupled with higher standards of data security and protection of personal data.[78] Universities and other public sector research are also required to publish, share and make results freely available as such, research emanates from public funding. Although this need for sharing is regarded as the essence of

71. D.L. Burk, Misappropriation of trade secrets in biotechnology licensing, *Albany Law Journal of Science and Technology*. 1994; 4: 121, 139.
72. Protecting Innovation Through Trade Secrets and Patents: Determinants for European Union Firms, EUIPO July 2017.
73. *Ibid*.
74. The aim of the Lisbon Strategy 2000–2010, launched in March 2000 by the EU heads of State and government, was to make Europe 'the most competitive and dynamic knowledge-based economy in the world, capable of sustainable economic growth with more and better jobs and greater social cohesion'.
75. European Union Parliament Website Lisbon European Council 23 and 24 March Presidency Conclusion.
76. Brussels, 3 March 2010 COM(2010) 2020 final, Communication from the Commission Europe 2020 A strategy for smart, sustainable and inclusive growth. The EU 2020 while requiring strengthening of research partnerships in achieving commercialization goals also requires improvement of the conditions for enforcing intellectual property.
77. Communication from the Commission to the Council, the European Parliament, the European Economic and Social Committee and the Committee of the Regions Improving knowledge transfer between research institutions and industry across Europe: embracing open innovation: Implementing the Lisbon agenda, EUR 22836 ENCOM(2007)182.
78. *Supra* note 37, 39.

university research, it often becomes incompatible with industry's need to keep information confidential and protected by IPR.[79] Promoting innovation and disseminating new knowledge can be compatible, provided that IPR are applied suiting the needs of the research in question. Apart from the traditional university sphere of research Europe has also been building platforms for technological innovation between public and private sectors in an attempt to develop solutions for concerns in different sectors such as energy, health, environment and the like.[80] These efforts have been furthered with the European research infrastructural platforms aiming to boost Big Data research in multiple fields such as biobanking, materials sciences, social sciences, humanities, life sciences, etc.[81] The emergence of such research platforms, faster computers and new mathematical techniques means it is possible to conduct large-scale study analysis over different periods of time. In addition, multiple collaborations, with research entities, cohorts and industrial partners enable the translation of such research into results. Against such changes in the frontiers of research information, trade secrets are increasingly being considered as an alternative to other IP rights. Within public research, commercial ventures may evolve relationships that may be modelled in different ways based on the purpose such relationship seeks to achieve. These may include co-funded research, commissioned works, consultancy or even the most popular model of collaboration the Public Private Partnership model (PPP).

With such strategic approaches to commercial collaborations within public sector and the need for balancing dissemination of publicly funded research, new alternatives may be essential to address competing interests involved in research. The question then becomes whether trade secrets can effectively function within the realm of public research. This question finds relevance in the light of the nature of genomic information and the features of trade secret as a mechanism to protect it. Genomic information includes a wide spectrum of information and associated data ranging from patient's genetic information, their inter relationships and other genomic research data.[82] Each of this information may be regard as confidential in nature; however they may not have the potential to be protected as a trade secret.[83] Trade secret essentially consists of two elements secrecy and commercial interest.[84] Only such information which has economic advantage and is subject to reasonable efforts to maintain its secrecy would be regarded as trade secret. However, in the context of genomic information this is an interesting paradox because genomic information covers an interrelated body of

79. *Ibid.*
80. Report on European Technology Platforms and Joint Technology Initiatives: Fostering Public-Private R&D Partnerships to Boost Europe's Industrial Competitiveness.
81. *See* the different areas of big data development through ERIC's https://ec.europa.eu/research/infrastructures/index_en.cfm?pg=eric-landscape.
82. Genomics and World Health: Report of the Advisory Committee on Health research, Geneva, WHO (2002); Biotechnology and Biopharmaceuticals: Transforming Proteins and Genes into Drugs, John Wiley & Sons, 19 September 2013 - Science.
83. J.M. Mohr, Rethinking trade secret protection, GEN 1 August 2013; 33(14).
84. Article 2, Directive (EU) 2016/943.

personal genomic data of the individual, their family members along with the co-relational scientific data derived by researchers.[85] Interestingly personal data relating to the contributor of the sample is kept confidential and efforts are taken continuously by the biobank cohorts to maintain its confidentiality. So also the wholeness of genomic information along with the participant data is what gives commercial value to 'genomic Big Data' as a resource.[86] This theoretically qualifies such information for protection under a trade secret regime.

On the factual side it can be seen that Recital 63 of General Data Protection Regulation[87] requires that the data subject should be offered access to his or her personal data and that right should not adversely affect the rights or freedoms of others, including trade secrets or IP. However, the result of those considerations should not be a refusal to provide all information to the data subject.[88] In the same vein the trade secret Directive 2016/943[89] acknowledges respect to the fundamental rights enshrined in the EU Charter of fundamental rights in respecting private life and personal data.[90] It follows that steps must be taken for the protection of personal data of any person whose personal data may be processed by the trade secret holder.[91] This caution must also be applied when taking steps to protect a trade secret, or the rights of any person involved in legal proceedings concerning the unlawful acquisition, use or disclosure of trade secrets.[92] Thus in terms of processing of genomic information the General Data Protection Regulation prevails over trade secret law. This possible conflict has been envisioned by European Data Protection Supervisor suggests, who was consulted in the formulation the EU trade secret directive and it was suggested that the Directive on Trade Secret should explicitly state that it does not interfere with data subject rights.[93] With regard to a data subject's access to the processing of his or her information the directive provides that the measures, procedures and remedies provided for shall be dismissed where the alleged acquisition, use or disclosure was for the purpose of protecting a legitimate interest recognized by union or national law.[94] This recognition

85. J. Kaye et al., Can I access my personal genome? The current legal position in the UK. *Medical Law Review*. 2014; 22(1): 64–86.
86. R. Mitchell, National biobanks: Clinical labor, risk production, and the creation of biovalue. *Science, Technology & Human Values*. 2010; 35(3): 330–355. http://doi.org/10.1177/01622439 09340267.
87. Regulation (EU) 2016/679 of the European Parliament and of the Council of 27 April 2016 on the protection of natural persons with regard to the processing of personal data and on the free movement of such data.
88. *Ibid.*
89. Recital 34, Directive (EU) 2016/943 of the European Parliament and of the Council of 8 June 2016 on the protection of undisclosed know-how and business information (trade secrets) against their unlawful acquisition, use and disclosure.
90. Article 7, Charter of Fundamental Rights of the European Union.
91. Recital 35, Directive (EU) 2016/943.
92. *Ibid.*
93. Opinion of the European Data Protection Supervisor on the proposal for a directive of the European Parliament and of the Council on the protection of undisclosed know-how and business information (trade secrets) against their unlawful acquisition, use and disclosure; *see also* for the general views on the conflict: G. Malgieri, Trade secrets v personal data: A possible solution for balancing rights. *International Data Privacy Law*, 1 May 2016; 6(2): 102–116.
94. Article 5, Directive (EU) 2016/943.

of a data subject's legitimate interest is also reflected in the words of the recital to the directive which requires that the trade secret law should not affect the rights of the data subject to access his or her personal data being processed and to obtain the rectification, erasure or blocking of the data where it is incomplete or inaccurate and, where appropriate, the obligation to process sensitive data in accordance with data protection law.[95] Thus from a practical stand point too, it appears that the European trade secret law is well founded within the norms of data protection of subjects. This means that biobank-based research could effectively venture to balance differing interests while choosing to protect genomic research results using trade secret law. In addressing the legal possibilities of applying trade secrets to biobanks the other question to be address is whether the nature of being publicly funded imposes any limitation on the use of trade secrets as such. As discussed above there is an increase in collaborative research partnerships between publicly and private sectors which are seen as a paradigm shift in different sectors. While universities obtain a source of funding and a way of meeting the financial burden necessary to develop inventions commercially, industry gains access to new technology and excellent researchers.[96] Apart from this traditional notion of an upstream university research there is also an observable phenomenon of public sector and private sector linking in partnerships for formation of platforms and strategic alliances which are large-scale, independent and self-financing entities.[97] These are involved in a large-scale research and development of specific disease-oriented studies, laboratory diagnostics, testing devices, or broader therapeutic protocols or modalities, such as particular forms of gene therapy to development pathways for specific diseases.[98] Protecting research results through IPR within such relationship is indeed a challenge. Biotech industries tend to use patents or trade secrets which are designed to protect commercial interests by allowing companies and individuals to keep secret, for a potentially unlimited time, formulas, processes and inventions that offer a pecuniary gain especially when not known by competitors.[99] This stands in stark contrast to the directions of publicly funded institutions whose goal is openness, wider dissemination and sharing of research with other entities.[100] At the same time it can also be argued that while the creation of innovations often requires openness, their

95. *Supra* note 91.
96. D.E. Korn, Patent and trade secret protections in university-industry research relationships in biotechnology. *Harvard Journal on Legislation.* 1987; 24: 191; P. Shockley, The availability of trade secret protection for university research. *Journal of College and University Law.* 1993–1994; 20: 309.
97. http://ec.europa.eu/research/innovation-union/index_en.cfm?pg=etp.
98. J.S. Sherkow, Protecting products versus platforms. *Bio entrepreneur Nature Biotech.* 14 April 2016, doi:10.1038/bioe.2016.4.
99. D.S. Levine, 'The impact of trade secrecy on public transparency', Rochelle C. Dreyfuss and Katherine J. Strandburg, (eds), 'The law and theory of trade secrecy: A handbook of contemporary research', Edward Elgar Publishing, 2010.
100. Improving knowledge transfer between research institutions and industry across Europe: embracing open innovation, European Commission Directorate-General for Research Directorate-General for Enterprise and Industry EUR 22836 EN COM(2007)182; *see also* David S. Levine, *supra* note 99.

commercialization necessitates their protection.[101] In a commission working document on improving knowledge transfer between research institutions and industry across Europe, the finer balancing of trade secret law was considered in detail. It provided that, 'research institutions should accept to keep confidential the trade secrets and knowledge belonging to other partners as a general rule.[102] Nevertheless, research institutions should only exceptionally accept to keep their own research results confidential, on the basis of a detailed assessment and justification of this need.[103] Companies may have a legitimate interest in keeping certain results secret, to make it easier for them to reap the associated commercial benefits. The general principle that if the industry partner wants greater control over the publication and confidentiality of the results it must increase its contribution to the research institution seems to be a useful one in this context. This will have to be matched with any legal requirements for the research institution to publish results. Indeed, confidentiality can only be accepted to the extent that this is not contrary to any general legal act or regulations relating to the access to information in the research institution's Member State'.[104]

This means that collaborative research can no longer ignore the needs of research commercialization which may be pursued through the protection of such research results. Further, these obligations also apply to public research enterprises (including platforms or alliance) which may be required protection of trade secrets or other IP rights. The mere fact of private sector involvement in research should not, in itself be a reason to restrict access to the data or reuse of data.[105] As suggested by OECD in their recommendation on Access to Research Data from Public Funding, balancing differing interests may find possible solution in measures that promote non-commercial access and use while protecting commercial interests.[106] Such measures could involve trade secrets or partial or delayed release of data which can ensure that the primary participants of such project may exploit the collaboration to the fullest extent.[107]

Another possible application of law within the discourse of trade secrets in the context of public sector is the reuse of Public Sector Information Directive, which will also be briefly touched upon herein to appreciate its importance to public-funded research.[108] The directive offers an openness principle to public sector information by default in freely making it available for commercial and non-commercial reuse.[109] The term 'public sector' under the directive includes, bodies governed by public law which has been defined to mean those established for the specific purpose of meeting needs

101. K. Laursen and A.J. Salter, The paradox of openness: Appropriability, external search and collaboration, *Research Policy*. 2014; 43(5): 867–878.
102. Directive (EU) 2016/943 of the European Parliament and of the Council of 8 June 2016 on the protection of undisclosed know-how and business information (trade secrets) against their unlawful acquisition, use and disclosure.
103. *Ibid.*
104. *Ibid.*
105. *Infra* note 715.
106. OECD, Principles and Guidelines for Access to Research Data from Public Funding, 2007.
107. *Ibid.*
108. Directive 2013/37/EU of the European Parliament and of the Council of 26 June 2013 amending Directive 2003/98/EC on the reuse of public sector.
109. Article 3(1), Directive 2013/37/EU.

in the general interest, not having an industrial or commercial character; having legal personality; and financed, for the most part by the State, or regional or local authorities, or other bodies governed by public law; or subject to management supervision by those bodies; or having an administrative, managerial or supervisory board, more than half of whose members are appointed by the State, regional or local authorities or by other bodies governed by public law.[110]

Thus public research establishments and universities may come under the purview of the directive. However under the directive it excludes documents held by educational and research establishments, including organizations established for the transfer of research results, schools and universities from reuse.[111] So also commercial confidentiality (e.g., business, professional or company secrets) are also excluded from such reuse. On the contrary, it does not exclude documents held by libraries, museums and archives.[112] The directive also re-clarifies that it shall neither affect the existence or ownership of IPR of public sector bodies, nor does it limit the exercise of these rights in any way.[113] To this end, it also promotes licensing on reasonable terms by such public entities.[114] In addition a refusal to a third-party access or refusal to offer a licecse in respect to trade secrets shall also include grounds for refusal to the applicant.[115] In *Cambridge University Hospitals NHS Foundation Trust*[116] the information claimed to be under trade secret containing personal data was refused for third-party access by the university hospital, on the grounds that the information constituted a trade secret and that its disclosure would be likely to prejudice its commercial and technical interests. The information commissioner, UK[117] observed that in addressing the refusal of trade secret information by a public authority it was necessary to consider the actual harm caused to the commercial interest of the public authority. This according to the commissioner can be derived by examining the causal relationship that existed between the potential disclosure of the information being withheld and the prejudice to those commercial interests.[118] This means that publicly authorities can apply trade secrets to protect valuable information and even limit their sharing in commercial interest which are essential to the concern as such. However, this will also be a challenge for public authorities and research institutions if access to that data is denied for other actors who may generate additional knowledge from such information.[119]

110. Article 2(2), Directive 2013/37/EU.
111. Article 1(e), Directive 2013/37/EU, 'reuse' means the use by persons or legal entities of documents held by public sector bodies, for commercial or non-commercial purposes other than the initial purpose within the public task for which the documents were produced. Exchange of documents between public sector bodies purely in pursuit of their public tasks does not constitute reuse.
112. Article 1(e), (f), Directive 2013/37/EU.
113. Recital 22, Directive 2013/37/EU.
114. Aritcle 8, Directive 2013/37/EU.
115. Article 4(3), Directive 2013/37/EU.
116. Cambridge University Hospitals NHS Foundation Trust (Health (NHS)) [2016] UKICO FS50608319 (18 July 2016).
117. Under UK Freedom of Information Act 2000 (FOIA).
118. *Ibid.*
119. J. Drexl, Designing competitive markets for industrial data in Europe – between propertisation and access, JIPITEC, 2016.

[D] Different Approaches for Evolving Secrecy Measures Within Biobanks

Trade secrets have achieved unexpected prominence over the recent years owing to their capacity to cover different types of data within its folds with minimal efforts.[120] Although the investment in their creation maybe nominal, their value is generally considered to be more difficult to determine.[121] Therefore, it is much of a challenge to justify when secrecy is sought in a public setting. The way research collaborations are structured often determines the way in which valuable information or results are protected through trade secrecy. The literature offers three divergent views on how knowledge appropriation could proceed within collaboration and how collaborators can transform knowledge into commercial success using trade secrets as a tool. There are three evolving approaches to involving secrecy in commercial research namely the spill over prevention approach, openness and a hybrid approach each of which will be briefly discussed herein.

The spill over prevention approach which considers that firms are more likely to seek external collaborators if they can protect their innovation by patents, and more generally, guard against unintended knowledge spillovers to partners. This can be effectively dealt with by strategic protection measures such as protecting the outflow of commercially sensitive information. This according to the proponents of the approach reduces the potential for freeriding within and beyond the cooperative agreement and improves the stability of such agreements.[122] Based on the type of collaboration and the firm-specific characteristic of the partners involved, the spill over approach recommends adjusting the level of strategic protection such as secrecy.[123] The spillover approach offers protectionist strategies for firms involved in collaboration and regards that incoming spill overs that often emerge from public research are increasingly beneficial for firms employed in cooperation with them.

The openness approach posits that firms seeking external knowledge for innovation are less likely to involve exclusivity as it impedes their ability to gain from collaboration, and because they want to be attractive partners for potential collaborators. In contrast to patent, trade secrets limits the openness in the channels of knowledge sharing and often posits complexities in protecting them, particularly while being engaged in collaborative exchange with external actors.[124]

The spill over and open approaches presents two distinct directions for information appropriation in external relations. While the one represents maximization of appropriability, the other seeks to limit this in the interest of increased openness as means for flow of knowledge. However, while these approaches suit specific scenarios,

120. K. Linton, The unexpected importance of trade secrets: New directions in international trade policy making and empirical research, June 2016.
121. *Supra* note 59.
122. *Supra* note 100.
123. E. Giannopoulou, et al., Same but different? research and technology organizations, universities and the innovation activities of firms. *Research Policy*. 2018.
124. J.P. Liebeskind, Keeping organizational secrets: Protective institutional mechanisms and their costs. *Industrial and Corporate Change*. 1997; 6: 623–663.

they may not be of uniform applicability. Within a publicly funded research environment, collaborations may seek different needs based on the nature or stage in which the innovation collaboration proceeds. Therefore such public collaborations particularly those within biomedical sectors, which involve multiple partners, must find distinct measures suited to the needs of collaboration. This flexible approach commonly referred to as hybrid approach in essence finds a middle path to applying protectionist regime and openness. A hybrid approach thus allows for building new capacities and capabilities in wider sectoral areas of business and research, and supports innovation diffusion across sectors.[125] In this process, standard norms for knowledge appropriation through legal and strategic measures such as patents and trade secrets along with ownership are replaced by a case-to-case approach to ensure better results from different collaborations.[126] For example the Integrated Medicines Initiative (IMI), being the biggest public private partnership in the context of health research involved both academic and commercial partners in its research collaborations. IMI has found a unique way to mediate the needs of commercial partners and the need for disclosure of public research. Under the IMI Regulation, the IMI joint undertaking shall ensure the protection of sensitive information the disclosure of which could damage the interests of its members or of participants in the activities of the joint undertaking.[127] Further the IMI model agreement stipulates that during implementation of the action and for four years after the period any data, documents or other material (in any form) that is identified as confidential information at the time it is disclosed will be kept confidential.[128] This period may be extended at the request of a beneficiary for an additional period beyond the initial four years. The use of confidential information is generally limited to implementation of the agreement unless otherwise agreed. Within the PPP, the beneficiaries or private entities may disclose confidential information to their personnel or third parties involved in the action only if they are essential for the implementation of the agreement and such persons to whom the information is being disclosed are bound by an obligation of confidentiality. However the IMI would not have any obligations to protect the confidential information where:

(a) the disclosing party agrees to release the other party;
(b) the information was already known by the recipient or is given to him without obligation of confidentiality by a third party that was not bound by any obligation of confidentiality;
(c) the recipient proves that the information was developed without the use of confidential information;
(d) the information becomes generally and publicly available, without breaching any confidentiality obligation; or
(e) where the disclosure of the information is required by EU or national law.

125. *Ibid.*
126. *Supra* note 124.
127. Article 15, Regulation No. 557/2014.
128. Article 36, confidentiality, Model agreement for IMI 2020 grants.

The rationale behind the efforts of IMI in evolving a strategic framework for PPP, is to assemble a critical mass of expertise and resources that cannot only solve highly complex challenges of drug discovery and development but also ensure that scientific breakthroughs are exploited by the pharmaceutical industry and regulatory agencies to benefit patients and society.[129] Collaboration between industrial and academic partners requires greater participation, flexibility and dynamicity.[130] This in-turn requires tailoring the partnership to its innate needs. Such innovate modelling of research collaboration offers strength for publicly funded biobank-based research in involving trade secrets for protection of research data or other commercially relevant information. So also, the directive on reuse of public sector information will not affect trade secrets, which are a result of public private sector collaborations. Even though 'archives' have not been defined in the directive it can be construed to include biobanks. Biobanks while employing confidentiality to honour partnership interests must also ensure that the free flow of data is not affected. Trade secrets are alternative measures to protect investments in information. It also dually functions as a system for slow percolation and sharing with the research community, thus uniquely balancing differing interests. While sui generis database discussed under Chapter 4, also functions to protect investments, trade secrets protection has the obvious advantage of protecting specific information (even those that are not part of a database structure) and ensuring a system of liability for specific tortious conduct rather than a property right.[131]

129. M. Gunn et al., Benchmarking the scientific output of the innovative medicines initiative, *Nature Biotechnology*. 2015; 33: 811–812.
130. Guidelines for Successful Public – Private Partnerships, European commission, 2003.
131. *Supra* note 99.

Part IV Commercial Collaboration in Biobanks, Guidelines, Practices and Good Governance

CHAPTER 7

Contractual Agreements and IP Policies of Biobanks

§7.01 INTRODUCTION

This chapter will analyse various clauses found in agreements between biobanks, researchers and the industry. This will specifically include MTAs/DTAs (Data Transfer Agreements) and collaborative agreements. In general collaborations within biobanks are mainly of two types namely service collaborations and research collaborations:[1]

(1) Service collaborations: deal in the normal biobanking transaction of offering samples and minimal data sets to users who are in need of such samples for research purposes. The collaboration is based purely on the ability of the biobank to provide the samples, minimum data set and basic services required by the bio-industry company.[2] A fee is usually charged for the processing of the samples and not the samples per se as trading HBMs are prohibited by law and convention. Sample transfers are usually processed through MTAs and any minimal associated data may be transferred to researchers through a DTA. Many biobanks have DTA within the clause of their MTAs.

(2) Research collaboration: range from a study cohort to a large collaboration project with multiple partners working collectively towards a particular research problem. These collaborations involve biobank as a partner for samples, data or research expertise. Such collaborations may be a single

1. R.T. Lawlor, 'Models of collaboration and experiences between bio-industry and academic biobanks' in E. Salvaterra (ed.) 'Advances in biobanking practice through public and private collaborations', Bentham, 2017.
2. *Ibid.*

location or multilocation projects. As discussed in Chapter 2 such collaborations may also be brought through the expert centres which may connect the biobank resources with the needs of the industrial partner's research. Research collaborations are brought about by contractual agreements that specify terms and conditions of such partnership.

However it is also pointed out that apart from the above two collaborations there are certain other types of studies which are conducted based on agreements between biobanks and the research partner such as validity research. Such studies are often to test an industrially developed product or process using biobank samples and do not need informed consent as they are considered as improvement studies.[3] Such validation research does not involve IPR as the base technology has already been developed by the industrial partner, unless where the biobanks were previously engaged in the product development.[4] Both service collaborations and research collaborations contain IP clauses, which will be considered within the context of the present chapter. The concern over disclosure of information regarding research collaborations were expressed by many biobanks. One biobanker even conveyed that 'sample alone cannot give sustainability to a biobank; we need to have more research collaboration with the industry, however we need to play safe in such dealings'.[5] Thus for reasons of such concerns of a competitive biobanking market and reasons of confidentiality, non-disclosure arrangements (entered by the author with biobanks), the specific industrial partners, biobanks, collaborative clauses, etc. will not be expressly stated herein. However national biobank nodes, research and academic institutions working within the field of biobanking have developed templates for collaboration which are distributed publicly, for e.g., IPAG,[6] P3G elements of access policy, BBMRI-ERIC tool,[7] biobank sverige research agreement,[8] Lambert toolkit,[9] Brunswick Template Agreements[10] and the like. Inspiration will be drawn from such documents as these templates are widely used as standard tools within biobanking circles. So also MTA's and DTAs analysed in this chapter will not be identified expressly to avoid any prejudice (See table of MTAs and DTAs in Annex I).

Further the content of this document, including the examples cited herein are purely for the sake of information and analysis only and is not intended to be judgmental of any policy or practice of the biobank. To ensure this the various clauses and agreements will be discussed together under two parts a) MTAs involved in service agreements and b) research collaboration agreements

3. N. D'Haene et al., 'Clinical validation of targeted next generation sequencing for colon and lung cancers.' A. Scarpa (ed.) *PLoS One*. 2015; 10(9): e0138245. PMC. Web. 6 October 2017. *See also* note 1.
4. *Supra* note 1.
5. Interview notes.
6. http://bbmri.at/biomaterial-mta.
7. http://www.bbmri-eric.eu/services/other-services/.
8. http://biobanksverige.se/research/basic-information-in-english/.
9. https://www.gov.uk/guidance/model-agreements-for-collaborative-research.
10. https://www.praxisunico.org.uk/resource/brunswick-template-agreements.

[A] MTAs in Service Agreements

The transfer of materials between universities and public research institutions with researchers is affected through the legal instrument in the form of MTA. It is regarded as tool for sharing of biological materials that may be protected by different legal tools, such as patents, trade secret or confidential information, copyright, database rights, privacy or even a sum of all.[11] The task of an MTA is multifold; it seeks to set the boundaries for the use of the materials; it determines the relationship between the parties to such agreement; it contributes to avoiding liabilities for misuse of the materials and helps to preserve the IP and attribution rights with regard to the use of such samples.[12] MTAs thus involve different legal requirements such as those of contract, IP, liability, indemnity, etc.[13]

Its importance in biomedical research has also been recognized by the WMA Declaration of Taipei on Ethical Considerations,[14] which requires that governance arrangement of biobanks must include a systematic use of MTA when necessary.[15] While access is provided both to publicly funded research as well as private research partners, there are often differences in fees sought from industrial partners. MTAs also serve to exchange materials between biobank partners involved in other research collaborations. Once a project is floated, researchers are free to select the biobank offering the samples of their choice. Most biobanks seek an application specifying the nature of study, type or range of the sample, the purpose of research, the institution within which the researcher or the research project functions. Some biobanks do not honour similar research projects in the same year. This often depends on the research policy of the biobank or its partnership interests. Additional data may also be requested from such biobanks. Upon review of such application an MTA will be entered into between both parties offering access to the material so requested. The use of samples may be followed by a number of obligations which the researcher needs to fulfil. When data is involved, it is usually a licence that is granted to use the data according to certain conditions. However, lack of uniformity and harmonization of MTAs have led to mixed structures which deal in samples and data which has been regarded by many scientific writers as inappropriate.[16] Further the distinction between scientific needs and financial nature of MTAs are not always clearly demarcated.[17] Amidst such concerns the BBMRI-ERIC platform offers two standard MTAs and DTAs for researchers, so also other national nodes have been seeking to use standard forms within such regional biobanks. However, this is not yet completely harmonized and efforts have

11. T. Margoni, The roles of material transfer agreements in genetics databases and bio-Banks, In: G. Pascuzzi et al., *Comparative issues in the governance of research biobanks: property, privacy, intellectual property, and the role of technology*. Springer 231–249.
12. *Supra* note 5.
13. The KTI Practical Guide on MTA.
14. Revised by the 67th WMA General Assembly, Taipei, Taiwan, October 2016.
15. Point 21, Taipei Decleration, 2016.
16. S. Pathmasiri and B.M. Knoppers, Material and data access agreements: Core elements, P3G Ethics and Policymaking Core.
17. *Supra* note 6; *See also* D. Mascalzoni et al., International charter of principles for sharing bio-specimens and data. *European Journal of Human Genetics*. 2015; 23: 721–728.

been underway within BBMRI to seek enforcement of standard norms.[18] The present assessment will touch upon a three points of enquiry namely: (1) ownership; (2) IPR; and (3) data emerging from the samples.

[1] Ownership

The concept ownership over materials have been differently addressed within the agreements, with some specifying the nature of ownership while others with the word 'possession' as in Type 1. The governance principles under the 'EU recommendation on research on biological materials of human origin',[19] requires that the person and/or institution responsible for the collection should be designated and this information should be publicly available. However beyond this the concept of ownership is not fully explored and is widely debated among the academic as to its nature.[20] The transfer of materials to researchers within other projects or institutions or even across the borders brings forth the issue of ownership over the resources. In order to avoid such concerns some biobanks tend to use the idea of ownership as can be seen from type samples.

Type 1

The Biobank is in possession of certain HBMs (the 'Materials') with associated Personal Data, which needs to be analysed within the framework of a study project. The Biobank collaborates with the Responsible Researcher for the Project. The Parties wish the Recipient to be able to analyse the Material for the Project and the Biobank agrees to make the Material and associated coded Personal Data available to the Recipient for the purposes of the Project

18. Workshop on MTA and IPR issues, 26 September 2014.
19. Article 16, Recommendation CM/Rec(2016)6 of the Committee of Ministers to Member States on research on biological materials of human origin (Adopted by the Committee of Ministers on 11 May 2016 at the 1256th meeting of the Ministers' Deputies).
20. *See* for instance: C. Rhodes, 'Potential international approaches to ownership/control of human genetic resources. *Health Care Analysis*. 2016; 24: 260–277. PMC. Web. 8 October 2017; C. Petrini, Ethical and legal considerations regarding the ownership and commercial use of human biological materials and their derivatives. *Journal of Blood Medicine*. 2012; 3: 87–96. PMC. Web. 8 October 2017. S. Munzer, A theory of property. Cambridge University Press, 1990, p. 41; I. Goold, et al., Persons, parts and property: How should we regulate human tissue in the 21st Century?, Hart Publishing 2014.

Type 2

(1) **Sample 1**
X Biobank is the owner of the property in the Samples in the Resource. The Biobank hereby grants the Applicant a limited, revocable, worldwide, royalty-free, non-exclusive licence (but not any ownership rights) to use the Samples for the Permitted Purpose only.

No transfer of Rights: RECIPIENT acknowledges that X retains ownership of all materials, Modifications and data including of all related IPR relating to the materials, its Modifications and DATA. X hereby grants RECIPIENT the right to use the materials and data for the Research Purpose. Except as provided in this Agreement, no express or implied licenses or other rights are granted to RECIPIENT.

(2) **Sample 2**
Biobank shall be the sole owner of any and all data and materials including all data obtained by the bioanalysis of Material or derivate data (i.e., data derived from the original data), and other information as well as any and all IPR related thereto.

(3) **Sample 3**
Ownership Rights. X confirms that it has acquired the Material and has the right to provide access to it in accordance with the Y Act. The Biobank X and its owners retain ownership and all IPR pertaining to the Material.

The Type 1 MTAs seeks to offer a sense of custodianship of materials by explicitly using the term 'possession'. The term possession has been defined as the actual control of property combined with the intention to use it, rightly or wrongly, as one's own.[21] As discussed under Chapter 3 ownership refers to an exercise of dominion over a thing or claims. On the contrary the existence of possessory rights implies that the person in possession of the thing is not the true owner but had limited rights to perform specified acts with regard to the thing.[22] In this sense Type I claims are more aligned to the concept of stewardship which was elaborately discussed under Chapter 1.

On the contrary 'ownership' conveys an exclusive right to use, possess and dispose of property, subject only to the rights of persons having a superior interest and to any restrictions on the owner's rights imposed by agreement with or by act of third parties or by operation of law.[23] The Type 2 MTAs not only exhibit ownership over the corporeal materials but also extends its rights over any incorporeal rights that may arise on account of such biological materials including upstream IP rights. There is also a third category found within the MTAs analysed which seeks property rights where any

21. J. Law, A dictionary of law (Eighth edition, edited by Jonathan Law ed., Oxford quick reference). Oxford University Press, 2015.
22. Nordic Health Law in a European Context: Welfare State Perspectives on Patients' Rights and Biomedicine, edited by Elisabeth Rynning, and Mette Hartlev, BRILL, 2011 at p. 273.
23. *Ibid.*

IPR arise on account of the use of such samples. In such cases there may be a claim to the use of such information or even joint inventorship based on sample contribution.

Type 3
Where the research involving the Material or a Modification results in an invention or patentable modification of the Material, the Recipient and its Researcher/s shall promptly disclose this development to the X. Recipient and X shall decide jointly about the inventorship, taking into due consideration the X's contribution to the invention through its Material. Decisions about all further proceedings, such as filing of a patent application or exploitation, shall be made after inventorship is determined.

Type 3 claims while not invoking ownership of possessory rights make claims to the modification of the material leading to an invention. In a more positive sense this ensures biobank's control over the resources while at the same time being neutral about the issue of ownership. However in the light of Recommendation CM/Rec(2016)6 of the Committee of Ministers to Member States on research on biological materials of human origin,[24] it would be essential for biobanks to ensure responsibility to the collection and designation of such information, which must be made publicly available. Thus MTAs must seek to carefully choose terms that express their responsibility. In this regard Type 1 would be more suited to the principles and ethical practices of biobanks.

[2] Intellectual Property Rights

Biobanks normally have extensive polices on research and inventions related to such research. Hence, most MTAs address the issue of IPR. The terms of access also involves conditions on how the exploitation of IPR must be meted out. Biobank MTAs may contain various provisions relating to IPR including inventions resulting from research, data, trademarks relating to the biobank and the like.

Type 1
X claims no ownership to new IP invented or developed solely by or for the Recipient in connection with the Project, except that X will own the raw analysis and assay data to the extent it performs the analyses and assays, unless otherwise expressly agreed, as well as any generic improvements or inventions related to X's laboratory, sample or information handling methods or procedures
Non-Assert. The Recipient covenants not to assert its IPR arisen from the Project and the Material against X, its owners or their successors, in any court or administrative agency, and it shall ensure that its assignees and licensees commit to the same. This covenant applies only with regard to activities in the fields of public sector (i) research and/or development and (ii) health/medical services, including biobank

24. Article 16 – Governance principles.

Type 2

- Each Party (and/or its researchers) shall retain title to any IPR made under the Research Plan. Nothing herein shall be deemed to constitute the grant of any licence under any intellectual property right. Before Recipient (and/or its researchers) files a patent application regarding an invention made under the Research Plan, Recipient (and/or its researchers) shall agree with X (and/or its researchers) in a separate written agreement regarding ownership of the invention and conditions for its use. X shall always retain the right to use the results for non-commercial research and education.
- The Recipient shall be entitled to any inventions to the extent that these result from its own independent use of the data and/or Material. Recipient shall grant Biobank a worldwide non-exclusive royalty free irrevocable research licence with respect to any such inventions. If the Recipient elects not to seek any IP protection with respect to such inventions he shall transfer any such rights to Biobank at no cost.
- **Rights to inventions/developments made by the Applicant** -Subject to an exception the Biobank confirms that it will have no rights or licence to the IPR in relation to any inventions or findings developed by the Applicant as a result of using the Materials ('Applicant-Generated Inventions'). The exception would apply where Applicant-Generated Inventions are, or are in the process of being, used unreasonably to restrict health-related research and/or access to healthcare anywhere in the world ('Unreasonable Restriction'). If, at its reasonable discretion, the Biobank considers that an Unreasonable Restriction exists or is likely to exist then it shall promptly notify the Applicant and automatically, on receipt of such notification, the Applicant shall be deemed to grant a perpetual, irrevocable, worldwide, fully paid-up, royalty-free, fully sublicensable licence to the Biobank to use such Applicant-Generated Invention in order to remove or mitigate the Unreasonable Restriction.

Type 3

- The Parties shall have the joint ownership of the Results and all IP pertaining to the Results.By 'joint ownership', the Parties understand that each Party shall have the right to use the results for any purposes including research and commercial purposes, with the right to sublicense. If such use of the results by either Party causes the disclosure of any results, which have not already been published, the Party using the results shall limit the disclosure to the extent strictly required for its good-faith use of the results. No disclosure shall occur before ...... has had the opportunity to file the appropriate patent applications or other IPR covering the results, or confirmed that it does not intend to file such applications.
- Inventions: All right, title and interest in any identifiable or separately registrable item of IP arising from the RECIPIENT'S use of or access to the materials and/or data in course of the Research Purpose, including any Inventions created by the RECIPIENT with the exception of Modifications and Inventions made in course of Prohibited Use, will be owned by the RECIPIENT or in case of a joint invention to the party/s who created or made a contribution to the Invention. Each party will be entitled to use joint Inventions for its own commercial and non-commercial purposes unless otherwise agreed in a separate agreement. The RECIPIENT will provide details on any Inventions to X in the form of a report at the completion of the Research Purpose.

MTAs enable biobanks to determine the pursuit of upstream or downstream IPR. Apart from the samples which were discussed above, IPR also emerge from inventions created based on the usage of the samples sought from the biobank. These may involve different scenarios as follows:

(a) Where the invention is sole creation of the applicant of the MTA.
(b) Where such invention proceeds from a joint investigation by the biobank and the researcher.
(c) Where a validation of results are done with the biobank in relation to the results of the invention which have already been developed by the applicant.

In most cases the biobank neither seek any claims for downstream invention nor validation studies.[25] However where such research samples are used in a joint study involving any research contribution form the part of the biobanks the nature of such contribution decides the claim over IPR. So also where there are generic modifications to the samples or processing methods the IP may be claimed by biobanks as in the case of Type 1.

Such arrangements for claiming IP and its exploitation will be made in additional clauses of the MTAs or through separate contractual agreements between the biobank and the researcher. Even where such claims are not made to any IPR as in Type 1 and Type 3, yet there may be claim to use such IP on a non-commercial basis in the interest of public research and dissemination. Type 2 categories of material transfer arrangements actively ensure that the rights over the inventions are freely available to the recipient at the same time ensures biobank's use of the inventions for non-commercial research and educational activities. Thus, while promoting research and innovation by research partners it seeks a fair balance for public research. So also Type 2 is broad enough to seek any IP rights for public research which are not being pursued by the recipient. Type 2 may also be noted for its activism in terms of any inventions or findings developed by the recipient. Where the exploitation of the invention limits health research or access the biobank may intervene. As Chapters 1 and 8 notes there is a need for a creative use of contractual and licensing arrangements within biobanks and such actions are well within the control of biobanks who being the stewards of the resources have a responsibility to ensure its effective use without affecting public research and dissemination. However such measures may also raise the question of validity under competition law rules which is beyond the scope of the present enquiry.

[3] Data Relating to the Samples

Data in relation to a material may be of varying types which have been discussed elsewhere within the work and under Chapter 4. The MTAs may seek to exert its interest in certain data like assay data[26] while leaving out others like researchers data.

25. E. Salvaterra, Advances in biobanking practice through public and private collaborations, Bentham Science Publishers 2017.

> X Biobank shall be the owner of the IPR in any and all Assay Data generated during the Approved Research Project; X Biobank hereby grants the Applicant a limited, revocable, worldwide, royalty-free, non-exclusive licence (but not any ownership rights) to use the Assay Data for the Permitted Purpose only; and
> Subject to the license-back provisions below, the IPR in the Results Data deriving from use of the Resource for the Permitted Purpose will belong to the Applicant.

while biobanks retain all IP rights over data shared to the recipient, derived data[27] sought from research or analysis of original data including assay data may also controlled by biobanks.

> Biobank shall be the sole owner of any and all data and materials including all data obtained by the bioanalysis of the Material or derivate data (i.e., data derived from the original data), and other information as well as any and all IPR related thereto. In case the Recipient creates data from the bioanalysis of the Biobank's Material, the data must be returned to the Biobank

However, seeking an assumption of an all-inclusive claim over data ownership may be problematic and challengeable especially considering the lack of uniformity in approaches over the nature of biological data (*see* Chapter 4 for discussion).

Apart from expressing rights over data, MTAs also require that the use of such data sought from the biobank be acknowledged in various publications resulting from the use of such data. Publication is an important result of data access for research hence it must seek to comply with the standards of authorship and good scientific practices. Where such research is not published within stipulated time as required by the DTA, the biobanks may retain the power to publish such results with relevant acknowledgment. While this is often seen as a matter of policy for research sharing within public domain, it tends to affect the rights of the author stipulated under Articles 2 and 4 of the Information Society Directive.[28] (*See* box below for examples)

> 1. Authorship and contributions will be determined in accordance with scientific standards (International Committee of Medical Journal Editors). In general, it is of good scientific practice to include author(s) from the Cohort in the publication(s). If there is foreseen a deviation from this practice and the Recipient's plans are not to include authors from the Cohort, the Cohort contact person will be notified of this at least one month before the first submission of the scientific manuscript or similar publication.

26. Assay Data: these are data generated from analyses of the samples.
27. Derived Data: these are data generated from analyses or functional combinations of the biobank data or Assay data.
28. Right of reproduction and distribution (Directive 2001/29/EC of the European Parliament and of the Council of 22 May 2001 on the harmonisation of certain aspects of copyright and related rights in the information society).

2. In the event that Recipient has not published the Results within twelve months after completion of the Research, Biobank is, in view of its policy to make results of research by use of data and Material in the Biobank publicly available, nevertheless entitled to publish the Results on its website, again clearly labeled as Results of the Research with a unique project code for unambiguous identification linking it to the Research and under acknowledgement of the Investigator and other relevant members of the Research Group.

[B] Collaborative Research Contracts

Research collaborations within biobanks are increasingly becoming more visible and are considered essential for the sustainability of the biobanks as well as to ensure cost effective means of accelerating translational research.[29] Biomarker development, molecular characterization, clinical trials where pharmaceutical companies can collaborate to investigate molecular pathways as potential targets for targeted therapies are often the subject of such collaborations. Such collaboration may be structured as a one-on-one research to form a research cohort or one to many collaborations such a research structure.[30] Thus there may be small scale studies to larger partnerships which may extend even across different national borders. Often the biobank is a partner to such research endeavors in terms of resource and scientific expertise. The development and testing of biomedical interventions seek effective partnership. The aim of such partnership must be to resolve real or perceived disparities in power or expertise in a manner that ensures equity in decision-making and action.[31] One of the essential considerations in such collaborations is how to handle the IPR. This may depend on how the partnership is actually being brought about. So also it may involve the nature of institutions in such partnerships e.g., it depends on whether the biobank is an independent entity or part of an academic structure such as a university. The normal practice is to use a standard contract which has been built in cooperation with legal departments of the universities/biobank and legal advisers which incorporates the needs of the industrial partner. So also biobank partnership contracts may involve separate clauses such as an annex involving service contracts (for shipment, storage, laboratory usage) MTAs along with DTAs. So also where any technical process, methods or other background technology[32] is to be used by either party to the

29. Chalmers et al. (2015).
30. *Supra* note 1.
31. International Ethical Guidelines for Health-related Research Involving Humans, CIOMS, guideline 8.
32. Background Technology or Background or Pre-Existing Intellectual Property refers to Results which were acquired or generated by one Party prior to the Effective Date or outside the scope of the Project.

collaboration, there will be specific clauses to that effect. One of the important clauses of such collaboration involves the use and access of background IP or IP that was previously generated by one or more of the parties to the partnership. So also the use of project IP or foreground IP will also be decided well in advance between the collaborators of such partnerships.

> a. Access to Background for the implementation of the Project
>
> The owner of Background which is necessary for the project-related work of a Party shall grant to said Party a free, non-transferable and non-exclusive Access Right that is limited to the duration and purposes of its project-related work, unless this infringed the rights of Third Parties. Necessary Access Rights shall be Access Rights without the granting of which the requesting Party would either not be able to perform its tasks in the Project or exploit the Foreground it has developed at all or would only be able to do so subject to considerable delay or at unreasonable extra cost. It shall be incumbent upon the requesting Party to justify such necessity.
>
> b. Access to Background for use or exploitation outside the Project
>
> To the extent that a Party requires another Party's Background for the purpose of making economic use of or exploiting its own Foreground arising from the Project outside the Project, the other Party shall grant the relevant Party Access Rights thereto, subject to fair conditions that conform to market practice, within the framework of a licensing agreement to be concluded separately.
> Necessary Access Rights to Background can be applied for in writing with the relevant Party

> If one Party makes any of its Background IP available to the other Party in the course of the Project, the Party receiving such Background IP shall treat it as Confidential Information and may not reveal it to others or use it in any manner except as agreed Where it is necessary for the project to use Background IP belonging to X to carry out the Project, X shall grant a free, non-exclusive, non-transferable licence to use such Background IP solely for that purpose. If one Party require a licence to use Background IP belonging to the other in order to use or commercially exploit the research results of the Project, the Party owning the Background IP shall, grant such a licence to the other Party on mutually agreed terms

Where the biobank performs the analysis themselves, or shares expertise the IPR will be performed based on such contribution. Aggressive use of IPR is usually meted out through a non-assertion clause or limited licences to such results. However the general policy is to jointly hold any research results patentable or otherwise developed in the course of the project.

- The results of the Project, including any IPR and commercially valuable know-how ('Project IP') shall be owned by the Party which generates it.
- Foreground IP which is generated by both Parties shall be jointly owned by those Parties with each jointly owning, having an undivided interest in it and being free to use such Project IP for its own non-commercial purposes; except where there is a confidentiality obligation.
- Further no Party jointly owning any Project IP shall do anything which would prejudice the rights of the other joint owner.

The IP so generated from the collaboration shall be licensed to each other on a royalty-free, non-transferable, non-exclusive manner. The parties may also make mutually agreed arrangements to use the project IP in any other projects in which such parties may be involved. Clauses for exceptions are also seen to be made for academic purposes such as research, teaching or other forms of dissemination. However, publications are often required to be agreed for in advance and often limit any confidential information of the other party involved. Some clauses tend to push for more rights with regard to the project IP. For instance:

Results arising from the project shall jointly belong to ....(the project parties)

Such clauses while seeking joint ownership over project IP is often onerous, particularly where the results have to be shared even when there is effectively only one party deemed as the actual inventor. Further it may require relevant permissions from other parties for any commercial exploitation of the IP generated by the part to the project. Parties may seek to negotiate such clauses or add deviations to standards in the exceptions. Apart from this some collaboration agreements may also offer strategies for seeking IP rights, cost and finance relating to such pursuit including asserting the rights in a timely manner. They may also involve clauses pertaining to third party use or access of such research results.

- The Parties shall mutually inform one another without delay of any and all Foreground generated as well as on the content of any related invention disclosures made by their employees.
- If none of the Parties waives its share or the share is not transferred to another Party, Joint IP Rights shall be jointly registered as IP Rights, explicitly stating the co-ownership shares, which are determined by the respective inventor's shares.
- Prior to registering IP Rights, the co-owners shall lay down their related rights and obligations in a written agreement. Each co-owner shall be individually entitled to make unrestricted use of the Joint IP Right and to grant non-exclusive rights of use to Third Parties.

Either parties may also seek to register the IP right where the other is no longer interested in it. Such arrangements for taking control over the IP may involve time frames or waiver arrangements from the party seeking to leave the pursuit of the IP right.

- If a Party, within a period of ......months from the point in time at which the information required for the registration of an IP Right is available, fails to register an IP Right, or if a Party is no longer interested in maintaining an IP Right, it shall immediately notify the other Parties thereof in writing.
- Within ....weeks from this notification, the other Parties shall have the opportunity to state, in writing, their interest in assuming or taking over and continuing the IP Right. The holder of the IP Right shall transfer it to the interested Party or Parties based on its/their shares or have it re-registered in the latters' name.
- The costs of registering and maintaining IP Rights shall be borne by the owner of the relevant IP Right. In the event of the exploitation of IP Rights, separate pertinent agreements may be concluded.

Integrating the control over research results are essential particularly where they lead to an intellectual property right. As can be seen from the above-mentioned clauses there is a stronger vision of governing such rights within biobank projects. While most of contractual clauses referred to IP in general the mention of 'registration' and 'patentable modification' etc. suggest the focus on patentable inventions resulting from the use of biobank resources. Also only one of the agreements referred to claims for authorship and joint authorship while the others sought only an acknowledgment of the research support or expertise resulting in such publication. While the MTAs reflected a stronger control of biobanks over resources in exercising a custodian role and also endeavouring to step in when unreasonable restrictions arises to access, the partnership agreements were pinpointed and focused on the conduct of research and sharing the research results and IP between the parties. Research exemption or non-commercial uses for either party to the contract was provided. Beyond this the agreements considered here did not offer much in terms of access for other public institutions or any benefit sharing arrangement. However research contracts may have 'good cause clauses' which may seek to terminate the contract where the purpose of the partnership is not being fulfilled by the other party or where funding arrangements are revoked or altered. Such clauses are effective to enable publicly funded institutions to ensure effective control over such partnerships. As Chapter 8 will demonstrate there are other successful models from different parts of the globe which are beginning to redesign the way in which traditional PPP function.

CHAPTER 8
Consequences of Involving IPR Within Biobanks

§8.01 PRIMARY CONSEQUENCES WHILE INVOLVING IPRs

In the previous Chapters 3, 4 and 5 the importance, role and application of IPR along with its involvement in the practices within biobanks has been analysed. Many concerns were also raised while addressing these issues such as ownership, consent, sharing of resources, etc. There are different views on commercial involvement and collaboration within biobanks. Some consider it essential for development of big sciences particularly from a technical, economic and organizational point of view to strengthen research in particular areas of genomic research.[1] On the contrary it is also considered that industrial involvement in biobanks may tend to intensify ethical and legal issues and may create more complexities to the governance of biobanks.[2] In indulging the discussion, actual experiences with commercialization and IPR within biomedical research needs to be examined. In this respect this chapter will consider examples from real world commercial involvement of biobanks along with protection of research results through IPR. The aim of such an examination is to consider the pointers for a successful commercial partnership and lessons for incorporating IPR within a systemic functioning of biobanking. Three distinct examples will be examined herein namely deCode genetics or the Icelandic biobanking experience, the Uman Genomics a Swedish biobanking initiative and the Sardinian Biobank from Italy. These examples from Europe are prominent and sought a lot of attention for their failure to indulge in an effective commercial partnership. All of these cases related to private entities within a publicly funded biobank setting which also involved IPR for protection of their research results.

---

1. D.N. Wholley, Public-private partnerships in biomarker research, *Genomic and Personalized Medicine.* (Second Edition, 2013).
2. T. Caulfield et al., Industry involvement in publicly funded biobanks. *Nature.* April 2014; 15.

[A] Icelandic Biobanking Experience

Iceland has been systematically collecting health data on its population since the eighteenth century. From 1930 to 1966 Iceland's Directorate of Health published individually identifiable health information about the Icelandic population, including information such as birthdate, initials and diagnosis.[3] However a plan for a more formalized pharmacogenomics database was developed by Dr Kari Stefansson an Icelander and the founder of a private company deCODE genetics along with his collaborator.[4] The promise of genomic science coupled with the unique genes of a small population group of Iceland made it an ideal study. This plan was backed up by the Government of Iceland which offered deCODE a contract to develop, operate and maintain a health sector database for a period of twelve years. After that time, the disposal and operation of the health sector database was to be decided by the Ministry of Health and Social Security. The Ministry of Health and Social Security has further clarified that deCODE will create and operate the database for research but that deCODE does not have exclusive rights to using the health sector database. On this basis, deCODE genetics established agreements with several Icelandic hospitals to enable to secure health information which was to be incorporated into the health sector database. Thus researchers who wanted to access the database had to access is through deCODE.[5] The functioning of deCODE's plan for seeking health information and creating the database was enabled by the Health Sector Database Act (HSD) passed by the Althing (the Icelandic Parliament) in December 1998.[6] The core of the HSD Act was the authorization of the database's creation and operation in Iceland by a private sector licensee. Further it was possible for such licensee to seek data derived from medical records for entry into a health sector database, with the consent of health institutions or self-employed health workers.[7] Interestingly the right of the patients under the act was a right to opt out of such inclusion within the database.[8] Thus where the patients failed to opt out, the licensee who was deCODE in this case could carry out the collection, use and incorporation of genetic information belonging to patients within the database without their individual consent per se. This formed the major criticism against the formation and use of genetic database although many efforts were provided in the act to ensure the privacy and security of the Icelandic citizen's whose information was being gathered.[9] While the company being founded by an Icelander was able

3. Iceland's Research Resources: The Health Sector Database, Genealogy Databases, and Biobanks; *see also* G. Árnason, Icelandic Biobank. A Report for GenBenefit (2007).
4. H. Gottweis and A. Petersen, Biobank governance in comparative perspectives, Routledge 2008.
5. *Ibid.*
6. D.E. Winickoff. Genome and nation: Iceland's health sector database and its legacy. *Innovations: Technology, Governance, Globalization.* 2006; 1(2): 80–105.
7. Article 7, Act on a Health Sector Database, No. 139/1998.
8. Article 8, Act on a Health Sector Database, No. 139/1998.
9. *Supra* note 4. for instance Winickoff notes The act authorized the licensee to use the data for profit, but it provided for the protection of privacy in a number of ways. First, the licensee could not grant direct access to the database or information it contained to third parties. Second, it would have to process the information itself in ways that could not be linked to identifiable individuals. The act provided that the licensee could be civilly liable for negligent disclosure of

to convince a political support to the control of the health sector database by the single private entity, it soon became the centre of criticism as any access or collaboration of other private research entities would invariably have to involve deCODE's consent along with fee payment.[10] The hype of identifying the qualities of the 'Viking genes' along with the government support enabled greater investments for deCODE by the public in its shares. The database of Icelanders was thus made a 'for profit' database handled by a private party which could use the database for their research or other collaborations. The activity of deCODE was also a promise to boost the employment of Icelanders along with substantial contributions for public sector in terms of monetary contributions.[11] deCODE also made a five-year agreement with pharmaceutical giant Hoffmann-La Roche. According to the benefit-sharing plan, Roche would provide the Icelandic people free of charge with pharmaceutical and diagnostics products that emerge from the collaboration.[12] However deCODE finally became bankrupt in 2009 and was auctioned to a private investment company by the bankruptcy court and was later brought by Amgen a leading pharmaceutical company.[13] The failure of the Icelandic biobank's commercial public partnership has been widely attributed to the twin issues of consent and privacy.[14] The Supreme Court of Iceland also considered presumed consent to be less meaningful while acknowledging the rights of the relatives to make decision about the data involved in the Icelandic database.[15] With regard to the health sector database Act, the court observed that the act opened up the possibility of a private entity, who was neither a medical institution nor a self-employed health service worker to obtain information from medical records without the explicit consent of the person whose information is so obtained. While this per se did not violate of any constitutional right, the fact of inadequate protection of the kinds of information to be transmitted to third parties violated the constitutional rights of privacy of the citizens.[16] In an assessment of the Icelandic partnership with the private entity deCODE, it is clear from the observation of the Icelandic Supreme Court that the issue was not whether commercialization was appropriate or whether private partnership ought to be involved in genetic research. Instead the question rested on the adequacy of privacy and security of the information of Icelanders. At the heart of whole conflict depicted by

information, and the act authorized other penalties, including fines, imprisonment and possible revocation of the licence for violations of the act, the licence, or government regulations under the act.

10. H.C. Mitchell, The intellectual commons: Toward an ecology of intellectual property, Lexington Books 16 September 2005.
11. G. Palsson, 'The rise and fall of a biobank: The case of Iceland', in H. Gottweis and A. Petersen (eds), 'Biobanks governance in comparative perspectives', Routledge, 2008.
12. *Supra* note 1.
13. https://www.genomicslawreport.com/index.php/2010/01/25/meet-the-new-decode-same-as-the-old-decode/ (last accessed on 29 October 2017).
14. H. Rose, From hype to mothballs in four years: troubles in the development of large-scale DNA biobanks in Europe. *Community Genetics*. 2006; 9(3): 184–189.
15. *Ragnhildur Guðmundsdóttir v The State of Iceland*, Icelandic Supreme Court No. 151/2003.
16. *Ibid.*

general writers and media as an attempt on 'patenting a nation's genes',[17] was the role and responsibility of the State in developing governance adept to the research needs of biomedical research along with creating the norms of developing a responsible partnership with private entities. This has led scholars to questions the nexus of innovation and governance.[18] Palsson identified several issues that led to the failure of the health sector database none of which points to the involvement of commercial partnership or IPR. Hence he calls it an event of 'bio politics of the dispossessed' reflecting the strategies of resistance developed by segments of Icelandic Medical establishment which felt threatened by the loss of control and security created by the biobank.[19] Further the immense power offered by a governmental backing to a single private entity added to the bio-political fury in medical research, which has been seen competitive in every part of the world.[20] Thus the example of deCODE stands to ratify the need to address ethical and legal issues of precompetitive research partnership rather than blaming the woes on IPR per se. This point can be further assessed through the next example.

[B] Uman Genomics

Iceland had been a focus of many biobanks in developing their policies so much so that Icelandic experience has been marked and ranked as a failure story.[21] Based on this, many other biobanks which were in the stage of development then, began to have extensive ethical policies, purportedly to overcome that 'Icelandic Scenario'.[22] The new Swedish company had been developed out of the shared wish of the University of Umeå and the County Council of Västerbotten to commercialize the medical bank located at the large teaching hospital in Umeå in an ethical manner.[23] Uman Genomics had exclusive rights to generate and sell genetic information from blood samples stored in a medical bank based on samples from 60% of the geographically isolated population of Västerbotten, a county in Northern Sweden.[24] However, spite of the hype it created on modelling a highly ethical system of biobanking it went down to become almost bankrupt just like deCODE. The failure of Uman Genomics was attributed to its lack of planning and vision and immense focus on ethics.[25] They also failed to seek contracts from private companies on this account. Owing to this the company had to change its plans. The county council under which the company was functioning revised the contract under which the company was no longer required to report its

17. M. Canellopoulou-Bottis, Decode Iceland and genetic databanks: Where 'consent' to genetic research means patenting a Nation's genes, (conference paper presented at ETHICOMP Conference, Sweden, September 2005)
18. *Supra* note 4.
19. *Supra* note 9 at p. 42.
20. *Supra* note 11.
21. Nature 400, 3; 1999.
22. J.R. Gulcher, and K. Stefansson, Ethics of population genomics research. *Nature*. 22 July 1999; 400(6742): 307–308.
23. *Supra* note 11.
24. A. Abbot, Sweden sets ethical standards for use of genetic 'biobanks', *Nature* 1 July 1999; 400.
25. *Supra* note 11.

results to the biobank until patents were filed. The requisite for a majority of public ownership was also altered for the ease of its functioning.[26] However, the renewed contract model was challenged by the founding researchers of the biobank who considered that a social enterprise model of reinventing the benefits of research into the biobank had to be adopted.[27] This created tensions between the county and the research scientists involved in the biobank. Another prominent reason pointed is the lack of a vision in IP policy as to who has the rights over research results. While Sweden considers the scientific researchers as the creative inventors having the right to seek patents over the results, the policy of the Uman Genomics was that the county and the university was having the ultimate rights over the biobank including its research activities. Hence it became confusing and conflicting to the interest of the researchers involved in research within the biobank.[28] This created tensions and bitter battles between researchers and the biobank leading to researchers even rescinding previous contracts. This example while claiming to try to rectify the damage deCODE did to the reputation of the biobank failed in terms of balancing the research interests and having a vision for an IP policy while maintaining ethical standards.[29]

[C] The Sardinian Biobank

The Sardinian biobank is a more contemporary example of public sector involvement with private entities in a commercial setting. Sardinia is one of the islands of Italy and consists of a population which has been developed thousands of years ago by the original settlors. It involves families through consanguineous marriages with in the Sardinian community.[30] On this account the genetic pool has been considered to be isolated and unique just like the Icelandic population. A noted feature of the genetic pool was that the inhabitants of the Sardinian island region were exceptionally long-lived and hence Sardinia was considered as a longevity hotspot.[31] And within each town, people's DNA is not very genetically diverse, because they have lived in relative isolation for centuries. Scientists hoped that by matching people's DNA with their medical history and genealogy, they can discover genes that confer protection from ageing and disease and this created Sardinia the focus point for genetic research.[32] To unravel the genetic mysteries related to age-related traits and diseases, the Italian National Research Council (CNR) Institute of Cagliari and the US National Institute on

26. G. Gaskell, et al., Genomics and society: 'Legal, ethical and social dimensions', Routledge 17 June 2013.
27. *Supra* note 11.
28. *Supra* note 11 *see also* M.G. Hansson (ed), The human use of biobanks, Uppsala University 2001; M.G. Hansson and M. Levin (eds), Biobanks as resources for health, Uppsala University 2003.
29. S. Roselle, Sweden's answer to genomics ethics, *Nature*, 16 September1999; 401.
30. C. Piciocchi et al., Legal issues in governing genetic biobanks: The Italian framework as a case study for the implications for citizen's health through public-private initiatives, *Journal of Community Genetics* 2017.
31. N. Nosengo, DNA heist that was not sparks data questions, Alleged theft from Italian gene bank dismissed – but ownership of samples remains under investigation, *Nature Biotech.* 16 September 2016.
32. *Ibid.*

Ageing (NIA) carried out the Sardinia project called 'Progenia' for the Sardinian public.[33] In the year 2000 Shardna Life Sciences was formulated. It was a partnership between the public and the private sector involving the Institute of Population Genetics of the Italian National Research Council (CNR) Bank of Sardinia, a local private clinic and the Sardinian Holding Company SFIRS.[34] With such inspired initiative the biological samples were collected within a biobank and studies were conducted giving publications along with patents.[35] Almost ten years after its creation there was a transition on the top of the company where one of the majority shareholders sold his shares to an Italian foundation involved in scientific and medical research and health and charitable activities and this foundation was hit by financial instability leading to the bankruptcy of Shardna. A British biotech company Tiziana Life Sciences bought Shardna in 2016. However Nature (in September 2016) also reported a heist of samples from the facility which was later identified as a transfer of samples and not an actual heist. While it was reported that a part of the samples were shifted to a hospital facility before it was sold to the new company, there was confusion as to the ownership of the resources. The event of bankruptcy and resale brought in a huge void over the fate of the resources and the prospects or possibilities for a new study by the British company, which Nature reported, would have to seek new consent from the Sardinians for any research to proceed.[36] The chaos of events also led to concerns in the EU commission and parliamentary questions were raised by a member of the EU Parliament as provided in Box (1)[37] and it received a reply from the commission *see* Box (2).[38] As can be clearly seen from the question and response reproduced above, the concerns raised in the question were not completely addressed by the response from the commission. The nature of public private partnership, bankruptcy procedures in the context of biobanks, ownership rights and the scope of commercialization were clearly avoided in the response. While it stands true that no commercially oriented genetic research can function without appropriate consent, the importance of commercial results benefiting the human community cannot be ignored. Further alteration of governing structures must be focused to avoid pitfalls as it happened in the case of Sardinian Biobank.

33. https://sardinia.nia.nih.gov/ (last accessed on 3 November 2017).
34. A. Meldolesi, Italy toasts sardinia with SharDNA. *Nature Biotechnol.* 2000; 18: 1032.
35. *Supra* note 27.
36. *Supra* note 28.
37. Parliamentary questions: P-005318-16, Question for written answer to the Commission Rule 130 Giulia Moi (EFDD), 30 June 2016. Available at: http://www.europarl.europa.eu/sides/getAllAnswers.do?reference=P-2016-005318&language=EN (last accessed on 4 November 2017).
38. Parliamentary questions: P-005318/2016, Answer given by Ms Jourová on behalf of the Commission, 25 August 2016.

BOX: (1) Questions to the commission

Shardna a (mostly publicly-owned) research company specializing in genomics, over the years has tested some 13,000 DNA samples donated by the inhabitants of ten towns and villages in the Ogliastra area, thus building up an extremely valuable genetic database. The events that resulted in the bankruptcy of Shardna in 2012 have changed the purpose of the research, transforming it into a commercial activity. The importance of this database is due to the fact that the samples relate to one of the longest living populations in the world, living in an isolation that has enabled ancient genes to be preserved unchanged over the centuries. Given that, for genetic data, a high level of protection of the right to the protection of personal data is always required, taking into account the UNESCO Declaration on Human Genetic Data, whereby the collection of genetic material must be based on the principle of 'prior, free, informed and express consent, without inducement by financial or other personal gain', can the Commission answer the following questions:

- In its view, should legislation not be drawn up in order to prevent the commercial use of such sensitive information?
- What tools are currently available to the Commission to prevent the marketing of such an important heritage?
- Will it encourage the adoption of instruments with a view to protecting such personal rights, a task that is currently left to the discretion of individual Member States?

BOX (2). Reply by commission

Directive 95/46/EC(1) on the protection of personal data and the national implementing legislation apply to the processing of personal data by Shardna. Personal data must be processed fairly and lawfully, collected for specified, explicit and legitimate purposes, not be further processed in a way incompatible with those purposes and not kept longer than necessary for those purposes. According to Article 8 of Directive 95/46/EC the processing of special categories of data e.g., concerning health, which include genetic data, is prohibited except if the data subject explicitly consents to the processing or for the purpose of preventive medicine, medical diagnosis or the management of healthcare services or for reasons of substantial public interest.

The Commission understands that the inhabitants have consented to the use of their genetic data in a genetic database by Shardna for research purposes. Any further processing for commercial purposes cannot be done without their consent.

The EU General Data Protection Regulation(2), which will apply as of 25 May 2018, will strengthen the right to protection of personal data including the conditions for consent and the data subjects' right to correction, deletion and blocking of personal data. Genetic data will be expressly listed under the special categories of data.

Without prejudice to the powers of the Commission as guardian of the Treaties, the supervision and enforcement of data protection legislation falls under the competence of national authorities, in particular the data protection supervisory authorities, and courts.

---

(1) Directive 95/46/EC of the European Parliament and of the Council of 24.10.1995 on the protection of individuals with regard to the processing of personal data and on the free movement of such data, OJ, L 281, 23.11.1995, p. 31.
(2) Regulation (EU) 2016/679 of the European Parliament and of the Council of 27.4.2016 on the protection of natural persons with regard to the processing of personal data and on the free movement of such data, and repealing Directive 95/46/EC (General Data Protection Regulation), OJ L 119, 4.5.2016, pp. 1–88.

[D] The Three Examples from Europe and the Concern over IP Involvement

Three prominent examples of biobank's commercial involvement were analysed above. Each of the examples demonstrates differing situations but a commonality existing in terms of commercial involvement with the private sector in terms of genetic research. Many scholars have pointed out Iceland as a 'controversial example' in the context of IP involvement and commercialization,[39] however this pertains to structural and political factors rather than IPR.[40] In fact none of the examples of biobank failures in Europe discussed above were caused by involvement of IPR per se. Instead governance, political actions, lack of vision, or absence of policy formulations essential for preparing the collaboration with private entities failed the cases cited above. For instance it was reported that deCODE along with Roche was to develop commercial products and a benefit sharing was to be made with Icelandic population in the form of free medication and diagnostic products if such results were developed, however this was not the main bone of contention or the actual cause for its fall. So also it was reported that in 2006 five former deCODE employees, were sued by deCODE for, among other things, stealing information about trade secrets, standardized research methods and procedures, financial contracts, software and data owned by deCODE.[41] This gave rise to concerns over loss of personal information of participants. While this may be attributable to faculty encryption procedures and data handling, it was not the case of an IP exploitation claim unlike, for instance, the John Moore case.[42] Also it appears particularly from the Uman Genomics and Shardna Biobank case that protectable research results were in fact developed and other research were effectively

---

39. D.M. Gitter, 'The challenges of achieving open source sharing of biobank data', in G. Pascuzzi et al. (eds) 'Comparative issues in the governance of research biobanks', Springer, 2013; K. Beier, Biobanking strategies and regulative approaches in the EU: Recent perspectives. *Journal of Biorepository Science for Applied Medicine.* 2015; M. Canellopoulou-Bottis, Decode Iceland and genetic databanks: Where 'consent' to genetic research means patenting a nation's genes, 2005.
40. *Supra* notes 6 and 9.
41. http://www.vb.is/frettir/ifn-decode-files-suit-to-defend-intellectual-prope/38625/.
42. *Moore v Regents of the University of California* (51 Cal. 3d 120; 271 Cal. Rptr. 146; 793 P.2d 479.

proceeding while such events happened on account of other factors.[43] The different factors that contributed to the concerns over public private partnership within the above-mentioned biobanks largely focused on the issues of consent, privacy and security of the genetic materials collected. The differing concerns in relation to the case studies above that were raised in reports, news and literature in relation to the use and commercial exploitation of genetic resources can be seen under table (1) below. As seen from the above table, concerns in the area of commercial involvement focuses on lack of clarity over:

- ownership over resources;
- control and access by single private entities;
- concerns over IP ownerships;
- transfer of data to third parties.

These issues reflect the fact that just like the issue of consent and privacy, commercial involvement seeks attention in terms of the need and purpose of the biobank within a localized setting, along with a realistic functioning within approved ethical and legal paradigms. For instance, while there is a strong ethical foundation for seeking consent under the Helsinki Declaration of biomedical research, any perceived practice contrary to this norm would be disapproved as it happened in the Icelandic case. Similar public outburst occurred in the recent case of NHS, UK's secret deal with Google where the NHS Foundation failed to comply with data protection rules. It failed to seek consent and inform patients when it gave 1.6 million patient records to Google-owned artificial intelligence company DeepMind for a trial to use technology to monitor and diagnose acute kidney injury.[44] The value of health-related data is immense. In a positive sense creating value from such resources is essential in the push towards increasing the information on diseases, monitoring and enabling technology to seek answers to the woes of mankind. However in seeking value from the resources there is a need if not a responsibility to aligning public and private interests around the public's data so that both sides benefit from such partnerships.[45] Thus imbibing such ethical consideration in health-related research is not only essential but indispensable to a vigilant informed society. This also stands to apply to any involvement of IPR within such collaborations. The primary purpose of all the biobank-based collaboration (discussed above) were creation of genetic sample repositories and data for future use by members of the scientific community, both in the public and private sector through collaborative efforts. But where it fails, it raises questions of seeking effective partnership, control and access mechanisms for the perpetuation of such projects.[46]

43. *Supra* note 27.
44. http://www.telegraph.co.uk/technology/2017/07/03/googles-deepmind-nhs-misused-patient-data-trial-watchdog - says/;http://www.dailymail.co.uk/sciencetech/article-4662060/Google-DeepMind-deal-use-NHS-patient-files ILLEGAL.html.
45. J. Powles and H. Hodson, Google deepMind and healthcare in an age of algorithms, *Health Technol.* November 2016.
46. S.M.C. Gibbons et al., Lessons from European population genetic databases: Comparing the law in Estonia, Iceland, Sweden and the United Kingdom, 12 European journal of health law. 2005; 103, 134.

Table 8.1 Concerns Raised over Commercial Involvement Based on Case Study among Others[47]

Country	*Consent*	*Privacy and Security*	*IPR/Ownership/ Control*	*National Legislation*
Iceland	- Informed consent - Presumed consent - Procedure of opt-out consent	- Data protection by third-party encryption - Security of cross-border transmission of data	- Ownership - Control over database by a single private entitySale of information to other institutions/ corporation abroad	- Health Sector-Database Act, 1998 - Biobanks Act, No– 110/2000
Sweden	- Informed consent - Consent for previous samples	- Access limited to encoded samples, hence concerns form follow up research	- Control over biobank - Who owned IP rights from research using biobank samples (main contention in Uman Genomics)	- The Swedish Act on Biobanks (2002:297) - The Act concerning the Ethical Review of Research involving Humans (2003:460) - The Personal Data Act (1998:204)
Italy	- Informed consent for new research - Informed consent by new undertaking	- Displacement of data - Security over genetic information	- Realignment of collaboration and consequent control over samples	- Italian Data Protection Code (Legislative Decree no. 196 of 30 June 2003, IDPC) General Authorization for the Processing of Genetic Data (No. 8/2016)

47. Developed and Modified from H. Swede et al., National population-based biobanks for genetic research, Genetics in Medicine. March 2007; 9(3):141–149.

[E] Other Secondary Consequences of IP Involvement for Biobank Based Research

The cases discussed above demonstrate that at a primary level within biobanks, there is in fact a greater challenge for commercial involvement including IP practices owing to the need for balancing varied ethical interests rather direct consequence flowing from IPR. This does not however exclude secondary consequences of IP involvement for biobank-based research and drug development. This particularly visible in the area of PM and rare diseases.

Translational research infrastructures along with harmonization of structured, semi-structured and unstructured data are a central component for research in PM.[48] Evolving innovation within such data centred research tangents with a complex set of legal rights such as patents, database rights, copyrights, trade secrets and personal data-related rights. IPR in general are regarded as an incentive regime to encourage innovators to engage in the product and development of information.[49] In their absence, innovators will have too little incentive to engage in innovation, creation, discovery and commercialization.[50] Pharmaceutical innovation is both time consuming and expensive. The cost of researching and developing a new chemical or biological entity in 2016 was estimated at EUR 1,926 million.[51] So also by the time a medicinal product reaches the market, an average of twelve to thirteen years will have elapsed since the first synthesis of the new active substance.[52] Within such prolonged span and capital investment in health, patents act as an essential incentive for the development of pharmaceuticals. In addition, patents enable the promotion of knowledge sharing by requiring the details of the patented invention to be placed in the public domain in return for the exclusive right to exploit the invention.[53] In addition to patents there exits other incentives in Europe for pharmaceutical sector. This includes SPC's for compensating the loss of effective patent protection due to the length of regulatory approval processes.[54] Apart from this data exclusivity and market, protection offers additional incentives for pharmaceuticals to develop existing molecules or indications further or for creating improved versions of existing drugs.[55] An innovating company has eight years of 'data exclusivity', during which their preclinical and clinical trial data may not be referenced in the marketing authorization dossier of another company (generic company) for the same active substance. Market protection ensures that the products may not be placed on the market until ten years after the initial authorization of the

48. M. Aguirreet al: PerMed, Shaping Europe's vision for personalised medicine, strategic research and innovation agenda (SRIA), June 2015.
49. H.E Smith, Intellectual property as property: Delineating entitlements in information. *Yale Law Journal*. 2007; 116(8); Yale Law & Economics Research Paper No. 355.
50. *Ibid.*
51. EFPIA, www.efpia.euThe Pharmaceutical Industry in Figures, 2017.
52. *Ibid.*
53. J. Goldstein and E. Golod, Human gene patents, *Academic Medicine*. 2002; 77: 1315.
54. F. Papadopoulou, Supplementary protection certificates: Still a grey area?, *Journal of Intellectual Property Law & Practice*. 2016: 372.
55. S. Shorthose, Guide to EU pharmaceutical regulatory law, Kluwer Law International; Fourth Edition, August 2013 at p. 375.

innovative product.[56] When an application is made for a new indication for a well-established substance, a non-cumulative period of data exclusivity is granted, provided that significant preclinical or clinical studies were carried out for the new indication.[57] Further EU regulations also offer Orphan Medicinal Products (OMPs) that eventually make it to the market, ten years of market protection.

Thus it appears that there is no dearth in incentive structures for pharmaceutical innovation and development, there seems to be lesser incentives for involving such structures in the context of PM. Personalised medical strategies include, rare and ultra-rare genetic diseases for which there may be no or limited cure only.[58] Common diseases including genetic diseases, such as cancer, diabetes mellitus, or Alzheimer's disease, affect a large segment of the population, which justifies the enormous financial allocations for translational and clinical research. In contrast, the less than 5,000 known rare disorders affect only very few patients each, even though the cumulative disease burden is substantial.[59] So how does existing incentives affect rare and orphan disease research?

First, in the absence of a sufficient market there may be lesser impetus for PM research in general and advanced data driven studies in particular. Scholars content that, the prospect of obtaining exclusive rights to exclude competitors from marketing an innovation designed for an individual, or even a few individuals, hardly seems sufficient to attract the investment needed to develop the PM-based innovations.[60] Even though there has been a reported increase in the marketing authorization for orphan diseases between 2011 and 2012, these have fallen since then.[61] In addition, a large percentage of them do not reach marketing approval spite of seeking an orphan drug designation.[62] Thus implying that the drive for bringing drugs for orphan and rare diseases, to the market is constantly diminishing.

Second, even considering the existence of a sufficient market and potential possibilities for IP exploitation, there exists the likelihood for exploitation of patients by charging higher price for their access.[63] Although, the incentives issued by the regulations have greatly encouraged the number of medicines for rare diseases these

56. *Ibid.*
57. Article 10(5) Dir. 2001/83/EC; *see also* Art. 14(11) Reg. (EC) No. 726/2004.
58. S. Lee, and M. Choi, Ultra-rare disease and genomics-driven precision medicine. *Genomics & Informatics.* 2016; 14(2): 42–45. PMC.
59. C. Klein and W.A. Gahl, Patients with rare diseases: From therapeutic orphans to pioneers of personalized treatments. *EMBO Molecular Medicine.* 2018; 10(1): 1–3. PMC. Web.
60. D.L. Burk, Patents as data aggregators in personalized medicine. *Boston University Journal of Science and Technology Law.* 22 April 2015; 21(2): 2015; UC Irvine School of Law Research Paper No. 2015–47. *See also* V.G. Koch, Incentivizing the utilization of pharmacogenomics in drug development, *Journal Health Care Law & Policy.* 2012; 15: 263.
61. V. Giannuzzi et al., Orphan medicinal products in Europe and United States to cover needs of patients with rare diseases: An increased common effort is to be foreseen. *Orphanet Journal of Rare Diseases.* 2017; 12: 64. PMC. Web. 20 June 2018. *See also,* Bio business briefs regulatory watch, where do new medicines originate from in the EU?, 2014 and EMA facts sheet, 2017.
62. V. Giannuzzi et al., Failures to further developing orphan medicinal products after designation granted in Europe: an analysis of marketing authorisation failures and abandoned drugs, *BMJ Open* 2017.
63. *Supra* note 30.

have led to increasing price structures for such drugs.[64] While there exists differential pricing for drugs across Europe, orphan diseases with the lowest prevalence are likely to have the highest price across European countries.[65] The rising cost of drugs is often a general concern in terms of access; nonetheless, this is elevated in the context of orphan diseases or rare disease.[66] Moreover, market exclusivity for orphan drugs is related to its orphan designation and not the product as such. This could lead to product ever-greening practices by the initial sponsor where a number of designations are obtained for the same product.[67] This has also led many to question whether paying for expansive treatment for few individuals are sustainable.[68] This is particularly problematic because of the access by patients may often be depended on the reimbursement which in many countries are denied because of the exorbitant prices.[69] Nonetheless, these drugs have important social value for improving patient's quality of life and increasing highly limited treatment options for rare diseases, thus also enabling a personalized healthcare regime, which is actively being pursued in Europe.[70]

Third, in the absence of IP-based incentives there also exits tendencies for pharmaceutical companies to seek secrecy of their research data.[71] The disclosure requirements under patent law ensure scientific or technical openness in the promotion of innovation. In the absence of this exchange, inventors might protect the details of new inventions through other measures such as trade secrets which are increasingly becoming prominent in Europe with the EU's Trade secret Directive.[72] The clinical and non-clinical data captured by the various systems during clinical trials for drugs are

64. *Ibid.*
65. *See* for instance: A. Detiček et al., Patient access to medicines for rare diseases in European countries, *Value in health: The Journal of the International Society for Pharmacoeconomics and Outcomes Research*, ISSN: 1524-4733; 21(5): 553-560. *See also* K. Cockerill, White paper, orphan drug pricing in EU; W. Hughes-Wilson et al., Paying for the orphan drug system: Break or bend? Is it time for a new evaluation system for payers in Europe to take account of new rare disease treatments?, *Orphanet Journal of Rare Diseases*. 2012; 7:74.
66. https://www.politico.eu/article/future-of-pharma-incentives-fine-line-between-incentives-and-favoritism-drug-research/ (last accessed on 9 July 2018).
67. Under Art. 8(3) of Regulation (EC) No. 141/2000, a similar medicinal product may be granted an MA for the same therapeutic indication if the second applicant [for an MA] can establish that its medicinal product, although similar to the orphan medicinal product already authorised, is safer, more effective or otherwise clinically superior. *See also*, M. Minn, Development of orphan drugs under European regulatory incentives and patent protection, *European Journal of Health Law*. 2017; 24: 239-263.
68. W. Hughes-Wilson et al., Paying for the orphan drug system: Break or bend? Is it time for a new evaluation system for payers in Europe to take account of new rare disease treatments?, *Orphanet Journal of Rare Diseases*. 2012; 7: 74.
69. A. Co^te et al., What is wrong with orphan drug policies?, *Value in Health*. December 2012; 15(8): 1185-1191.
70. D. Horgan et al., Personalised medicine - bringing innovation to the healthcare system, Biomedicine *Hub*. June 2017; 2(suppl 1): 479674.
71. V. Giannuzzi et al., Orphan medicinal products in Europe and United States to cover needs of patients with rare diseases: An increased common effort is to be foreseen. *Orphanet Journal of Rare Diseases*. 2017; 12: 64. PMC. Web. 20 June 2018. *See also*, Bio business briefs regulatory watch, where do new medicines originate from in the EU?, 2014 and EMA facts sheet, 2017.
72. Directive (EU) 2016/943 of the European Parliament and of the Council of 8 June 2016 on the protection of undisclosed know-how and business information (trade secrets) against their unlawful acquisition, use and disclosure.

invariably valuable in itself. Such information even though not part of the patented inventions is often driven by the invention.[73] For example, data gathered during genetic tests including those recorded in the formation of such devices or data collected during the trial for personalized drugs. Such information are of great value and remains to the exclusion of the patent holder.[74] This is also the case irrespective of the validity of the patent per se.[75] This poses concerns for PM-based generic research for personalized drugs that is limited by the lack of disclosure of clinical and other associated data. So also diagnostic methods, which are subject to patents, may involve differing types of technical data that could enhance or limit the working of the invention. The patent holder may withhold such valuable information. Thus while patent disclosure offers greater information value[76] yet it does not offer much in terms of *actual working knowledge-data*' or '*data generated knowledge* derived in the course of clinical research, which makes patent holders the aggregators of data.[77]

Against this background the role of biobanks and biobank-based upstream research have a greater role to contribute particularly for rare disease and orphan drug research. Biobanks can provide critical research and infrastructure support for clinical genetics in the era of PM. Studies using biobanks can effectively support discovery and validation of genetic associations and gene-environment interactions, which will inform general biological insights on disease pathogenesis and can ultimately be translated for risk assessment/stratification, new diagnostics, pharmacogenomics and drug development. These are important to supporting the practice of clinical genetics.[78] In addition, publicly funded research has increased incentives to involve in PM and rare disease initiatives in the interest of the donors who have contributed the samples for research. At the same time as discussed elsewhere sustainability of biobanking infrastructures also poses a challenge for research.[79] Against this background, it is essential to consider policies for collaboration for bringing together public research and the pharmaceutical industry. It is only through commercial involvement within multisectoral and interdisciplinary partnerships can scientific research progress towards the path of translation. In considering the above examples and the need for the commercial involvement of biobanks, it is essential to address the determinants of effective PPP, which offers an environment to involve IP rights and at the same time address the concerns relating to commercial involvement in biobank-based research.

73. *Supra* note 71.
74. *Ibid.*
75. *Supra* note 29; A.K. Rai, Risk regulation and innovation: The case of rights-encumbered biomedical data silos, *Notre Dame Law Review*. 2017; 92(4); Duke I & E Research Paper No. 2017-08; Duke Law School Public Law & Legal Theory Series No. 2017-31.
76. C.D. Asay, The informational value of patents. *Berkeley Technology Law Journal.* 2016; 31: 259.
77. B.M. Simon and T. Sichelman, Data-genrating patents. *Northwestern Law Review*. 2017; 111: 377.
78. J.E Olson et al., Biobanks and personalized medicine. *Clinical genetics*. 2014; 86(1): 50–55.
79. B. Clément et al., Public biobanks: Calculation and recovery of costs, *Science Translational Medicine.* 5 November 2014; 6(261): 261fs45.

§8.02 GOVERNING PUBLIC-PRIVATE COLLABORATION WITHIN BIOBANKS

Genetic research within biobanks has progressed rapidly over the last two decades from individual projects to biobank platforms to large-scale collaborative research involving multiple partners in multiple jurisdictions.[80] The rapid pace of change in research paradigms within biobanks have produced distinct social reactions; on the one hand there is a strong support towards commercial partnerships aiming to produce socially useful products and on the other hand there are different dilemmas involving ethical issues, such as preventing exploitation, ensuring fairness to study participants, and balancing costs and benefits.[81] While commercialization is indispensable, the ability to exploit genomic resources for commercially oriented result comes with great responsibilities. Within traditional research collaboration in publicly funded biobank setting, there exists the problem of 'opposing force'. While academic institution, biobanks and other public research is predominantly oriented towards creating knowledge, value creation, dissemination and building trust in research. Industry on the other hand is more focused on seeking protectable research results, protecting such results through IPR and seeking returns on their valuable investments.[82] Over emphasis of either side of the force tends to limit the potential for collaboration and may even jeopardize research. In order to avoid these, new solutions were proposed by EU grant funding schemes in the form of public private partnership.[83] Public private partnership refers to contractual arrangements between a not-for-profit organization and a profit-oriented organization with the aim to jointly address issues pertaining to the use of resources, accountability, transparency and management of conflict of interests.[84] Public private partnership models aim to seek advantages from both sectors such as knowledge, skill sets, resources, industrial tools and the like offering to create a win-win for both parties involved in such partnerships. But as noted in the examples earlier evolving and maintaining such partnership can often be onerous. There are certain factors that need to be considered for a successful partnership which will be explored under various heads herein.

[A] Models of Collaboration

There are different models of partnership some of which have been touched upon under Chapter 2. Public Private Partnership (PPP) models may take different forms

80. D. Chalmers et al., Has the biobank bubble burst? Withstanding the challenges for sustainable biobanking in the digital era, *BMC Medical Ethics*, BMC series – open, inclusive and trusted 2016; 17: 39.
81. D. Budimir et al., Ethical aspects of human biobanks: A systematic review. *Croatian Medical Journal.* 2011; 52(3): 262–279. PMC.
82. E. Salvaterra et al., Advances in biobanking practice through public and private collaborations, Bentham Science Publishers 2017.
83. European Commission, (2010), Europe 2020 –A strategy for smart, sustainable and inclusive growth, COM(2010) 2020, p. 20.
84. H. Stevens et al., Perspectives and opportunities for precompetitive public-private partnership in the biomedical sector, *Biotechnology Law Report*, 2013; 32: 131.

guided by their scope, duration or the aims they pursue. Whatever form it takes, it comes with a balance of responsibilities for both the academic/public sector entity and the private sector.[85] Within the area of genomic research and translation of the research there are different phases. These may consist of a precompetitive phase involving upstream research involved in biomarker identification, discoveries, screening platforms and the like. The competitive phase on the other hand may involve drug discovery, development and access.[86] Biobanks have an indispensable role in both these expanded phases of precompetitive and competitive research. They are platforms of collaboration which help to accelerate translation.[87] Investigation of biological samples from patients (diseased) and corresponding non-affected tissue, blood cells or bodily fluids provides insight into the molecular pathogenesis of diseases, which may lead to the identification of new targets for therapy.[88] Human biological samples are also required to establish the relevance of findings generated in model organisms and also in validation of drug targets thereby critically contributing to translation from bench to bedside.[89] In each of the phases biobanks have distinct role to play as in Fig (8.1). Based on these differing phases there can be partnerships arising in each phase. For instance knowledge generation PPP (precompetitive) focused on optimizing knowledge e.g., C-Path (critical path institute).[90] Integrated Drug Discovery Partnerships aims to test proof of concept of promising molecules. Such partnership develops after target identification and drug discovery[91] e.g., CD3 (Center for drug design & discovery). Product development are the oldest models of PPP and are created to seek successful public-private inputs in the development of products useful to the community. This type of partnership has been applied in the context of product development for neglected diseases e.g., Medicines for Malaria Venture (MMV). Product Access Partnership is aimed at distribution of drugs or vaccines e.g., PPP GAVI (Global alliance for vaccines and Immunization).[92]

However biobanks in Europe are more focused on precompetitive research partnerships. Precompetitive research partnership concentrates on generation of knowledge with an aim to develop answers to fundamental research questions. Precompetitive public private partnership often falling in the early phase of research is directed towards building and improving on knowledge for all actors involved. The aim of such partnership is not to develop a product per se,[93] although product may also result in early stages e.g., bioRaids project involved in cervical cancer research also tended to develop vaccination during such research. Thus it is essential to identify early on the target of research and develop the right partnership model suiting the needs of

85. O. Yildrim et al., Opportunities and challenges for drug development: Public private partnership, adaptive designs and big data, *Frontiers in Pharmacology,* 2016; 7: 461.
86. *Ibid.*
87. *Supra* note 46.
88. K. Zatloukal and P. Hainaut, Human tissue biobanks as instruments for drug discovery and development: Impact on personalized medicine. *Biomarkers in Medicine.* 2010; 4(6).
89. *Ibid.*
90. https://c-path.org/.
91. *Supra* note 49.
92. *Supra* note 50.
93. *Supra* note 49.

such target. In this process it is essential to focus on the purposes of the biobank and most importantly the local needs of the community contributing to such samples.[94] Lack of common tangents to this goal may often lead to the failure of the partnership and most importantly the public trust involved in such research.

Figure 8.1 Collaboration in Translation (modified from H. Stevens et al. Perspectives and opportunities for precompetitive public-private partnership in the biomedical sector, Biotechnology Law Report, 2013)

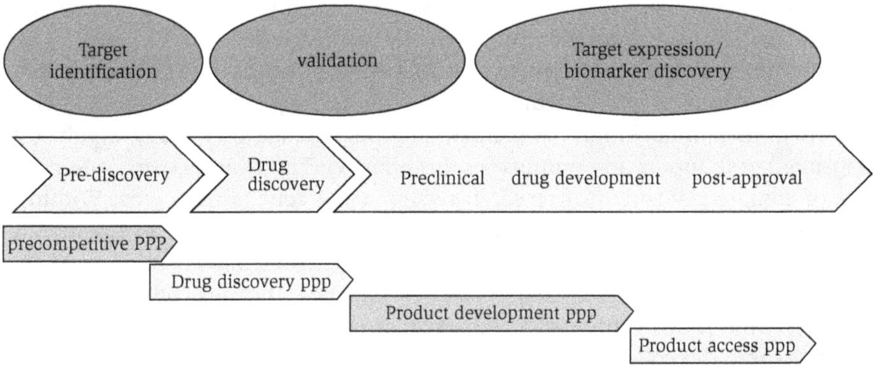

[1] Creating Contractual Relationships and IP Management

Collaborative partnerships can result in benefits for the parties involved in the research. This may involve creating compromise along with flexibility in collaborative arrangements.[95] However such limitations or flexibilities must be fair and must enable the realization of purpose.[96] Scientific collaborations tend to focus on the research that is being pursued leaving contracts to be determined by those in the legal wing or technology transfer offices, making it a formality of administration.[97] Instead, laying the foundations of such partnership must reflect the needs of science and ensure adherence of scientific good practices.[98] So also the use and exploitation of samples and data must befit the ethical standards of genomic research. Another essential consideration is to include provision for unforeseen events which could impact collaboration and tend to affect the structures involved in the research. Such events like bankruptcy, change of directions of research, changes in the research environments must be provided for under the contract for partnership. This will enable the protection of

94. P. Hofman et al., Public–private relationships in biobanking: A still underestimated key component of open innovation, *Virchows Arch*, Springer 2013.
95. M. Parker and P. Kingori, Good and bad research collaborations: researchers' views on science and ethics in global health research. *PLoS One.* 2016; 11(10): e0163579.
96. R. Mahoney and A. Krattiger, 'Agreements: A review of essential tools of IP management'. in A. Krattiger (ed.). 'Intellectual property management in health and agricultural innovation: A handbook of best practices'. MIHR and PIPRA: Davis, 2007. pp. 675–687.
97. *Supra* note 59.
98. *Supra* note 60.

investments involved in such research as personnel may change over time, or changes may occur within the public-private collaboration which may tend to lose its purpose.[99] Such changes must neither affect the confidentiality and privacy of research partners nor the loss of valuable resources collected for the original purpose. For example in the Sardinian biobank the lack of foreseeability in agreements led to a bigger question what will be the fate of the resources? How will the valuable resources be protected? What will be the fate of research use of the samples?[100]

Research collaborations, should not only define the means by which the ends may be achieved, but also must seek to ensure a sustainable use of valuable resources for research. So also it is essential that genomic resources including data relating to the donors be under the governance of public sector institutions or be held by such institutions in any unforeseeable event as it happened in the case of Sardinian biobank.

The success of a good partnership rests in seeking value for the knowledge generated from mutual inputs. Managing such knowledge essentially involves the management of IP inputs and outputs. In this effort PPP must also ensure attention to modes of commercialization of research results using genetic resources. Within the context of publicly funded biobanks and research pursued by them in collaboration with private sector, efforts to commercialize research results must involve creating an environment for sharing knowledge without affecting the possibilities to protect innovation using IPR. In this regard research agreements should include provisions that outline how the collaborators would make decisions about joint commercialization, including ownership of IP and the distribution and form of benefits.[101] Such decision is complex and needs to consider different models that may suit the goals of the partnership. The IP management may take shape through different strategies. Broadly the research and commercial environments expressly consider three different strategies which will be touched upon here with a view to consider the needs of a biobank partnership. These include a) interest balancing PPP (or open innovation)[102] b) open collaboration and c) intermediate or hybrid strategies.[103]

[a] Interest Balancing Partnership

The idea of seeking an 'open innovation' policy was promoted by Henry Chesbrough, an organizational theorist from University of California. His idea suggests that companies should make money by leveraging multiple paths to market for their technologies. Open innovation in his terms meant that valuable ideas can come from inside or

99. J. Geary et al., Access and benefits sharing of genetic resources and associated traditional knowledge in northern Canada: Understanding the legal environment and creating effective research agreements. *International Journal of Circumpolar Health* 72 (2013).
100. https://www.theguardian.com/world/2016/aug/12/ethical-questions-raised-in-search-for-sardinian- centenarians-secrets (last accessed on 1 November 2017).
101. *Supra* note 64.
102. H. Chesbrough Open innovation: The new imperative for creating and profiting from technology, Harvard Business School Press 2003.
103. H. Stevens et al., Intellectual property policies in early phase research in public-private partnerships, *Nature Biotech.* May 2016; 34(5).

outside the company and can go to market from inside or outside the company as well.[104] The R&D departments should not restrict their goal to exclusively inventing new knowledge. In addition, they should be open to accessing and integrating external knowledge or in other words keeping openness towards developing an innovation policy. Thus as per this approach instead of managing IP to exclude everyone else from using it, companies should manage IP to advance their own business models and to profit from others' use. One of the main business decisions of a firm becomes what necessary pieces of an innovation should be internally versus externally supplied, followed by how to integrate the pieces together.[105] This idea of integrating different knowledge to evolve a firm centred innovation could also be applied to partnerships which are more commercially focused with increasing IP policies and vigorous licensing arrangements.[106] Interest-oriented partnership limits use of background IP only to the purpose and development of the project IP. Project IP may belong jointly or may be shared by the creators and are made only available to the member of such collaboration.[107] Interest balancing partnership while being open to generating new knowledge by involving different partners, yet tends to be more commercially focused and as such may not suit precompetitive needs of biobank-based research. This is particularly the case where generating public trust in early on partnership is essential in the interest of research.

[b] Open Collaboration

While 'open innovation' approach sees flow of ideas from within and outside an industrial partner in ways suitable to its commercial development, an open collaboration on the contrary is motivated by a desire to foster research collaboration in a non-competitive environment.[108] Open collaboration rests on the idea of creating something together with the aim of sharing it commonly for all.[109] The foundation for this approach in genetic research was laid by the HGP with rapid release of sequencing information.[110] The non-profit approach seeks sharing and access for all. Different forms of open collaboration have also been applied such as open source and open access with the aim to negate the effects of a strict application of IPR.[111] Open source is in fact used in software licensing as a model in which the source code is open to the

104. *Supra* note 67.
105. *Ibid.*
106. *Supra* note 68.
107. *Supra* note 68; *see also* M. Perkmann, 'Trading off revealing and appropriating in drug discovery: The role of trusted intermediaries,' Best Paper Proceedings of the 2009 Academy of Management Meeting, (August 2009).
108. C. Mimura, 'Nuanced management of IP rights: Shaping industry-university relationships to promote social impact' (15 July 2009) R. Dreyfuss, H. First and D. Zimmerman (eds) 'Working within the boundaries of intellectual property', Oxford University Press, 2010.
109. A. Forte and C. Lampe, Defining, understanding, and supporting open collaboration: Lessons from the literature, *American Behavioral Scientist*, 2012; 57(5): 535–547 SAGE Publications.
110. E.R Gold and D. Nicol in Comparative Issues in the Governance of Research Biobanks – Property, Privacy, Intellectual Property, and the Role of Technology (eds G. Pascuzzi, U. Izzo and M. Macilotti) 191–208 (Springer, 2013).
111. *Ibid.*

public with an effort to encourage peer production. Within such a model the holder of initial result seeks IP protection over such knowledge and provided licence to all takers who agrees to license out their improvement and additions to everyone else on the exact same terms.[112] Open access though similar to open source in terms of philosophy, ensures that access to the resources is regulated by the norms of research community than through property rights. The UK biobank is considered as an example of this model under which bona fide scientists, undertaking health-related research in the public good. Approved scientists from academia, government, charity and commercial companies can request access to the biobank. UK Biobank requests return of results deemed of interest to the global research community and an acknowledgement to the effect that 'the research has been conducted using the UK Biobank Resource'.[113] Another prominent example is the Structural Genomics Consortium (SGC) which is a public private partnership consortium of pharmaceutical companies, universities and public and charitable organizations that do research on 3D structures of proteins relevant for human health. The research results are made freely available by publishing and depositing protein structures in an open protein databank.[114] SGC acts as the trust partner and enables its commercial participants to disclose strategically sensitive information, simultaneously minimizing the risk of appropriation losses.[115] Biobanks may find it potentially difficult to seek complete openness in the real sense as it contains personal data of a sensitive nature.[116] An open collaboration model may have greater limitations in terms of incentivizing innovation. Studies in relation to the SGC point out that firms may only be prepared to engage in an open collaboration PPP only when IP appropriation is of lesser importance compared to the benefits arising from a program.[117] This may be a tough call for biobank-based research particularly if it does not enable incentivizing research outcomes. As pointed out elsewhere in this work that value creation for research in biobanks is of particular significance and as such an open collaboration tends to limit this possibility effectively.

[c] Intermediate Models for Partnership

An intermediate collaboration seeks to find a balance between the two extremes of commercial focus and open collaboration. Under such a strategy the IP management policy is negotiated based on the project at hand but with a vision to protect essential IP wherever necessary and to offer as much access to resources to the public.[118] One of the best examples of such a balanced partnership is the MMV. The MMV, a not-for-profit foundation based in Geneva, aims to develop new antimalarial drugs for

112. *Ibid.*; *See also* A. Rai and J. Boyle, Synthetic biology: Caught between property rights, the public domain and the common, *PLos Biol* 5: e58.
113. *Supra* note 48.
114. B. Leten, et al., IP models to orchestrate innovation ecosystems, *Californian Management Review.* 2013; 55: 51–64.
115. *Supra* note 74.
116. *Supra* note 75.
117. *Supra* notes 74 and 79.
118. *Supra* note 70.

developing countries through public private partnership. There are pressing challenges development of antimalarial drugs. These include financial, interest in neglected diseases, managerial difficulties of partnering with public-private institutions, commercialization and cost-effectiveness.[119] The developments of such drugs are essential for the less developed countries where the prevalence of malarial diseases is very high.

The MMV partnerships are structured to meet the needs of all its partners pharmaceutical companies, academia as well as contractors within different jurisdictions. As per this approach where the collaborative effort succeeds in producing a drug to treat malaria, the MMV project gets the IPR relating to its use within the scope of MMV's 'field', a supply of the drug that results from the collaboration to developing countries at cost or at preferential prices; and rights to use it in disease-endemic countries.[120] In addition to these, MMV also seeks the right to a licence to continue manufacture of the drug with another partner if its initial partner pulls out for any reason.[121] The welcome Trust, UK has also coordinated with the other projects of MMV. For instance the trust along with the MMV and the Singapore Economic Development Board agreed to fund the Novartis Institute for Tropical Diseases (NITD) to carry out a programme of drug discovery in the field of malaria in Singapore. This was also a PPP modelled in the same lines of balanced intermediate partnership. Under this Novartis agreed to make contributions in kind to the cost of the programme. NITD also owns (or in the case of IP generated by collaborators, has rights to acquire rights to) all IP generated during the funded programme, but the Trust and MMV have a non-commercial research licence, to enable basic research on any findings of the programme. The Trust and MMV have rights to step-in if NITD fails to file or prosecute patents so that valuable IP protection is not lost. In addition, NITD has agreed to covenants not to sue for infringement of the programme patents any not-for-profit institutions that may carry out non-commercial research. So also NITD cannot commercialize products without the consent of the Trust and MMV to the process of development. The program seeks informed consent from the participants and also involves a benefit-sharing arrangement for them. In the event that NITD puts development on hold for certain periods, or fails to make any sales into developing countries within a certain period following launch, the Trust and MMV have the option to take over the necessary IP rights, to ensure that developing countries benefit from the outcomes of the research.[122] While MMV is one example of an intermediate approach, it is not an ultimate standard. A balanced approach must be pursued on a case-to-case basis depending on the goals of research and the tangential interests of the collaborating partners.[123]

119. S. Nwaka, Drug discovery and beyond: The role of public-private partnerships in improving access to new malaria medicines. *Transactions of the Royal Society of Tropical Medicine and Hygiene.* 2005; 99S, S20–S29.
120. *Supra* note 86.
121. *Ibid.*; *see also* Transactions of the Royal Society of Tropical Medicine and Hygiene (2005) 99, 1.
122. https://wellcome.ac.uk/funding/managing-grant/approach-wellcome-trust-managing-intellectual-property-maximise-public-health-benefit; *See also* S. Nwaka et al., Medicines for malaria venture – new developments in antimalarials. *Travel Medicine Infectious Disease.* 2004; 2: 161–170.
123. *Supra* note 61.

[B] Seeking Value Through Licensing Arrangements

Licensing IP rights is often a major part of negotiating collaborations or guiding the handling of IP arising from such collaborations.[124] Patenting provides important incentives for research and development leading to advancement in genetic tests and treatments. Nonetheless, there is a perceived concern with regard to patents on gene sequence-related inventions.[125] The commercialization and involvement of IP is controversial in genetics due concerns over access and availability of treatments.[126] So also research undertaken by research bodies operating with limited capital, may not be able to use patents within their research because of high licence costs. This is particularly the case in the context of SME's or university startups and the like.[127] So also experiences have shown difficulties in seeking access by needy patients to products resulting from genomic research.[128] These concerns are deeper in the context of biobanks where there is a constant threat of exploitation of altruistically donated samples and sensitive information transferred for research purposes which may also affect the privacy and security of donors.[129] Apart from this the traditional concerns of limiting scientific access to research data spikes these concerns.[130] Building Public Private Collaboration seeks to limit those fears or concerns with the involvement of a public institution who shares the responsibility to deal in the samples and data and seek potential use for the resources. In such circumstances licensing arrangements can be effectively used to contribute to mitigate such concerns. One of the prominent and most successful licensing models has been the Cohen-Boyer patent licence for a patent method for combining DNA from different organisms developed by the Stanford University.[131] The Cohen and Boyer discovery provided tools for genetic engineering and was the subject of controversy that led to a lively public debate on recombinant DNA and commercialization during 1970s in US.[132] Given the early controversy surrounding the Cohen-Boyer patent, the eventual success required a great deal of creativity, strategy and persistence.[133]

The Cohen-Boyer Model was guided essentially by certain factors such as:

---

124. J. Wilbanks, 'Intellectual property aspects of collaboration', in S. Ekins et al., 'Collaborative computational technologies for biomedical research'. John Wiley & Sons, 4 August 2011.
125. M. Henry et al., DNA patenting and licensing. *Science.* 2002; 297.5585: 1279.
126. J.G Kers et al., Trends in genetic patent applications: The commercialization of academic intellectual property. *European Journal of Human Genetics.* 2014; 22(10): 1155–1159.
127. L. Bernier, Justice in genetics intellectual property and human rights from a cosmopolitan liberal perspective, Edward Elgar 2010.
128. *Greenberg v Miami Childrens Hospital*, 264 F. Supp. 2d 1064, 2003.
129. Public opinion about the importance of privacy in biobank research, D.J. Kaufman et al., *American Journal of Human Genetics* November 2009; 85(5): 643–654.
130. S. Fortin et al., 'Access arrangements' for biobanks: a fine line between facilitating and hindering collaboration. *Public Health Genomics* 2011; 14: 104–114.
131. A.K. Rai and S. Rebecca, Eisenberg Bayh-Dole reform and the progress of biomedicine, *American Scientist.* 2003; 91(1): 52–59.
132. S.S. Hughes. Making dollars out of DNA. The first major patent in biotechnology and the commercialization of molecular biology, 1974–1980. *Isis.* 2001; 92: 541–575.
133. M.P. Feldman et al., 'Lessons from the commercilization of cohen-boyer patents: The Stanford university licensing program', in A. Krattiger et al., 'Intellectual property management in health and agricultural innovation: A handbook of best practices', MIHR Oxford. 2007.

(a) Public sector ideals.
(b) Incentives to commercialize and develop innovations.
(c) Provide for research and educational purposes.[134]

In evolving the licensing policy the university sought royalties under a non-exclusive licensing strategy in keeping with the goals it sought to achieve. There were also wider consultations in building consensus along with flexibility in approaches that enabled the commercial success of the patents and evolved a group of companies that pushed the innovation forward.[135]

In the same vein, biobank-based research and partnerships must evolve licensing models that incorporate the use of the resources while ensuring other research is not limited in the process. IP licence is an essential tool which lays out the conditions under which the rights granted, the freedoms given, and the requirements imposed. It is a conditional grant, that is, if the licensee does not comply with the requirements and obligations, then the right to practice is terminated.[136] Licensing may vary in types and in strategy, for instance it may be limited to a particular IP or inclusive of all IP that may arise as a part of a project/venture or it may be for use of background IP for the purposes of the project. Collaborative agreement terms may outline the use of the background or foreground (project) IP as is essential to the needs of the collaboration. This apart separate licensing agreements may be formulated as additions to the partnership terms. Such licensing terms must essential be flexible to include ethical requirements suited to the needs of biobank-based research. The essential guidelines for licensing in genomic research have been discussed in Europe by the OECD and the ESHG.[137] The OECD recommendation from 2006 elaborates the principles applicable to the licensing of genetic inventions together with the related best practices that have to be adopted in relation to such inventions. While the guidelines are paths to a better licensing strategy, even the OECD guidelines require that the licensors and licensees should, while meeting their economic needs, design their licensing arrangements so that patients have access to new health products and services.[138] The ESHG recommendations offer larger perspectives on genetic inventions and licensing issues. There are four essential licensing strategies considered by ESHG namely:

(a) *Promoting respect for IP*: international licensing standards such as the OECD guidelines on licensing should be largely diffused in the research community. So also licensing as a practice must not be just drafted by legal experts or the tech transfer centre but it must involve a greater participation of other member of genetic research such as the researchers and clinicians. Participant education in licensing practices is also an essential part of the process

134. *Ibid.*
135. *Ibid.*
136. *Supra* note 91.
137. Patenting and licensing in genetic testing Recommendations of the European Society of Human Genetics European Journal of Human Genetics (2007), 1-7.
138. *See* point 19 OECD guidelines on genetic Inventions 2006.

know-how to handle licences and patents, and whom to contact for advice and assistance in the processing of such agreements.

(b) *Protecting Genetic information*: licence agreements should not provide the licensor with exclusive control over human genetic information. Rightholders should license genetic inventions for health applications, including diagnostic testing, on terms and conditions that seek to ensure the widest public access to, and variety of, products and services based on the inventions. Foundational genetic inventions and methods for diagnosis should be licensed so as to be broadly accessible, at a fair and reasonable price.

(c) *Compulsory Licensing*: seeking compulsory licences serve a purpose in keeping patentees from exerting extreme monopoly rights. This may be of great support to essential invention in the field of health.

(d) *Seeking and developing alternative models*: the ESHG strategy calls upon all stakeholders to start the process of developing a code of conduct for partners with patents, covering ethical aspects as well as smooth licensing arrangements. The strategy also seeks setting up specific licensing guidelines, especially for IP generated by means of public funding, and to pose incentives for reasonable licensing behaviour.

Thus creatively seeking novel models that can accommodate varying preferences must be ardently pursued by collaborator's. The OECD guidelines recommend a non-exclusive licensing as a standard strategy. Under this the licensee is granted the right to use the licensed technology covered by the licensed IPR during the term of the licence. However, the licensor retains the right to use the licensed technology and associated intellectual property right itself and retains the right to grant other licences to third parties.[139] While this strategy may fit well for standard and traditional partnerships, it may not be the case of PPP. Project partnerships[140] with private entities and other biobanking institutions are seen to use a co-ownership strategy with each granting the other a royalty-free licence to use the IP. In such cases biobank-based research by publicly funded entities must seek licensing practices that develop value for the public private partnership in general.[141] While there are no rigid directions in this regard collaborative research partnerships may evolve models like co-exclusive licensing arrangements. Under a co-exclusive arrangement the licensor grants a licence to more than one licensee, but agrees that it will only grant licences to a limited group of other licensees. The group of licensees may be identified by name, description (a licence will only be granted to licensees who meet certain criteria), or simply by number (a limited number of licences will be granted by the licensor).[142] It is a hybrid of a non-exclusive license and an exclusive license, under which both the licensor and

139. OECD 2006.
140. *See* Chapter 5.
141. D. Mindruta, Value creation in university-firm research collaborations: A matching approach. *Strategic Management Journal*, 2013; 34(6): 644–665.
142. https://unitedkingdom.taylorwessing.com/synapse/commerical_exclusive_nonexclusive.html.

a single licensee may exercise rights in the subject of IP.[143] Setting conditions is often done by non-exclusive licensing arrangements e.g., Non-assert declarations and immunity-from-suit agreements are an explicit set of conditions which may be prescribed. Apart from these hybrid models could also ensure that conditions may be set to the exploitation of the IP. Often projects particularly those focusing on rare diseases develop studies or collaborations from sample collection of patients who are eager to seek solutions to their woes. If the product so developed from such resources tends to be restrictive of a fair and reasonable access by such patient groups, it harms the research possibilities through diminished public trust which may in turn affect the future activities of the biobank involved in such partnerships. Licensing arrangements must thus seek affordable access to any genetic tests developed using the samples from the biobank and must also facilitate the development of research for new and improved treatment for particular diseases.[144] Thus not only can ethical norms be effectively sought but also benefit-sharing arrangement possibilities for patient groups can be worked along the lines of licensing. For instance 'Humanitarian Use Licensing' has been effectively used in agriculture in the context of plant varieties as well as in seeking essential pharmaceutical drugs for patients.[145] Humanitarian use licences set the conditions for the provision of access to innovations for people in need at a royalty-free basis or at lower costs. Humanitarian use licences assure that products of research and development stay publicly available and that at the same time the incentive functions of exclusive IPR are maintained.[146] Such technology transfer licensing models can well be adapted to products resulting from biobank-based research collaboration with private entities. Such adaptive moves have been employed by the PXE international[147] in their licensing arrangements by being flexible in their licensing arrangements and by seeking to secure favourable licensing conditions suited to the ends of their research.[148] Endorsing community/social goals in seeking value creation can thus be incorporated in the licensing policies by a creative involvement by publicly funded biobanks, research institutions and university technology transfer offices. Needless to say this calls for attention to the role of public institutions in genomic research as well.

[C] Bridging the Gap Between Genomic Research and Local Considerations

It is now widely accepted that innovation cannot be fully understood independent of the social and institutional conditions of the location from where the research

143. https://www.iprhelpdesk.eu/kb/3189-what-difference-between-exclusive-and-non-exclusive-licence.
144. P. Atkinson, et al., New genetics, new identities Routledge, 2006.
145. W. Kaplan, Using IP agreements to promote the objectives of public private partnerships in developing affordable products for developing countries, WHO.
146. A.L. Brewster, et al., Facilitating humanitarian access to pharmaceutical and agricultural innovation. *Innovation Strategy Today*. 2005; 1(3).
147. International Research and patient support organization working on pseudoxanthoma elasticum (PXE).
148. *Supra* note 111.

evolves.[149] Territoriality as a variable is a factor widely being explored in innovation research.[150] Biobank while acting as a support mechanism for all types of research, are also involved with samples collected locally e.g., population biobanks or research cohorts studying specific genetic traits such as the Sardinian and Icelandic biobanks discussed above.

As seen from the examples discussed early on in this chapter, much of the public concerns were raised locally and moved on to international attention. Collaborations often take place across borders however the local consideration must be taken into account for the following reasons:

(a) Biobanks' accreditation is often sought with the competent national authorities which is usually the Ministry for Health, the Ministry of Research or local pharmacology agency.[151] Sometimes biobanks may be placed within local hospitals or research clinics which may fall under the local authorities.
(b) Existence of local interest in genetic resources within biobank which consists of patients in a given geographic space. This also means that samples and data are collected locally.[152]
(c) Existence of special genomic entities with special genotypic characteristics within a geographical location.
(d) Presence of ethics committees which function locally.[153]
(e) Existence of National IP laws and Ethical regulations governing the biobank's research.
(f) Supervisory authorities under the data protection regulation handle data processing locally.[154]
(g) Biobanks have access committees to protect participants' interests and to ensure that the resource is not depleted or misused. Such decisions are based on local sentiments of the biobank in seeking a chain of trust between the participants and the custodians of the biobanks.[155]

Thus as can be seen from the list the legal and institutional arrangements for biobanks are linked territorially. Thus biobank-based research must invariably seek attention to local consideration while involving in research partnerships. The recognition of the territorial variable in stimulating innovations must pay heed to the local concerns faced by research. There are varying concerns for innovation locally. Seeking

149. M. Ferretti and A. Parmentola, The creation of local innovation systems in emerging countries, the role of governments, firms and universities, SpringerBriefs in regional science 2015.
150. O. Crevoisier. Beyond territorial innovation models: The pertinence of the territorial approach. Regional Studies 2014; 48(3):551–561.
151. H. Gottweis et al., Biobanks for Europe a challenge for governance, Directorate-General for Research and Innovation Science in society, EU 2012.
152. E. Zika et al., Biobanks in Europe: Prospects for harmonisation and networking, 2010.
153. *Supra* note 116.
154. Regulation (EU) 2016/679 of the European Parliament and of the Council of 27 April 2016.
155. N.R. Anderson and K.A Edwards, Building a chain of trust: Using policy and practice to enhance trustworthy clinical data discovery and sharing. ACM Annual Meeting December 2010.

skilled expertise locally, remoteness of the region with sparse local innovation assets (e.g., Sardinian island) and lack of trust in external expertise particularly multinational companies of a commercial origin are some of the glaring concerns for research and innovation.[156] In fact this schism is at the root of the many dilemmas of biobanking in Europe.

The OECD policy brief 'Regions and Innovation Policy'[157] recommends that a strategic innovation policy must seek to:

(i) identify and build on the region's existing asset base and its current advantages;
(ii) support socio-economic transformation (including reconversion or seeking new specializations, training, attracting and retaining human capital);
(iii) evolve locally through the creation of knowledge-based capability, upgrading or expanding strategic infrastructure in the region;
(iv) improve local private sector input into innovation strategy development. Governance arrangements should allow for ongoing feedback into innovation policy which involved non-governmental actors, including SMEs, scientists, academics, training institutions and other stakeholders essential to the effective and efficient implementation of innovation strategy.

Promoting local innovation while seeking a larger outreach for the research should be the aim of collaboration. While Icelandic biobank involved an Icelander to deal with the health database, it jeopardized the mission by involving a single private entity and offering it with immense powers in terms of commercialization. In this light aggregate participatory collaborations have been reported in biobank-based research which not only encourages multiple commercial entities locally but also competitive partnership within public-private collaboration.[158] It is also essential in this respect that there exists local involvement of a public partner as trusted partner in the research collaboration.[159]

So also biobanks must ensure that science communication must go beyond the simple dissemination of basic information towards a dialogue with the public including the local communities whose samples are used in research to explain the purpose of biobanks and how they operate, and to give people an opportunity to voice their concerns and conditions for their support and participation.[160] For instance IBBL Luxembourg has been engaged in outreach programs for the local community and integrating with community activities including educational and informative programs

156. S. Kinnear, et al., Regional advantage and innovation, Springer Science & Business Media, 4 December 2012.
157. OECD, 4 May 2011.
158. K. Meir, The human face of biobank networks for translational research, *Biopreservation and Biobanking*, 2011; 9(3).
159. M. Ferretti and A. Parmentola, The creation of local innovation systems in emerging countries the role of governments, firms and universities, Springer 2015.
160. G. Gaskell and H. Gottweis, Biobanks need publicity. *Nature*, 2011; 471(7337): 159–160.

to seek better participation.[161] The CIOMS health research guidelines[162] recommend that engaging the community strengthens local ownership of the research. An open and active process of community engagement is critical for building and maintaining trust among researchers, participants and other members of the local community. While mutual disagreements must be sorted through negotiation, the policy also states that the community must not be permitted to insist on including or omitting certain procedures that could threaten the scientific validity of the research. At the same time, the research team must be sensitive to cultural norms of communities in order to support collaborative partnerships, preserve trust and ensure relevance.[163] In other words there must be realistic balance between the conflicting interests. Such a move assists in demonstrating community benefits arising from research and offers to strengthen public support of research. This is not only essential for building trust but also in promoting consent for innovation in biomedical research.

[D] Policy Considerations for Data Sharing

Data sharing is increasingly being considered as an essential policy in the field of genomics, pursuant to open-access policies that pursued in the other fields such as software and computer programs. More so its importance is voiced for publicly funded research within biobanks.[164] Such a realization also comes from an understanding that in science, research advances through cooperation, sharing and collaboration.[165] Historically the human genomic research has encountered tensions on account of competitive research between the HGP and its private sector rival Celera Genomics which was focused on restricting data. To defeat data restrictions all data generated by the HGP were made freely and rapidly available on the Internet, serving to accelerate the pace of medical discovery around the globe.[166] In 1996, an international group of scientists came together in Bermuda to discuss how sequence data from the HGP should be released. The meeting concluded in the formation of the 'Bermuda Principles', a set of rules ensuring the data would be immediately shared on publicly accessible databases as it was generated. It involved three main principles of 1) primary genomic sequence must be in the public domain 2) rapid data sharing 3)

161. https://www.ibbl.lu/report/lab-real-world/; *see also* on community engagement D. Chalmers et al., New avenues within community engagement: Addressing the ingenuity gap in our approach to health research and future provision of health care. *Journal of Responsible Innovation,* 2014: 1–14.
162. Guideline 7, International Ethical Guidelines for Health-related Research Involving Humans, Fourth Edition. Geneva. Council for International Organizations of Medical Sciences (CIOMS); 2016.
163. *Supra* note 129.
164. J. Kaye and N. Hawkins, Data sharing policy design for consortia: Challenges for sustainability. *Genome Medicine.* 2014.
165. R. Caso R and R. Ducato, 'Opening research biobanks: An overview'. in G. Pascuzzi, U. Izzo and M. Macilotti (eds) 'Comparative issues in the governance of research biobanks'. Springer, Berlin, Heidelberg, 2013.
166. B.M. Simon, How to get a fair share: IP policies for publicly supported Biobanks, *Stanford Journal of Law Science and Policy*, May 2009.

coordination of sequencing activities amongst research institutions with widest possible information for the research community.[167] This groundbreaking accord contravened the conventional practice of releasing data only after publication in scientific journals.[168] Apart from this there have been other international efforts such as the Fort Lauderdale Agreement (2003) which sought a tripartite sharing of responsibility for generating community resources involving three constituencies within the scientific research community namely the resource producers, resource users and funding agencies; each having a unique and critical role to play in ensuring the growth and development of the community resource system.[169] The Paris guidelines on proteomic sequence 2005 and its follow on the International Summit on Proteomics Data Release (2008) focused on the challenges of sharing proteomics data;[170] the Budapest open access initiative seeking an open access for research data.[171] Another important agreement is the Toronto Statement on Pre-publication Data Sharing (2009) which followed upon the Bermuda statement endorsed the value of rapid data release for other biological data sets, including chemical structure, metabolomics and RNAi data, and annotated clinical resources, such as tissue banks, cohorts and case control studies. It also offered best practices for data sharing for funding agencies who are involved in genomic research.[172] While these international policy statements offer a scientific approach on sharing of different data, there has been no conclusive norm in Europe enforcing the sharing of genomic research data. Unlike sequencing data which is out in the public domain (except novel) sequences, biobank-based research often evolves critical data relating genetic correlations, genetic epidemiological studies or even phamacogenomic studies.[173] Such studies are often conducted by multiple research partners who take the time to carefully control and reproduce experiments, generalize the findings or research to understand the biological underpinnings involved in such biomedical research. IPR in varying forms which have already been dealt in the previous chapters often protect such data. The question then becomes what data may be shared? and how or when can it be shared?. While privacy and protection of data protects sensitive data from being transferred, other types of data may be classified into sharable and restricted data. For example the UK biobank categories differing types of data and holds that it may restrict the type of data based on its origins

---

167. http://web.ornl.gov/sci/techresources/Human_Genome/research/bermuda.shtml#1.
168. The Human Genome Project led to a paradigm shift in the way science is conducted and data is shared, Nature Blog. *See also* https://report.nih.gov/NIHfactsheets/ViewFactSheet.aspx?csid=45.
169. Sharing Data from Large-scale Biological Research Projects: A System of Tripartite Responsibility Report of a meeting organized by the Welcome Trust and held on 14–15 January 2003 at Fort Lauderdale, USA.
170. H. Rodriguez et al., Recommendations from the 2008 international summit on proteomics data release and sharing policy - The Amsterdam principles. *Journal of Proteome Research.* 2009; 8(7): 3689–3692. PMC.
171. http://www.budapestopenaccessinitiative.org/boai-10-recommendations (last accessed on 16 November 2017).
172. Prepublication data sharing, Toronto International Data Release Workshop Authors, Nature sept 9, 2009.
173. Australian Law Reforms Commission and Australian health ethics committee report, 2003.

i.e., if it is subject to a different ownership or existence of other rights.[174] Such data may only be shared through a DTA upon the payment of a processing fee.[175] Existence of IP rights over data may also limit sharing of data. The Concordat on Open Research Data policy 2016, developed by multiple stakeholders in UK considers open access to research data as a standard practice. However it supports justifiable restrictions on data sharing where it would infringe IPR, confidentiality requirements or any other legal restrictions.[176] This apart larger consortia working in specific areas of biomedical research have data management policies that are often suited to their goals. For instance the Malaria Gen project, international cancer genome consortium[177] have differing policies with regard to data sharing and management. Hence there is no uniform standard as how a public-private partner must design its data policy. However smaller markets such as those for rare diseases may be inhibited by IPR to a greater extent than others. In this regard collaboration focused on rare disease have sought brokerage model in seeking a balance. In this model a single entity creates its direct specific network and acts as a structural intermediary for all its partners e.g., international rare disease consortium (IRDiRC). The IRDiRC for instance seeks a high level of visibility of research results which ought to be rapidly shared to the scientific, healthcare, patient and pharmaceutical communities. In this direction its policy requires that research projects should publish their results in a timely manner in peer-reviewed scientific journals, preferably with open access. In the same vein it also recognizes that IP is an important factor for the public and the private sector, in particular to cover the significant cost of developing new therapies. Issues related to IP rights need to be assessed and handled in accordance with fundamental ethical rules and principles. In this respect IRDiRC policy IP issues and confidentiality agreements need to be balanced with the need to share information for the benefit of research and the patient community.[178] Similar approach has also been adopted by the International Charter of principles for sharing biospecimens and data, developed by a group of researchers and bioethicists[179] which seeks respect for IP: the sharing of data and biospecimens needs to protect proprietary information and address the requirements of institutions and third-party funders. Thus different institutional approaches seek to resound a common balance in terms of data sharing and restrictions through IPR. PPP are intended to seek increase in information in particular areas of biomedical research and must seek to offer limited open access i.e., amongst the partnership within the

174. http://www.ukbiobank.ac.uk/wp-content/uploads/2013/10/ukbiobank-data-management.pdf.
175. https://www.technologyreview.com/s/609184/uk-biobank-supercharges-medicine-with-gene-data-on-500000-brits/ (last accessed on 15 November 2017).
176. Concordat on Open Research Data, July 2016 available at: http://www.rcuk.ac.uk/documents/documents/concordatonopenresearchdata-pdf/ (last accessed on 15 November 2017).
177. International cancer Genome consortium for instance follows the Fort Lauderdale guidelines and does not seek IP rights over primary data *see*: https://dcc.icgc.org/.
178. IRDiRC. Policies and Guidelines 2013. Available from http://www.irdirc.org/wp-content/uploads/2013/06/IRDiRC_Policies_Longversion_24May2013.pdf (accessed on 16 November 2017).
179. D. Mascalzoni et al., International charter of principles for sharing bio-specimens and data. *European Journal of Human Genetics*. 2015; 23(6): 721–728.

collaboration including access to academic institutions seeking to develop in existing research frameworks e.g., the Malarigen Model.[180] Data sharing could also be beyond the collaboration to other research groups on a quid pro quo basis or upon the assessment of a bona fide status through a DTA for example the welcome trust case control consortium access arrangement and the Expert Advisory Group on Data Access (EAGDA) data access recommendation both offer such modalities for external access.[181]

The OECD guideline on access to research data observes that:

> As public/private partnerships in the funding of research and related data production are increasing, balanced public/private arrangements should facilitate broad access to research data where appropriate. The fact that there is private sector involvement in the data collection should not, in itself, be used as a reason to restrict access to the data. Consideration should be given to measures that promote non-commercial access and use while protecting commercial interests, such as delayed or partial release of such data, or the voluntary adoption of licensing mechanisms. Such measures can allow the primary participants to fully exploit the research data without unnecessarily shutting off access.[182]

Thus a balanced model founded on the goals of research must govern the data-sharing plans of public private collaborations. The EU 2020 FAIR data management manual reflects the balance in the phrase '*as open as possible, as closed as necessary*' and leaves out the possibility to exclude research data from sharing in an EU project where it is aimed to protect IPR.[183]

[E] Trans-national Sharing of Data in Commercial Partnerships

Sharing of data across national border or even internationally has been a traditional concern for research partnerships which are spread out in different jurisdictions. Rec(2006)4[184] provides that transborder flows, biological materials and associated personal data should only be transferred to another state if that state ensures an adequate level of protection. On the same lines the CM/Rec(2016)6[185] on research on biological materials of human origin consider the transborder flow of biological materials and requires transfer to another State only if an appropriate level of protection is either ensured by the law of that State or by legally binding and enforceable instruments adopted and implemented by the parties involved in the

180. D.A. Choksi et al., Data sharing and intellectual property in a genomic epidemiology network: Policies for large scale collaboration, *Bulletin of the World Health Organization* 84: 382–387.
181. *Ibid.*, note 147.
182. OECD, Principles and Guidelines for Access to Research Data from Public Funding, 2007.
183. H2020 Programme Guidelines on FAIR Data Management in Horizon 2020, EU commission July 2016, *see also*: http://ec.europa.eu/research/participants/docs/h2020-funding-guide/cross-cutting-issues/open-access-dissemination_en.htm (last accessed on 16 November 2017).
184. Article 16 Recommendation Rec(2006)4 of the Committee of Ministers to Member States on research on biological materials of human origin and its Explanatory Memorandum.
185. Article 19, Recommendation CM/Rec(2016)6 of the Committee of Ministers to Member States on research on biological materials of human origin (Adopted by the Committee of Ministers on 11 May 2016, at the 1256th meeting of the Ministers' Deputies).

transfer for future research activities.[186] Apart from this there are in fact no guidelines as to transborder sharing of genetic resources. With regard to materials many biobanks have stricter policies for limiting transmission abroad. Personal data on the contrary is dealt by the General Data Protection Regulation[187] which requires that where personal data is transferred to a third country or organization, such entity receiving the personal data must provide adequate safeguards with enforceable rights for and effective legal remedies for data subjects.[188] Other types of research data (excluding personal data) are protected by contractual agreements such as DTA and this also involves provisions for any IPR that are involved. In this respect collaborations must also seek to protect IP rights in data and seek to clarify the IP associated with the data for the benefit of any potential users.[189] Protecting IP rights also includes seeking appropriate enforcement procedures where infringement takes place.[190]

[F] Creating a Culture of Responsible Research and Entrepreneurship

Public research may take shape in varying forms through differing channels such as universities, public sector institutions or non-profit entities which may be wholly or partly funded through public resources. Dissemination of such research occurs though varying forms such as technology transfer, spin-offs, collaborations, publications and other protectable research results.[191] One of the major difficulties within PPP is a strong but consensus-driven leadership, adaptive governance and, above all, efficient resource and operational planning.[192] In addition the current drive in EU on increased access, data sharing[193] and on creating value-oriented research results[194] for economic development is an added positive challenge for collaboration, research institutions as well as its partners. Biobank-based research equally faced with the challenge of developing policies on the commercialization of HBM and data, IPRs, the sharing in scientific advancements and its benefits along with the sharing of research results.[195]

186. *Supra* note 151.
187. Regulation (EU) 2016/679 of the European Parliament and of the Council of 27 April 2016 on the protection of natural persons with regard to the processing of personal data and on the free movement of such data, and repealing Directive 95/46/EC (General Data Protection Regulation).
188. Article 46, Regulation (EU) 2016/679.
189. M.W. Caroll, Sharing research data and intellectual property law: A primer, *PLoS* biology 13(8): e 1002235.
190. Directive 2004/48/EC on the enforcement of intellectual property rights ('the Enforcement Directive') offers different measures and deals in the procedure relating to enforcement of any IP right.
191. R. Gold et al., 'Commercializing university research: Beyond economic incentives', in S. Kieff and T.A. Paredes, 'Perspectives on commercializing innovation', Cambridge University Press, 2015.
192. M. Said and E. Zerhouni, The role of public private partnerships in addressing the biomedical innovation challenge, *Nature.* November 2014; 13.
193. https://ec.europa.eu/digital-single-market/.
194. L. Georghiou, Value of research policy paper by the Research, Innovation, and Science Policy Experts (RISE), *European Commission*, 2015.
195. OECD, OECD Guidelines on Human Biobanks and Genetic Research Databases. *European Journal of Health Law.* 2009: 191–204.

The need for sustainability and balanced innovation within such research seeks the creation of innovation culture that may offer an environment for realization of the different challenges faced by the research. In this regard ***three*** main cultural parameters are identified which will be briefly discussed herein.

[1] Creating a Culture for Balanced Commercial Involvement and Entrepreneurship

Health research in general and biomedical research in particular, is seen as formal contributor to humanity. This is so because health is regarded as a fundamental right in Europe.[196] Achievements in health have been driven by research and innovation and by the high value placed on science in a free and open spirit of (self) critical thinking.[197] Scientific research within academia has been traditionally built into a structure with set values such as non-profit making, open, accessible and for public perspectives. In The Social Structure of Science, Robert Merton (1942) identified four norms which he believed applied to scientific research, these include:

(1) 'Communism': academics communism implied that the results of their research should be the common property of the whole scientific community. The scientist's claim to his IP is limited to that of recognition and esteem.
(2) Universalism: this implied that true claims are thus related to objective data and transcend race, class, political and/or religious barriers.
(3) Disinterestedness: Merton assigned high moral standards of personal integrity to scientists who, he argued, were motivated and rewarded through recognition of their achievements rather than monetary gain.
(4) Organized scepticism: This demands remaining sceptical about the results of research, including the potential shortcomings of one's own work, until all the facts are established.[198]

These norms aim to place scientific research in high pedestal and are essential to research particularly within publicly funded institutions. However such norms must be realistic to the needs of research and development. IPR promote innovation in many ways through efficient use of research tools bringing forth scientific innovation in the form of new products, process and technical knowledge which perhaps would not have

196. Article 35, EU charter of fundamental rights, Everyone has the right of access to preventive healthcare and the right to benefit from medical treatment under the conditions established by national laws and practices. A high level of human health protection shall be ensured in the definition and implementation of all union policies and activities.
197. Better Research for better health: A vision for health and biomedical research from EU Scientific Panel for Health, vision on 'Better Research for Better Health', May 2016.
198. B. Macfarlane et al., Communism, universalism and disinterestedness: Re-examining contemporary support among academics for merton's scientific norms. Journal of Academic Ethics. 2008; 6: 67–78; M.S Anderson et al., Extending the Mertonian norms: Scientists' subscription to norms of research. *The Journal of Higher Education*. 2010; 81(3): 366–393.

sought attention in the absence of an incentivized paradigm.[199] In the US, an effective innovation policy and entrepreneurship paradigm within public sector research was brought about through the federal Bayh-Dole Act.[200] The Bayh-Dole Act permits government grantees and contractors to retain title to federally funded inventions and encourages universities to license inventions to industry.[201] The act was aimed to facilitate technology transfer to the private sector and enable developing university discoveries into commercial innovations that would have otherwise been lost in academia.[202] While this created immense boost to public funded research it often put university research out of the reach which is regarded as of its main defects.[203] Unlike this, the situation in Europe is different. There is no law similar to the Bayh-Dole Act in Europe. At the same time there exist immense public contributions towards research. However it has often been criticized that European public sector knowledge and technology transfer between public sector and industry is missing a link in innovation value chain. One of the reasons for this is the absence of a balanced entrepreneurial culture in academic and other public funded research.[204] Biomedical research has great economic value in enabling competitiveness and innovative capacity and equally facilitating economic growth.[205] While EU has greater capacity measures and polices for enhancing biomedical research such as research infrastructures and ERIC platforms, concerns have also been raised about value creation, lack of competitiveness and innovation in EU.[206] In an evaluation report of the Scientific Panel for Health (SPH) under Horizon 2020 framework, which examined health and biomedical research, pointed out the excellent research potential of EU both in public and private spheres; however it also raised concerns for the lessening of innovation and competitiveness pushing many biotech industries away from Europe. A reason for this among others pointed out in the report was a lack of adaptedness to the new challenges of research[207] such as public private collaborations and industrial orientation to secure coordinated research results. Seeking an entrepreneurial outlook in publicly funded biomedical research does not imply a blind commercial-oriented strategy stalling biomedical research. Instead it aims to consider organizational or structural visions which enable shaping research in a dynamic environment with an orientation towards future goals. Within an R&D management perspective, an entrepreneurial vision is an image of what the future ought to be like. Development of such as vision is preceded by forecasting

199. P. Lee, Patents, paradigm shifts, and progress in biomedical science. *Yale Law Journal.* 2004; 114: 659.
200. Bayh-Dole University and Small Business Patent Act 96–517.
201. A. Stajano, Research, quality, competitiveness: European Union Technology Policy for the knowledge-based society, Springer Science & Business Media 2008; A. Stajano, Making academia aware of Intellectual Property Rights (IPR) – comparing US and EU experiences.(conference proceedings).
202. A.K. Rai and R.S. Eisenberg, Bayh-Dole reform and the progress of biomedicine. *American Scientist.* 2003; 91(1): 52–59.
203. *Ibid.*
204. M. Granieri and A. Renda, Innovation law and policy in the European Union: Towards horizon 2020, Springer Science & Business Media 2012.
205. *Supra* note 164.
206. *Ibid.*
207. *Ibid.*

the actual, matter of fact, realistic and pragmatic future to create an estimate of what the future is likely to be.[208] The role of public research in seeking such a vision would involve an acceptance of a realistic environment with a goal of organized translation of research objectives into practical realities. Seeking such policy objectives in biomedical research also involves the involvement of IPR and finding the appropriate levers to leave enough scope for positive benefits to the society at large.[209]

This process requires a self-evaluation by public research entities in the following:

(a) Improving existing knowledge.
(b) Seeking and improving the knowledge base.
(c) Seeking opportunities for profit.
(d) Greater involvement of private entities through a PPP incentivizing research.
(e) Sharing and access wherever possible.
(f) Avoiding a freeriding problem in public research[210] and protection of research results through different IPR wherever essential and suitable to the needs of the organization.
(g) Modelling non-profit clearing houses within public research. In cases where the IP rights covering those upstream units of knowledge are widely dispersed, it could be helpful in mutual interest of academia and private research to allow others to use the knowledge controlled by their IP in exchange for access to the knowledge of those others through systemic mechanism such as clearing houses.[211] e.g., European Mouse Mutant Archive (EMMA).[212]
(h) Seeking and designing value creation models within commercial spaces.
(i) Finding strategies to seek impact assessment of research projects.

208. I. Drori and D. Landau, Vision and change in institutional entrepreneurship: The transformation from science to commercialization, Berghahn Books 2011.
209. B. Verspagen, University research, intellectual property rights and European innovation system. *Journal of Economic Survey*. 2006; 20(4).
210. *Supra* note 171.
211. Collaborative Mechanisms for Intellectual Property Management in the Life Sciences, OECD 2011.
212. The European Mouse Mutant Archive (EMMA) is a researcher-led clearing house that seeks to archive and distribute mouse mutant lines to the biomedical research community for non-commercial research and teaching purposes. EMMA is one of several institutions that facilitate the exchange of mouse lines by acting as a broker for those lines and associated IP. In order to become a member of the EMMA network, several conditions must be met, including the ability and capacity to archive mouse lines and involvement in the mouse research field, being a signatory to a cooperation agreement to provide long-term, stable funding for EMMA. EMMA requests that all depositors grant EMMA a licence covering all relevant IP held by them to allow EMMA to distribute the mouse lines and to permit users to use the mouse line for non-commercial and educational uses. Beyond this, EMMA does not get involved with clearing rights to the mice strains. That is, if a user wishes to either transfer a mouse line or use it for commercial purposes, the user will need to negotiate a licence with whoever holds IP rights over that line. *See*: M. Hagn, et al., EMMA–The European mouse mutant archive, *Briefings in Functional Genomics*. 1 September 2007; 6(3): 186–192.

While the list is not limited to the ones mentioned herein, it must be assessed by the goals such publicly funded research seeks to attain. Publicly funded research must seek policies like entrepreneurs, ready to implement new ideas, willing to take the risk of failure and able to admit when this has happened.[213] Such preparedness is particularly essential in volatile areas such as biomedical research.

[2] Evolving a Value-Based Innovation Culture

Publicly funded research is often exploited through spin-offs or collaboration with industrial partners. The success of such partnership however depends on a matching synergy between public sector and private sector. While it is essential for public sector to have an entrepreneurial outlook, it is equally essential for European industries collaborating with academic/public partners to be well versed in the innovation norms and the ends of public research. The OECD Innovation Strategy calls mechanisms that facilitate the circulation of knowledge in the form of 'knowledge networks and markets' (KNM), which it defines as 'arrangements which govern the transfer of various types of knowledge between independent parties'.[214] These good practices include joint collaborative mechanisms through which two or more actors (public-private) co-operate to (i) share knowledge, (ii) share the legal rights to use knowledge or (iii) create new knowledge through joint effort. Thus creating new knowledge and seeking value from existing knowledge irrespective of whether it becomes a protectable IP. This is highly essential for both public and private partners. However unlike public sector which is less focused on economic concerns, private organizations, focuses on profit orientation. Hence they tend to focus more on applied research and the exploitation of knowledge; including refinement and extension of existing technologies.[215] Seeking value-oriented research outcome involves designing partnerships in ways that enables the incentives and motivations of the individual parties to converge on a shared vision for the project. For industries and commercial partners such as SMEs, the approach to valorization must evolve:

(a) Creating a sensitive approach to value orientation in research projects with public institutions.
(b) Evolving IP policy and management within a value-based model. This implies that rather than focusing on maximizing one's individual IP position, the partners should maximize the value of IP to the partnership as a whole vis-à-vis outside parties while maintaining a free flow of knowledge within the network.[216]

213. *Supra* note 176.
214. *Supra* note 178.
215. P.J.P Garbade et al. The impact of the product generation life cycle on knowledge valorization at the public private research partnership, the Centre for Bio Systems Genomics, *NJAS – Wageningen Journal of Life Sciences*. 2013; 67: 1–10.
216. *Supra* note 178.

(c) Seeking rights for explorative research rather than seeking ownership rights in research.[217]
(d) Offering research exemption for academic purposes including nominal sharing arrangements through MTAs or DTAs or licensing contracts where there exists an IP over research result.
(e) Opening CSR in seeking distribution of benefits for community who may be a part of the biomedical research.
(f) Corporate involvement in academic dissemination: such as publications enable sharing of information within the research community of the efforts or ongoing research within collaborative research with such industrial partners. Training and skill development programs to public researchers are also seen as an emerging practice. Industrial partners are increasingly setting up units for research within academia to collaborate and disseminate effectively e.g., Mitsubishi Genetic Therapy Center at Imperial College, London (GTC).

Above all such efforts value creation approach seeks creating a culture of larger societal value for research emanating within public research. And as noted by the European Commission this approach must move along the lines of a realization that research is a part of the culture of Europe and should be valued for its role in creating a critical and reflexive society.[218]

[3] Seeking a Culture for Imbibing Liability Roles

Social needs give rise to technological changes and this enable the means to create changes in scientific research. However, much of the niches for technology are created not from human needs but from the needs of technology themselves.[219] For instance the technique of cryopreservation and biobanking lead to technological changes in bioinformatics enabling the possibilities to understand genomic correlations. In similar fashion social changes in scientific culture brings forth ethical concerns in research. Evolving solutions for patient's concerns or health issues of a community involves the seeking of consent to use their samples for research. This gives rise to a liability on the part of the researchers to honour the commitment to the rightful use of the sample within the scope of consent. In the absence of clarity on the rights of ownership over resources, liability ought to form the foundation of an ethical control over biomedical research.[220] Liability must be viewed legally as well as socially in seeking responsibility in biomedical research. The rules of legal liability are often pressed in after fact and questions any use of resources beyond permitted use as defined by contract or data

217. *Ibid.*
218. Value of Research, Policy Paper by the Research, Innovation, and Science Policy Experts (RISE) European Commission, Directorate-General for Research and Innovation 2015.
219. W.B. Arthur, The nature of technology: What it is and how it evolves, Simon and Schuster 2009 at p. 175.
220. L.I. Palmer, Should liability play a role in social control of biobanks, *Journal of Law, Medicine and Ethics*, 2005.

protection laws.[221] Social liability kicks in with accepted norms of given communities. Norms of science and good clinical practices enables the duties of scientific researchers including institutions involved in such research.[222] Currently BBMRI-ERIC is involved in the process of developing a code of conduct for health research to ensure compliance by the research community to accept norms of health research including data protection and privacy.[223] Expanding a culture for integrating liability rules for different role players in biomedical research also helps to remove uncertainties of biobank-based research while ensuring to control the behaviour of the agents of research.

221. *Ibid.*
222. http://www.ema.europa.eu/ema/index.jsp?curl = pages/regulation/general/general_content_ 000486.jsp&mid = WC0b01ac058006e00b.
223. http://code-of-conduct-for-health-research.eu/ (last accessed on 18 November 2017).

Part V Conclusion and Way Forward

CHAPTER 9

End of Biobanks and the Role of IPR: From Resources in Common to Utilization for Common

'Research using Health Databases and Biobanks can often significantly accelerate the improvement in the understanding of health, diseases, and the effectiveness, efficiency, safety and quality of preventive, diagnostic and therapeutic interventions. Health research represents a common good that is in the interest of individual patients, as well as the population and the society'.

Taipei Declaration Ethical Considerations regarding Health Databases and Biobanks, 2016.

§9.01 ROLE OF IPR WITHIN BIOBANKS

In the light of the above reflections about biobank-based research this chapter aims to revisit the present research to draw conclusions, implication and way forward. Within this research the role, application and possibilities of different IPR in biobank-based research were examined. In this assessment, the role and application of IPR were examined both from a data and sample perspective. So also the consequences for involving IPR within biobank-based research collaborations were examined. Biobanks are designed systems for collection processing and storage of HBMs and data for the ends of research. However over the years biobanks have become more diverse in terms of their role and contribution towards genomic research. Within the realms of this role patentability of HBMs reflected a two-way tension between patent technicalities and its impact from a moral perspective.

A functionality perspective revealed enough foundations for patentability of biotechnology invention using HBMs. Elements isolated from its natural environment or produced by means of a technical process could be the subject of an invention even if it previously occurred in nature. Thus under Article 5(2) of the biotech directive the isolation of HBMs from its natural state through a technical process is considered as an 'invention' under European patent law. One of the prominent implications for patentability within biobank-based research is in the area of PM. As established in Chapter 3, genetic diagnostic methods, biomarker research and dosage regimes are prominent areas of biomedical and life science research where patentability has developed innovation in Europe.

The nature of biotechnological patents and its impact on social norms sought an enquiry into ordre public and morality under Article 53. The technical exception of excluding certain inventions from patentability (even when substantive and formal conditions were met) is offered under the EPC. However the applicability of this provision to exclude inventions developed without adequate consent procedures is far from clear. The commission's deliberate avoidance to indulge and the CJEU's observations in C-377/98[1] on consent issues as a 'misplaced' idealism have set aside issues of pre-patent research from the purview of patent law. In this light, Article 53 of EPC as a mechanism to identify and regulate issues of consent are bleak. Hence it can be seen that spite of the potential role that patents offer within biobank-based research it placed with structural limitations to involve research norms such as consent. On the contrary there is a visible push for enforcing norms for biomedical research from the ECtHR. This disjoint requires a mechanism to stabilize this void which is discussed under Chapter 2.

Biobank's involvement with genetic information and development of repositories with collection of data along with the samples led the inquiry into sui generis rights in Europe. The underlying question was whether integrating wet data into a database along with its associated information meant the protection of the content of the database. Article 7(1) of the Directive 96/9 aims to protect the substantial investment in the obtaining, verification or presentation of the contents of the database and this object is fulfilled by preventing 'extraction' or 'reutilization' of the contents. The analysis under Chapter 4 synthesizes the concept of autonomous value for biological material in combination with data to form database giving it protection as 'contents' of such database. This implies an expanded possibility for biological databases. However, under the directive a lawful user of a database may not be prevented from extracting or reutilizing insubstantial parts of the contents or part of the database where the user has been required to access only part of such database. Thus sui generis rights cannot apply to biobank databases which may place restriction on lawful users' access on account of the sensitive nature of materials under Article 8 of the Database Directive.

While the analysis reveal that data as such could become intrinsically the subject of a sui generis protection, the equally important question is whether it is essential in the context of health research where databases tends to offer a lot in terms of research support. It has been debated that data as such is non-rivalrous and non-exclusive to seek control over such data. Further public-funded bodies and research entities are required to share and offer access to researchers the data generated under such publicly funded research. They are also required to promote data access and sharing among other research institutions and national research agencies digitally. This is in fact

1. *Kingdom of Netherlands v European Parliament and Council of EU.*

regarded as the first pillar of the digital agenda for Europe.[2] At the same time biobanks being involved with personal data must seek to protect wherever needed. So also there is a need to recognize and take into consideration other types of data such as research data over which IPR may apply. The exploration of such a question is essential to the context of Big Data within genomic science where there is dearth of an EU legal framework on the ownership of such data. In its vivid absence sui generis rights and copyrights at best protect the rights of investors and creators of data. In addition Chapter 6 dealt with the use of trade secret law as an alternative model for protecting data. It was expressed in the analysis that with the new changes in the EU law governing trade secrets, it could play a fundamental in protecting different kinds of data including those produced as a result of publicly funded research entities and also enable dissemination of such data in a balanced method. At the same time trade secrets bear the innate limitation of data hauling and limiting access even in the absence of patent rights over such data. For instance, when Myriad Genetics lost their patents for breast cancer genes, the company did not lose value. This was because of the fact that they held the data from patients and had access to all publically sequenced tumours equally. This enabled them to claim better results for AI-dependent determination of genetic variants more effectively. At the same time, their data and databases were effectively protected through trade secrecy.[3] Such commercial oriented practices from biotech firms and pharmaceuticals may have greater impact on patient-related data and knowledge sharing. Such examples ought to guide public research particularly research collaborations to seek limited used of secrecy to the interests of collaborative innovation to avoid the pitfall of data silos. Straight jacket norms do not fit different scientific cultures. At the same time it is also not possible to remould legal norms to fit each and every situation. However where essential legal norms and legal practices must ensure openness to political and moral cultures (Touri, K, 2002). This reconfiguring tension is mostly centred in the discussion over patentability in the context of biotechnology as demonstrated in Chapter 3. The need for clearing the legal vacuum is heightened as is seen in the discourse over biobanks. Essentially any biomedical research involving HBM would be deterred in the absence of the clarity over 'ownership' rights and the essential legal controls in ensuring an ethical 'pre-patent' phase. Within the context of biobanks the collection, storage and process of samples follows definitive standard procedures to maintain quality and legitimacy to the collection so developed. The access and secondary use of such resources in research cohorts ultimately takes the research process from upstream to its downstream end result where the possibility over IP involvement increasingly arises. This creates a need for developing a culture for responsible research innovation within biomedical research in general and pre-patent research in particular as enlisted in Chapter 2. The practice and procedures of IP law must also be adjusted to incorporate issues such as consent. Adjusting the legal practices can offer better changes in social process and relationships within the

2. https://ec.europa.eu/digital-single-market/en/policies/shaping-digital-single-market (last accessed on 20 November 2017).
3. C.J. Guerrini, et al., Myriad take two: Can genomic databases remain secret?, *Science.* 12 May 2017; 356(6338): 586–587.

scientific culture. What is at stake as witness in the literature review is the concern over self-determination not only in terms of seeking samples or data for research but also a sense of self-fulfilment in ensuring that one's sample or data is not serving the goals for which it was contributed. Such stakeholder concerns are at the heart of the discussion on commercialization and IPR. A myopic view of legal norms runs counter to the perceived notions for any positive role for IP. The push on one side for seeking an effective regime for protecting research results in fact distances social notions of its role which would invariably be judged by property norms than a norm of incentivizing research. This is essentially an age old wisdom discussed in the John Moore case where the court observed:

> One may earnestly wish to protect privacy and dignity without accepting the extremely problematic conclusion that interference with those interests amounts to a conversion of personal property. Nor is it necessary to force the round pegs of 'privacy' and 'dignity' into the square hole of 'property' in order to protect the patient, since the fiduciary-duty and informed-consent theories protect these interests directly by requiring full disclosure.[4]

In this regard, it is also hard to forgo the innate nature of Big Data and the new market value of data. In biomedical research, the analysis of Big Data has become a major driver of innovation and success. Research in epidemiology, infectious, rare diseases, and genomics and genetics are greatly impacted by aggregated datasets which help to improve medical knowledge and clinical care.[5] At the same time the data that offers value essentially involves the personal data of the donors. This uniqueness of genomic data offers a tight rope for commercial research and ethical consideration at the same time. To ensure a balanced approach to data management in the paradigm of value oriented data research, FAIR principles have been proposed by scholars and adopted by the European commission under Horizon 2020. These principles provide guidance for public research for a scientific data management and stewardship and are relevant to all stakeholders in the digital economy.[6] They provide the accessible, interoperable and reusable (FAIR) access to data.[7] However, FAIR principles are criticized for not understanding research in its varying dimensions.[8] Data does not always find use by making it available in the public domain.[9] In addition, the standard of such principles vary within different data spaces and may not be ideal for genomic data. For instance, genomic research needs to protect participant's rights and at the same time incentivize more research and innovation in the interest of the health of patients. Balancing these needs no doubt calls for data stewardship and management, but with a vision of what is at stake in the process. Achieving such standards is as much

4. 51 Cal. 3d 120; *see also Foulders v Willoughby* (1841) 8 M & W 540, 151 ER 1153.
5. M. Brent Daniel et al., The ethics of biomedical big data, Springer 2016.
6. M.D. Wilkinson, et al., The FAIR guiding principles for scientific data management and stewardship. *Scientific Data*, 2016; 3: 160018. doi:10.1038/sdata.2016.18.
7. *Ibid.*
8. http://www.bio-itworld.com/2018/04/23/fair-data-at-the-right-time-what-researchers-are-saying-about-data-stewardship.aspx (last accessed on 4 February 2019).
9. K. Høyer et al., OECD guidelines on open access: commercialization in disguise?, *Trends in Biotechnology* 26(9): 480.

a collective effort involving standard-setting and is an individual requirement on the part of researchers and data producers.[10] Therefore it is essential that the standards reflect the three principles of discussed under Chapter 1.

Biobanks designed systems for collection processing and storage of HBMs and data for the ends of research. However, over the years biobanks have become more diverse in terms of their role as a service provider, research infrastructure and contributor towards genomic research. The manifold role and complexities involved in plying these roles are stupendous. Within the purview of these distinct roles this work has considered the interaction of biobanks with market forces which is often an ignored 'elephant' in the room. The interrelationship of IP rights and markets within genetic research is often meted out with suspicion, distrust and concern. This is on account of several conceptions some of which are have a realistic base with incidents ranging from unconsented use of tissues to consented use in research leading towards commercialize without informing the subject and even charging exorbitant amounts from the same donors who contributed the samples. Thus the landscape of commercialization in genetic research is not so bright. Nevertheless, these instances are not completely the result of IP inclusion. Instead such perceptions are based on multiple issues each of which are distinct in itself such as the issue of 'ownership', 'consent' or 'access'. The opponents of commercial involvement and IP, base their arguments based on 'ownership over bodies' or more importantly the genetic information of the person as such. Seeking property rights according to them is an 'objectification of human body'. On the contrary, supporter of commercial exploitation view IP as a tool for fostering innovation offering welfare to the community. However, these two extremities demonstrate the rather unclear picture of the requisites of scientific research, social perceptions and the application of legal norms of IP within scientific domains. The present work reconfigures and identifies this divergence in the legal norms and its application for biomedical research. It proceeds with the realization that any idea of 'property' within genetic research has devolved into an exploitative regime. This can be seen in the way the conception of 'property' in its multidimensional aspects of possession and exclusion is often misconceived in the context of genetic research. Ownership over HBMs collected for research still remains under a veil of obscurity. On the contrary, property rights in innovation rests with the holder of the patent right. The intertwining of these within academic discussions have muddied the actual issues involved within an IP regime in the context of genetic research. Assigning all the woes to commercial research or IPR does not absolve the needs of the community in terms of health research outcome. Maximizing benefits from commercial research, requires a strong incentive for a non-commercial research agenda to counterbalance and supplement commercial efforts.[11] This means that the metaphor of IP as an incentive structure for innovation in biomedical research must seek more common denominations that match the social needs in order to match such optimism. One of the limitations to this reshaping is growth of genomic research outstripping the ability of legal norms to seek

10. M. Boeckhout et al., The FAIR guiding principles for data stewardship: fair enough? *European Journal of Human Genetics: EJHG.* 2018; 26(7): 931–936.
11. *Supra* note 9.

their innate limitations within scientific disciplines. Having said this, the task of researchers, biobanks and the commercial partners is to find those seminal spaces for balancing social needs and scientific goals. Working within a reality that scientific community most likely seek IPR to protect their research results and to enforce them, biobanking policies ought to move towards the framing of IP policies in a manner that not only offers access to genetic information but also ensures translation of results to health innovation. Biobanks being the first point of offering access to researchers and collaborators have a greater scope for maintaining accurate flood gates to enable the realization of this balance. In the words of BBMRI-ERIC, biobanks are designed to be instruments that help the scientific community to go beyond the frontier of knowledge and capacity of what they can achieve alone.[12] In building a scientific practice for biobanking, the legal structures are often, placed within the box of technology transfer officers or law firms who efficiently process documents to the needs of the law. This tends to create the lacuna between scientific research and legal practice. The legal landscape of scientific research is characterized by the existence of layers of heterogeneity in both legal principles as well as contextual application. It is thus essential for scientific researchers to appreciate legal norms and evolve a participatory role in the process of securing mechanisms for involving ethical norms within scientific collaborations, which can enable a valourized outcome. The research has highlighted the principles essential to genomic research namely 'stewardship', 'public trust' and 'valorization'. In the absence of these principles, the legitimacy of biobanks and its research would be affected. Chapter 2 and Chapter 7 of this book demonstrate that there are varying initiatives and policy statements that draw attention to such principles but without an actual incorporation into practice with the result that such principles often remain ideological. The analysis of the present work highlights the need to incorporate such principles in actual practice and a need for framing realistic policies suiting the local concerns of the community contributing the samples. Public-private collaboration has emerged as model endorsed in EU for resolving some of the issues faced by biobank research. Nevertheless, PPP also fails where the visions of research and conflicting interests are not harmonious. Some of the innate limitations are also exhibited in the contractual arrangements as Chapter 7 points out. Legal agreements such as MTAs, DTAs and licensing arrangements must effectively be used as tools to bolt the ethical considerations within commercial relationships as this work underlines. As such the research demonstrates an abyss between various IP policies and the ethical norms of scientific research and data management within the context of biobank-based research in Europe. Resurrecting from this valley of death requires building bridges in the form of creating an environment for balancing different interests within research partnerships particularly in finding a creative role for IP.

12. BBMRI stakeholders forum report 2010.

[A] Finding a Role of IP

In identifying the functional role of IPR within biobanks and also in recognizing the gaps within institutional structures to deal with genetic research practices, the question remains as to what is the role IP right in genetic research?

A starting point to this discourse is the reasoned belief that IPR in genetics are the means by which the value of common are turned into private benefits.[13] Governance of commons in property has received much attending through Hardinian concept of 'commons'.[14] The opponents of this approach believe in seeking utility from commons which enables innovation and economic progress. Further it is also argued that technological progress would not have occurred in the absence of commercialization. Also knowledge development would also have been much slower in the absence of IP rights.[15] At the same time granting exclusive rights have been considered to hinder access to innovation and data. Both these arguments holds true in differing senses. Historically, the grant of patent has always represented a bargain between the inventor and the society: in exchange for the disclosure of invention.[16] Based on grant of such information the inventor is granted an exclusive right in quid pro quo. So also grant of copyright over creative works is with the aim to seek the public availability of such creative works. Thus, exclusivity has been a hard balance for regulated information. Like any other technology that has come across, genomic research also reflects these tension with greater emphasis that human genetic resources could neither be owned and/or appropriated by anyone, nor could they be subject to exclusive rights being a common heritage for humankind.[17] While these traditional two faced arguments continue to go in circles, there is an obvious need for realistic considerations. The fact of the matter being that such views often tend to focus on genetic patents as such and tend to view genes a common resources or an IP. The value of human genetic resource emerges from the actual or potential information it holds.[18] The commercial potential of genetic information and their nucleotide sequences is acknowledged particularly in the preparation of human products such as insulin, growth hormone, developing diagnostic kits for genetic diseases and prenatal diagnosis and ultimately for gene therapy.[19] Apart from these traditional uses HBMs also enable the wider understanding of molecular biology and pathology. For instance, the identification of pathways that leads to evidence-based therapies that are selected for their effectiveness such as in

13. J. Boyle, The second enclosure movement and the construction of the public domain. *Law and Contemporary Problems*. 2003; 66:33–74.
14. G. Hardin, The tragedy of the commons. *Science*. 1968; 162: 1243.
15. G. Dutfield, Intellectual property rights and the life science industries: past, present and future. *World Scientific*. 2009; 325–337.
16. J.Straus, 'Biotechnology and intellectual property', in H.-J. Rehm and G. Reed (eds) 'Biotechnology set', Second Edition, Wiley-VCH Verlag GmbH, Weinheim, Germany, 2001.
17. C. Rhodes, Potential international approaches to ownership/control of human genetic resources. Health Care Analysis. 2016; 24: 260–277.
18. L. Bernier, Justice in genetics: Intellectual property and human rights from a cosmopolitan liberal perspective, Edward Elgar 2010.
19. A. Pompidou, Research on the human genome and patentability – the ethical consequences. *Journal of Medical Ethics*. 1995; 21: 69–71.

cancer cells carrying particular molecular alterations. The advent of the omics technologies makes it possible to accelerate the identification of potential new targets for specific drugs through the systematic analysis of the molecular characteristics of large series of tumour samples.[20] Thus drug discovery, validation, biomarker development and other molecular and pathological studies have dominated the research scenario governing genomic science. Against this background the question no longer limits itself to gene patents but to secondary use and development of genetic data in seeking research results. Thus the modern genomic era represents the era of Big Data and control over the use and access of such data. The role of IP in genetic research ought to shift towards a role in creating the best conditions for research and in translating that research into tangible healthcare benefits. In other words creating an environment where the use of IPR enables greater drive towards health care innovation while at the same time ensuring that enough remains in common. This role of IP can be fulfilled only by a common effort of all the stakeholders involved in genetic research both public and private. IPR within biomedical and health innovations enable the essential incentives for collaborative partners in research involving industrial partners. The examples of innovative medicines initiative (IMI) and the MMV project clearly seek to utilize this incentive in driving industrial innovation within the limits and control of the PPP. Collaboration in life sciences involves a role for IP at different cycles of research. In a public consultation conducted by the European commission on public private partnership in life sciences research and innovation,[21] 90% of the stakeholder response was the challenge to incorporate novel technologies into bringing innovations for the benefit of patients. 88% of the responses were also concerned about societal issues and the role of life sciences and suggested PPP but also observed that there existed challenges in bringing public and industrial partners together. While IP is an essential incentive to research partnerships its relentless pursuit can be harmful for both collaboration and public trust in such research.[22] Studies in Europe have also been reporting successful modalities for seeking balanced approaches to IP within research partnerships particularly by regulating the IP rights in the early precompetitive phase of research.[23] The essence of a successful IP policy lies in designing the points where IP can be sought and left out and where its pursuit is futile. In the present scenario of biomedical research the social role of IP is becoming the new face and challenge in collaborative research. This implies a shift from resources held in common to utilization for common policy.

20. K. Zatloukal and P. Hainaut, Human tissue biobanks as instruments for drug discovery and development: Impact on personalized medicine. Biomarkers in medicine. 2010; 4(6): 895–903 ISSN 1752.
21. European commission, Directorate general for research and innovation, 30 January 2013.
22. J. Wilbanks, 'Intellectual property aspects of collaboration', in S. Ekins et al. (eds) 'Collaborative computational technologies for biomedical research', Wiley and sons, 2011.
23. R. Belderbosa et al., Co-ownership of intellectual property: Exploring the value-appropriation and value-creation implications of co-patenting with different partners, *Research Policy.* 2014; 43: 841–852; H. Stevens et al., Innovative medicines initiative (IMI) case study analysis reveals the true added value of early-phase public-private partnerships (PPPs). *Biotechnology Law Report.* 2015; 34(4): 153.

[B] 'Resources in Common' to 'Utilisation for Common'

Turning to the implications of IP over the 'resources in common', it is essential to note that this argument has been frequently raised in literature in defence of genetic resources. More prominent are those statements which consider genetic resources as owned by humanity in general and hence biobanks are mere stewards in possessing the property that belongs to all. This philosophy has been used to barricade any commercial exploitation of these resources. The 'common heritage of mankind' (CHM), sometimes also referred to as the common heritage of humankind, represents the notion that certain global commons or elements regarded as beneficial to humanity as a whole and should not be unilaterally exploited by individual states or their nationals nor by corporations or other entities, but rather should be exploited under some sort of international arrangement or regime for the benefit of mankind as a whole.[24] It developed internationally through the UN in 1967 wherein there was a calling for protecting the deep seabed beyond national jurisdiction and the resources contained therein to be declared the common heritage of mankind.[25] Form this; the concept has spread to different fields including genetic research. Appropriation of genetic resource through IPR dissociates the resources from the common heritage. This idea has two innate problems one, it does not explain the 'ownership' right by the 'common' including property rights being held by researchers, scientists, patients or other individuals who are a part of this 'common' except being distinctive by their professional identities. Second the idea of 'property' in genetic resources still binds the common heritage doctrine which is in fact prohibited by ethical norms creating a divide in the identity of what common heritage stands for.[26] IPR do not enable control over human body as such; it only offers the holder, rights to an invention in its functional perspective. In addition, use and exploitation of IPR is an essential condition under law which is often exercised through licensing arrangements. Use of resources creates value for such resources instead of holding them as stagnant resources of the 'common'. The concerns are however rightfully placed where research or access is held up on account of unjust licensing policies or other restrictive controls which limits access for other scientific researchers. As rightly pointed out by a scholar if the common heritage designation confers rights to 'the human genome,' then clear arguments must be constructed to explain how far common heritage rights and interests can reach.[27] In the absence of this clarity, the concept of common heritage at best serves the moral obligations without practical notions. In this context, the reader is also reminded of the principle of 'stewardship', which was discussed in detail under Chapter 1. The principle of stewardship is seen an expression of the common heritage

24. E. Egede, Common heritage of mankind in international law, OUP 2014.
25. C. Rhodes, Potential international approaches to ownership/control of human genetic resources. *Health Care Analysis*. 2016; 24: 260–277.
26. *See* D. Dickenson, Me medicine vs. we medicine: Reclaiming biotechnology for the common good, Columbia University Press 28 May 2013.
27. P.N. Ossorio, The human genome as common heritage: Common sense or legal nonsense?. *The Journal of Law, Medicine & Ethics*. 2007; 35(3): 425–439.

doctrine.[28] However, the concept of 'stewardship' is much more oriented towards responsibility than just being beholders of resources. Steward is at liberty to put the property in question to use, seek returns from it and align practicable imperatives to 'property' which also includes enriching the resource. Hence, stewardship is more ideally suited as a metaphor in the context of biobanks holding their resources for the purposes of research use. As demonstrated in this research, biobanks and biobank-based partnerships are evolving under new legal and soft legal structures which are to be followed both by public or private research institutions. Over the years this has become an imperative for any collaborative research to proceed. The author has herself personally encountered during her empirical study visits, that a research project within a public-private collaboration which was to be finalized had to called off on account of the limited purview of consent, which came across in the project review meeting. This incident demonstrates that research collaborations proceeds in Europe with greater value for the ethical norms of scientific culture. Ensuring such imperatives within research in the use of common resources for evolving socially useful innovation within health thus becomes the researcher's stewardship role. In shifting the focus from 'resources in common' towards 'utilization for common', the role of IPRs in genomic research would involve stewardship of both data and resources while ensuring valorization of research results and increased dissemination of results where possible.

[C] Implications for Biobanks

[1] Sample Management

Tissues stored within biobanks are the essential source of biomedical research. Hence the use of samples within a research paradigm must seek focused attention. Often research proceeds without foreseeing an actual protectable research result over which IP rights may be claimed; although these may be contemplated within the collaborative contracts. Hence all research using HBMs is a prepatent research. Therefore care must be taken to ensure that the human biological samples seek the standards as required by law and practice within biobanks. In Europe the Council Recommendation CM/Rec(2016)6[29] recognizes the value of biomedical research for the advancement of healthcare and the improvement of the quality of life and at the same time offers to protect the personal life of individuals who have contributed their samples for biomedical research. The recommendation requires that appropriate consent ought to be respected in using the biological materials for research purposes, particularly if they are identifiable. If the proposed use of identifiable biological materials in a research project is not within the scope of prior consent given by the person concerned, efforts must be made to obtain such consent unless the individual, at the time of offering her samples, expressed the wish not to be contacted. In situations in which contacting a

28. K. Baslar, The concept of the common heritage of mankind in international law, Martinus Nijhoff, 1998 at 85–91.
29. Adopted by the Committee of Ministers on 11 May 2016 at the 1256th meeting of the Ministers' Deputies.

donor has been unsuccessful, the research project may still be able to use the biological materials and data, where the research addresses an important scientific interest and is in accordance with the principle of proportionality.[30] This means that the interference with a fundamental right affected must be proportional in relation to the legitimate interest pursued by the researcher. Non-identifiable materials on the contrary could be used in a research project provided that such use does not violate any restrictions defined by the person concerned before the materials have been rendered non-identifiable. While the recommendation provides for special cases wherein samples may be used in research where consent is unobtainable, it is essential that such decisions to proceed with the research must be made in accordance with the directions of an independent ethics committee. Research collaborations must ensure the revenant approval and consent for sharing with commercial partners. In the present scenario one of the difficulties pointed out by biobankers (from the interviews) is the difficulty to trace the research chain. This creates difficulties for regulating prepatent research. The Havasupai tribe case which met with public opposition is a glaring example of samples that were collected for one single purpose but used in others without consent. Such concerns reflect the need for a system of tracking research using biological samples just like the EMA's Clinical trial registry which seeks a mandatory record of the various clinical trials in EU.[31] Further, as pointed out in Chapter 3, the EPC neither expressly requires applicants to submit evidence of previously informed consent of the donor of the cells or a benefit-sharing agreement, nor has its approach been broad enough to include an assessment of consent under the substantive provisions of patent law. It is thus essential for research to demonstrate the rightful consent and use as per the approved norms. Creating such a norm for research flowing from biobanks can help resolving the issues of prepatent research.

[2] Data Governance

Data within biomedical research is often the gold mine that forms the source of most research. 'Data' has immense value beyond the purpose for which they are collected.[32] In Europe database rights and copyrights and trade secrets largely govern rights over data. However seeking both these could be a burden to the needs of a data economy.[33] Limiting access to upstream research databases runs counter to the norms of access and sharing of such data. Research databases for instance those compiled by a specific research cohort or partnership can seek the benefit of protection offered by database rights. However, care must be taken to ensure that arrangements are in place for controlled access to such data that does not limit the lawful user's right to exploit such data. Other measures such as copyright or contractual arrangements for biobank

30. CM/Rec (2016) 6, Art. 21.
31. https://www.clinicaltrialsregister.eu/.
32. P. Burton et al., Policies and strategies to facilitate secondary use of research data in health sciences, *International Journal of Epidemology*. 2017; 1-5.
33. White Paper – Data ownership in the context of the European data economy: proposal for a new right, 2017.

databases must be fully explored in the interest of protecting such data. An advantage of copyrights is that it imposes no restriction on the sharing of the basic building blocks of knowledge such as facts or ideas. However, their suitability to genetic data varies (*see* Chapter 5). Secrecy can be another effective tool to enable the exploitation of research result to the fullest, however public research collaborations must use mechanisms such as time-bound strategies to ensure that secrecy is limited to a certain period of time after which such data must be made publicly available. The ability of the research infrastructure to share, access and reuse data, as well as to integrate data from diverse sources for research or other purposes requires effective technical and legal interoperability rules and practices. Thus, it is essential to appreciate the nature of data involved along with identifying the relevant IP laws governing them. Similarly, the identification of ownership or control over data is also imperative. Further users of research data must also abide by the national laws relating to the use of such data along with other international obligations (e.g., responsible conduct of research, FAIR data management, declaration on data citation) for the responsible sharing and use of resources.[34] However, without using straight jacket standards, it is essential that each biobank sets standards essential to its needs and outlook.

[3] Biobank Clearing Houses

Clearing houses are platforms or intermediaries bringing together owners and users of goods, services and information to lower transaction costs.[35] Under this arrangement IP holders enter into a standard-form licence with the clearinghouse that they select. Those wishing to clear IP rights over particular units of knowledge falling within the clearinghouse enter into standard-form licences to cover those individual units.[36] Clearing houses are similar to patent pools in ideology. Patent pool involves collecting a series of patents that relate to the use of a particular technology so that they can be efficiently licensed to those making, using or selling that technology. These are licensed to users under a defined package.[37] The distinction between patent pools and clearinghouses is that, in the former, the agent or patent holders determine which IP is to be licensed (through bundling) while in the latter it is the user who decides.[38] Clearing houses are widely becoming popular in biomedical research as a means of overcoming tedious licensing process through a one-stop destination. Clearing houses are aptly suited to inventions and for licensing data within biobanks. Prominent examples from biomedical research include EMMA, 'International Policy interoperability and data Access Clearinghouse' (IPAC) is provided by the P3G. The MMV have also announced an information clearing house for licensing research data involving malarial research.[39]

34. Legal Interoperability of Research Data: Principles and Implementation Guidelines, 2016.
35. E. van Zimmeren et al., Patent pools and clearinghouses in the life sciences. *Review trends in biotechnology*. November 2011; 29(11).
36. Collaborative Mechanisms for Intellectual Property Management in the Life Sciences, OECD 2011.
37. *Ibid.*
38. *Ibid.*
39. MMV Business Plan 2017.

Such efforts would enable greater access and inducement for sharing of data through formal structures. However, such efforts are formative in Europe within the area of biobanks.

[4] Innovation Impact Assessment of Biobank-Based Research

There is increasing recognition that health research investment should lead to value creation and improvements in policy practice, resource allocation, and, ultimately, the health of the community.[40] Most of the research funding in EU seek a report of research progress. However beyond this there isn't much of a follow-up. One of the key questions in genomic research is in understanding how biobank-based research contributing to any visible benefits to the community. Researchers are involved in a process of creating identifiable and protectable results from their research; in other words, transforming knowledge into IPR. IPR no doubt creates value for research, however valorization involves much more that seeking patents.[41] As discussed in Chapter 2 it involves making knowledge suitable, economically viable and socially useful. Impact assessment for various policies have been devise in EU[42] and also on an international level, in the context of innovation in climate-related technologies.[43] Research impact assessment has different functions including monitoring performance, accountability and a source of funding information.[44] Impact assessment of publicly funded biobank-based research helps to demonstrate to the different stakeholders the value of research and most importantly how the taxpayer's money is being put to use. It can also enable identification of the gaps in research or innovation policies which could be addressed in particular areas of genomic research upon such assessment. Besides genomics and the health agenda demands a novel vision that reaches beyond the research horizon to arrive at application and health impact assessment of novel technologies assists in this understanding.[45] Added to this, such assessment has an educative value for common public and the research participants whose perception of biobank-based research may be limited on multiple accounts.

[5] Governance Sand Box for Biobanks

Complex research environments must ensure adaptive strategies that suit research in general and collaborative research in particular. When public research expands its role

40. A.J Milat, et al., A narrative review of research impact assessment models and methods. *Health Research Policy and Systems*. 2015; 13: 18. PMC. Web. 22 November 2017.
41. D. Stemerding and R. Nahuis, Implicit and explicit notions of valorization in genomics research. *New Genetics and Society*. 2014; 33(1): 79–95.
42. https://ec.europa.eu/info/law-making-process/planning-and-proposing-law/impact-assessments_en (last assessed on 22 November 2017).
43. Technology Needs Assessment for Climate Change, UNDP.
44. T. Penfield, et al., Assessment, evaluations, and definitions of research impact: A review. *Research Evaluation*. 1 January 2014; 23(1): 21–32.
45. A. Brand et al., 'Probst-Hensch biobanking for public health', in Peter Dabrock (ed.) 'Trust in biobanking: Dealing with ethical, legal and social issues in an emerging field of biotechnology', Springer, 2012.

as a commercial collaborator, it needs to strategically balance different legal and governance parameters. Where precompetitive space rapidly evolves along with emerging technologies such as Big Data and artificial intelligence, it may be less clear as to how such technology can be governed, or what impact property rights will have in the context. Involving IPR within such research can be a challenge for collaborators. It is therefore essential that a sandbox-structured platform is created for different phases of biobank research which offers a structured and controlled environment within which the collaboration's governance and other external legal parameters can be successfully tested in developing new strategies suited for innovation.[46] The sandbox modelling also provides collaborators with the ability to test the safeguards for protection for IPRs or secrecy measures and assess its impact on other ethical polices. Rather than a set standard criterion for collaboration, flexible sandbox modelling of contractual arrangements in varying projects can enable public research to have equitable control in collaboration with other industrial collaborators. However other essential parameters such as data protection must be strictly ensured within such measures.

§9.02 POLICY RECOMMENDATIONS: A NUANCED MANAGEMENT OF IP WITHIN BIOBANKS

Biomedical research is rapidly advancing and so is the role of biobanks, which are becoming more diverse in perspectives and approaches. Over the span of two decades research within biobanks have immensely increased in Europe and so are the efforts on the part of biobank, legislators and other stakeholders to push new models for research involving greater participation of stakeholders. This has been on account of the exorbitant amount of investments poured into the creation of biobank resources which did not seek much returns as expected. Further sustainability of biobanks could not be ensured which considerably affected the very existence of many biobanks. PPP have gained acceptance in the recent years. However involving a ppp model requires balancing of research purposes with social needs. Achieving this balance with the inclusion of IPRs is not an easy task. Planning strategies and modelling them into sandbox models early on can enable a healthier partnership within the parameters of maintaining public trust and value creation. Hybrid models are recommended for biobanks but these have to be drawn from the goals of the biobank or of its research .Such models of partnership must also be governed by the concerns or interests of the local community.

It is essential to accept commercialization as an essential process for seek monetary resources for research and innovation to proceed effectively. By this it is not implied sale or rent seeking from HBMs. Such a view runs contrary to law as well and ethics. PPP as a means for commercial development of research results must be viewed holistically in meeting the demands of sustenance and innovation into an equation of

46. Such measures are being tested and evolved to regulate complex financial decision. https://www.finextra.com/blogposting/15759/the-role-of-regulatory-sandboxes-in-fintech-innovation.

balance. Involving industrial partners ensures continuance of the structures which are hard to maintain on a daily basis. It must also involve adequate sharing of resources where ever possible. Collaboration is highly essential to balance out profit maximization with value production.

IP arrangements within collaboration must seek to clarify the use of background and foreground IP. Upon completion of such research participants and their affiliated entities must have the right to academic use of the research results. Thus, research use must be exempted for both the parties involved in the partnership in the interest of academic dissemination. Involving open access for sharing of data must be evolved as an essential practice but with a care to find the spectrum of openness of different kinds of results or data.

While sector specific legal regime may not be essential for biobanks and their research, law must play a dynamic role in calibrating the systemic functioning of biotechnological inventions within life sciences. In this respect, there is also an urgent need for legislators to clarify the issues of ownership in the context of Big Data research and in the context of HBMs. HBMs must be regarded as resource under stewardship of research infrastructures. Research data and other results, on the contrary may be owned and protected using IPR. This also implies the need to classify and elaborate on the types of data within biobanks. Patent filing procedures must require consent form for the samples used in research leading to the patent. Evolving such practices remains within the purview of national patent offices and the EPO who are required to take a proactive role in this process.

The changing role and approaches of biobank research must also seek to create codes of conduct for research which can function as useful tools in the context of a RRI. Enforcing a culture for RRI in genetic research is also essential.

§9.03 SEEKING THE END OF BIOBANKS

Creating curiosity cabinets of knowledge to present day biobanking has been a long stride of vision, science, research and technology. Pickstone in the 'ways of Knowing: A New History of Science, Technology, and Medicine'[47] classifies the understanding of knowledge into science, technology and medicine. Science offers a historical perspective of nature in differing manifestations, experimentalism seeks an analytical refinement of the technical process involved and medicine imbibes the techno-science knowledge to transform it into scientific commodities.[48] In the context of biomedical research this transformation from genomic science to biobanks represents the phase of transformation of science to technology with the aim of seeking products which are fruits of such research. In tracing the end of biobank, its purpose offers some directions. Academic and industrial research for seeking solutions for health-related ills along with educating generations about the hidden knowledge of genomics offer to support the novelty of biobanking as a systemic model and as a field of research.

47. J.V. Pickstone, Ways of knowing: A new history of science, technology, and medicine, University of Chicago Press, 2001.
48. *Ibid.*

Biobanks are thus embedded within the realms of 'knowledge creation', 'knowledge translation' and 'knowledge exchange' each as an essential limb for the subsistence and continuity of biobanks. Law creates the essential order within in which such systems operate transform and develop products for the benefit of mankind. However as this work demonstrates visions for knowledge translations often do not match practical realities. These have contributed to pitfalls in research activities within genomic research. But, as is often said errors enable truth to come out just as the diverse experiences of commercial involvement of biobank within Europe have revealed.[49] Invoking cohesion between research, innovation and bioethics towards a social transformation for greater good is the end of biobanks. The role of law in this process of realistic transformation is analogous to Hegel's owl of Minerva spreading its wings only with the fall of the dusk seeking to find those conditions essential for a new dawn in biobanks.

49. Quote of Sir Francis bacon, see Guibbory, Achsah. 'Francis Bacon's view of history: The cycles of error and the progress of truth.' *The Journal of English and Germanic Philology*. 1975; 74(3): 336–350. *JSTOR*.

Annex I

1. Supplementary Table for Chapter 7

Sl.No	Name of Organisation / Biobank	Type of Document	Country/Region	Remarks
1	Auria biobank, Turku(biobank)	MTA, Terms of transfer	Finland	Upon request
2	EORTC (Non-profit)	policy detailing the conditions for access to data and samples	Belgium	Publicly available
3	Biobank Sverige, Uppsala (Biobank Sweden)	MTA, Partnership template	Sweden	Available online
4	BioMedBridges, Cambridge (research collaboration)	MTA, DTA, Tool for IP, provider agreement	UK	Available online
5	Latvian Biomedical Research and Study Centre(BMC, Biobank)	MTA, consent	Latvia	Upon request
6	Brunswick Group,Brunswick Template Agreements	MTA, research collaboration	UK	Available online
7	CARTaGENE (public research platform)	MTA, DTA	Canada	Upon request
8	Denmark National Biobank	MTA, Consent form	Denmark	Upon request

9	European Molecular Biology Laboratory(EMBL) (intergovernmental org)	MTA	Heidelberg	Upon request
10	Euro Biobank, Milan(non-profit federation)	MTA	Italy	Upon request
11	FINRISK Study (THL, biobank, public research institution)	MTA	Finland	Upon request
12	GENETHON (non-profit)	Service contract	France	Upon request
13	Biobank,GRAZ	MTA, Consent form	Austria	Upon request
14	IBBL	MTA, Consent form	Luxemburg	On request
15	Instituto de Salud Carlos III (ISCIII)	MTA	Spain	Available on request
16	Karolinska Institute Biobank	MTA, research agreements	Sweden	Standard form of Swedish biobank
17	Life Gene (non-profit)	DTA, MTS, access policy, IP policy	Sweden	Available online
18	Lifelines Cohorts & Biobank Initiative (Non-profit, company)	MTA	Netherland	Upon request
19	Malta Biobank	MTA	Malta	Available online
20	Myobank-AFM,Paris (Non-profit)	MTA	France	Upon request
21	Public Population Project in Genomics(P3G)	Sample and Data Access: Core Elements, template	Canada	Available online
22	Parelsnoer Institute (public research institution)	MTA, DTA	Netherland	Available online, Eng. Version on request
23	Telethon network genetic biobank (Non-profit network)	MTA	Italy	On request
24	UCL (university biobank)	MTA, model template	UK	On request
25	UK Biobank	MTA, DTA, data management and sharing plan	UK	Available online

26	Walton center NHS (hospital trust and publicly funded research center)	MTA	UK	Upon request
27	Wellcome Trust Sanger Institute (Registered charity)	MTA, data sharing protocols	UK	Available online
28	WHO (International org.)	MTA	Geneva	Available online
29	BBMRI-ERIC	Standard Contracts (e.g., MTA/DTAs)	Austria	Available online
30	IPAG (Project of Austrian Universities and Enterprise network)	IPAG (Intellectual Property Agreement Guide) Model Agreements	Austria	Available online
31	Estonian Genome Center (biobank)	MTA	Estonia	Upon request

Bibliography

List of Original Publications

R. Neethu. What the role out of EU data protection means for you, Nature biotech 2017.

R. Neethu et al. Clinical trials data transparency & GDPR compliance: What does it imply for data sharing and open innovation?, Oxford Journal of Science and Public Policy (accepted for publication, 2019).

R. Neethu and Nana Kongsholm et al. Sustainability of university-run biobanks (Joint paper, published by Biopreservation and Biobanking, August 2018).

R. Neethu. ELBERTE v LATVIA: The to be or not to be question of consent, Medical Law Review vol. 25, no. 3 (1 August 2017): 484–493.

R. Neethu. Biobank-related research and intellectual property rights: Deconstructing the obscurity, Journal of Intellectual Property Law & Practice vol. 12, no. 4 (1 April 2017).

R. Neethu. Sovereign trusteeship and multilateral protection of intellectual property rights, Journal of Intellectual Property Law & Practice vol. 10, no. 2 (1 February 2015): 89–97.

Articles

Adams, M., Prentice, E.D., Oki, G.S. Ethical considerations in informed consent for potential future use of human tissue samples, IRB vol. 18, no. 2 (1996): pp. 6–7.

Holzinger, A., Jurisica, I. (eds). Knowledge discovery and data mining, LNCS 8401 (2014): 1–18.

Aicardi, C. et al. Emerging ethical issues regarding digital health data. On the World Medical Association Draft Declaration on Ethical Considerations regarding Health Databases and Biobanks. Croatian Medical Journal vol. 57, no. 2 (2016): 207–213. PMC. Web. 16 January 2017.

Alessia, C. et al. The European Research Infrastructures of the ESFRI roadmap in biological and medical sciences: Status and perspectives, Ann Ist Super Sanita vol. 50, no. 2 (2014).

Capron, A.M. et al. Ethical issues in governing biobanks: Global perspectives, Ashgate Publishing Ltd., UK 2013.

Cambon-Thomson, A. The social and ethical issues of post-genomic human biobanks. Nature Reviews Genetics vol. 5 (2004): 866–873.

Ohly, A. Reverse engineering: Unfair competition or catalyst for innovation?. In: Straus J, ed., Patents and Technological Progress in a Globalised World: Liber. Berlin: Springer, 2009, 535–552.

Konski, A.F. Genetic data, patents, and trade secrets, Personalized Medicine Bulletin, 9 November 2012.

Hugenholtz, B., Senftleben, M.R.F. Fair use in Europe: In search of flexibilities, November 2011.

Blatt, R.J.R. Banking biological collections: Data warehousing, data mining, and data dilemmas in genomics and global health policy, Community Genetics vol. 3, no. 4 (2000): 204–211.

Leiter, B., Weisberg, M. Why evolutionary biology is so far irrelevant to legal regulation, Law and Philosophy, vol. 29 (2010): 31.

Bubela, T., Guebert, J., Mishra, A. Use and misuse of material transfer agreements: Lessons in proportionality from research, repositories, and litigation, PLoS Biology vol. 13, no. 2 (2015): e1002060. PMC. Web. 8 October 2017.

Camporesi, S., Vaccarella, M., Davis, M. Investigating public trust in expert knowledge: Narrative, ethics, and engagement, Bioethical Inquiry vol. 14, no. 23 (2017).

Weil, C.J., Compton, C. Trade-secret model: Potential pitfalls, Science vol. 333 (2011).

Caulfield, T., et al. A review of the key issues associated with the commercialization of biobanks, Journal of Law and the Biosciences vol. 1, no. 1 (2014): 94–110. PMC.

Caulfield, T., et al. DNA databanks and consent: A suggested policy option involving an authorization model, BMC Medical Ethics vol. 4, no. 1 (2003).

Chalmers, D., et al. Has the biobank bubble burst? Withstanding the challenges for sustainable biobanking in the digital era, BMC Medical Ethics (2016).

Díaz, C.L. (2005): Intellectual Property Rights and Biological Resources: An Overview of Key Issues and Current Debates, Wuppertal Papers, No. 151, Wuppertal Institut für Klima, Umwelt, Energie, Wuppertal, http://nbn-resolving.de/urn:nbn:de:101:1-200910062169.

Lenk, C., et al. Biobanks and tissue research: The public, the patient and the regulation, Springer (2011): 20–23.

Reed, C. Information in the cloud: Ownership, control and accountability. In: Anne S.Y. Cheung, Rolf H. Weber, Privacy and Legal Issues in Cloud Computing. Edward Elgar, UK, 2015.

Christensen E. Biobanks and our common good. In: Solbakk J., Holm S., Hofmann B., eds. The Ethics of Research Biobanking. Boston, MA: Springer, 2009.

Heaney, C., et al. The perils of taking property too far, Stanford Journal of Law Science and Policy vol. 1 (May 2009): 46–64.

Rodgers, C. Natures place? Property rights property rules and environmental stewardship, Cambridge Law Journal vol. 68, no. 3 (November 2009): 550–574.

Conley, J.M., et al. A trade secret model for genomic biobanking. The Journal of Law, Medicine & Ethics: A Journal of the American Society of Law, Medicine & Ethics vol. 40, no. 3 (2012): 612–629.

Council of Europe Convention on Human Rights and Biomedicine (1997) Article 21 – Prohibition of financial gain, http://conventions.coe.int/Treaty/en/Treaties/Html/164.ht.

Trouet, C. New European guidelines for the use of stored human biological materials in biomedical research, Journal of Medical Ethics vol. 30 (2004): 99–103.

D'Abramo, F., et al. Research participants' perceptions and views on consent for biobank research: A review of empirical data and ethical analysis. BMC Medical Ethics vol. 16 (2015): 60. PMC. Web. 23 March 2016.

Burke, D.L., Copyrightability of recombinant DNS sequences, Jurimetrics vol. 29, no. 4 (Summer 1989): 469–532.

Burk, D.L., Misappropriation of trade secrets in biotechnology licensing, Albany Law Journal of Science and Technology vol. 4 (1994): 121, 139.

Burk,D.L., Lemley, M.A., Policy levers in patent law, University of Minnesota Law School Public Law & Legal Theory Research Paper Series, Research Paper No. 03-11(2003).

Korn, D.E., Patent and trade secret protections in University-Industry research relationships in biotechnology, Harvard Journal on Legislation vol. 24 (1987): 191.

Gurwitz, D., Pirmohammad, M., Pharmacogenomics: The importance of accurate phenotypes, Pharmacogenomics vol. 11, no. 4 (2010): 469–470.

Levine, D.S., The impact of trade secrecy on public transparency. In: Dreyfuss, R.C., Strandburg, K.J., eds. The Law and Theory of Trade Secrecy: A Handbook of Contemporary Research. Edward Elgar Publishing, UK 2010.

D'Haene, N., et al., Clinical validation of targeted next generation sequencing for colon and lung cancers. PLoS ONE vol. 10, no. 9 (2015): e0138245. PMC. Web. 6 October 2017.

Gervais, D., The Tangled Web of UGC: Making Copyright Sense of User-Generated Content, Vanderbilt Journal of Entertainment & Technology Law vol. 11 (2008–2009): 841 ff.

DG Internal Market and services working paper: First evaluation of Directive 96/9/EC, 12 on the legal protection of databases, December, 2005.

Elger, D.M., et al., What is a biobank? Differing definition among biobank stakeholders, Clinical Genetics, 3 September 2013.

Mascalzoni, D. (ed.), Ethics, law and governance of biobanking, Springer NL, 2015.

Dodds, S., Ankeny, R., Regulations of hESC research in Australia: Promises and pitfalls for deliberative democratic approaches, Bioethical Inquiry vol. 3 (2006): 95–107.

Gitter, D.M., The challenges of achieving open source sharing of biobanks. In: Pascuzzi, G. et al. Comprarative issues in the governance of research biobanks, Springer, 2013 165.

Schovsbo, J., Minssen, T., 'Legal aspects of biobanking as key issue for personalized medicine and translational exploitation', Journal of Personalised Medicine vol. 11, no. 5 (2014).

Dove, E.S., Joly, Y., Knoppers, B.M., Trade-secret model: Legal limitations, Science vol. 333, no. 6049 (2011): 1575.

Estape, E.S., Mays, M.H., Sternke, E.A., Translation in data mining to advance personalized medicine for health equity. Intelligent Information Management vol. 8, no. 1 (2016): 9–16.

Richard Gold, E., Nicol, D., Beyond open source: Patents, biobanks and sharing. In: Pascuzzi, G., Comparative issues in the governance of research biobanks. Springer 2013.

Bulygin, E., et al., Essays in Legal Philosophy, Oxford University Press, 2015.

Appel Blue, E.E., Redefining Stewardship over body parts, Journal of Law and Health vol. 21 (2007): 75, 122.

Barraclough, E., What Myriad means for biotech, WIPO Magazine, August 2013.

Dove, E.S., Joly, Y., The contested futures of biobanks and intellectual property, Teoria y Derecho vol. 11, no. 1 (2012): 132–146.

European commission staff working paper on the review of the EC legal framework in the field of copyright and related rights, SEC 995 (2004).

France, UK and Germany; See more in White Paper - Data ownership in the context of the European data economy: proposal for a new right, 6 February 2017.

Marodin, G., et al., 'Biobanking for health research in Brazil: Present challenges and future directions', Rev Panam Salud Publica vol. 31, no. 6 (2012).

Van Overwalle, G., Uncorking trade secrets: Sparking the interaction between trade secrecy and open biotechnology. In Dreyfuss, R.C., Strandburg, K.J., eds, The Law and theory of trade secrecy: A handbook of contemporary research. Cheltenham: Edward Elgar Publishing Ltd, 2011, 246.

Gibbons, S.M.C., Regulating biobanks: A twelve point typological tool, Medical Law Review vol. 17 (Autumn 2009): 313–346.

Gold, E.R., et al., Are patents impeding medical care and innovation?, PLoS Med vol. 7, no. 1 (2010): e1000208.

Gottweiss, H., Zatloukal, K., Biobank governance: Trends and perspectives, pathobiology, vol. 74 (2007): 206–211.

Griffiths, J., The 'three-step test' in European Copyright Law: Problems and solutions, Intellectual Property Law Quarterly (2009): 489.

Hallinan, D., Friedewald, M., Open consent, biobanking and data protection law: can open consent be 'informed' under the forthcoming data protection regulation?, Life Sciences, Society and Policy vol 11, no. 1 (2015).

Hargreaves, Supporting Document T to the Hargreaves report on text mining and data analytics in call for evidence responses (May 2011).

Holman, C.M. Biotechnology Law Report vol. 35, no. 2 (April 2016): 45–54. See also Seldon, T., Beyond patents: Effective intellectual property strategy in biotechnology, Innovation, Management Policy and Practice vol. 13, no. 1 (2011): 55–61.

HUGO Ethics Committee – Statement on Human Genomic Databases, Eubios Journal of Asian and International Bioethics vol. 13 (2003): 99.

Sherkow, J.S., Protecting products versus platforms: Bio entrepreneur, Nature Biotech (14 April 2016).

Drexl, J., Designing competitive markets for industrial data in Europe - Between Propertisation and Access 8 (2017) JIPITEC 257 para. 1.

Lunshof, J.E., et al., From genetic privacy to open consent, Nature Biotech vol. 9 (May 2008).

Matsuura, J.H., Trade-secret model: Privacy rights, Science vol. 333 (16 September 2011).

Seddona, J.J.M., Currie, W.L., Cloud computing and trans-border health data: Unpacking U.S. and EU healthcare regulation and compliance, Health Policy and Technology vol. 2 (2013): 229–241.

Mohr, J.M., Rethinking trade secret protection, GEN vol. 33, no. 14 (2013).

Schovsbo, J., et al., Legal aspects of biobanking as key issues for personalized medicine and translational exploitation, Personalized Medicine vol. 11, no. 5 (2014): 497–508.

Weinstein, J., Coming of Age: Recognizing the Importance of Interdisciplinary Education in Law Practice, Washington Law Review vol. 74 (1999): 319, at 353.

Vaught, J., et al., Biobankonomics: Developing a sustainable business model approach for the formation of a human tissue biobank, DOI: 10.1093/jncimonographs/lgr009.

Sandor, J., The case of biobank with law: Between legal and scientific fiction, Journal or Medical Ethics (2011).

Gregory, J., Bowker, G.C., The data citizen, the quantified self, and personal renomics. In: Nafus, D., Quantified, biosensing technologies in everyday Life. MIT Press, online 2016.

Davis, J.H., Schoorman, F.D., Donaldson, L., Toward a Stewardship theory of management, Academy of manaement Review vol. 22, no. 2 (1997).

Forsberg, J.S., Changing perspectives in Biobank research: From individual rights to concerns about public health regarding the return of results, European Journal of Human Genetics vol. 17 (2009): 1544–1549.

Hughes, J., The philosophy of intellectual property, Georgetown Law Journal 77 (1988): 287.

de Jong, S., Engaging scientists: Organising valorisation in the Netherlands. Rathenau Instituut,NL, 2015.

Jacob, M., Lundqvist, M., Hellsmark, H., Entrepreneurial transformations in the Swedish university system: The case of Chalmers University of Technology, Research Policy, vol. 32, no. 9 (2003): 1555–1568.

Jolly, Y., et al. Moving beyond commercialization: Strategies to maximines the economic and social impact of genomic research, Plicy Brief, 5, 212, 2012.

Cameron, J., et al., The precautionary principle: A fundamental principle of law and policy for the protection of the global environment, Boston College of International and Comparative Law Review vol. 14, no. 1 (1991).

Hsiao, J.I.-H., Wang, W.-L., Dosage patenting in personalized medicine, Boston College Intellectual Property & Technology Forum, 2012.

Gaster, J.-L., Der Rechtsschutz von Datenbanken: Kommentar zur Richtlinie 96/9 EG;mit Erläuterungen zur Umsetzung in das deutsche und österreichische Recht, Köln-Berlin-Bonn-München: Heymanns Verlag 1999.

Bovernberg, J.A., Should genomic companies set up Database in EU? The EU database Directive revisited, EIPR (2001): 364.

Chang, J., Xuezhong zhu, Bioinfomatics databases: Intellectual property strategy, Journal of Intellectual Property Rights, vol. 15 (2010): 447–454.

Wu, J.-R., Zeng, R., Molecular basis for population variation: From SNPs to SAPs, FEBS Letters, vol. 586, no. 18 (2012): 2841–2845; Jordan, R.A., On the scope of protection for computer programs under copyright. (Computer Programs: the Patent/Copyright Interface), AIPLA Quarterly Journal vol. 17, no. 3 (Summer 1989): 199–214.

Kaye, J., et al., Can I access my personal genome? The current legal position in the UK, Medical Law Review vol. 22, no. 1 (2014): 64–86.

Kinkorová, J., Biobanks in the Era of personalized medicine: Objectives, challenges, and innovation: Overview, The EPMA Journal vol. 7 (2015): 4. PMC. Web. 17 December 2016.

Hoeyer, K.L., Size matters: The ethical, legal, and social issues surrounding large-scale genetic biobank initiatives, Norsk Epidemiologi vol. 21, no. 2 (2012): 211–220.

Hunter, K.G., Laurie, G.T., Involving publics in biobank governance: Moving beyond existing approaches. In: Widdos, H., Mullen, C., The governance of genetic information: Who decides?. Cambridge University Press, 2009.

Kiley, T.D., Learning to live with the living invention, APLA Quarterly Journal vol. 7 (1980): 220.

Kayton, I. Copyright in genetically engineered works, The George Washington Law Review vol. 50 (1982): 191–218.

Kariyawasam, K., Talagala, C., Cloud computing and the future of copyright law, EIPR vol. 39, no. 2, (2017): 102–116; See also Storing Content in the Cloud: Copyright Law Issues, copyrightlaws.com.

Laursen, K., Salter, A.J., The paradox of openness: appropriability, external search and collaboration, Research Policy vol. 43, no. 5 (2014): 867–878.

Truyens, M., Van Eecke, P., Legal aspects of text mining, Computer Law & Security Review vol. 30 (2014): 153–170.

Madhavan, M., Copyright versus database right protection in the UK: The bioinfomatic bone of contention, Journal of World Intellectual Property, vol. 1 (2006): 61–90.

Melzer, M.A., Copyright enforcement in the Cloud, Fordham Intellectual Property, Media and Entertainment Law Journal vol. 21 (2011): 403, 404.

Margoni, T., The roles of material transfer agreements in genetics databases and bio-banks (2013).

Lemley, M.A., The surprising virtues of treating trade secrets as IP rights, Stanford Law Review vol. 61 (2008): 118.

Mascalzoni, D, et al., International charter of principles for sharing bio-specimens and data, European Journal of Human Genetics vol. 23, no. 6 (2015): 721–728.

Worsman, M., Copyright in health records, Health law Bulletin Mondaq Business Briefing (18 November 2010).

Marx, V., Biology: The big challenges of big data, Nature vol. 498, no. 7453 (2013): 255–260.

Zvelebil, M.J., Baum, J.O., Understanding bioinformatics. Garland Science,NY,USA 2008.

Senftleben, M., Breathing space for Cloud-Based Business Models exploring the Matrix of copyright limitations, Safe Harbours and Injunctions, JIPITEC vol. 4, no. 2 (2013): paragraph 87.

Partington, M., Empirical legal research and policy-making. In Cane, P., Kritzer, H.M., The Oxford Handbook of Empirical Legal Research, Oxford Handbooks online, 2010.

Senftleben, M., The international three-step test: A model provision for EC fair use legislation, JIPITEC vol. 1 (2010): 67.

Van Hoecke, M. Methodologies of legal research: Which kind of method for what kind of dDiscipline?. Bloomsbury Publishing,UK, 2011.

Travers, M., Banakar, R., Theory and method in socio-legal research, Oxford Hart Publishing, 2005.

Limb, M., Patients in wales to take control of medical records. BMJ 2017; 357: j2982.

Hansson, M.G., Ethics and biobanks. British Journal of Cancer vol. 100, no. 1 (2009): 8–12.

Molnár-Gábor et al., Computing patient data in the cloud: practical and legal considerations for genetics and genomics research in Europe and internationally. Genome Medicine vol. 9 (2017): 58

Ficsor, M.J., The WIPO 'Internet Treaties' and copyright in the 'Cloud', copyright and related rights in the 'Cloud' environment. ALAI 2012 Congress, Kyoto, 16–18 October 2012.

McGinnis, R., Originality and intellectual property in the French and English enlightenment, Routledge, 2009.

Mitchell, R. National biobanks: Clinical labor, risk production, and the creation of biovalue. Science, Technology & Human Values vol. 35, no. 3 (2010): 330–355.

Munzer, S., A Theory of Property. Cambridge University Press, 1990, p. 41.

Scudellari, M. Biobank managers bemoan underuse of collected samples, Nature Medicine vol. 19, no. 3 (March 2013).

Morente M.M., Alonso, S., Current challenges of human tumour banking, Journal of Hematology Oncology vol. 23 (2005): 54–56.

Murphy, M., et al., Engaging diverse stakeholders to inform biobank governance, biopreservation and biobanking, Journal of Hematology Oncology vol. 15, no. 4 (2017).

Mason, J.K., Laurie, G.T., Consent or property? Dealing with the body and its parts in the shadow of Bristol and Alder Hey, The Modern Law Review, vol. 64 (September 2001): 710–729.

Vatter, M., The Republic of the living: Biopolitics and the critique of civil society, Fordham University Press, NY,2014.

Murtagh, M.J., et al., Realizing the promise of population biobanks: A new model for translation, Human Genetics vol. 130, no. 3 (2011): 333–345.

Mazur, D.J., Full disclosure of the 'Raw Data' of research on humans: Citizens' rights, product manufacturers' obligations and the quality of the scientific database, philosophy compass, Blackwell Publishing Ltd, 2011.

Melham, K., et al.. The evolution of withdrawal: Negotiating research relationships in biobanking, Life Sciences, Society and Policy vol. 10 (2014): 16. PMC. Web. 12 December 2016.

Herder, M., Patents & the progress of personalized medicine: Biomarkers research as lens, Annual Health Law vol. 18 (2009): 187.

McCarty, C.A., Wilke, R.A., Biobanking and pharmacogenomics, Pharmacogenomics vol. 11 (2010): 637–641.

Chow, M., Intellectual property strategy in bioinformatics, Journal of Intellectual Property Rights vol. 8 (March 2003): 130–137.

Korn, N., Oppenheim, C., Duncan, C., IPR and licensing issues in derived data, May 2007.

Nelson, B., Empty archives, Nature 461 (2009):160–163.

Moran, N., The rise of trade secrets in biotechnology, Science Business (26 June 2008).

Olson, J.E., et al., Biobanks and personalized medicine, Clinical Genetics vol. 86, no. 1 (2014): 50–55.

Holmes, O.W., The path of the law, Harvard Law Review vol. 10 (1897): 343.

Jones, O.D., Behavioural economics meets behavioural biology', North-western University Law Review vol. 95 (2001): 1141 ff.

Olson, J.E., et al. Biobanks and Personalized Medicine, Clinical Genetics vol. 86, no. 1 (2014): 50–55. PMC. Web. 16 January 2017.

Shockley, P., The availability of trade secret protection for university research. Journal of College and Univrsity Law vol. 20, no. 3 (Win 1994): 309-332.

Patino, R.M., Moving research to patient applications through commercialization: Understanding and evaluating the role of intellectual property, Journal of the American Association for Laboratory Animal Science vol. 49, no. 2 (2010): 147–154.

Torremans, P.L.C., The road towards the harmonisation of trade secrets law in the European Union, Revista La Propiedad Inmaterial, no. 20 (JULIO-DICIEMBRE DE 2015).

Jensen, P.B., Jensen, L.J., Brunak, S., Mining electronic health records: Towards better research applications and clinical care, Nature Genetics vol. 13 (June 2012).

Puchois, P., Finding ways to improve the use of biobanks, Nature Medicine vol. 19, no. 7 (2013): 814-815.

Parry, B., Gere, C., Contested bodies: Property models and the commodification of human biological artefacts, Science as Culture, vol. 15 (2006): 139–158.

Cane, P., Conaghan, J., The New Oxford Companion to Law, Oxford University Press, 2008.

Pottage, A., The socio-legal implications of the new biotechnologies, Annual Review of Law and Social Sciences vol. 3 (2007): 321-344.

Petrini, C., Ethical and legal considerations regarding the ownership and commercial use of human biological materials (Dove Medical Press, 2012)

Prokosch, H.U., et al. IT infrastructure components for biobanking, Applied Clinical Informatics vol. 1, no. 4 (2010): 419–429. doi:10.4338/ACI-2010-05-RA-0034.

Palsson, G., The rise and fall of a biobank: The case of Iceland. In: Gottweis H., Petersen A., eds, Biobanks: Governance in comparative perspective. Abingdon: Routledge (2008), pp. 41–55.

Ramsey, P., as cited in Elizabeth E. Appel Blue, Redefining Stewardship over body parts, J.L. & Health vol. 21 (2007): 75, 122.

Withers, P.J.A., et al., Stewardship to tackle global phosphorus inefficiency: The case of Europe, AMBIO 44 (Suppl. 2) (2015): S193–S206.

Pellegrino, E.D., Toward a virtue-based normative ethics for the health professions, Kennedy Institute of Ethics Journal vol. 5, no. 3 (1995): 253–277.

Pirnay, J., et al., Beware of the commercialization of human cells and tissues: Situation in the European Union. Cell Tissue Bank vol. 13, no. 3 (2012): 487–498

Andanda, P.A., Human tissue related inventions: Ownership and intellectual property rights in international collaborative research in developing countries', Journal of Medical Ethics vol. 34 (2008): 171–179.

Purcell, S., et al., PLINK: A tool set for whole-genome association and population-based linkage analyses, American Journal of Human Genetics vol. 81, no. 3 (2007): 559–575.

Bernt Hugenholtz, P., Implementing the European Database Directive, 11 March 1996, IVIR.

Thomas, D., Karnell, G.W.G., Originality of the copyrighted work: A European perspective, Journal of the Copyright Society of the U.S.A. vol. 39, no. 4 (Summer 1992): 289–302.

Petersen, C., DeMuro, P. Legal and regulatory considerations associated with use of patient-generated health data from Social Media and Mobile Health (mHealth) Devices, Applied Clinical Informatics vol. 6, no. 1 (2015): 16–26.

Petrini, C., Ethical and legal considerations regarding the ownership and commercial use of human biological materials and their derivatives, Journal of Blood Medicine vol. 3 (2012): 87–96. PMC. Web. 8 October 2017.

Rai, A.K., Regulating scientific research: Intellectual property rights and the norms of science, Northwestern University Law Review vol. 94, no. 1 (Fall 1999): 77–152.

Reichman, J.H., Okediji, R.L., When copyright law and science collide: Empowering digitally integrated research methods on a global scale, Minnesto Law Review vol. 96, no. 4 (2012): 1362–1480.

Rhodes, C. Potential international approaches to ownership/control of human genetic resources, Health Care Analysis vol. 24 (2016): 260–277. PMC. Web. 8 October 2017.

Lawlor, R.T., Models of collaboration and experiences between bio-industry and academic biobanks. In: Elena Salvaterra, ed., Advances in biobanking practice through public and private collaborations Bentham eBooks, 2017.

Cook-Deegan, R., et al, The next controversy in genetic testing: Clinical data as trade secrets?, European Journal of Human Genetics vol. 21, no. 6 (2013): 585–588.

Mitchell, R., et al., A trade secret model for genomic biobanking, The Journal of Law Medicine & Ethics (September 2012).

Rothstein, M.A., Expanding the ethical analysis of biobanks, Journal of Law, Medicine & Ethics vol. 33 (2005): 89–101.

Schultz, M., Lippoldt, D., Approaches to protection of undisclosed information (trade secrets): Background paper, OECD Trade Policy Papers, no. 162, (Paris: OECD Publishing, 2014).

Pathmasiri, S., et al. Intellectual property rights in publicly funded biobanks: Much ado about nothing?, Nature Biotechnology vol. 29, no. 4 (April 2011).

Solbakk, J.H., et al. The Ethics of Research Biobanking. Springer US, 2009.

Samuel, G., Interdisciplinarity and the authority paradigm: Should law Be taken seriously by scientists and social scientists?, Journal of Law and Society vol. 36, no. 4 (December 2009): 431–459.

Salzberger, E.M., The law and economics analysis of intellectual property: Paradigmatic shift from incentives to traditional property, Review of Law & Economics vol. 7, no. 2 (2011): 435–480.

Simonsen, H., Brandt, N.J., Nørregrade-Pedersen, B. Neonatal screening in Denmark: Status and future perspectives, Ugeskr. Laeger vol. 160 (1998): 5777–5782.

Nussbeck, S.Y., et al., 'Life in data' – Outcome of a multi-disciplinary, interactive biobanking Conference Session on sample data, biopreservation and biobanking vol. 14, no. 1 (2016).

Holm, S., From Steward to Stuart: Some problems in deciding for others, Northern Ireland Legal Quarterly vol. 62 (2011): 617, 632.

O'Brien, S.J. Stewardship of human biospecimens, DNA, genotype, and clinical data in the GWAS Era, Annual Review of Genomics and Human Genetics vol. 10 (2009): 193–209.

Fullerton, S.M., et al., Meeting the governance challenges of next-generation biorepository research, Science Translational Medicine (20 January 2010)

Sargsyan, K., et al., Sustainability in biobanking: Model of biobank graz., Biopreserv Biobank vol. 13 (2015): 410–420.

Stilgoe, J., Owen, R., Macnaghten, P., Developing a framework for responsible innovation. Research Policy vol. 42, no. 9 (November 2013): 1568–1580.

Aymé, S., et al., Patenting and licensing in genetic testing: Recommendations of the European Society of Human Genetics, European Journal of Human Genetics vol. 16 (2008): 405–411.

Pathmasiri, S., et al., Intellectual property rights in publicly funded biobanks: Much ado about nothing?, Nature Biotechnology vol 29, no. 4 (April 2011).

Sobradillo, P., Pozo, F., Agustí, A., P4 Medicine: The future around the corner. Archivos de Bronconeumología 47, no. 1 (2011): 35–40. doi: 10.1016/j.arbres.2010.09.009.

Strimbu, K., Tavel, J.A., 'What are biomarkers?' Current opinion in HIV and AIDS vol. 5, no. 6 (2010): 463–466. PMC. Web. 19 December 2016.

Armstrong, S., Patient access to health records: Striving for the Swedish ideal, BMJ (2017).

Stein, L.D., The case for cloud computing in genome informatics, Genome Biology vol. 11 (2010): 207.

Paul, S., Gade, A., Mallipeddi, S., The state of Cloud-Based Biospecimen and Biobank Data Management Tools, Biopreservation and Biobanking vol. 15, no. 2 (2017).

Seddon, J.J.M., Currie, W.L., Cloud computing and trans-border health data: Unpacking U.S. and EU healthcare regulation and compliance. Health Policy Technology vol. 2 (2013): 229–241.

Caulfield, T., et al., Industry involvement in publicly funded biobanks: Ethics watch, Nature Genetics vol. 15 (April 2014).

Simson, T., What is trust?, Pacific Philosophical Quarterly vol. 93, no. 4 (2012): 550-569.

Turner, A., et al., Biobank economics and commecialization problem, Spontaneous Generation vol. 7, no. 1 (2013): 69–80.

Tucker, J.B., Zilinskas, R.A., The promises and perils of synthetic biology, The New Atlantis 12 (Spring 2006): 25–45.

Cook, T., Exceptions and limitations in European Union Copyright Law, Journal of Intellectual Property Rights vol. 17 (May 2012): 243–245.

Verissimo, P.E., Bessani, A., E-biobanking: What have you done to my cell samples?, IEEE Security & Privacy, vol. 11, no. 6 (November–December 2013): 62, 65,

Waltz, E., Genentech's Cabilly victory (NEWS), Nature Biotechnology vol. 27, no. 4 (April 2009): 307.

Winickoff, D.E., Partnership in U.K. Biobank: A third way for genomic property?, The Journal of Law, Medicine & Ethics vol. 35, no. 3 (Fall 2007) 440–456.

Watkins, D., Burton, M. (eds), Research methods in law. Abingdon: Routledge, 2011.

Walker, R.L., Morrissey, C., Bioethics methods in the ethical, legal, and social implications of the human genome project literature, Bioethics vol. 28, no. 9 (2014): 481–490.

Waldby, C., Stem cells, tissue cultures and the production of biovalue, Health: An Interdisciplinary Journal for the Social Study of Health, Illness and Medicine vol. 6 (2002): 305–323.

Wilsdon, J., Wynne, B., Stilgoe, J., The public value of science. London: Demos, 2005.

Brian Arthur, W., The nature of technology: What it is and how it evolves', Penguin books 2010.

van Est, R., Intimate technology: The battle for our body and behaviour, *Rathenau Instituut* (12April 2015).

Fisher, W., Theories of intellectual property. In Muzer, S.R., ed., New essays in the legal and political theory of property (Cambridge University Press, 2001) 168-199.

Streitz, W.D., et al., Material transfer agreements: A university perspective, Plant Physiology vol. 133 (2003): 10–13.

Lades, W.M., Posner, R.A., The economic structure of intellectual property law, Chapter 2, at p. 40 Belknap Press; First Edition (US) First Printing edition (2003)

Wade, T.D., Traits and types of health data repositories. Health Information Science and Systems vol. 2 (2014): 4. PMC. Web. 29 March 2017.

Legal Resources

COMMISSION IMPLEMENTING DECISION, of 22 November 2013, on setting up the Biobanks and Biomolecular Resources Research Infrastructure Consortium

(BBMRI-ERIC) as a European Research Infrastructure Consortium (2013/701/EU).
Legal framework for a European Research Infrastructure Consortium - ERIC, Practical Guidelines, April 2010.
Council Regulation (EC) No 723/2009 of 25 June 2009 on the Community legal framework for a European Research Infrastructure Consortium (ERIC).
European Patent Convention, 1973.
Additional Protocol to the Convention for the Protection of Human Rights and Dignity of the Human Being with regard to the Application of Biology and Medicine, on the Prohibition of Cloning Human Beings, ETS No.168, 01/03/2001.
Additional Protocol to the Convention on Human Rights and Biomedicine concerning Genetic Testing for Health Purposes, CETS No. 203, 01/07/201.8.
Transplantation of Organs and Tissues of Human Origin, 01/05/2006.
Additional Protocol to the Convention on Human Rights and Biomedicine concerning Genetic.
Testing for Health Purposes, Strasbourg, 27/11/2008.
Tissues and Cells Directive (2004/23/EC).
Directive 2010/45/EU.
Directive 98/44/EC, on the legal protection of biotechnological inventions.
Directive No 96/9/EC on the Legal Protection of Databases in Europe.
Directive 2010/53/EU / 2010 on standards of quality and safety of human organs intended for transplantation.
European Biotechnology directive 98/44/EC 1998.
Implementing Regulations, 1973.
Regulation (EU) 2016/679.
EPC Guidelines for examination, 2014.

Table of Cases

Index

Q

R

S

www.ingramcontent.com/pod-product-compliance
Lightning Source LLC
LaVergne TN
LVHW020644300926
849161LV00004B/806